British Design from 1948

British Design from 1948
Innovation in the Modern Age

—Christopher Breward & Ghislaine Wood

V&A Publishing

First published by V&A Publishing, 2012

V&A Publishing
Victoria and Albert Museum
South Kensington
London SW7 2RL

Distributed in North America by Harry N. Abrams Inc., New York

Hardback edition
ISBN 978 1 85177 674 0

Paperback edition
ISBN 978 1 85177 675 7

Library of Congress Catalog Control Number: 2011935128

10 9 8 7 6 5 4 3 2 1
2016 2015 2014 2013 2012

A catalogue record for this book is available from the British Library.

● [FRONT JACKET/COVER IMAGE] Collage by Daniel Streat (Barnbrook). For credits on this, and the section and chapter opening images see pages 390–91. ● [PAGE 5] *Queen Elizabeth II on Coronation Day*, Cecil Beaton, 1953 (see plate 1.33) ● [PAGE 8–9] Pharmacy restaurant and bar, Damien Hirst, 1997 (see plate 2.19) ● [PAGE 10] *David Bowie*, Brian Duffy, 1973 (see plate 2.93) ● [PAGE 12] 'Ian Dury with Love', poster, Barney Bubbles, 1977. All treatments by Daniel Streat (Barnbrook).

Designer: Daniel Streat (Barnbrook)
Copy-editor: Mandy Greenfield
Index: Hilary Bird
New photography by Pip Barnard, Richard Davis, James Stevenson and Sara Hodges, V&A Photographic Studio
Printed in Singapore by C.S. Graphics

This book is typeset in four British typefaces:

SECTION ONE: New Rail Alphabet
Rail Alphabet was designed by Kinneir Calvert Associates as part of British Rail's 1965 re-branding, and was also adopted by the National Health Service and British Airports Authority. It was adapted by Henrik Kubel and Margaret Calvert to create New Rail Alphabet in 2009.

SECTION TWO: Verdana
Matthew Carter designed Verdana for Microsoft Corporation in 1996. It is a humanist sans-serif typeface, which means that it is more calligraphic than other sans-serifs, increasing its legibility and making it easy to read at small sizes on computer screens.

SECTION THREE: Bourgeois
Bourgeois was designed by Jonathan Barnbrook and Marcus Leis Allion in 2005. It echoes letter forms from the early twentieth century, drawn in a contemporary style. The term 'bourgeois' was used historically in letterpress printing for a type size measuring approximately eight to nine point.

FRONT AND BACK MATTER: Parable
Parable was designed in 2002 by Christopher Burke. It is optimized for print in small text sizes, between six and ten point. Taking advantage of this quality, Parable was chosen for use in the eleventh edition of the *Concise Oxford English Dictionary*.

V&A Publishing
Supporting the world's leading museum of art and design, the Victoria and Albert Museum, London

Contents

SPONSOR'S FOREWORD

Ernst & Young is proud to sponsor 'British Design 1948–2012: Innovation in the Modern Age'. This unique exhibition brings together exceptional creative talents and design classics, from the everyday to the extraordinary, from art to architecture, Moore to Jaguar and Quant to McQueen.

'British Design 1948–2012' is the first of its kind, presenting designers born, trained or working in the UK. The exhibition highlights their bold, innovative and entrepreneurial spirit in an ever-changing world. It's a timely reminder of what makes the UK an important global influence.

As one of the world's leading business advisers, Ernst & Young recognizes the role entrepreneurship and innovation play in driving the growth of the broader economy. We've sponsored the arts for many years and we welcome this opportunity to contribute to cultural life.

We hope you enjoy this beautiful book and that it inspires your own entrepreneurial spirit and imagination.

ERNST & YOUNG
Quality In Everything We Do

'British Design 1948–2012: Innovation in the Modern Age' is a groundbreaking exhibition which celebrates more than 60 years of British art and design. From the last London Olympic Games held in 1948 to the current global competition, the exhibition traces how artists and designers have responded to a rapidly changing world. It is an exciting story, encompassing the diversity of British creativity and spanning everything from the ambition of grand state projects to the vibrancy of the nation's popular culture. Importantly, the exhibition helps trace the development of Britain's dynamic creative economy.

The exhibition has been three years in the making, and much research has focused on the V&A's rich collections. The Museum is world-renowned for its collections of British design, but this exhibition is the first to study intensively the post-war period. It brings together more than 350 works in all media, more than two-thirds of which are drawn from the V&A and many of which have never been on public display. The exhibition represents a significant advance in our understanding of post-war design and has provided a unique opportunity to assess the strengths, and weaknesses, of our collections. Almost 40 objects have been acquired for the show, ranging from Ernest Race's 'Antelope' bench from the Festival of Britain to the spectacular evening gown by Alexander McQueen from the 'Horn of Plenty' collection of 2009.

The show also includes more than 100 loans from public and private collections across the country and abroad. We are immensely grateful to the many lenders who have made this possible.

Finally, we would especially like to thank Ernst & Young for supporting both the exhibition and the wider programme of displays on British design that coincide with it. At a moment of great economic uncertainty it is fascinating to see how Britain has responded previously to hard times and tremendous change, to take stock of these achievements and look forward with confidence to the future.

—Martin Roth
Director, Victoria and Albert Museum

Ian Dury With Love

Introduction: British Design from 1948: Innovation in the Modern Age

— Christopher Breward & Ghislaine Wood

In the stifling summer of 1948, London, a city pole-axed by the physical, economic and emotional effects of seven years of conflict, hosted the first post-war Olympic Games with a sense of trepidation. Happily any worries soon evaporated, for as the Organizing Committee's Official Report remarked, the Opening Ceremony in Wembley Stadium was:

> packed with 85,000 people. The scarlet of the Guards Band, the white of the choirs, the many coloured dresses of the ladies and the shirts of the coatless male spectators blended with the orange red of the track, the vivid green of the grass in the centre and the gaily coloured flags, to form a never-to-be-forgotten spectacle.[1]

With great haste, no little ingenuity and at minimal cost, British sporting and governmental bodies had mustered once again the famous 'spirit of the Blitz' to ensure that the promotion, administration and accommodation of what would become known as the 'Austerity Games' were fit for purpose. Even the V&A played its part, presenting the last-ever Olympiad 'Sport in Art' competition exhibition through eight galleries at a total cost of £3,000.[2] By the time of the Closing Ceremony the Committee could report that:

> with this sad farewell, there was also combined a spirit of peaceful contentment, and indeed exaltation, that in spite of the trials and tribulations of a troubled world, and in spite of all the dismal prophecies as to the likely failure of the Games, they had risen, and triumphantly risen, to greater heights than they had ever reached before, and had stirred a real hope in the hearts of millions of men and women throughout the earth in the possibility of mankind living together in happiness and peace.[3]

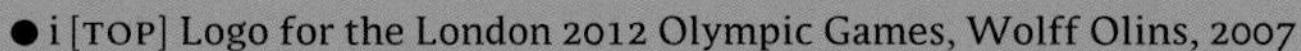

● i [TOP] Logo for the London 2012 Olympic Games, Wolff Olins, 2007
● ii [OPPOSITE] Poster for the London Olympic Games, Walter Herz, 1948 | Colour lithograph | V&A: E.331–2006

OLYMPIC GAMES
HERZ
29 JULY 1948 14 AUGUST
LONDON
Designed by HEROS PUBLICITY STUDIOS LTD.
Printed in Great Britain by McCORQUODALE & CO. LTD., LONDON, S.E.1.

Sixty-four years later, in the summer of 2012, London is set to host the Olympic Games once more. While the scale, sophistication and cost of the design of the Olympic Park in East London bear little comparison with 1948, there are some similarities in terms of the broader context – not least of a world facing significant long-term challenges in relation to natural and financial resources and political and social stability. The 'look' of the Games may have changed, but its 'spirit' remains remarkably unchanged; and this contradiction is perfectly captured in the twenty-first-century logo designed by Wolff Olins (although the bold design attracted some controversy on its initial release, to a British press traditionally sceptical of the value of corporate and public branding) [i]. As Olins's press release explains:

> London's Organizing Committee needed a powerful brand, one that could inspire and engage with a global audience of four billion people. A brand that could make the Olympic and Paralympic Games more relevant, accessible and inspiring than ever... These Games were to be everyone's. They would call for people to challenge themselves – to try new things, to go further, to discover new abilities... The emblem is 2012, an instantly recognizable symbol and a universal form... It is unconventionally bold, deliberately spirited and unexpectedly dissonant, echoing London's qualities of a modern, edgy city. Containing neither sporting images nor pictures of London landmarks, the emblem shows that the Games is more than London, more than sport. It is for everyone, regardless of age, culture and language.[4]

As in 1948, the V&A is staging a major exhibition that will open at the same time as the Olympics are hosted in London, of which this publication is the lasting record, though this time the focus is not sport. Instead *British Design from 1948: Innovation in the Modern Age* traces the changes that have informed the design, appearance and use of buildings, objects, images and ideas produced by designers who were born, trained or based in Britain since the 'make-do and mend' ethos of the Austerity Games. The range and scope of the project are huge, and its content echoes the connections and contrasts that link 1948 and 2012. The earlier examples from the 1940s and '50s support an interpretation of design in Britain that is in some ways paternalistic, parochial and fiercely patriotic, yet at the same time optimistic, democratic and highly principled; bent on creating a new and better world for its citizens. By the 1960s and through the '70s and '80s the selection of case studies demonstrates an increasing curiosity among artists and designers for the progressive character of design cultures in Europe and North America; but also a tendency towards individualism and creative anarchy informed by the economic, political and social crises of the era. And from the 1990s to the present the focus is on a slicker, more self-conscious, globally aware form of presentation; attuned to the ever-diversifying tastes of multiple audiences and consumers, and wryly critical of the models that succeeding Modernists, Postmodernists and neo-liberals have bequeathed to the youngest generation of British design talent.

● iii [LEFT] Poster for the Festival of Britain, featuring the Festival emblem designed by Abram Games, 1951 | Colour lithograph | V&A: E.307–2011 ● iv [OPPOSITE] 'Kangaroo', rocking chair, Ernest Race, 1953 | Commissioned for the roof terrace of the Time Life building, manufactured by Race Furniture Ltd, painted steel rod and flat section steel | V&A: W.36–2010

● V [ABOVE AND RIGHT] 'Carnival!!!!!', poster promoting a Rock Against Racism event, David King, *c.*1978 | Offset lithograph | V&A: E.204–2011

NF? NO!
Anti Nazi Leag
ROCK AGAINST RACISM
ARNIVA
AGAINST TH

● vi [OPPOSITE] 'Mandarin', furnishing textile, Linda Harper, 1960s | Manufactured by Hull Traders Ltd, printed cotton sateen V&A: T.168–1989 ● vii [LEFT] Mini, 1970; original design by Alec Issigonis, 1959 | Manufactured by the British Motor Corporation

Inevitably an exhibition and publication on British design will raise questions of definition, particularly around the whole issue of what might constitute the boundaries and characteristics of its subject. We are then indebted to the work of a number of scholars from several disciplines whose insights have informed our approach. Surprisingly the theme has not been a central concern to art and design historians (with some notable recent exceptions to be discussed later), but 'Britishness' is an idea that has continued to interest social and cultural historians since at least the late 1950s, when 'structuralist' and 'culturalist' professors of English literature, history and sociology in British universities argued over the place of theory in the arts and humanities and provided fuel for the emergence of the uniquely British cultural-studies project.[5] This line of academic enquiry, which connects Richard Hoggart to E.P. Thompson to Dick Hebdige to Raphael Samuel to Stuart Hall to Angela McRobbie, was one entirely focused on the issue of British identity and its relation especially to questions of social class and race and gender in a period of post-industrial and post-colonial decline.[6] The resulting literature – expansive, passionate and generally infused with Marxist good intentions – forms a bedrock for any project engaging with the material, visual and stylistic implications of post-war British design. However, its agendas and focus often work against the interpretation of representations and objects that are usually associated with this museum and with the cultural industry more generally.

The concept of Britishness has also provided a fruitful terrain for academic debate amongst political and social historians. Linda Colley in 1992 famously tracked the invention of the spatial, governmental and economic entity defined as the United Kingdom of Great Britain and Northern Ireland, from its initiation in the Act of Union of 1707 to the accession of Queen Victoria in 1837.[7] She demonstrated how relations with mainland Europe and North America and the effects of Empire encouraged the superimposition of an overarching British identity on much older regional and national identities. Crucial to her argument are the contributions of a 'pantheon' of British writers and artists to this patriotic project (interestingly the work of architects, scientists and engineers is rather underplayed), who are mobilized to suggest that the forging of Britishness has always been an essentially imaginative and creative process (an approach initiated by Nikolaus Pevsner in his examination of the characteristics of English art[8]). Even more usefully for our purposes, Colley's research suggests that some of the underlying identities that a homogenizing British identity supposedly replaced (Scottishness, Welshness, Englishness, Northernness...) have re-emerged and become far more important in the recent past and present, demonstrating the contingent nature of nationalistic and ethnic categories.

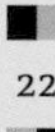

The 'imaginative' construct of Britishness evoked by Colley is one that has also concerned recent authors whose interest has focused on rather romantic (but nonetheless contested) conceptions of national belonging, rooted in the narratives of landscape, community and biography.[9] Benedict Anderson's influential work on 'imagined communities' first posited an understanding of modern nations as fluid cultural phenomena rather than material entities fixed on the map.[10] In the post-colonial, globalized, connected world of the twenty-first century the old imperialist desire to demarcate has been somewhat superseded by a consumerist tendency towards what geographer Steve Daniels has termed a 'symbolic activation' of nationhood, managed through an ongoing articulation of 'legends and landscapes, by stories of golden ages, enduring traditions, heroic deeds and dramatic destinies, located in ancient or promised homelands with hallowed sites and sceneries'.[11] The history of twentieth-century Europe is, of course, scarred by the adaptation of similar representations by the fascist ideologies of 1930s Germany and Italy, or by the rise of more recent extremist parties across the continent. But British institutions, politicians and activists – from the Crown, through William Morris to the National Trust and English Heritage – have, according to some, also tended to borrow from its nostalgic repertoire, albeit in gentler terms, inadvertently stifling technological and social innovation along the way.[12] The return to more radical concepts of Albion by anti-establishment writers, including Patrick Wright, Jon Savage, Ian Sinclair and Peter Ackroyd in the 1980s and '90s, and the rise of new independence movements and forms of local governance in Scotland, Northern Ireland and Wales more recently, suggest that the debate on nationhood and culture is not yet exhausted.[13]

● viii [OPPOSITE] 'The Ship' hat, Philip Treacy, 1994
Black satin, feather bones and antique bird-of-paradise feathers

Given the rich seam of literature generated by questions of British national identity, it is surprising how rarely histories of design engage directly with these complex issues. Fiona McCarthy and Cheryl Buckley have been the only design historians to face up to the challenge in a sustained manner.[14] With the exception of publications on fashion, film, craft and a recently developing scholarship on visual culture, the historiography of post-war British design and architecture has instead tended to concentrate (albeit very thoroughly) on institutionally-focused case studies couched in the constraining language of Modernism, rather than embracing the vibrant social, aesthetic and material narratives that imbue the terrain with colour and critical relevance.[15] Questions of identity and cultural value are more comprehensively addressed in recent literatures on late-twentieth-century popular cultures and subcultures, particularly histories of music and entertainment, but also exhibitions, consumer cultures, the built environment and urban life. The more perceptive cultural and social histories of Britain produced in the past decade have turned for inspiration to these themes of a peculiarly British sense of stylization and creativity.[16]

Beyond the academic disciplines, an accessible, almost touristic anthropology of 'British' character traits, typified by the journalism of Bill Bryson and Ian Jack, has enjoyed regular success in the non-fiction best-seller lists in recent years.[17] While there is a danger inherent in these sorts of texts of retreating into the comfort of stereotypes, they do offer another model for thinking through the ways in which the wider concept of Britishness in design culture might be applied in an accessible and stimulating manner; for an imaginative, object-centred survey of the make-up of modern Britain, drawing on these various lines of enquiry, is long overdue. It has become almost a truism to suggest that Britain's creative role in the world can be described through often opposing qualities that range from the eccentric and transgressive, through the romantic and sentimental, to the pragmatic and ingenious, but few have attempted to document the ways in which these characteristics have been consciously developed or inscribed in the nation's material landscape over time.

The exhibition 'British Design 1948–2012: Innovation in the Modern Age' attempts – by displaying more than 300 examples drawn from the fields of architecture, urban planning, fine art and sculpture, product, furniture, graphic, textile, ceramic, fashion and digital design, glass and metalworking, jewellery and illustration, design for performance, film and advertising – to construct just such a story. In so doing it follows a number of survey shows that have also presented the 'best of British' and have invited visitors to deconstruct the unique and shared qualities that define British manufacturing output: the Council of Industrial Design (CoID) sponsored 'Britain Can Make It' hosted by the V&A in 1946, and the less well-known 'Enterprise Scotland' at the Royal Scottish Museum, Edinburgh in 1947, 'Sheffield on its Mettle' in 1948 and 'The Story of Wool' at Bradford in 1949. All of these showcased contemporary British products and promoted the CoID line 'that exports were paramount, good design crucial and thoughtful consumption essential' in facing the challenges of post-war reconstruction.[18] The Arts Council (founded 1946) and British Council (founded 1934) have also played an important part in promoting British design both at home and abroad.

Alongside these organizations and events, the V&A has had a crucial role in the collecting and disseminating of contemporary British design in the post-war years, largely through the work of the Museum's Circulation Department. Described as a 'museum within a museum' and 'one of the real splendours of the V&A', the Circulation Department organized exhibitions that toured schools, colleges, museums and galleries throughout the country until the mid-1970s, while also developing an active contemporary acquisitions policy.[19] The educational remit of Circulation was paramount, and was clearly allied to the founding principles of the V&A. A broad exhibitions programme helped to inform and educate audiences and change attitudes towards contemporary design ideas, and important shows included Carol Hogben's 'Modern Chairs', held at the Whitechapel Art Gallery in 1970, which subsequently toured to Oxford, Aberdeen and Greenwich; and a number of single-media shows focusing, for example, on British studio pottery and modern glass. A thoughtful series paired contemporary designers, to explore the interrelatedness of different media – the jewellery of Gerda Flöckinger with the glass of Sam Herman, and the textiles of Peter Collingwood with ceramics by Hans Coper.[20]

This more experimental approach to themes and material typified the work of the Circulation Department, which actively explored the relationships between different disciplines. As Elizabeth Knowles, a curator in Circulation, described:

> contemporary fine art and design were dealt with together in a way that gave a specific current relevance through the sixties and early seventies. There was a rapid broadening of understanding of the interrelatedness of art and design, and of the recent history of art where design and photography, painting, graphic art, printmaking and so on had developed together. At one level, this was illuminated by the growth of 'Sunday Supplement' culture at that time.[21]

A particular strength of Circulation's collection and exhibition policy was in the area of textile design. Throughout the 1950s and '60s displays of contemporary textiles were sent around the country, predominantly to art schools, and the department built strong relationships with most of the leading manufacturers, including Liberty, Heal's, Edinburgh Weavers, Hull Traders, Helios and Horrockses. Through acquisition and gifts, thousands of examples entered the collection, making textiles one of the richest areas for the study of twentieth-century design in the V&A. A series of exhibitions also combined both historical and modern design and proved hugely influential. The 'English Chintz' exhibition of 1960 brought the story of chintz up to the present day and included work by Hans Tisdall, John Drummond and Lucienne Day. As *The Ambassador* magazine commented, 'the wealth of our design tradition becomes an inexhaustible point of departure for every kind of design from the most literal to the most abstract interpretation'.[22] And Barbara Griggs, writing in the *Evening Standard*, confidently predicted that the exhibition would 'exercise a major influence on fashion', reporting that 'Bernard Nevill, lecturer at the Royal College of Art, has persuaded the textile students there to produce a series of Morris-inspired designs.'[23] The V&A's historical collections throughout the period have continued to provide inspiration and a vast and well-used resource for contemporary designers and manufacturers.

● ix [OPPOSITE] *i-D*, issue 20, 1984 | Cover designed by Terry Jones | NAL: 38041800737660

WORLDWIDE MANUAL OF STYLE i-D No.20 NOVEMBER 19[illegible] £[illegible].00

THE FUN & GAMES ISSUE

i-D

YOW!

COME

INTO THE

BIRDCAGE

WITH THE

FASHION

FUN

BRIGADE!

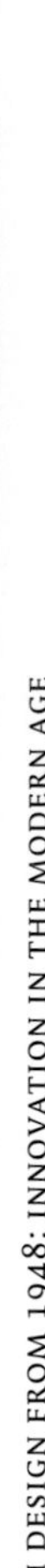

www.omlet.co.uk

● x [OPPOSITE TOP] 'Thinkingman's Chair', Jasper Morrison, 1986
Manufactured by Cappellini, 1989, painted tubular steel and strip steel | V&A: W.15–1989
● xi [OPPOSITE BOTTOM] 'Eglu' chicken house, 2007 | Manufactured by Omlet, moulded plastic

The controversial announcement of the closure of the Circulation Department in 1976 threw into stark relief the lack of cultural provision for the regions. The V&A was accused of 'metropolitan myopia', and a petition signed by more than 70 artists, art critics, college principals and historians was handed to the Department of Education and Science by David Hockney.[24] It stated, 'We cannot see why a cut of this order need necessarily deprive the whole country of a standard-setting and cost-effective service which continues to fulfil the vision of the original founders of the V&A.'

Despite the closure of Circulation, the V&A continued to showcase British design during the 1970s and early '80s through the activities of the materials departments (especially Prints, Drawings and Paintings – now part of Word and Image). Exhibitions such as Margaret Timmers's 'The Way We Live Now: Designs for Interiors 1950 to the Present Day', of 1978, not only provided an invaluable comprehensive survey of the British design scene at that date, but also brought a large number of important works on paper by designers into the collections. The collaboration with the Conran Foundation, which resulted in the opening of the Boilerhouse project within the V&A in 1981, finally provided a dedicated space for contemporary design shows, and a number of important exhibitions helped establish design as a genre separate from the decorative arts.[25] Subsequent development of the gallery of 'British Art and Design 1900–1960', in 1983, and of the Twentieth-Century Gallery in 1992 (partly redisplayed in the West Room of the National Art Library in 2008), together with a continuing series of thematic exhibitions, have ensured a long-standing engagement with, and consideration of, the shifting nature of British design practice, informed over the same period by the burgeoning discipline of design history.[26]

Beyond the V&A, the exhibition 'British Design: Image & Identity' – held by the Boijmans-Van Beuningen Museum, Rotterdam, in 1989 – offered a very different 'outsider' perspective, informed by (as the curators saw it) the collapse of British manufacturing in recent decades and the rise of a distinctive Postmodern British style-culture in the 1980s. In the words of the curator Frederique Huygen:

> The identity of British design is no easy thing to pin down... Fashionable tendencies intermingle with tradition, visual styles from elsewhere are quickly absorbed, and most design areas testify to a great diversity. Influences come from the street, from tradition, from modernism and classicism... There is little question of a single British Identity, in visual terms, that holds true for all design sectors. Any such leitmotiv is elusive indeed.[27]

In the spirit of a prevailing Postmodernism, Huygen favoured a pluralistic reading that emphasized diversity and the formation of multiple identities as a way of interpreting the 'character' of British creativity.

More recently, curators have chosen to set British design achievements in a sharper, more pragmatic, arguably Modernist perspective; where questions of local identity and 'personality' are subsumed by the greater demands of globalization. In 2009 the Design Museum in London staged and published 'Design In Britain: Big Ideas (small island)' in this spirit, celebrating the achievements of generations of British designers, but recognizing, once again, the challenges facing the sector in a world where 'there is no *British* design; there is only *design in Britain*'.[28] The context for this exhibition was a series of important monographic shows staged over the last 20 years and focusing on the work of major British designers, including practices as diverse as Archigram, Alan Fletcher and Philip Treacy.

British Design from 1948 incorporates elements of all these important predecessors, but in its approach – which aims to interrogate the constituents of an evolving design sensibility through an examination of the key places and spaces of the production and mediation of objects and ideas in Britain (the state, the city, the land, the home, the studio, the street, the factory, the laboratory and the architect's practice) – it offers what we believe is a more situated and nuanced account of how we got where we are, and how that journey has impacted on the look and feel of the objects and images that are all around us. Importantly, it also integrates the fine and decorative arts into broader cultural histories, breaking down the boundaries between disciplines. The three big themes of the exhibition: Tradition and Modernity, Subversion, and Innovation and Creativity, provide the section headers for the chapters in this book; and our overlapping chronological divisions are broadly the same (reconstruction in the 1950s and '60s, a challenge to consensus from the 1960s to the '90s, and the shift from a manufacturing to a service and creative economy from the 1970s to the present). Most crucially, we have invited prominent scholars from the disciplines of art and design history, leading critics and curators, and some of the most notable designers and makers of the past 60 years to tell the story of British design in all its forms and to reflect on its successes and failures. In 2012, as in 1948, we hope that all the training, teamwork and effort that went into the planning and execution of this timely project pay off!

Section One
Tradition and Modernity
1945–79

Tradition and Modernity 1945–79
— Christopher Breward & Ghislaine Wood

● 1.1 [BELOW] *Autumn Landscape*, William Gear, 1951 | Oil on canvas | Laing Art Gallery, Newcastle upon Tyne (Tyne & Wear Archives & Museums) ● 1.2 [BELOW RIGHT] The Prince of Wales's Investiture Coronet, Louis Osman, 1969 | Gold, platinum, diamonds and emeralds, the orb engraved by Malcolm Appleby, with velvet and ermine cap of estate | The Royal Collection ● 1.3 [OPPOSITE] View of a Modernist housing development, Ernö Goldfinger, 1942 | Print, watercolour and pastel on paper | RIBA Library Drawings Collection

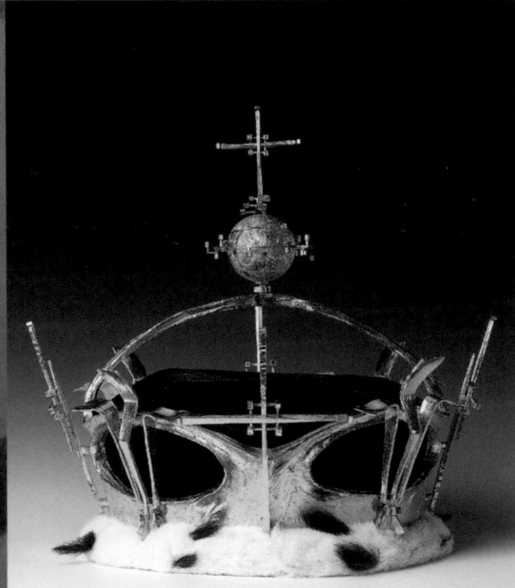

The immense impact of the war on the social, economic and physical fabric of Britain created a new politics of consensus. In 1945 a Labour Government, committed to equality, social reform and the task of reconstruction, swept to power, and its agenda for a comprehensive Welfare State was to be broadly supported by subsequent governments on both sides of the political divide for the next 30 years. As Arthur Marwick has observed:

> the ideology of consensus ... was of a well-disposed, well-educated upper class, cooperating with the various fractions of the middle class and with certain representatives of the working class, in running the country in the best interests of everyone, it being understood that those interests comprised spending money both on welfare services and, to a degree never envisaged before the war, on culture.[1]

This commitment to culture saw the creation of many new organizations, including CEMA (Council for the Encouragement of Music and the Arts), which in 1946 became the Arts Council; the CoID (Council of Industrial Design) in 1944; and, crucially, in 1964 the Labour appointment of the first Minister for the Arts, Jennie Lee, who issued the first White Paper on arts policy and funding in 1965. These new instruments of the state helped transform Britain's cultural landscape.

Initiatives such as the 'Britain Can Make It' exhibition, held in the V&A in 1946, and the Festival of Britain in 1951 engendered a design culture, one in which new concepts were corralled to meet the requirements of rebuilding Britain's infrastructure and influence overseas. In the designs for the Festival of Britain cultural policy was clearly allied with Modernist aesthetics to create a powerful vision of a modern, democratic nation. But this alliance did not go uncontested. The controversy over the inclusion and purchase of William Gear's *Autumn Landscape* in the exhibition '60 paintings for '51' clearly illustrated the resistance to Modernism in certain quarters [1.1]. Gear, it was argued in the national newspapers and private circles alike, was too European and his uncompromising abstraction thoroughly un-British. The war had brought to the fore the importance of preserving British traditions and heritage, for which people had fought and lost their lives. Alongside the promotion of certain figurative styles, various events also celebrated a Britain where tradition, stability and conservatism governed – and none was more important than the Queen's Coronation in 1953. In 1969 the investiture of the Prince of Wales also managed to convey the sense of an ancient rite reinterpreted for the modern world – its setting in Caernarfon Castle adding to the mysticism [1.2].

The drive for modernity in the reconstruction of Britain was often mediated by a preoccupation with the past and with British tradition, but much of the regeneration of urban Britain in the 1950s and '60s, the building of public housing and new towns, civic centres and schools, universities and hospitals was dominated by the discourses of Modernism [1.3]. In the New Towns the lessons of the nineteenth-century Garden City were adapted to meet the need of relocating large populations and industries from the overcrowded and bomb-damaged cities. Harlow, one of the first new towns, provided an early example of high-density housing, with the first residential tower block, The Lawn [1.4, 1.11, 1.60]. But the tower block would later become the focal point for much of the criticism of post-war Modernist architecture. As Frederick Gibberd, chief architect for Harlow, noted:

> The wholesale adoption of system-built tower blocks out of catalogues by local authorities as an easy way to reduce their waiting lists was one of the reasons why tower blocks became a symbol for all the ills of city centres. Other abuses were their expansion into monstrous slabs, their use as family flats and their high density.[2]

In the last new town, Milton Keynes, the planners and architects studiously avoided high-density towers and experimented with a wide range of housing, including innovative structures in new materials [1.9, 1.10]. The design of Milton Keynes in some ways signalled the rejection of many of the precepts of European Modernism by a generation influenced by the new thinking of the 1960s [1.61, 1.62].

The forces of change in larger society were also transforming the British home, and fundamental to this was the economic recovery of Britain, which had created new kinds of consumer demand. As Marwick suggests, these 'new consumers were in a position to reject the canons laid down by established authority, metropolitan, upper-class and old'.[3] A growing, affluent middle class embraced modern design, while the new kinds of living space created by denser living required new design solutions. As John Prizeman's drawing *Her House* of 1959 demonstrates, spaces in the modern home had to be flexible: kitchens, dining rooms and sitting rooms collapsing into a free flow of space and a new informality of living [1.5]. New types of space required affordable modern design, and many British furniture companies responded to the challenge, including G-Plan, Stag Furniture and Kandya [1.12]. These manufacturers, and high-end companies such as Hille and Archie Shine, often looked to Scandinavian Modernism for inspiration. A particular strength of British design for the home was in the area of textile design. Tibor Reich, Lucienne Day, Jacqueline Groag and Althea McNish, to name a few, created some of the best textile designs of the period, while companies like Hull Traders and Edinburgh Weavers experimented with new techniques and developed important relationships with fine artists [1.8, 1.16]. New types of objects also entered the home, and none had more influence on consumer taste than the television [1.6]. Still rare in the early 1950s, televisions were to be found in 75 per cent of homes by 1961, and in 91 per cent by 1971.

● 1.4 [ABOVE] Design for The Dashes, Harlow, Gerald Lacoste, 1954 | Drawn by Lawrence Wright, watercolour on card | RIBA Library Drawings Collection ● 1.5 [BELOW] Her House, design for a home limited to 1,070 square feet and a cost of £3,000, John Prizeman, 1959 | Published in the *Daily Express*, 15 October 1959, pen, ink and Letratone on paper | V&A: E.1135–1979 ● 1.6 [OPPOSITE TOP LEFT] 'CS17' television, Robin Day, 1957 | Manufactured by Pye Ltd, 17-inch screen and wooden cabinet, steel stand | V&A: Circ.231 & A–1963 ● 1.7 [OPPOSITE TOP RIGHT] 'Mambo' chair, Michael Inchbald, 1955 | Iron frame with cane arms and back, and foam cushions with linen upholstery | V&A: W.13: 1-3–1981 ● 1.8 [OPPOSITE BOTTOM] 'The Fisherman', furnishing textile, Keith Vaughan, 1956 | Manufactured by Edinburgh Weavers Ltd, screen-printed cotton | V&A: Circ.686–1956

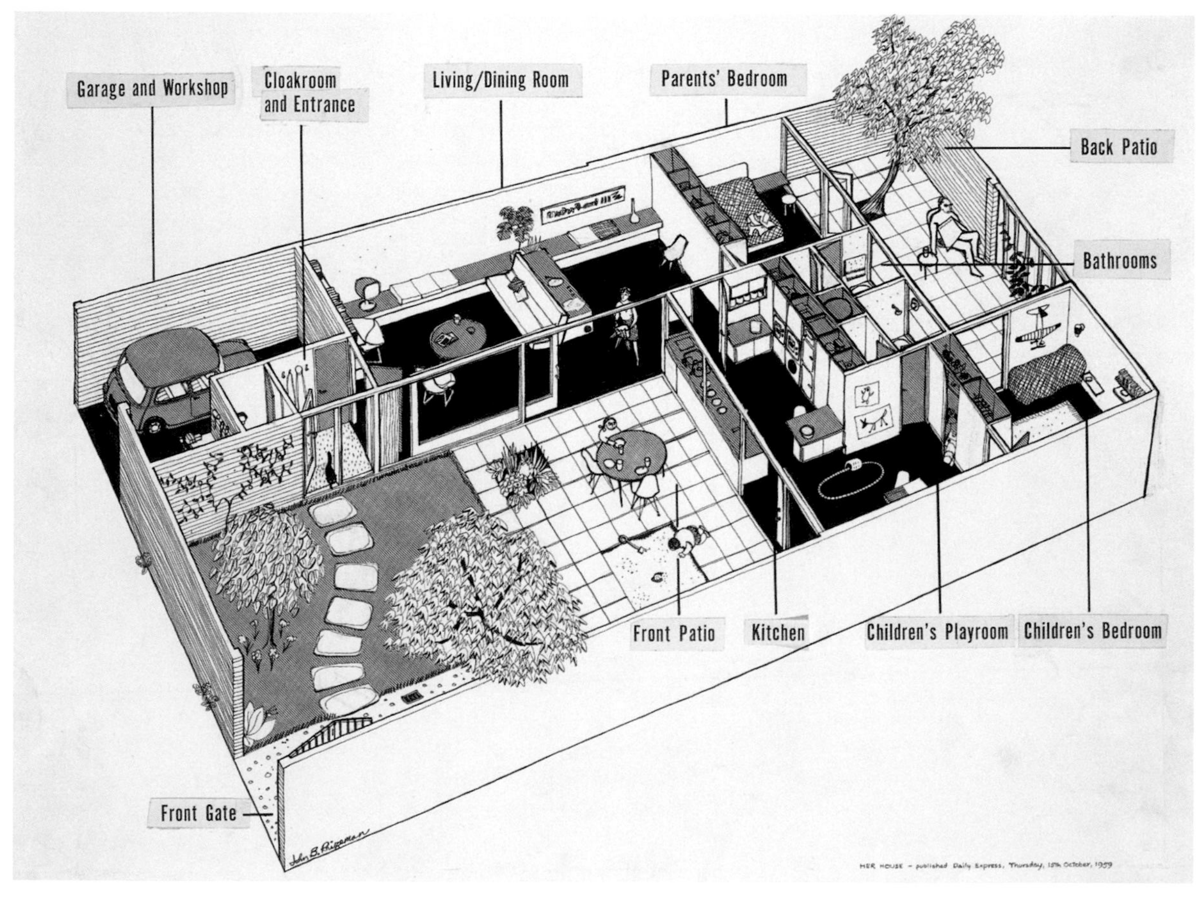

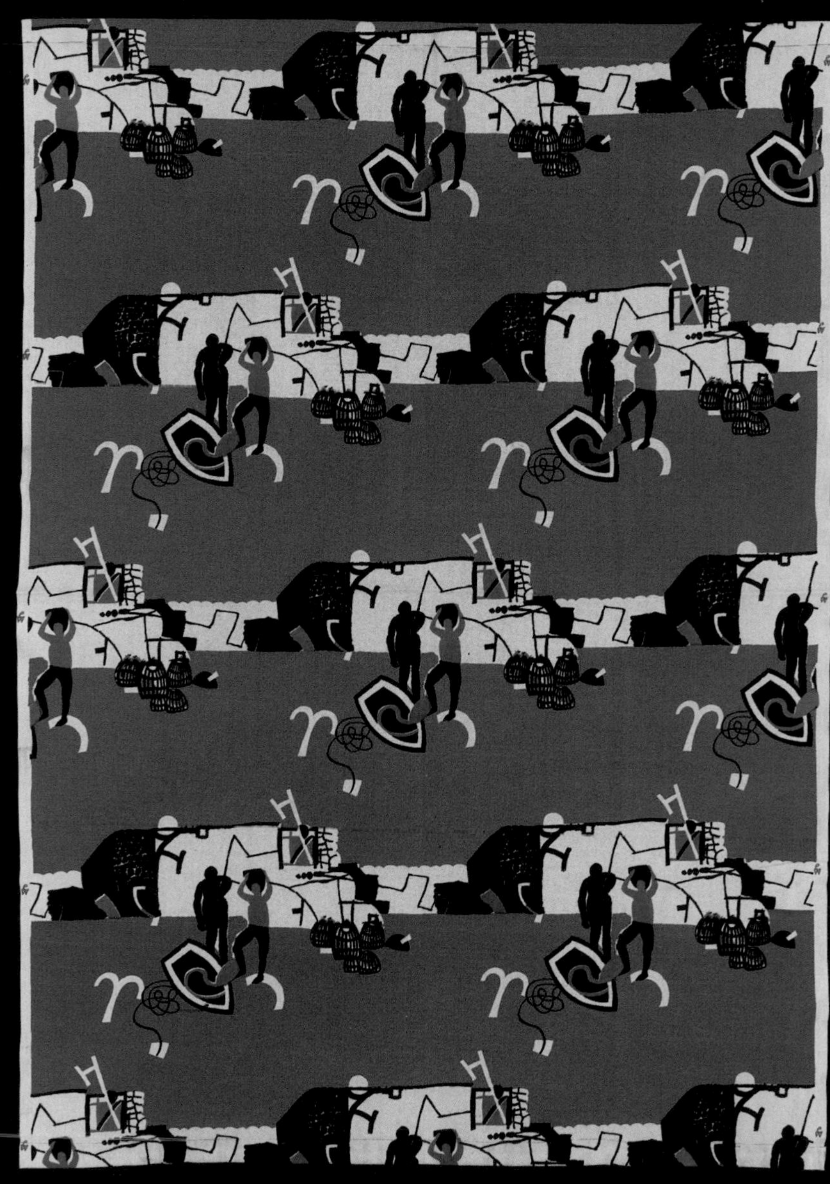

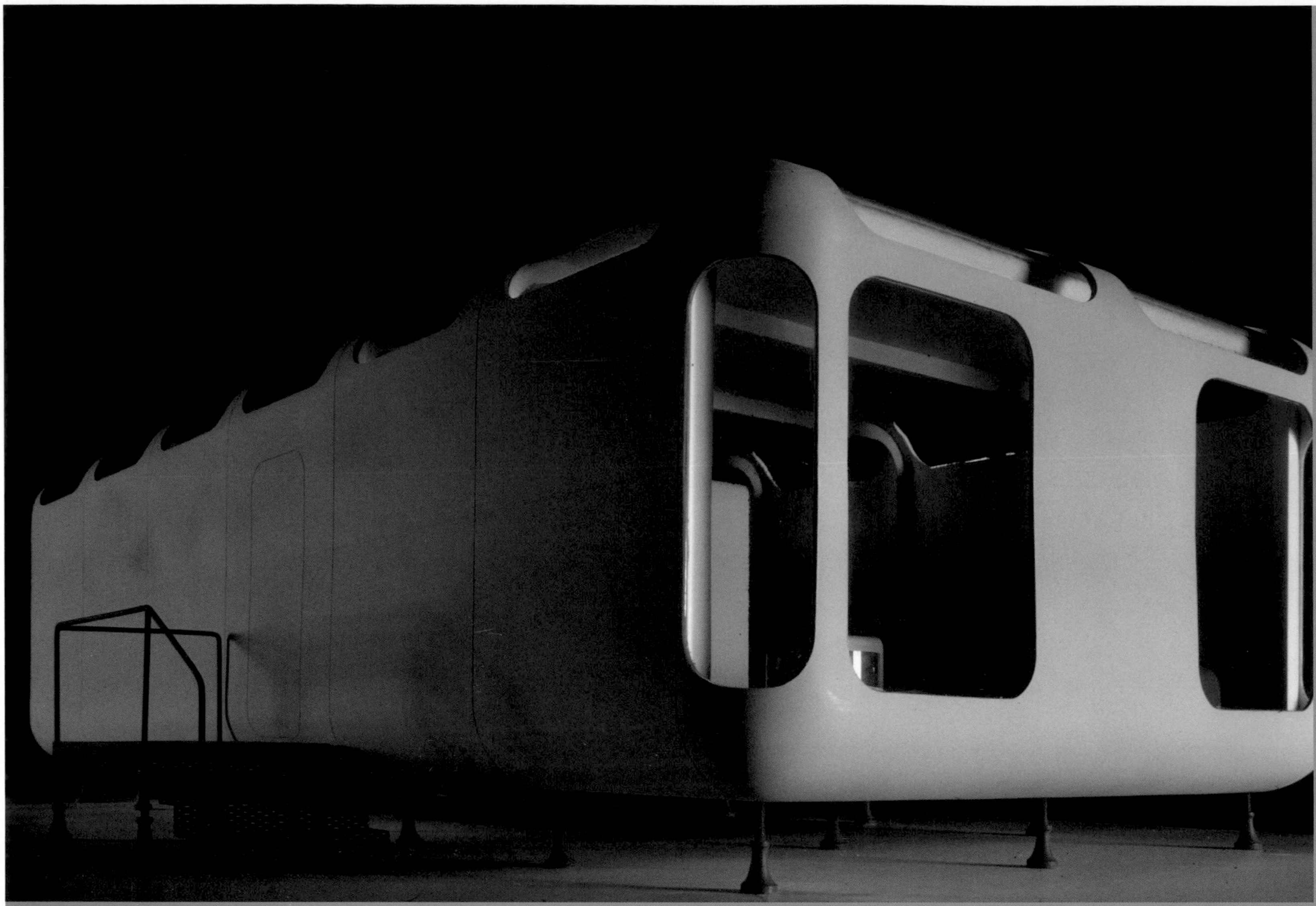

Where is Milton Keynes?

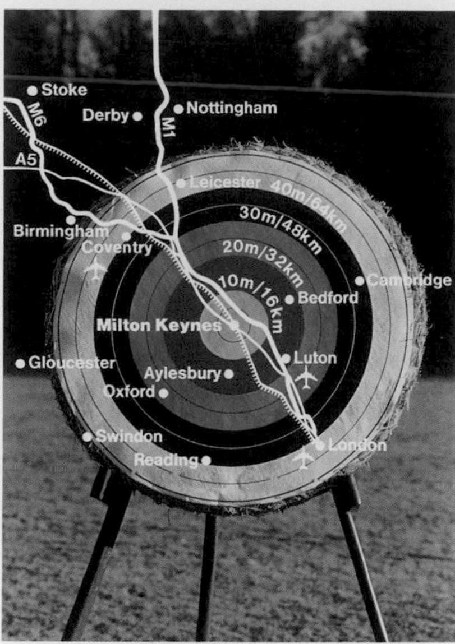

Milton Keynes is in North Buckinghamshire, an hour by road from London and just a bit longer from Birmingham.
Direct rail services bring you from many major cities like London, Liverpool, Manchester and Coventry, and the M1 and the proposed new motorway links will take you from Milton Keynes to ports and airports all over the country.
Within Milton Keynes a new system of roads has been designed so that you can travel around quickly and comfortably inside the city, too.

Milton Keynes Development Corporation, Wavendon Tower, Wavendon, Milton Keynes, MK17 8LX. Telephone: Bletchley 4000

Milton Keynes
The kind of city you'll want your family to grow up in

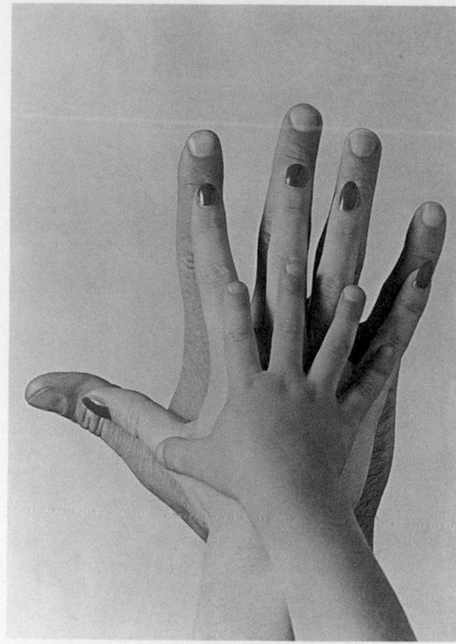

Milton Keynes will be different from the noisy, crowded and often ugly cities you know today. You'll be able to afford a place to live, find the kind of job you want and travel about easily.
In your spare time you'll have plenty of outdoor and indoor activities to choose from. And there'll be woodlands, hedgerows, rivers and streams to enjoy (things you wouldn't usually find in a city).
All kinds of people are coming to Milton Keynes. Many of them will be from London; people trying to get away from the problems of overcrowding and housing nightmares.
Maybe you're one of them.

Milton Keynes Development Corporation, Wavendon Tower, Wavendon, Milton Keynes, MK17 8LX. Telephone: Bletchley 4000

● 1.9 [OPPOSITE] Model of an experimental plastic house, 'GRP modular unit type 1', Milton Keynes Development Corporation Architects' Department, 1973
● 1.10 [ABOVE] Posters promoting Milton Keynes, Minale, Tattersfield, Provinciali, 1973 | Designed for the Milton Keynes Development Corporation, printed by Westerham Press, colour offset lithographs | V&A: E.174 & 175–2011

In the more rarefied world of interior decoration British designers were also making an important contribution. John Fowler's 'Country-House Style' was to have a widespread impact on the interiors of the rich, both in Britain and abroad [1.84]. His understanding of historical style and his sensitivity to detail brought about a reinvention of the idea of the aristocratic interior. He gave particular attention to soft furnishings and amassed a large collection of historic textiles and wallpapers. Fowler frequently adapted old designs, giving them a more contemporary feel by altering the scale, arrangement of details or colours. He said, 'I like the decoration of a room to be well behaved but free from too many rules, to have a sense of graciousness; to be mannered, yet casual and unselfconscious; to be stimulating, even provocative; and finally to be nameless of period.'[4]

The influence of Fowler was to be felt by the next generation, which included David Hicks and Michael Inchbald, both of whom developed their own unique styles, combining antiques, period-style furniture and modern design within the homes of wealthy and largely metropolitan clients [1.13, 1.14, 1.106]. Hicks's trademark was the use of bold pattern and strong colour, while Inchbald, who trained as an architect, designed modern furniture for many of his interiors. The work of Max Clendinning and Ralph Adron reflected a more contemporary pop aesthetic and a freeing-up of conventions, which appealed to a younger and more progressive audience [1.104, 1.108, 1.109]. As Lucia van der Post observed in the *Daily Telegraph*:

> I never did quite see all those girls in Courrèges boots and mini-skirts perching in a lady like manner on the edge of a Sheraton chair or even an Eames, come to that. In their own insistent, kooky way they were just crying out for furniture that was young, up-to-the-minute, visually provocative and had all the zing and impact of current fashion.[5]

Clendinning, alongside many other designers, experimented with new materials, processes and forms, such as spun polyurethane foam, reflecting the new, more relaxed style of the 1960s and the move away from functionalism. David Colwell's 'Contour' chair of 1968 is archetypal of the design of this period, with its use of transparent moulded plastic and clear Space Age imagery [1.15].

The shift in values towards the disposable and the contingent, which accompanied the expanding consumer landscape of the 1950s and '60s, also provoked reaction. Issues of ethical living, self-sufficiency and sustainability increasingly came to determine debates in the late 1960s and '70s, and the role of the British landscape and countryside as a source of inspiration and a place of work came into focus. Many artists and designers moved out of the metropolitan centres to locate their practices in the countryside, including craft practitioners such as the ceramist Michael Casson [1.97] and commercial designers like Laura Ashley. The Brotherhood of Ruralists – a group of painters that included Ann and Graham Arnold, Peter Blake, Jann Haworth, David Inshaw, and Annie and Graham Ovenden – left the city to focus on nature as a subject matter, recalling the move to St Ives by a group of artists almost 50 years before [1.18]. Themes of the romantic and the pastoral continued to exert an influence on much cultural production, and a particularly rich and idiosyncratic vein emerged in the realm of children's literature and illustration. J.R.R. Tolkien's extraordinary fantasy world of Middle Earth, explored in *The Lord of the Rings*, was made real in the illustrations of Pauline Baynes [1.90], while Kit Williams created a treasure hunt embedded in the British landscape. The magical 'Hare' jewel of the book *Masquerade* pricked the imagination of adults and children all over the country, and helped fuel the growing interest in the ancient, mystical sites of Britain [1.17].

The tensions between British traditions and the processes of modernization in the post-war period ripple through the areas discussed above: the state, city, land and home. The following essays explore these themes in more detail, throwing light on the way in which such tensions were articulated and resolved.

● 1.11 [ABOVE] The Lawn, Harlow, Frederick Gibberd, 1951 ● 1.12 [OPPOSITE TOP LEFT] Design for an interior furnished with G-Plan furniture, Leslie Dandy, 1960 | Pen and ink and watercolour on paper | V&A: E.335–1978 ● 1.13 [OPPOSITE TOP RIGHT] Drawing room, 10 Milner Street, London, Michael Inchbald, *c.*1959 | Furnishings include a swivel chair designed by Inchbald for the *QE2* ● 1.14 [OPPOSITE BOTTOM LEFT] Entrance lobby, apartment of Lady John Cholmondeley, Hyde Park, London, David Hicks, 1968 ● 1.15 [OPPOSITE BOTTOM RIGHT] 'Contour' chair, David Colwell, 1967–8 | Manufactured by 4's Company Ltd, 1968, acrylic shell with nylon-coated steel frame | V&A: Circ.64–1970

FLAMINGO
tibor foteurprint made in England.
FLAMINGO
tibor foteurprint made in England.

● 1.16 [OPPOSITE LEFT] 'Flamingo', furnishing textile, Tibor Reich, 1957 | Manufactured by Tibor Ltd, printed cotton with a design derived from photographs of leaves using the Fotexur process | V&A: Circ.463–1963 ● 1.17 [OPPOSITE RIGHT] Hare jewel, Kit Williams, 1978 | Made for the book *Masquerade*, published 1979, gold, faience, ruby, citrines, mother-of-pearl, quartz | Private collection ● 1.18 [ABOVE] *The Badminton Game*, David Inshaw, 1972–3 | Oil on canvas | Tate

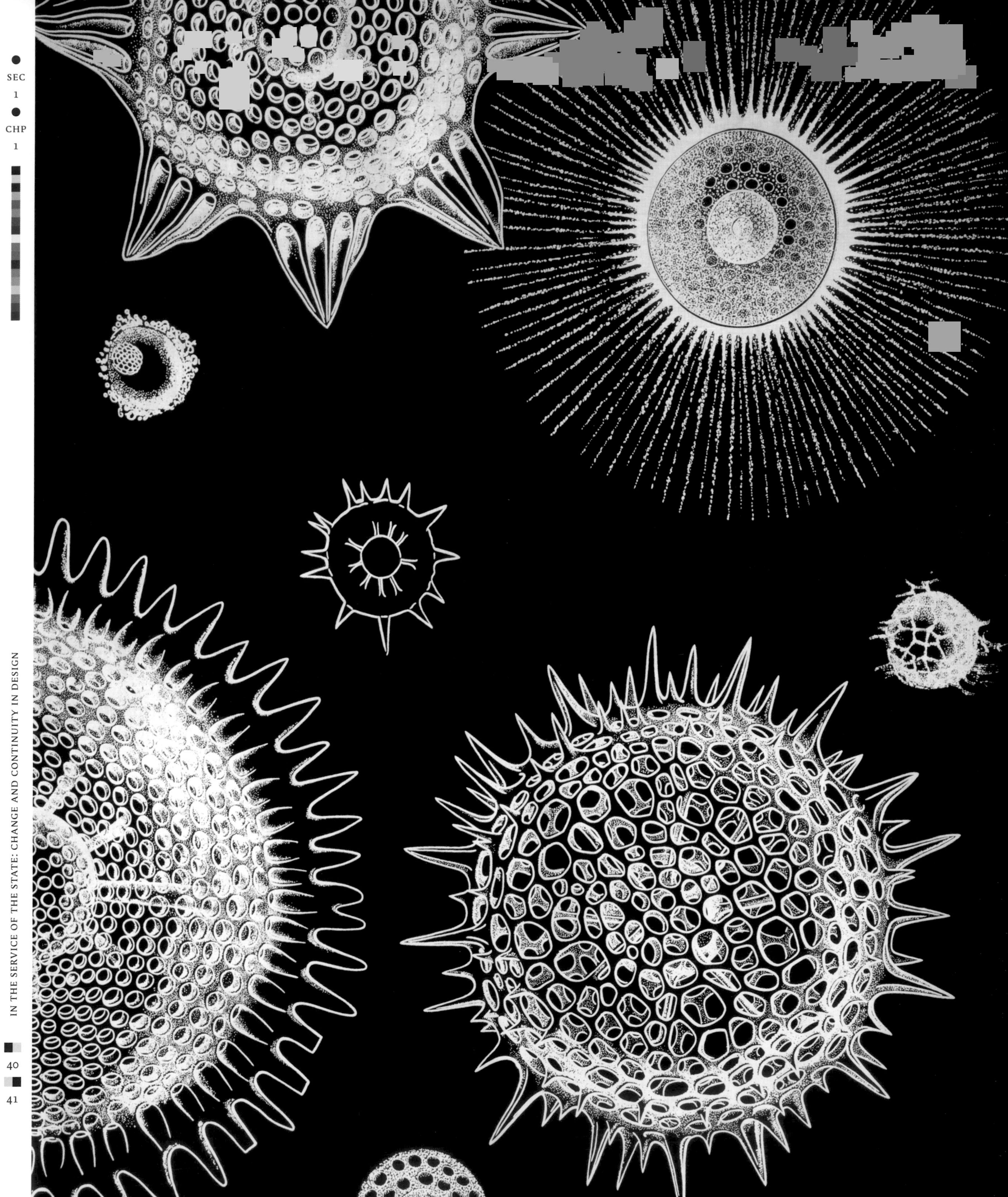

1 In the Service of the State: Change and Continuity in Design

— Christopher Breward & Ghislaine Wood

● 1.19 [ABOVE] Poster for the Festival of Britain, including the emblem designed by Abram Games, 1951 | Printed by W.S. Powell Ltd for HMSO, colour lithograph V&A: E.308–2011 ● 1.20 [OPPOSITE] Invitation to the Savoy Coronation Ball, Abram Games, 1953 | Printed by Lund Humphries, card | V&A: E.288–1981

The major state events of the Festival of Britain and the Coronation, held in 1951 and 1953 respectively, seem to lay bare the tensions between tradition and modernization that characterized British design culture as it emerged from the Second World War. On the one hand, the Festival, championed by a Labour government, provided a vision of modern Britain buoyed by a commitment to socialist welfarism and Modernism; on the other, the Coronation, held in that ancient locus of Church and state, Westminster Abbey, presented a spectacle redolent with tradition, which reaffirmed, for an awe-inspired audience, conservative structures of power and taste.

Yet these two occasions also revealed the interdependences existing in post-war Britain. Both presented scenarios where old and new cohered. If the South Bank site of the Festival promoted a more progressive view, then in related events through towns and villages all over the country Britain's ancient traditions and rituals were also celebrated. Many subsequent accounts of the Coronation have remarked on the multifaceted nature of the ceremony itself:

> Inside Westminster Abbey a privileged elite witnessed what was essentially a medieval rite... Outside ... a much larger audience saw the more familiar face of modern royalty, produced according to late nineteenth-century notions of official spectacle and tradition... [At the same time] the new medium of television magnified the pageantry, orchestrating the coronation as a world event and inserting it into a developing network of international communications.[1]

Many of the same figures were involved in the design of both projects. Sir Hugh Casson was Director of Architecture for the Festival and responsible for the street decorations at the Coronation; while Abram Games created memorably patriotic images for each, astutely adapting iconography to suit the different contexts. For the Festival, Games celebrated Britain's imperial past in the personification of Britannia, while for the Coronation Ball he played with the thoroughly royal symbolism of the lion and unicorn [1.19, 1.20]. Both were unambiguously decked in red, white and blue. This chapter describes the ways in which such key state-sponsored moments inscribed a series of design values and an attitude towards innovation that would have a profound influence on Britain's built environment and creative life for the remainder of the century.

THE FESTIVAL OF BRITAIN

As J.M. Richards, writing in the *Architectural Review*, remarked, 'Britain has for the first time this summer instead of a few freakish examples of a modern style, a whole quarter where the twentieth-century Englishman can wander about in a world of his own making.'[2] The astonishing structures of the Festival – the Dome of Discovery, the Skylon, the Festival Hall, the 'Sea and Ships' and 'Lion and Unicorn' Pavilions and the Regatta Restaurant – helped introduce the idea of modern architecture and the wider project of reconstruction to the general public, and all in the very heart of London. As

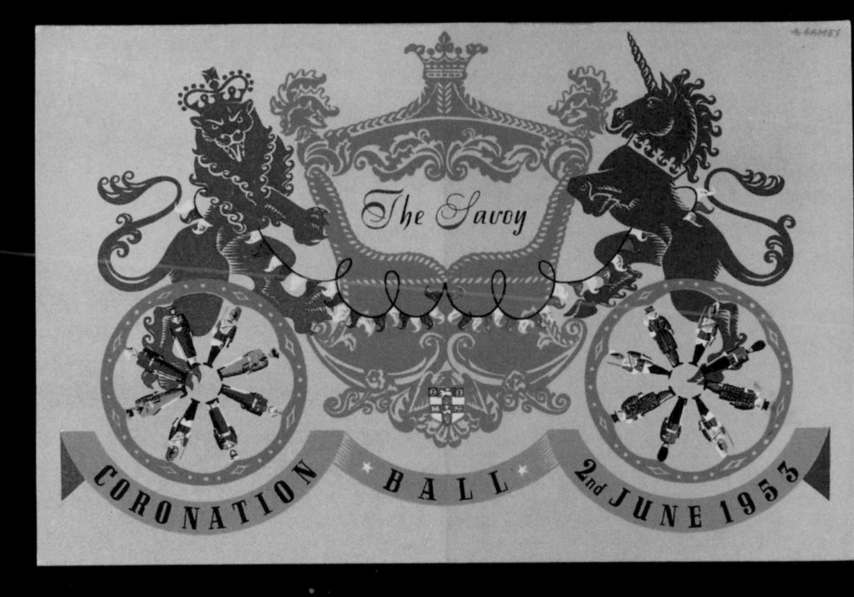

Misha Black, one of the designers of the Festival, noted, 'We vanquished those who claimed that modern architecture ... was unacceptable to the tradition-conscious British and could not be welded satisfactorily in the fabric of an ancient city.'[3] Much of the language of the South Bank was indebted to European Modernism and, like Misha Black, many of the architects and designers involved were European émigrés, having come to Britain before or during the war.

The Festival provided an opportunity for experiment. Ralph Tubb's Dome of Discovery was, at the time, the largest domed structure ever constructed, while Basil Spence's 'Sea and Ships' Pavilion used an exposed steel framework that proved extremely influential [1.22]. James Gowan, as a young architect, worked in the studio of Powell and Moya; he recently described drafting the impressive presentation drawing for the Skylon, but was most proud of the Newton Einstein House designed for a vacant site opposite the V&A in South Kensington and part of the Science exhibition [1.21, 1.23, 1.24].[4] This extraordinary building, sadly never built, aimed to demonstrate the Coriolis effect.[5] In these ways the Festival offered a testing ground that helped a generation of architects explore new ideas unfettered. As J.M. Richards noted, the Festival was 'conceived and built in a contemporary spirit, with no sign of the compromise usually thought necessary in order to placate conservative and official taste'.[6]

The utopian vision inherent in the Festival architecture was reinforced in the informal layout of the site, which avoided strong axes, in marked contrast to previous international exhibition plans. A 'democratic' informality permeated the entire experience, from the narrative of the displays and the way visitors wandered around the site to the focus on pleasure and entertainment.[7] The candy colours and delicate, almost fragile structures of Ernest Race and A.J. Milne's terrace furniture seemed to encapsulate the entire experience of ephemeral fun [1.25, 1.26]. As Dylan Thomas wrote, 'And what a lot of pink – rose, raspberry, strawberry, peach, flesh, blush, lobster, salmon, tally-ho – there is, plastered and doodled over this four-acre gay and soon-to-be-gone Festival City in sprawling London.'[8]

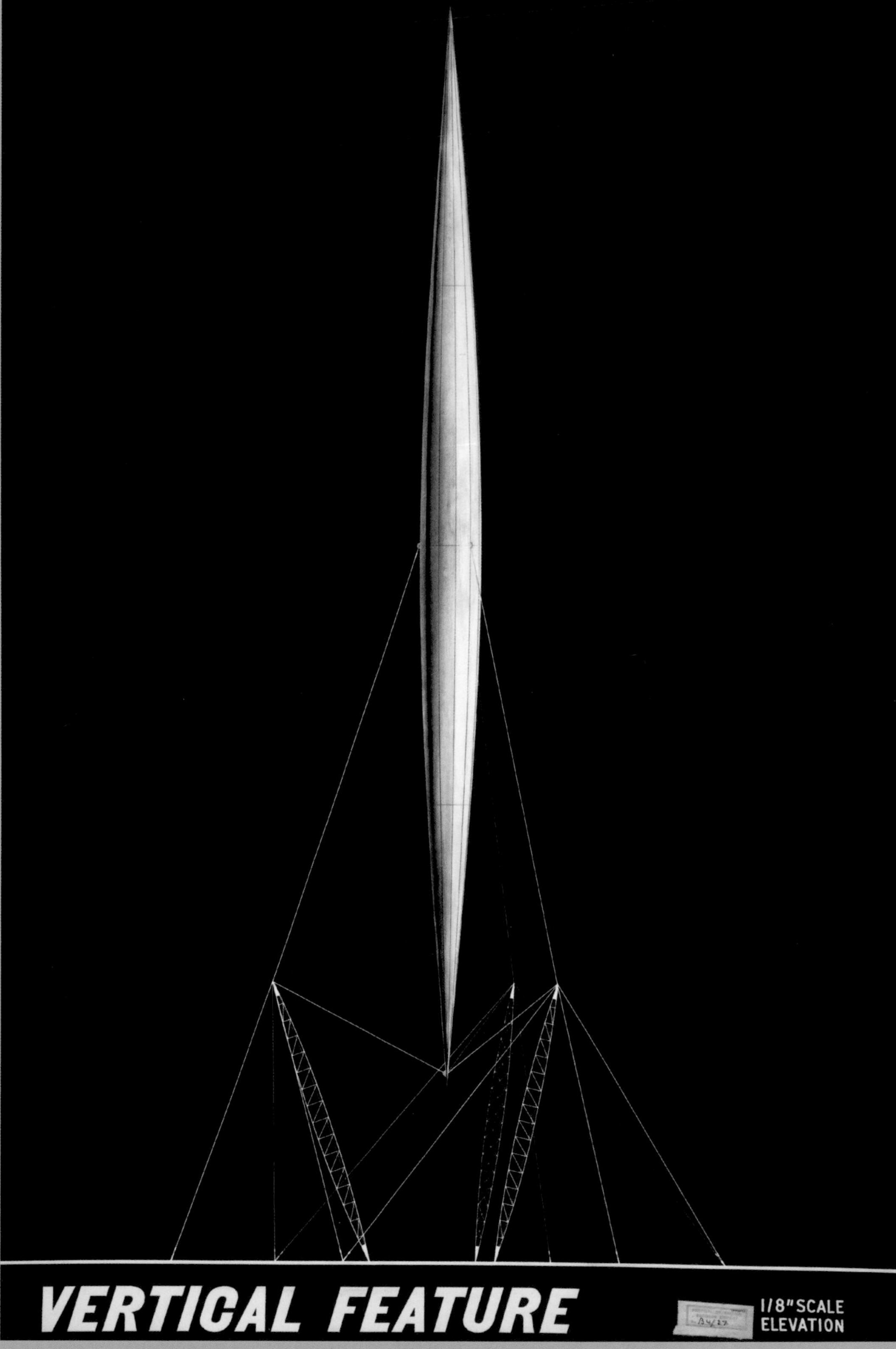

● 1.21 [ABOVE] Presentation drawing of the Vertical Feature, The Skylon, Powell and Moya, 1951 | Drawn by James Gowan, carbon-based ink on paper, backed onto millboard, with pen and ink drawing, pencil and charcoal | The National Archives ● 1.22 [OPPOSITE TOP] Presentation drawing of the South Bank with the Dome of Discovery, Douglas Stephen, 1951 | Pen and ink, wax resist, coloured ink wash and wax crayon on paper | The National Archives ● 1.23 [OPPOSITE BOTTOM LEFT] Poster advertising the Exhibition of Science held at South Kensington during the Festival of Britain, Robin Day, 1951 Issued by the London Press Exchange, colour offset lithograph | V&A: E.1923–1952 ● 1.24 [OPPOSITE BOTTOM RIGHT] Elevation and section of the Newton-Einstein House, designed for the Festival of Britain, Powell and Moya, 1951 | Drawn by James Gowan, dyeline print | The National Archives

FESTIVAL OF BRITAIN
RECORDS LIBRARY

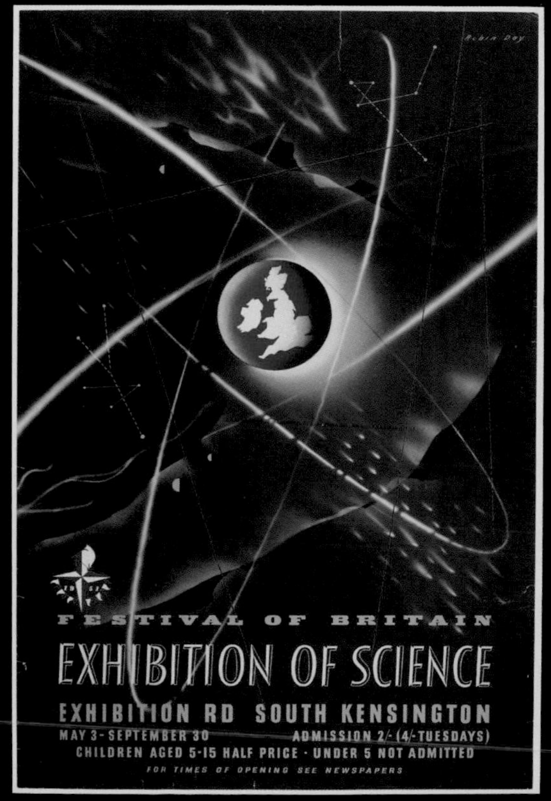
FESTIVAL OF BRITAIN
EXHIBITION OF SCIENCE
EXHIBITION RD SOUTH KENSINGTON
MAY 3 - SEPTEMBER 30
ADMISSION 2/- (4/- TUESDAYS)
CHILDREN AGED 5-15 HALF PRICE · UNDER 5 NOT ADMITTED
FOR TIMES OF OPENING SEE NEWSPAPERS

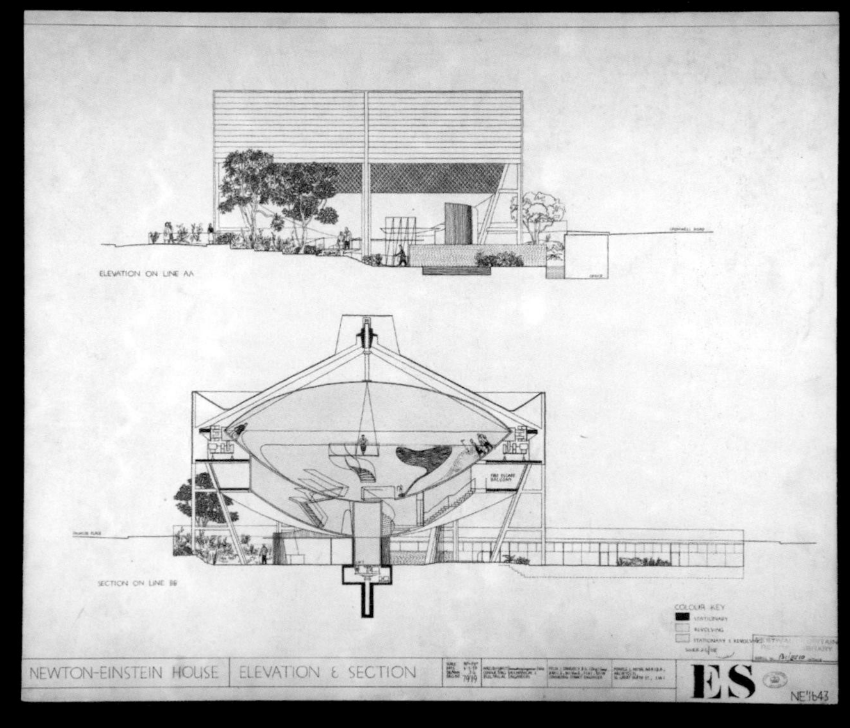
ELEVATION ON LINE AA
SECTION ON LINE BB
COLOUR KEY
STATIONARY
REVOLVING
NEWTON-EINSTEIN HOUSE
ELEVATION & SECTION
ES
NE 1643

● 1.25 [OPPOSITE] 'Antelope' bench, Ernest Race, 1951 | Manufactured by Race Furniture Ltd, bent steel-rod frame and moulded plywood seat | V&A: W.35–2010 ● 1.26 [ABOVE] Stacking outdoor chairs, A.J. Milne, 1951 | Manufactured by Heal & Son Ltd, perforated steel seat and back on a steel-rod frame | V&A: W.33 & 34–2010

Important also to the Festival organizers was the desire to integrate fine art throughout the site. Misha Black commented that they aimed 'to show that painters and sculptors could work with architects, landscape architects and exhibition designers to produce an aesthetic unity'.[9] A huge number of works were commissioned, with well over 80 items listed for dispersal at the end of the Festival.[10] Many leading British artists created pieces, including Eduardo Paolozzi, Lynn Chadwick, Barbara Hepworth, Henry Moore, Reg Butler and Victor Pasmore, but one of the most striking survivals is John Piper's huge mural *The Englishman's Home*, which was exhibited on the southern side of the 'Homes and Gardens' pavilion [1.28, 1.31, 1.32]. Painted in Ripolin on marine plywood to withstand outdoor conditions, the mural presented types, periods and styles of English domestic architecture, from stately home to Victorian terrace. The mural provided a romantic celebration of British architectural heritage and, like much of the Festival art, presented an ambiguous and rather tempered version of Modernism.

A central theme explored in the Festival, which perhaps presented a more radical agenda for the future, was the marriage of art and science. It was also the subject of the 'Growth and Form' exhibition, held at the Institute of Contemporary Arts (ICA) in the same year and organized by the Independent Group, one critic noting 'that modern science has provided the artist with a new subject matter, a "new landscape" ... is a truism'.[11] Various displays in the Dome of Discovery examined the subject, and Gerald Holtom's dramatic textile of plankton displayed in the Dome showed the decorative potential of magnification [p.40].[12] This closer relationship between science and art is perhaps best exemplified in the work of the Festival Pattern Group, where the modern science of crystallography literally became pattern [1.27, 1.30, 1.58]. Fabrics, wallpapers, floor coverings, glassware and crockery were covered with the molecular structures of insulin, haemoglobin, afwillite and so on, to create the ultimate in modern pattern-making. They were displayed both in the Dome of Discovery, and in the Regatta Restaurant, reinforcing their commercial potential [1.29]. Waitresses wore uniforms decorated in the patterns, and a display showed their range and versatility.

Writing later in 1975, Reyner Banham dissected the notion that the Festival had fostered great originality or had had lasting impact, arguing that much of it was derived from either European or American Modernism. He wrote:

> partly there is now a kind of mixture of sentimentality and astonishment about the whole enterprise. The idea of leadership in public taste with an almost formally constituted establishment is now almost as incredible as it is, to some minds, attractive – especially in the picture it presents of an apparently orderly structure of social castes who 'knew their place' in a way that teenagers, trade-unionists and trend-setters, among everybody else, no longer do.[13]

While the social and cultural changes of the 1960s made the Festival mission seem a century away, many of those who cut their teeth in the energy of the Festival were instrumental in reshaping the fabric and culture of British society – from schools, hospitals and universities to the consumer landscape of our high streets.[14]

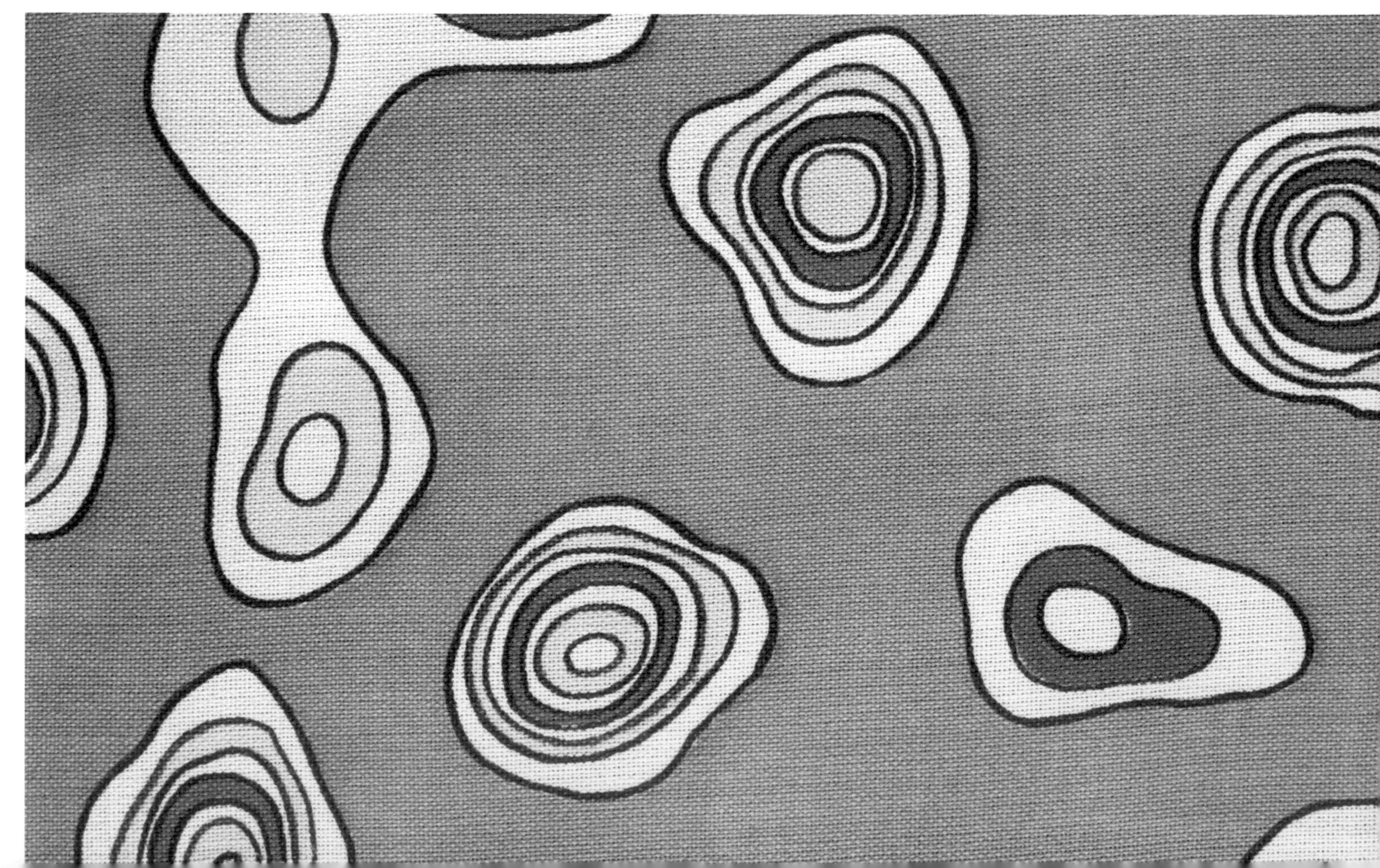

● 1.27 [OPPOSITE] Dress fabric, S.M. Slade, 1951 | Manufactured by British Celanese, screen-printed spun rayon with a design based on the crystal structure of afwillite | V&A: Circ.75B–1968 ● 1.28 [ABOVE LEFT] *Stabile (Cypress)*, Lynn Chadwick, 1951, in the sunken garden outside the Regatta Restaurant at the Festival of Britain ● 1.29 [ABOVE RIGHT] Display of products designed by the Festival Pattern Group, exhibited in the Regatta Restaurant at the Festival of Britain, 1951 ● 1.30 [BELOW] 'Surrey', furnishing fabric, Marianne Straub, 1951 | Manufactured by Warner & Sons, Jacquard woven wool, cotton and rayon with a design based on the crystal structure of afwillite | V&A: Circ.306–1951

● 1.31 [ABOVE] *The Englishman's Home*, mural painting, John Piper, 1950–1 | Ripolin paint on 42 panels of marine ply, made for the exterior of the 'Homes and Gardens' pavilion at the Festival of Britain | Courtesy of Liss Fine Art ● 1.32 [OPPOSITE] *Woman Resting*, Reg Butler, 1951 Welded steel, made for display at the Festival of Britain Exhibition of Industrial Power | Aberdeen Art Gallery & Museums Collections

Norman Hartnell

THE CORONATION

Two years later, while the Festival seemed almost forgotten, Britain was bracing itself for a rather different form of celebration. In common with every magazine of the time, *Country Life* produced a Coronation souvenir issue in June 1953, commemorating what its contributor Ivor Brown described as a 'crowning day' for London, 'a city with light in its eyes: a triumph of man over nature'. His article on the visual splendour of the ceremony set its material and symbolic importance in high relief:

> We are apt to be humdrum, even drab in our workaday lives, but there is before us, if we take our chances, the power to keep what is left of the ancient elegance while seeking new styles, not unworthy of the old. The two Coronation processions, as I watched from a window in Westminster, seemed far more than political and civic demonstrations. They were tributes to our submerged, yet undying, instinct for rare and lovely things... The monarchy ... is holding high a standard ... of joy in design and decoration as well as of modesty in conduct and decorum. Among the ordinances set before the Queen in the coronation service is a charge 'to restore the things that are gone to decay and maintain the things that are restored'. The monarchy is one of our guards against the vandal, one of our assertions that, in the world of use, beauty is no vanity, but chief among all useful things.[15]

Brown's portentous declaration was an apt summary of the important role played by the royal family and the institution of the monarchy in maintaining a sense of continuity, while carefully supporting modernizing trends in British life in the mid-twentieth-century.[16] Less remarked upon is the extent to which the Coronation was itself a sophisticated design event, operating across the fields of photography, fashion and performance to project a new version of the Crown's role in the life of the state. Cultural historian Robert Hewison identifies some of these tensions at play in Cecil Beaton's official photograph of the Queen, crowned and robed, with the interior of Westminster Abbey projected behind her [1.33].

As he points out: 'the different planes of foreground and background create an unsettling dynamic ... significantly the spectator's eyeline is not respectfully looking up at the monarch, but is on the same level, or even slightly above her.'[17] The image suggests the contingent and artificial nature of a grand state event in a democratic age. The bolt of blue and gold 'Queensway' rayon silk, designed for Warner and Sons by Royal College of Art professor Robert Goodden to decorate the Abbey interior, embodies the contradictions: a synthetic rendering of age-old symbols drawn back in a technicoloured sweep, like set-dressing on a Hollywood film set [1.35].

● 1.33 [OPPOSITE LEFT] *Queen Elizabeth II on Coronation Day*, Cecil Beaton, 2 June 1953 | Gelatin silver print, photographed at Buckingham Palace, in front of a studio backdrop of Westminster Abbey; the Queen wears the Coronation dress by Norman Hartnell, and robe embroidered by the Royal School of Needlework | V&A: PH.311–1987 ● 1.34 [OPPOSITE TOP RIGHT] *Queen Elizabeth II in Coronation Robes*, Norman Hartnell, 1953 | Pencil, watercolour and bodycolour on paper | The Royal Collection ● 1.35 [OPPOSITE BOTTOM RIGHT] 'Queensway', furnishing fabric, Robert Goodden, 1952 | Manufactured by Warner & Sons, designed to hang from the balconies of the nave in Westminster Abbey during the Coronation, woven silk, rayon, cotton and lurex | V&A: T.193–1953 ● 1.36 [ABOVE] *Flowers of the Fields of France*, state gown, Norman Hartnell, spring 1957 | Duchesse satin embroidered with pearls, beads, brilliants and gold thread, designed for the Queen's state visit to Paris | V&A: T.264–1974

At the centre of the image are the Coronation dress and robe, designed by Norman Hartnell, a leading member of the Incorporated Society of London Fashion Designers [1.34]. Hartnell's memoir, *Silver and Gold*, devotes some pages to the process of creation, from the October afternoon in 1952 on which the Queen placed the commission, requiring that it 'should conform in line to that of her wedding dress and that the material should be silk', to the morning in June 1953 when Hartnell, seated in Westminster Abbey, was witness as the 'Queen is come before our misty eyes. A slight and gentle figure, graceful in her glistering gown, her hands clasped and her eyes cast down. In beauty and solemnity, most slowly, she advances to her great and lonely station.'[18]

Following research on the coronations of previous British queens, from the first Elizabeth through Anne to Victoria, Hartnell 'retired to the seclusion of Windsor Forest and there spent many days making trial sketches. My mind was teeming with heraldic and floral ideas... I thought of altar clothes and sacred vestments ... and everything heavenly that might be embroidered upon a dress destined to be historic.'[19] The final design incorporated a complex interweaving of emblems representing every nation of the new Commonwealth: the English rose, the Scottish thistle, the Irish shamrock, the Welsh leek, the Canadian maple, the Australian wattle flower, the New Zealand fern, the South African protea, the Indian and Celanese lotus, and the wheat, cotton and jute of Pakistan (this use of symbolic motifs would be reprised in 1957 when Hartnell designed the formal gown, 'Flowers of the Fields of France', worn by the Queen on her state visit to France; the plants of the Commonwealth were here replaced by poppies, fleurs-de-lis, wheat-sheaves and Napoleonic bees in honour of the host nation) [1.36].[20] The accompanying purple velvet robe, its silk sourced (like that for the dress) from Lady Hart Dyke's silk farm at Lullingstone, included an embroidered gold border of olive branches and wheat ears (peace and plenty) completed by the Royal School of Needlework over 3,500 hours between March and May 1953.[21]

The ceremonial splendour of the Coronation, embodied in the glorious decoration of the Queen's body, played an important role in bolstering the political and social cohesion of the nation. As social historian Annette Kuhn has argued, 'ceremonial dress signifies that the occasion it celebrates subsumes the individualities of those taking part to larger communities; to attachments that go beyond, even overshadow, the personal lives of those pictured'.[22] This was true for the Queen herself, but it was also reflected in the amateur costumes that adorned the countless pageants and street-parties marking the event throughout the country and the Commonwealth. Similar sentiments were at play in the erection of street decorations along the route of the official procession, designed by Hugh Casson, and in the dressing of shops and offices with wildly festive designs (Selfridges, for example, was treated to a proto-pop evocation of Britannia in Edward Bawden and Richard Guyatt's proposed scheme). Ivor Brown captured the spirit precisely [1.37, 1.38]:

> London had done its best to look the capital part: there had been little official patterning of the décor. So the huge town beflagged was a People's Palace of Variety; each to his taste and purse... The floral dance of fluttering colour was all as free and easy as the 'English unofficial rose' beloved of Rupert Brooke.[23]

Such 'New Elizabethan' jollity, evoked in the series of celebratory lithographs completed by artists including Kenneth Rowntree and Edward Bawden at the Royal College of Art, offered a chance to 'recapture the sense of community lost in the years of austerity' [1.40, 1.41]. Robert Lacey suggests that:

> it was an opportunity to enjoy the weight of money in the pocket as the Churchill government dismantled the mechanism of socialist reconstruction. Ration books and Utility merchandise had undermined the Festival of Britain as a celebration of national rebirth. Now the first fancy pottery since the War was released from Staffordshire.[24]

Yet perhaps it is misleading to draw too many distinctions between a 'socialist' Festival of Britain and a 'conservative' Coronation. Churchill's administration may well have bulldozed the Festival site with indecent haste, but in retrospect it is striking how far the language of renewal and optimism was a shared one. In 1951 and 1953 politicians and planners were united in looking to build a golden future.

● 1.37 [OPPOSITE TOP AND BOTTOM RIGHT] Designs for Coronation street decorations for Hungerford Bridge and Whitehall, London, Hugh Casson, 1953 | Gouache and pastel on paper, and ink and watercolour on board | RIBA Library Drawings Collection ● 1.38 [OPPOSITE BOTTOM LEFT] Design for Coronation decorations for the Oxford Street frontage of Selfridges department store, London, Edward Bawden and Richard Guyatt, 1953 Pencil, watercolour and body-colour on paper | V&A: E.440–2010

UEEN
LONG MAY SHE REIGN
Edward Bawden
+

HUGH CASSON

1.39 [ABOVE] Perspective drawing of the British Embassy, Rome, Basil Spence, July 1962 | Graphite under-drawing, gouache, compressed charcoal and pastel on paper | RCAHMS: Sir Basil Spence Archive

If the Festival and Coronation presented differing, but not mutually exclusive, visions of modern Britain, then the way Britain presented herself abroad in this period of quickening decolonization and economic anxiety was a particularly sensitive and even more contested issue. A number of new embassy projects were undertaken during the 1950s and '60s, some in old centres of power and prestige and others in the new capitals of the post-colonial age. Buildings were planned for Rome, Warsaw, Mexico City, Colombo, Caracas, Islamabad, Lagos and Brasilia. In what style these ciphers of modern Britain were to be built and decorated was a concern for those in government and outside. As Anne Sharpley remarked in the *Evening Standard* with regard to Rome, 'anxiety sprang from a fear the Ministry might play safe and order something dull'.[25]

Increasingly Modernism, with its associations of utopian idealism, was seen as the most appropriate style in which to present Britain as a modern democratic partner rather than an imperial power.[26] And within the broad church of Modernism the architectural responses were extremely varied, ranging from utilitarian and conservative buildings to decorative high Modernism. The in-house architects of the Ministry of Public Building and Works were responsible for the majority of the new projects, but for certain buildings leading British architects were commissioned. For the new embassy in Rome, Sir Basil Spence was appointed [1.39].

In 1946 a Jewish terrorist attack had destroyed the old British Chancery building in the city, and the site, next to Michelangelo's Porta Pia and the Roman Aurelian Wall, was cleared and redesignated a park. During the 1950s the Ministry of Works drew up various proposals for a scheme, which were all turned down by the Italian authorities. Finally in 1959 the Foreign Office appointed Spence to design a building suitable for such a historically sensitive and high-profile site. His monumental and decorative Modernism, so elegantly expressed in his designs for Coventry Cathedral [1.78], was seen to be the solution for such a complex project, while his charisma, authority and personal charm also helped win over the Italian authorities.

Spence described the building as 'a British Palazzo in marble and concrete', and its massive structure with a giant central courtyard bore a clear relationship to Italian palazzo architecture. However, Spence made a daring and thoroughly modern statement in opening the building up to the surrounding gardens at ground level.[27] He raised the two-storey structure on columns to enable a flow between the internal and external spaces, commenting, 'there will be sheets of water and a great sense of space. Both water and space will flow underneath and through the building.'[28] Spence's bold spatial treatment and strongly articulated design were described by one critic in the *Daily Telegraph*: 'there is never any pettiness or indecision, everything is big-boned ... there is never the fussy overworked look that bedevils so much of English architecture.'[29] Sadly, due to financial pressures on the government, it was 10 years before the British Embassy in Rome was completed, and when it opened in 1971 it seemed rather old-fashioned – its decorative Modernism embedded in the architectural discourses of the late 1950s.

Running concurrently, the design for a new British Embassy in Brasilia presented a different, but equally problematic set of issues for the Ministry of Works. The new capital city of Brasilia, planned by Lucia Costa and Oscar Niemeyer, was to be the most ambitious statement of Modernist style and ideology ever created, and the way individual nations responded in their designs for their embassies became a focus of national prestige. A Ministry memo of July 1961 laid out the situation: 'We know from the President of RIBA, Sir William Holford, who was an assessor for the Brasilia plan, that the Brazilians are looking for the United Kingdom, together with United States and France, to make an outstanding architectural contribution to the new capital. We think this contribution can best be made by holding a competition.[30]

Rather than an open competition, the Ministry opted to invite entries from several practices, including Lasdun; Casson & Conder; Robert Mathew & Stirrat Johnson-Marshall; Yorke, Rosenberg & Mardall; Powell and Moya; and Alison and Peter Smithson. That the building should make a striking modern statement was beyond question. The job was offered to the Smithsons in spring 1964 and called for a preliminary design by the end of that year. Their long, low building, which dramatically used red-oxide-dyed concrete and dark wood, was conceived to ride 'into the landscape which is rust red as far as the eye can see'. They wrote of the building, 'the low lying "squashed crocodile" form of our project in some way arises out of a wish to ... give a glimpse of another social formulation – via the quiet shifting imagery of the façades and the internal arrangements they represent'.[31] The utopian symbolism of the building, an 'idealization ... of our own dream for a more egalitarian society', was of paramount importance to the Smithsons.[32] Of less concern was meeting the brief and the severe cost limits of the project, which (as with Rome) had drastically delayed the start of the build. In March 1965 Eric Bedford, chief architect of the Ministry of Works, expressed concerns over the project:

> The imaginative approach of Alison and Peter Smithson to present-day architectural problems was largely instrumental in them obtaining the commission... The appointment was received with general enthusiasm and acclamation throughout the architectural profession... The scheme is imaginative and unusual... Having said this, the obvious desire to achieve such a design has led them to proposals which are expensive in space, expensive to construct and eventually will be expensive to furnish and maintain ... it is difficult to see how the cost of the proposal will be reduced to the cost limit... The exciting idea of creating large open spaces by means of extensive spans and forming cubicles of various amorphous shapes can only lead to great waste of internal space ... one questions whether the architects have correctly understood the requirements of the Foreign Office and if this is the sort of image of Britain which is to be projected abroad.[33]

In 1968 a combination of factors finally led to the termination of the Smithsons' contract. Their design was expensive, and the economic conditions in Britain put overseas projects under particular pressure. The Brazilian government had also been slow to shift operations from Rio to the new capital, and as a result Britain (like several other countries) indefinitely postponed the building of a new permanent embassy. Work did not in fact begin until 1980.[34]

Under the auspices of the Ministry of Works, modern buildings were completed during the 1950s and '60s in a number of capitals, including Colombo, Warsaw and Mexico City [1.43]. Their decoration presented the Ministry with difficulties, as there were no stocks of contemporary-style furnishings, and period furniture was obviously inappropriate. To address the problem an Advisory Committee on Decoration and Furnishing was established in July 1960, which quickly became known as the Taste Committee. Its first members included Paul Reilly, Director of the Council of Industrial Design; Lady Balfour; Lady Eccles; James Smith, MP; and the chief architect and controller of supplies from the Ministry. Although the committee's remit covered both modern and traditional furnishings, it was quickly seen as 'likely to be dealing mainly with new buildings'.[35] One of its first tasks, and most significant contributions, was to advise on the design of glass and tableware [1.42]. The need for modern silverware was identified as a particular priority for the embassy in Warsaw, and David Mellor was commissioned to produce a design. His embassy-ware included an unconventional single candlestick, which typified the new informality of the post-war missions; it came in three different heights, which could be used in varying arrangements to suit the occasion, and was seen as a particularly modern reinterpretation of traditional candelabra. New glass and tableware were also commissioned from professors at the Royal College of Art, Robert Goodden and Richard Guyatt respectively. Again the choice of commissioning new designs from the College rather than selecting stock models from the manufacturers, as historically had been the process, revealed the Ministry's (and wider government's) commitment to showcasing and promoting contemporary British design. The new buildings and their interiors aimed to present Britain as a progressive and creative centre and, in so doing, helped establish an agenda for British trade in the post-war period. As one rather ambivalent High Commissioner wrote, '…even critics must grudgingly admit that Britain has shown herself still a pioneer'.[36]

● 1.40 [OPPOSITE] *Life Guards*, Edward Bawden, 1953 | From the Royal College of Art's celebratory Coronation series of prints, lithograph | V&A: Circ.326–1953 ● 1.41 [TOP] *Country Celebrations*, Kenneth Rowntree, 1953 | From the Royal College of Art's celebratory Coronation series of prints, lithograph | V&A: Circ.322–1953

CHANGE AND THE REALM

The design of Britain's stamps and coins is also an area where, historically, the state has had to tread a fine line between tradition and modernization, and where issues surrounding the reinterpretation of Britain's national symbols – particularly the image of the monarch – are powerfully contested. Importantly, it is also a field where the state continues to mediate a vision of Britain through the monarchy.

The accession of the young Queen in 1953 demanded new designs for stamps and coins, and work began immediately. The Queen sat for a series of photographs by Dorothy Wilding to be used for definitive stamps. Wilding's portrait helped promote the new Elizabethan iconography that marked the early years of the reign, as is clearly seen in Enid Marx's design for the penny stamp and Edmund Dulac's Coronation issue [1.48, 1.49]. This more traditional and romantic imagery also characterizes Mary Gillick's relief created for the new coinage, where the Queen, in girlish fashion, wears a wreath with fluttering ribbons [1.45]. The Wilding three-quarter-view portrait continued to be used for stamps until decimalization, while Gillick's relief was used on both coins until 1968 and exclusively on commemorative stamps until November 1967.

During the 1960s discussions on decimalization gained new energy and provided an opportunity for revised designs. As Christopher Ironside, the designer of the decimal coins, recalled: 'this major event would have to involve redesigning the coinage, but it was also an opportunity to change the shapes, sizes, metals and denominations of the coins in use by millions of United Kingdom businesses and individuals'.[37] Ironside's designs, which took six years to finalize, featured traditional heraldic imagery, with two of the most striking and complex designs created for the 10-pence piece, St George and the Dragon, and the two-pence piece, Britannia [1.46].

Decimalization was finally introduced on 15 February 1971, and Ironside's new designs were criticized by some for being too traditional.

A more progressive view was taken by Tony Benn, who was appointed Postmaster General in 1964. Under his direction, David Gentleman was asked to explore ways in which stamp design might develop in the future, and one particular area to be addressed was how UK stamps might be identified in a graphic element without the use of the monarch's head. In 1966 Gentleman's experimental album was made public [1.47]. Initially he explored ideas of using the lion-and-unicorn heraldry in silhouette. Later he developed the solution of using a silhouette of the Mary Gillick relief, but not before concerns had been raised over the apparent desire of the left-wing Postmaster General to replace the Queen's portrait. The event gained a political significance that clearly exposed the tensions between the forces of tradition and modernization in official British design circles.

Gentleman's experimental album established a whole new range of subjects for pictorial stamps and proved hugely influential, aided by the development in 1963 of multicoloured printing. The modern stamps introduced to the Post Office by Tony Benn signalled a freeing-up of constraints over design and a change in the way stamps were seen and collected by the public. Benn recalled that 'the new designs had been tremendously successful and admired all over the world. They had provided scope for a new art form, from this country's point of view, and the development of artistic possibilities that were simply prevented from being expressed in the old days'.[38] Arnold Machin's new definitive designs of 1967, in their bright modern colours, contributed to this progressive and populist vision [1.50].

The announcement by the Royal Mint in August 2005 of a public competition for a series of new reverses for the coinage, 40 years after decimalization, and the responses of 526 artists submitting more than 4,000 designs, demonstrated the continuing relevance of a peculiarly British design debate in which the old and the new reach a characteristic set of accommodations. As Sir Christopher Frayling, then Chair of the Royal Mint Advisory Committee, recalled:

> It was a fascinating process because what we were dealing with was nothing less than how Britain might be symbolized on the coinage in the early twenty-first century, at a time when discussions of 'Britishness' were, and are, very much in the news. Britishness, identity, inclusivity, citizenship ... heritage and contemporary – all were under discussion. How we see ourselves, and how much it matters.[39]

The winning designs, by recent University of Brighton graduate Matt Dent, launched in April 2008, proposed a series of deconstructed fragments of parts of the Royal Arms, which would be brought together to form a unified shield in the lower-value coins, while the whole was also represented singly on the one-pound coin [1.44]. As Dent suggested, 'This piecing together of the elements of the Royal Arms to form one design had a satisfying symbolism – that of unity, four countries of Britain under a single monarch.'[40] Six decades after the Festival of Britain and the Coronation the themes of change and continuity continue to inform the design of the public realm as powerfully as they did in 1951 and 1953.

● 1.42 [OPPOSITE] Display at the Design Centre, London, 1964, showing tableware designed for British embassies | Silverware designed by David Mellor, ceramics by Richard Guyatt for Minton & Co., glassware by Robert Goodden for Thomas Webb & Sons, commissioned by the Ministry of Works for the British Embassy, Warsaw
● 1.43 [ABOVE] British High Commission Offices, Colombo, Sri Lanka, Eric Bedford (chief architect) and C.R. Kidby (project architect) at the Ministry of Works, 1963–5

TEN PENCE
TWO PENCE
ONE PENNY
FIVE PENCE
TWENTY PENCE
FIFTY PENCE

Royal ciphers

● 1.44 [OPPOSITE] Designs for the reverses of coins, Matthew Dent, 2005–8 | Plaster The Royal Mint ● 1.45 [TOP LEFT] Model for the obverse of coins, Mary Gillick, 1952 Plaster | The British Museum ● 1.46 [BOTTOM LEFT] Competition design for 10-pence coin, Christopher Ironside, 1963–4 | Pencil on paper | The British Museum ● 1.47 [TOP RIGHT] Page from the 'Gentleman Album' of proposed stamp designs, David Gentleman, 1965 Printed paper | The British Postal Museum & Archive ● [BOTTOM RIGHT, CLOCKWISE FROM TOP RIGHT] 1.48 Definitive 1d. stamp, Enid Marx, 1952 | Photograph by Dorothy Wilding, printed paper | The British Postal Museum & Archive | 1.49 Coronation-issue 1s. 3d. stamp, Edmund Dulac, 1953 | Printed paper | The British Postal Museum & Archive | 1.50 Definitive 1s. stamp, Arnold Machin, 1967 | Printed paper | The British Postal Museum & Archive

Export Textiles in West Africa

—Nicola Stylianou

● 1.51 [ABOVE] Evening dress, Matilda Etches, 1948 | Printed cotton produced for the West African market | V&A: T.186–1969 ● 1.52 [OPPOSITE] Dress fabric for the West African market, 1947 | Manufactured by Logan, Muckelt & Co,. printed cotton | V&A: Circ. 82–1947

In 1948 Grace Lovat Fraser wrote *Textiles by Britain*, a history of textile production and a survey of the state of the British cloth industry at the time. She noted of the textiles manufactured in Lancashire for export that: 'These cloths though produced in enormous quantities are almost unknown to the rest of the country, for they are made exclusively for the native markets for which they are so carefully and brilliantly designed; yet they are some of the most beautiful and exciting materials produced by Great Britain.'[1] Although Britain was exporting textiles all over the world to India, the Far East and Southern and East Africa, it was West Africa that provided the largest market for cotton piece goods.[2] Despite not being widely known about, there seems to have been an increasing specialist interest in these textiles, which were known as wax prints, and the V&A had begun to actively collect them in 1947 [1.52]. However, by this time Britain's share of the West African cloth market was already decreasing.

Lovat Fraser described viewing Britain's export textiles as 'an unforgettable experience which transports one into a fantastic and romantic world of strange, heavy colours and exotic design'.[3] Due to their apparently 'exotic' appearance, and because they have come to be seen as archetypal examples of West African dress, the fact that these cloths were designed and made in England still comes as a surprise to many people. The wax prints for West Africa were originally produced as an attempt by Dutch manufacturers to imitate the batiks of Dutch East India and sell them back to the region, undercutting local production. The cloths did not sell well in the East Indies, but proved popular in West Africa and by the start of the twentieth century trade was thriving and European companies were competing with each other for a share of the market.

At the start of the 1930s India, Turkey, Egypt, Argentina, the Dutch East Indies and East Africa all consumed more British-made cloth than West Africa.[4] However, by 1936 West Africa was second only to India, as Britain lost out to new competitors such as Japan in other markets – for example, British East Africa. Frederika Launert has argued that Britain was able to hold on to the West African market in the 1930s because of the success of its designers, who continued to produce popular and fashionable patterns. By the end of the Second World War more British textiles were exported to West Africa than anywhere else. However, by 1948 Britain's share of the expanding West African market had almost halved and was still falling.[5] It is the importance of the West African market to Britain, and competition from abroad, that explains the increased interest in these cottons as Britain sought to promote her own industries in the face of post-war economic hardship.

British success in West Africa was based on a mixture of tradition and innovation. While many of the early designs remained popular, it was also necessary to supply new patterns, responding to fashion trends and regional preferences. New versions of proven popular themes were often produced. In 1952 Barbara Goalen was pictured draped in the 'Alphabet' design that had been in production since the early part of the twentieth century [1.53].[6] Patterns associated with learning were desirable, as a good education was an important status symbol and emphasized the modernity of the wearer. A similar cloth was being produced by the Calico Printers' Association in 1948 [1.55]. It still featured the block alphabet, but added cursive letters and centred the design around a clock, another sign of modernity; and versions of 'Alphabet' featuring computers instead of chalk boards remain in circulation today.

British designers were also being encouraged to make use of British-produced textiles. The V&A has two examples of dresses made in the late 1940s for the home market, but using textiles designed for West Africa: one by Hardy Amies and the other by Matilda Etches [1.51, 1.54].[7] The Etches dress reflects many elements of the history and development of wax prints. It was featured in *Vogue*, where it was described as a 'West African cotton dinner dress: flame and deep red print on copper: diagonal neck, sari edged'.[8] The use of Indonesian motifs and the 'crackled' effect reflect the origins of these textiles in the trade links between the Netherlands, West Africa, the Dutch East Indies and Britain. The pattern is also an example of a commemorative cloth; patterns marking important people or contemporary events had begun to be produced by British manufacturers in the early 1920s. This dress marks the end of the Second World War: the border of the fabric features both the letter V (for victory) and its Morse-code equivalent (...-).

Britain's textile exports to West Africa continued to fall during the 1950s, due to increasing competition initially from the Far East and, after 1960, from local manufacturers as newly independent countries such as Ghana and Nigeria established and promoted their own industries.[9] Today only one British company remains involved in the production of textiles designed specifically for the West African market: ABC Wax. However, all the manufacturing is done in Ghana by a sister company called Akosombo Textiles Ltd. Printed textiles are now exported from West Africa to Britain for sale to migrant communities and are widely available in many British cities.

● 1.53 [TOP] Barbara Goalen modelling 'African Alphabet' dress fabric, 1952 | Fabric manufactured by Grafton for the West African market, block-printed cotton, photographed by Elsbeth Juda for 'Milling Around Lancashire', *The Ambassador*, no.9, 1952 | AAD: 1987/1/113/48 ● 1.54 [OPPOSITE LEFT] Day dress, Hardy Amies, 1947 | Printed cotton produced for the West African market | V&A: T.236–1984 ● 1.55 [OPPOSITE RIGHT] Dress fabric for the West African market, 1947 | Manufactured by the Calico Printers' Association, printed cotton | V&A: Circ.396–1948

2 Urban Visions: Designing for the Welfare State

— Jonathan Woodham

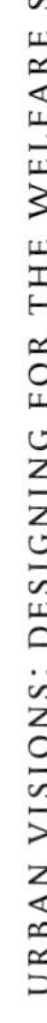

Comparing the period immediately following the Second World War with the early years of the second decade of the twenty-first century reveals a strongly contrasting outlook for design and the state. During the post-war years artists, architects and designers widely believed that the reconstruction period offered an unprecedented opportunity to participate in the shaping of a social, democratic and aesthetically charged vision of a new Britain. This assumed a wide variety of forms, including housing and everyday domestic furnishings and fittings, the building of new schools, New Towns, the remodelling of bomb-damaged city centres and urban spaces with improved standards of signage and street furniture, and the design of public transport systems on land, air and sea. The period also witnessed the election of a Labour government in 1945 and, under its aegis, the establishment of the Welfare State, as it is widely understood today.[1]

Returning to the present, architects, designers and others in the creative and cultural sectors face very different challenges from those of their counterparts in the 1940s, although they share the impact of economic crisis. However, in stark contrast to the reconstruction era that proffered many opportunities for state-funded commissions, including the 1951 Festival of Britain, the 2010s have seen the role of the state and centralized government challenged by the concept of the 'Big Society'.[2] This, it is argued, gives individuals and communities more control over their destinies, a line of thought strongly reminiscent of Margaret Thatcher's critique of the 'nanny' state in the 1980s.[3]

● 1.56 [OPPOSITE] Churchill Gardens, London, Powell and Moya, 1947–62

DESIGN DURING THE RECONSTRUCTION YEARS

It has been suggested that there was a comparatively narrow social, professional and educational spectrum from which many of the leading advocates of improved standards of British design were drawn in the interwar years.[4] And importantly many people, like Lord Reith at the BBC, believed that aesthetic judgement demanded talent, training, discrimination and taste. It has also been argued that 'there was a considerable continuity in aesthetic hegemony from the pre- to post-Second World War period', with a number of prominent figures from the ranks of the Board of Trade's (BoT's) pre-war Council for Art and Industry and the wartime Utility Furniture Committee being appointed to the government's Council of Industrial Design (CoID), which was established in 1944.[5]

But it was not just individuals associated with BoT committees who formed powerful, often interlocking design alliances that proved highly influential in promoting a well-designed and socially progressive urban vision of Britain. The Ministry of Information's Exhibition Division, led by artist and designer Milner Gray, also included many notable post-war designers. These included Misha Black and Kenneth Bayes, co-founder members with Gray of the highly influential Design Research Unit (DRU). It, in turn, employed multidisciplinary designers who became involved with the Festival of Britain in 1951. The Camouflage Development and Training Centre in Farnham, Surrey, was another wartime body that brought together many architects, designers and artists. They included the influential post-war architects of new schools, Stirrat Johnson-Marshall and David Medd, who trained under Major James Gardner, a leading exhibition designer in the post-war years, with important roles at the 1946 'Britain Can Make It' exhibition, the Festival of Britain, Brussels Expo '58 and Montreal '67.

Hugh Casson, Director of Architecture at the 1951 Festival, had joined the Camouflage Development and Training Centre on the outbreak of war, as had the architect Basil Spence, who later collaborated with Gardner on 'Britain Can Make It'. Spence received several important commissions for the Festival of Britain and, subsequently, for Coventry Cathedral and the 'plate-glass universities' (see below). Underlining the metropolitan outlook of the tight-knit coterie of architects and designers involved with the Festival, Edinburgh-based Spence 'was the only architect from outside the close circle of London designers to be given work on any scale'.[6] Also important in underlining London as a major source of architectural and artistic influence were leading educational institutions, such as the Architectural Association's School of Architecture and the Royal College of Art.

THE FESTIVAL OF BRITAIN, 1951

Although established under the BoT during the wartime coalition government, in the following decades the CoID continued to play a significant national role in promoting the benefits of high standards of design to manufacturers, retailers and the general public. Its organization of 'Britain Can Make It' at the V&A in 1946 provided a useful apprenticeship for its central role in the much larger national 1951 Festival of Britain.

The Council's most significant task at the Festival was to promote modern industrial design. Deeply involved in the Festival's organization, it was charged with the selection of all industrially manufactured goods on display. To facilitate this, it initiated in 1948 the 1951 Stock List (later Design Review), a photographic card index of designs selected by panels drawn from a wide range of design disciplines for possible inclusion at the Festival. All products had to be in current production and designed and manufactured in Britain.

As a major architectural, design and cultural embodiment of a social and democratic vision of Britain after the war, the 1951 Festival has attracted considerable analysis, not least because it became something of a political and ideological battleground in the economically difficult climate of the times.[7] Although promoted as apolitical, the Festival was clearly a project close to Labour's heart, strongly steered by Herbert Morrison, Deputy Prime Minister and architect of the Labour Party's 1945 manifesto *Let Us Face the Future*. Originally conceived as an international exhibition, the Festival was downgraded in 1947 to a national exhibition with four principal sites in London (the South Bank, Lansbury, Battersea and South Kensington) and others in Glasgow ('Industrial Power'), Edinburgh ('Living Traditions') and Ulster ('Farm & Factory'). Inhabitants of other major cities were able to experience condensed versions of the modernizing message of the London South Bank exhibition by means of the Land Travelling Exhibition, which visited four cities in the Midlands and the North of England, and the Festival Ship *Campania*, which visited 10 major ports in England, Scotland, Northern Ireland and Wales. Although the Festival may be more fully understood through a variety of interpretations, such as 'a summation of the planner-preservationist vision [that] also allows us to detect fractures in the landscape of modern consensus' where 'traditional landscape, local heritage, and pastoral anti-modernity line up against visions of a planned and ordered country'[8] as 'a "new picturesque" pattern-book'[9] or 'an imagined community of all-white British people moving forward into a more egalitarian future',[10] the progressive South Bank site and the 'Live Architecture' exhibition in Poplar, East London, provide a key focus for this chapter.

The *Architectural Review* described the Festival's South Bank site as 'the first modern townscape'.[11] Characterized by a series of coordinated open public spaces set between modern buildings, such as the Festival Hall, the Skylon, the 'Transport', 'Sea and Ships' and 'Schools' pavilions, the site greeted the 8,455,863 visitors with an alluring vision of a progressive contemporary face of urban Britain. With raised walkways, gushing water fountains and gardens, its communal spaces were populated with contemporary street furniture, such as Ernest Race's 'Antelope' and 'Springbok' chairs and Maria Shephard's ubiquitous concrete planters [1.57].[12] Visitors also strolled past bollards with lighting elements designed by Hugh Casson or H.T. Cadbury-Brown, drinking fountains by James Cubitt and litter bins by Jack Howe.

Although predominantly concerned with contemporary architecture and design with a strong Modernist tinge, the South Bank also played host to science as an inspiration for design, as seen particularly in the work of the Festival Pattern Group.[13] Conceived by the CoID's Chief Industrial Officer, Mark Hartland Thomas, the aim was to convince manufacturers that crystallography – a field in which Britain led the world – could provide a fresh impetus for surface pattern in fields such as textiles, carpets, wallpapers, ceramics, metals, plastics and glass [1.58]. Eighty patterns based on the magnifications of boric acid, insulin, haemoglobin and other substances attracted 28 manufacturers, such as Wedgwood, Warner & Sons and Warerite, to participate. However, many of the patterns applied to everyday products came together in the public eye in the furnishings, decor and tableware in Misha Black's and Alexander Gibson's Regatta Restaurant on the South Bank, where even the waitresses wore collars made from hydrargillite-inspired lace.

● 1.57 [OPPOSITE] Terrace outside the 'Land of Britain' pavilion at the Festival of Britain, 1951 | Outdoor furniture includes 'Antelope' chairs, Ernest Race, manufactured by Race Furniture, and stacking chairs, A.J. Milne, manufactured by Heal & Son

● 1.58 [OPPOSITE] Wallpaper, Robert Sevant, 1951 | Manufactured by John Line & Sons, screen-printed paper with a design based on the crystal structure of insulin | V&A: E.888–1978

THE FESTIVAL AT LANSBURY: THE 'LIVE ARCHITECTURE' EXHIBITION AT POPLAR

In its 'Plan for Posterity' the 1951 *Exhibition of Architecture: Poplar, Festival Guide* drew attention to the nationwide display of architectural heritage in the form of cathedrals, churches, castles, palaces, country houses and villages, in marked contrast to 'what architecture in the true sense can do for us in the future [that] is presented on the South Bank. Here, at Lansbury, can be seen what is being done today.'[14] Pinpointing the Lansbury exhibition site from a distance was a large construction crane, a symbolic emblem of building construction. In order to contextualize the 'Live Architecture' of the Lansbury Estate itself – a contemporary 'urban village' of housing, schools, churches, a market square and shopping precinct – visitors were greeted by a 'Town Planning' Pavilion and 'Building Research' Pavilion, which sought to explain to them the principles of modern planning and architecture.

During the war years Patrick Abercrombie and London County Council (LCC) architect J.H. Forshaw had considered London's future in the 1943 *County of London Plan*, in which it was considered that 'a sense of community, of neighbourly responsibility, satisfies the essential human need' and that 'each community should be composed of several units of convenient size to be known as "neighbourhoods"'.[15] The Lansbury Estate represented just such a unit, and its open spaces and community spaces were aligned closely to the principles of the Labour government's 1946 New Towns and 1947 Town and Country Planning Acts. The former was concerned with the rebuilding of the urban environment and identified a need to construct a series of New Towns; the latter came into effect on 1 July 1948 and legislated for greater control by local authorities of planning and redevelopment.

The architect behind the 'Live Architecture' display was Frederick Gibberd, who had been a strong advocate of siting the exhibition in bomb-damaged Poplar in order to demonstrate graphically to the public how reconstruction could benefit people's daily lives. He designed the central focus of the new estate, the market square and precinct, which provided what was, in effect, a template for many subsequent pedestrianized shopping centres across Britain. In the square and precinct were a series of three-storey maisonettes above shops, as well as two pubs and a clock tower from which visitors could view the development as a whole. F.R.S. Yorke, a contemporary of Gibberd at the Birmingham School of Architecture, was commissioned to design the Susan Lawrence Primary School (1949–51) and Elizabeth Lansbury Secondary School (1951–2) as part of the Lansbury site. Importantly, the widely influential prefabricated construction system adopted was that pioneered by Hertfordshire County Council (see below). Underlining his commitment to a stimulating learning environment, Yorke worked with art teacher and designer Peggy Angus, who adorned the nursery school's entrance hall with a striking design of decorated tiles manufactured by Carters of Poole.[16]

However, the 'Live Architecture' exhibition failed to attract more than a modest number of visitors (86,646) when compared with those to the South Bank site (8,455,863). As Gibberd himself wrote 25 years later:

> In terms of architecture it was all too modest and lacking in 'architectural statements' like the Dome of Discovery to attract the younger generation of architects. But it was immensely important, and I suppose everyone who was in any way involved in the rebuilding of Britain was influenced by it.[17]

THE NEW TOWN VISION

The New Town vision was very much a part of Gibberd's ideas about the rebuilding of Britain. To meet the needs of post-war housing demand, the New Town programme provided seemingly utopian solutions to the problems of overcrowded and war-damaged inner cities, through the creation of new urban communities in less-populated areas. Following the New Towns Act of 1946, 32 New Towns in England, Scotland, Wales and Northern Ireland were planned in three phases over more than 20 years, commencing with Stevenage and Harlow, which were designated in 1946 and 1947 as part of a group of eight New Towns combining people and industries in the South-East. There were six others in England, including Corby, Peterlee and Newton Aycliffe, together with Glenrothes and East Kilbride in Scotland. A final phase that included Milton Keynes and Telford was designated in 1967 and 1968.

The New Towns sought to satisfy the human and communal needs of future residents through the adoption of the 'neighbourhood' principles suggested in the City of London Plan. Lord Reith, chair of the post-war Labour government's New Towns Committee, even went so far as to describe them as 'essays in civilization'.[18] This didactic, almost paternalistic approach typified those who believed they knew best what the public wanted or needed, at a time when neither public consultation nor an authentic consumer voice was a significant consideration. The New Towns – something of an ideological battleground for many years – received the final *coup de grâce* in 1992 when the New Town Development Corporations were closed down and their assets sold off by the Conservative government. A leader in *The Times*, entitled 'Paradise Mislaid', fulminated that 'Milton Keynes was the last desperate throw of a generation of British planners who were distasteful of the traditional British cities and towns and had the political power and public money to fashion the environment to their will... The architect was god and history was the devil.'[19]

From 1946 Frederick Gibberd played a seminal role in the creation of Harlow New Town, drawing up the master plan and serving as planner and chief architect [1.59]. Like its early counterparts elsewhere, Harlow was divided into a series of neighbourhoods, complete with housing, pub, shopping precinct and other communal facilities. Gibberd's housing schemes were generally low-rise mixed developments of flats and terraced houses, although at Harlow he also introduced a nine-storey block of flats, The Lawn, often regarded as one of the earlier tower blocks of architectural note in Britain [1.11]. Gibberd also commissioned many contemporary architects to contribute buildings to the town, including Yorke, who designed the Ladyshot housing area. Landscaping was a feature of Harlow, where green spaces and plantings intersected with housing [1.4].[20] However, the New Towns began to attract criticism even from the early years, most notably at the hands of the architectural critic J.M. Richards in his 1953 article on 'The Failure of the New Towns' in the *Architectural Review*.[21] This failure was centred on three counts: social, economic and architectural.

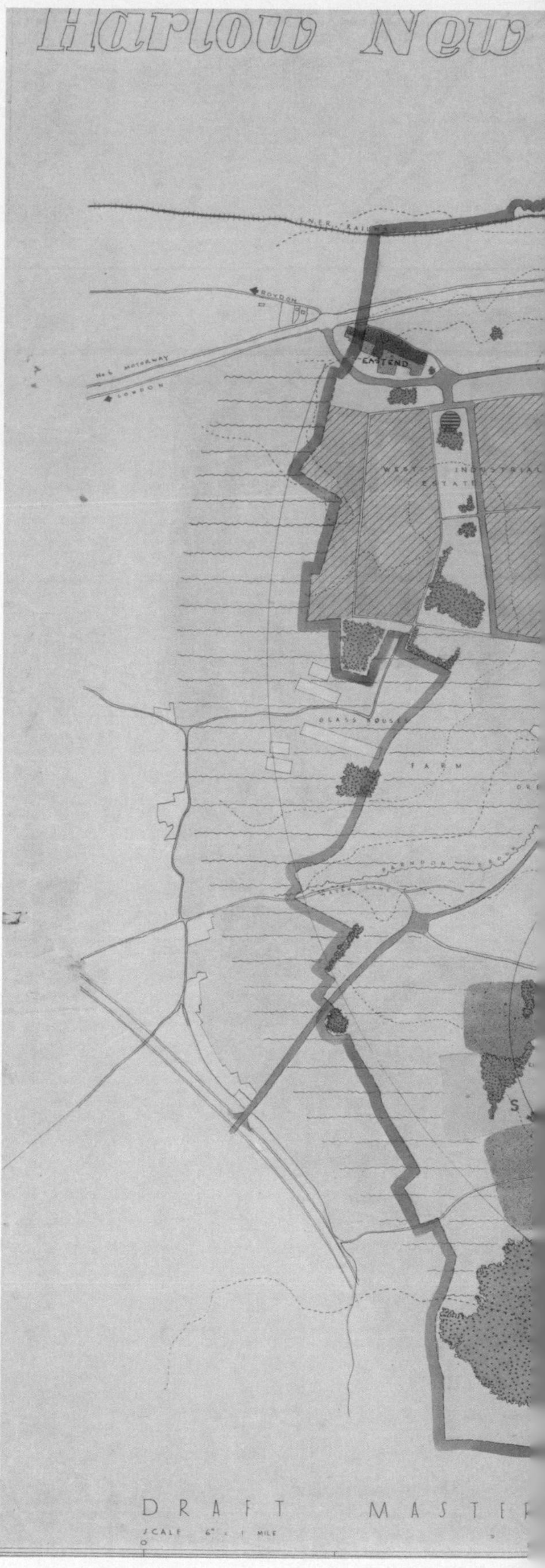

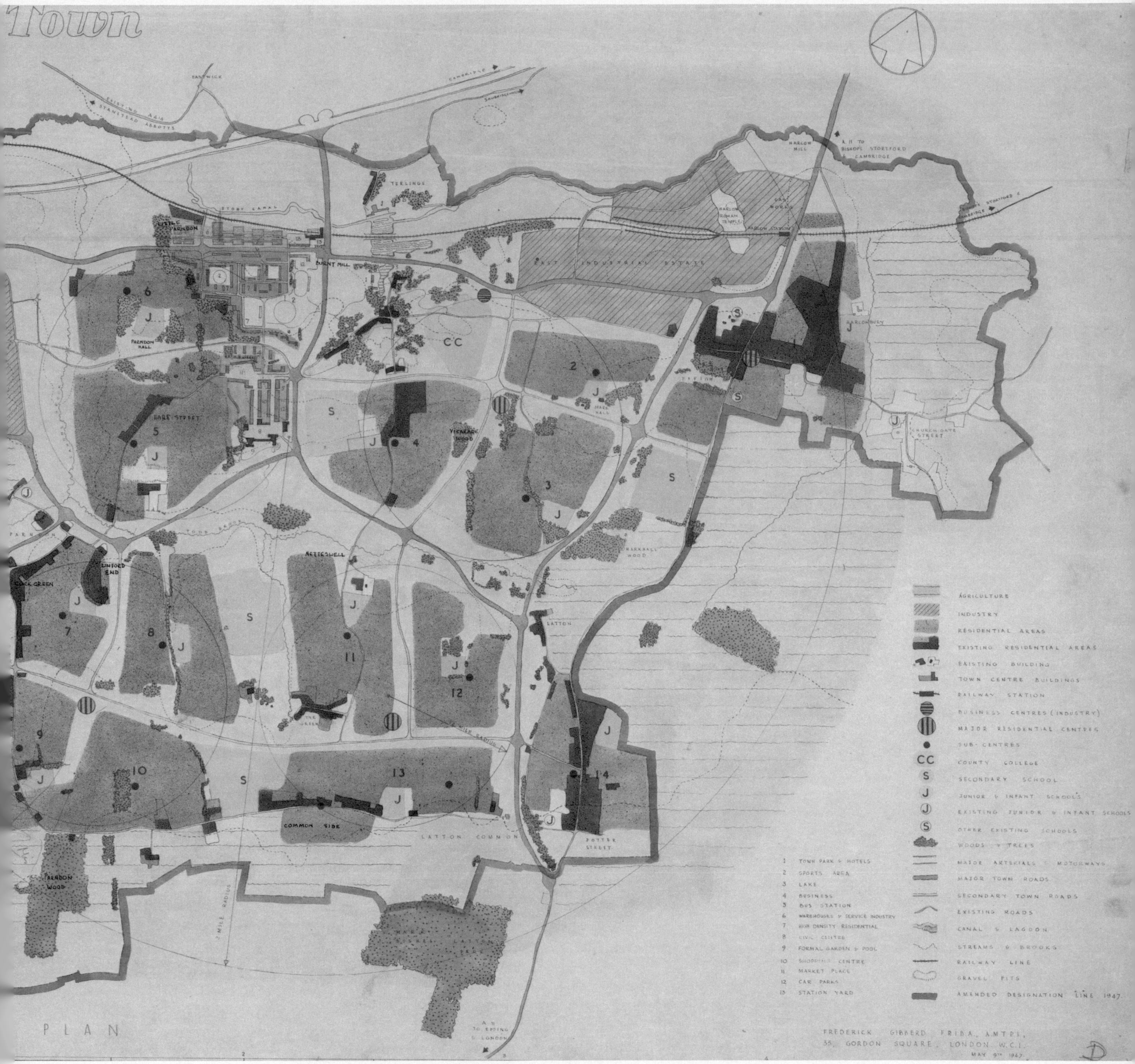

● 1.59 [ABOVE] Draft plan of Harlow New Town, Frederick Gibberd, 1947 | Hand-coloured print | Gibberd Garden Trust

● 1.60 [ABOVE] *Family Group*, Henry Moore, 1954, installed in Harlow town centre | Photograph by Henk Snoek, 1972 ● 1.61 [OPPOSITE TOP] Design for Calverton End Adventure Playground, Milton Keynes, Ron Herron of Archigram Architects, 1972 | Dyeline print with added colour felt-tip pen, film and collage mounted on board | Archigram Archive ● 1.62 [OPPOSITE BOTTOM] Design drawing for Milton Keynes shopping centre, Derek Walker, Stuart Mosscrop, Chris Woodward and Syd Green, 1973 | Drawing by Helmut Jacoby, pen and ink | RIBA Library Drawings Collection

House-building had been a national priority, which, in the case of New Towns, resulted in the fact that the 'neighbourhood' shops, schools, industries, hospitals and the cultural and recreational facilities essential to their successful realization were slow to materialize. In effect, their inhabitants were seen to lack the essentially social urban (or town-related) qualities of street life or living in close-knit social communities, and to be located in an impersonal landscaped environment that differed little from many pre-war garden-suburb housing estates.

Space does not permit a fuller examination of the New Towns' history or the full variety of approaches, such as that embodied in the pedestrian-traffic segregation of Cumbernauld (designated in 1955) in Scotland; designed to accommodate a population drawn from the poor housing conditions in Glasgow, its Corbusian-influenced Brutalist town-centre megastructure attracted considerable attention. However, a brief look at Milton Keynes is warranted, as the 'last desperate throw of a generation of British planners', as *The Times* put it, on the 25th anniversary of its designation in 1967.[22]

Unlike many of the earlier New Towns – conceived in an era when a coordinated public-transport policy was anticipated, but never arrived – Milton Keynes was planned as a fresh alternative to the perceived failures of earlier New Towns, yet was informed by a knowledge of Garden City principles. In its first iteration of 1967, Buckinghamshire's County Architect and Planner had envisaged it as a town of high-rise clusters linked by monorail. However, the second 1969 master plan, drawn up by Milton Keynes's Chief Architect and Planner Derek Walker and others, envisaged it very differently. Low-rise and low-density, it was characterized by varied housing types, with an emphasis on planting and landscaping [1.9, 1.61]. Unlike earlier New Towns, Milton Keynes also recognized the reality of car ownership, with a design that consisted of a central business and shopping district with a grid road system that connected it to a series of local centres. A Miesian simplicity of form, with external use of mirrored glass complemented by its internal glazing and marble finishes, characterized the shopping centre, which was opened by Prime Minister Thatcher in 1979 [1.62].[23] Although Milton Keynes still attracted criticism from a number of quarters, by the first decade of the twenty-first century its population had risen from 40,000 to 230,000, with more than 10,000 businesses. Boasting an extensive network of pedestrian walkways, cycleways and affordable housing, it proved to be a desirable place in which to live and raise families [1.10].[24]

CALVERTON END
ADV PLAYGROUND
14.9.72
RH
165 : 006
ARCHIGRAM
ARCHITECTS

SOCIAL HOUSING

Despite the large investment in New Towns, social housing in the cities also remained a high priority, becoming something of a political barometer in the post-war decades. Serious social problems had resulted from the incapacity of cities such as London, Liverpool, Manchester and Glasgow to find acceptable solutions to the housing crisis, causing unprecedented pressure to build upwards on high-density, predominantly urban sites.[25] There were plans to accelerate the housing programme through the initiation of council subsidies for building tower blocks in 1957, followed by further subsidies in 1962 to adopt new prefabricated building techniques for tower blocks and multi-deck access flats, a seemingly cost-effective and rapid way forward. Despite the doubts of many local authorities and the prevailing lack of enthusiasm of the new tenants, a massive programme was initiated, and 26 per cent of all housing built by local authorities in 1966 was in the form of tower blocks.

However, serious doubts were raised with the partial collapse in 1968 of Ronan Point tower block in Newham, East London, following a gas explosion. Built using a system of prefabricated concrete panels, it had been completed only two months earlier. This media-worthy event sharpened the debate about tower blocks as the best solutions to housing problems, with more questions being posed about their suitability for families, their lack of social space and the difficulties of maintenance – especially essential services such as lifts – as well as the growing fears of crime. Nonetheless, there were also positive architectural responses to the inner-city housing crisis, as evidenced by a number of high-density developments spanning the period of this chapter, most notably for the LCC. A number of them will be briefly considered.

One early solution to London's acute housing shortage attuned to the social-democratic aspirations of many architects and planners of the post-war years was the large-scale development at Churchill Gardens, Westminster [1.56]. Designed by Powell and Moya, architects of the Skylon on the South Bank at the Festival of Britain, the high-density scheme looked to continental (particularly Dutch) Modernism and was designed to house 5,000 residents on a 33-acre site. A mixed development of blocks of flats 9–11 storeys high, with a number of lower blocks of maisonettes and flats of five storeys, it was built in several phases between 1945 and 1961, the first of which was completed in 1950.[26] A key feature was that it conformed to the 'neighbourhood' unit concept identified in the City of London Plan (1943), which was also at the heart of early New Town thinking. The fact that many subsequent developments nationally were to ignore this dimension was a significant ingredient in their failure.

Other notable social-housing landmarks of these years designed for the LCC included the 27-storey Balfron Tower and its neighbour Carradale House in the Brownfield Estate, Poplar [1.63, 1.64]. Designed in the Brutalist style and clearly articulating their internal functions through their external forms, they were commissioned from architect Ernö Goldfinger in 1963 and completed in 1967 and 1970 respectively. Goldfinger's commitment to social housing was such that he moved into a flat in the Balfron Tower and listened to residents' views about living in the block. Such critiques were responded to in another Goldfinger building, the 31-storey Trellick Tower, commissioned in 1966 and completed in 1972 – a time when such tower blocks were increasingly being associated with social problems. Despite Goldfinger's concern for the residents' needs, Trellick Tower subsequently became known to some as the 'Tower of Terror'. However, as has been considered by a number of historians, vandalism and anti-social behaviour in tower blocks such as this were not so much due to their architects' failings as to the financial constraints of local authorities, preventing the provision of caretakers.[27] Although tarred by the same brush, Trellick Tower was conceptually very different from the anonymous blocks erected by building companies such as Wimpey, which provided attractively low-priced, anonymous, standardized 'packages' for local authorities, but gave rise to an increasingly hostile public, media and architectural press.

● 1.63 [ABOVE] Balfron Tower, Rowlett Street, London, Ernö Goldfinger, 1965–7 ● 1.64 [OPPOSITE] Elevation drawing of Balfron Tower, Rowlett Street, London, Ernö Goldfinger, 1965 | Photomechanical print on drafting film | RIBA Library Drawings Collection

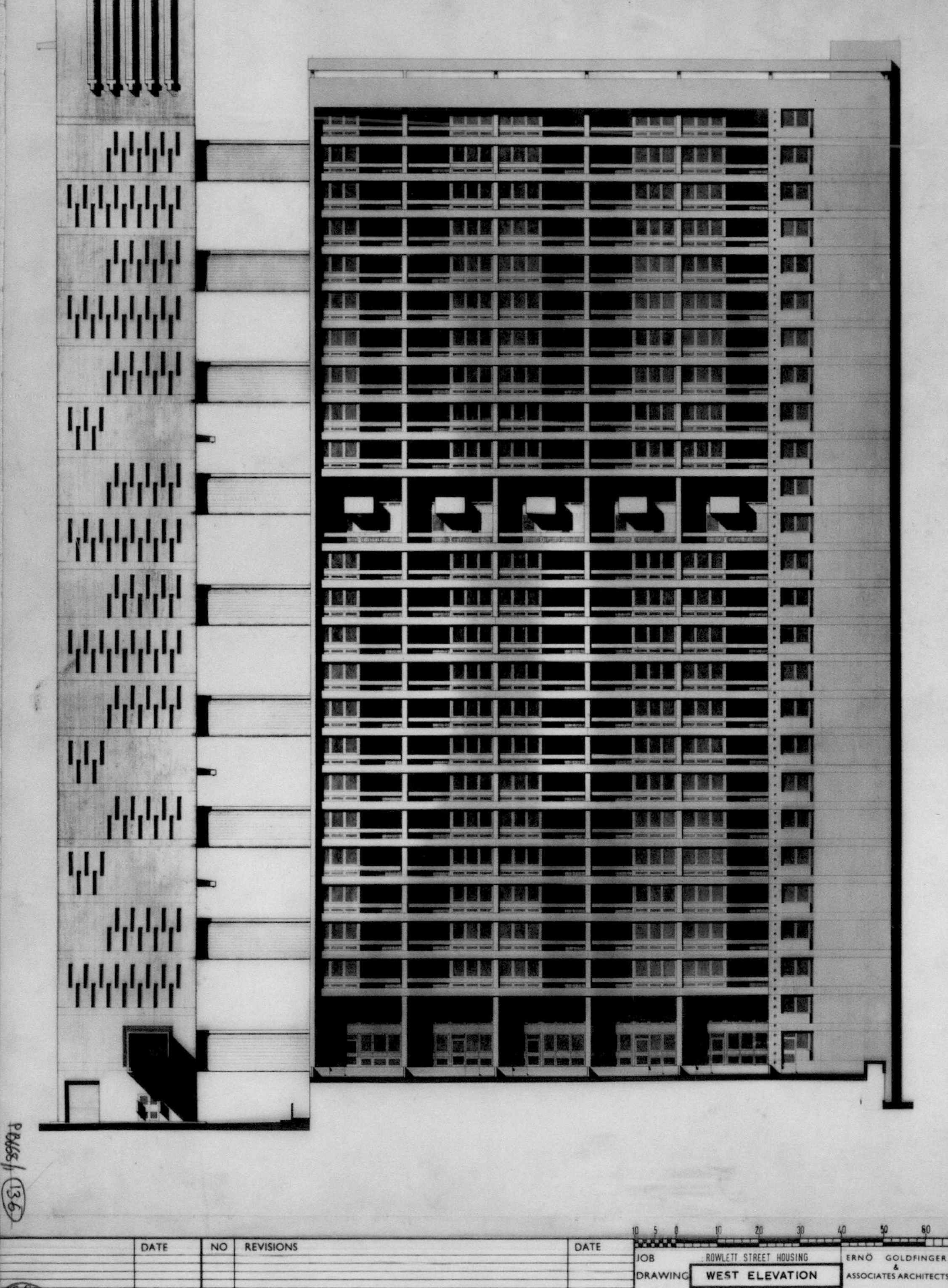
DATE
NO
REVISIONS
DATE
JOB : ROWLETT STREET HOUSING
DRAWING WEST ELEVATION
CLIENT : L.C.C.
SCALE : 1/16" = 1'-0"
DRAWN
DATE : 6.3.65.
ERNÖ GOLDFINGER & ASSOCIATES ARCHITECTS
69-70 PICCADILLY
LONDON W1
HYDe Park 5657-8 / 5210
No RSH/528.5
ISSUE
RIBA

● 1.65 [ABOVE] Perspective drawing of the Albert Sloman Library, University of Essex, Architects Co-Partnership, *c.*1964 | Ink on architectural tracing paper | Architects Co-Partnership ● 1.66 [OPPOSITE] Falmer House, University of Sussex, Basil Spence, 1959

THE NEW SCHOOLS AGENDA AND OTHER EDUCATIONAL DESIGN INITIATIVES

Like public housing, the provision of new school buildings was very much a part of post-war ambitions. Expectations were high in the wake of the 1944 'Butler' Education Act, which had raised the school leaving age, made secondary education free and opened up for many the future possibility of further and higher education. With more than 5,000 schools damaged in the war, as well as a significant increase in birth rates, there was a pressing need for the rapid provision of new school buildings.[28]

There was considerable innovation in school building techniques, most notably at Hertfordshire County Council, where, with the approval of the Ministry of Education, expertise in prefabrication was swiftly developed.[29] The leading figure in the 'Hertfordshire experiment', as it became known, was Stirrat Johnson-Marshall, who, as Deputy Architect at the County Council and working closely with the county's Chief Education Officer, headed a team of specialists who sought to provide educationalists with appropriate buildings. Other key figures working with Johnson-Marshall included David Medd, Bruce Martin and Mary Crowley, all of whom became widely recognized as specialists in the field.[30] New prefabrication techniques aligned to new educational ideas and 'child-centred' learning were applied to Burleigh Infants School, Cheshunt (1946–7), and the Village School at Essenden (1947–8). The latter gave off a Scandinavian feel, no doubt influenced by Medd, who had visited Scandinavia and met Alvar Aalto, Sven Markelius and Gunnar Asplund. These were just two of the programme of 10 new primary schools in the county's 1947 programme. Medd's prototypes were marked by their lack of internal columns and the use of glass clerestories and warm colours to brighten the internal spaces. Important too, in the Hertfordshire schools, was the design of appropriate sanitaryware for young children, and the team worked closely with the ceramics manufacturing firm of Adamsez to bring this about. The prevailing low-quality design of school furniture was another area of investigation.

In 1948 Johnson-Marshall moved from Hertfordshire to become Chief Architect of the Architects' and Buildings' Branch at the Ministry of Education (MoE), working alongside a progressive and enlightened civil servant, and he was joined by David and Mary Medd (née Crowley) in 1949. The Hertfordshire programme, well embedded by this time, continued to flourish and complete 10–12 schools annually: 100 new schools had been built by 1954 and doubled by 1961. The research-and-development unit at the MoE also built prototype schools: one of the Medds' significant achievements was the Village School at Finmere, Oxfordshire, completed in 1960 for £10,000. By working closely with Oxfordshire's Deputy Education Officer, the provision of interlinked teaching and other accommodation, as well as the placing of equipment, was based on careful observation of classroom teaching aligned to the close involvement of many architects, teachers and educationists who visited it. Thus an effective philosophy was set in place for the county's schools. However, such a coordinated and user-intensive approach was not shared by many education authorities, resulting in less effective results elsewhere.

Not all schools at the time were designed in line with contemporary educational principles. The *enfant terrible* in this respect was the avant-garde competition-winning design by Alison and Peter Smithson for Hunstanton Secondary School, which was completed in 1954 [1.68]. Known by many locals as 'the glasshouse' and ridiculed by the public, its glass, brick and concrete forms and exposed services were acclaimed by numerous progressive architects and contemporary critics, such as Reyner Banham. However, its stark Mies-influenced forms were not highly compatible with the educational needs of children or teachers and represented the Smithsons' reaffirmation of the importance of architecture itself.

Later examples of the Medds' work included the Eveline Lowe Nursery and Primary School in Camberwell, London (1965–6), and the Delf Hill Middle School in Bradford (1966–9), both of which were built in the reinvigorated educational climate following the 1964 Labour general-election victory, when the party's *New Britain* manifesto had restated many of its post-war aspirations [1.69]. The design of the Eveline Lowe School promoted the intermingling of age groups and shared teaching across a range of different areas devoted to reading, writing, sewing, painting, domestic science and other activities. It also involved the design of furniture and equipment – a national problem, as few education authorities had the resources to establish their own design departments to compensate for the furniture industry's lack of interest. The LCC was one of the few that had one, along with a small number of others, including Hertfordshire, Kent and Nottinghamshire. Other solutions were pioneered in the 1960s, including the Counties Furniture Group established in 1961, led by Shropshire in collaboration with West Sussex, Northamptonshire and, subsequently, Worcestershire and Denbighshire.[31]

Other Local Education Authorities also contributed to innovations in school-building, including Nottinghamshire, which established a design development group that included former employees at Hertfordshire. By 1957 this alternative approach, with the help of the MoE, had evolved into CLASP (Consortium of Local Authorities Special Programme) with a membership of Coventry, Durham, Leicester, Nottinghamshire, Glamorgan and the West Riding of Yorkshire councils. Mainly applied to multi-storey secondary-school buildings, it brought together the resources of different local authorities to produce lower-cost, but effective solutions to school design.

● 1.67 [OPPOSITE TOP] Norfolk Terrace, University of East Anglia, Denys Lasdun, 1964–8
● 1.68 [OPPOSITE BOTTOM] Hunstanton School, Norfolk, Alison and Peter Smithson, 1949–54

The post-war years also offered considerable opportunities for the design of what became known as 'plate-glass universities'. Accommodating the expanding population bulge of the post-war years, this momentum gathered pace following publication of the 1963 Robbins Report on Higher Education, which had recommended immediate university expansion. Early examples included the universities of Sussex, York and East Anglia, the first three to be approved by the government. Basil Spence and Partners were commissioned to design the University of Sussex in 1959 [1.66]. Low-rise and using brick with sculptural overhanging roofs, the design exuded a gentle primitive aesthetic with echoes of late Corbusier.[32] The task of designing the University of York fell to the firm of Matthew, Johnson-Marshall and Partners, using a construction system derived from CLASP in which the university became a consortium member in order to undertake a tailored development programme for its particular needs. By way of contrast, Denys Lasdun, the designer of the National Theatre (1963–76), was appointed in 1962 to produce a design that reflected the University of East Anglia's interdisciplinary academic structure [1.67]. Trained at the Architectural Association and inspired by Corbusier, his designs included the Library, the Teaching Wall, the Central Square, the ziggurat-like residential Norfolk and Suffolk Terraces, and a matrix of raised walkways that embraced the concept that no campus building should be more than four minutes' walk away from any other. This concrete aesthetic influenced the design of other early 'plate-glass' universities, such as Essex, which had been approved in 1961 and developed an architectural plan spatially inspired by the squares and towers of medieval San Gimignano [1.65].

The commissioning of Gowan and Stirling to design the Engineering Faculty at Leicester University marked an interesting moment in British contemporary architectural design. Completed in 1963, the Engineering Faculty's red tile and engineering bricks, patent glazing and cantilevered lecture theatres resulted in a striking appearance that was widely praised by critics as a visual embodiment of the marriage of art and technology. However, this seemingly successful bonding of innovative materials and progressive aesthetics subsequently proved to be problematic and damaging to Stirling's reputation. This was compounded by technical problems encountered in his design for the History Faculty at Cambridge University of 1968, giving clients and users additional opportunity to condemn his work and question aspects of contemporary architecture. This paralleled wider public doubts associated with the consequences of untested technical innovations in housing during the later 1960s.

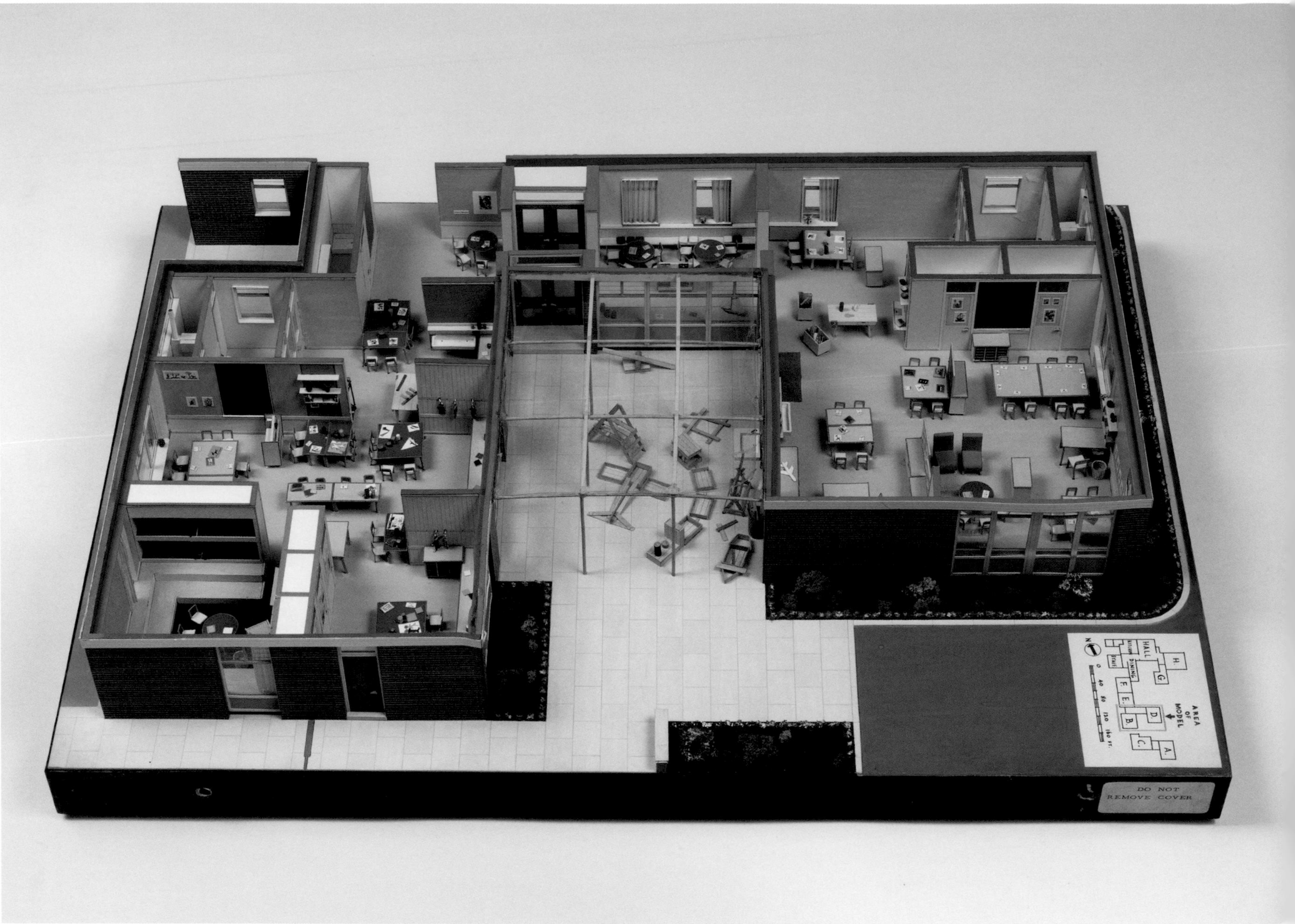

Aspirations for the development of a forward-looking transport and communications infrastructure were at the core of the vision for redesigning a new Britain after the war. Many facets of rail, road, freight and air transportation systems were publicly owned and under state control. Inevitably the post-war decades saw considerable developments in public-transport design, ranging from architecture and industrial engineering to signage, printed ephemera and uniforms. The emerging breed of British design consultancies was increasingly involved in the widespread drive to promote a modern, efficient and aesthetically conscious outlook in public transport, their multidisciplinary skills being applicable to the design of everything experienced by the travelling public and employees.

Following the introduction of the 1947 Transport Act, the British Transport Commission (BTC) was established as part of Labour's transport nationalization programme in January 1948. Its responsibility was to oversee docks and inland waterways, road transport, railways and the already nationalized London Passenger Transport Board. British Railways was established as part of this package, an amalgamation of the 'big four' pre-war companies: the Great Western Railway; the London, Midland and Scottish Railway; the London and North Eastern Railway; and the Southern Railway. Major changes were enacted in the following decade under the Conservatives, following the publication by the BTC of the *Modernization and Re-Equipment of British Railways* report in 1954, which recommended the replacement of steam locomotives with diesel and electric units, commissioning new passenger and freight rolling stock and the initiation of a programme of signalling and track renewal.[33] A £1.2 billion modernization programme was announced the following year, although its failure to achieve its financial targets by the early 1960s resulted in the 1963 'Beeching' Report on *The Reshaping of British Railways*, which led to a drastic programme of station closures and curtailment of passenger services. The BTC itself was axed following the 1962 British Transport Act and was re-formed into five new organizations, including the British Railways Board and London Transport Board.

This period of significant structural change was accompanied by major shifts in design outlook. In 1956, through its chairman Brian Robertson, the BTC established the British Railways Design Panel, with George Williams (a former CoID staff member who had also worked for the DRU) as its first Design Director. Royal Designer for Industry Christian Barman also served on the panel as Chief Publicity Officer. The panel was charged with advising on the best means of raising performance levels through improved standards of equipment and amenity design. It was immediately accepted that independent design consultants could be employed, and the DRU – one of the first generation of British design consultancies to offer a range of services across the full design spectrum – was a major beneficiary. Early DRU designs for British Railways included a series of seven locomotives designed in 1956 by Misha Black in consultation with J. Beresford-Evans.

Considerable public interest in the redesign of British Railways was evidenced by a weekly attendance of more than 28,500 at the 1963 'New Designs for British Railways' exhibition at the CoID's London Design Centre.[34] On display were the early results of the British Railways design. modernization programme commissioned from the DRU. The exhibition included mock-ups of first- and second-class coaches, with new upholstery fabrics, plastic laminates and improved luggage racks, litter bins, lighting, graphic design and lettering, and prototype uniforms that were to be trialled at selected stations. Further design developments were exhibited at a subsequent Design Centre exhibition in January 1965, devoted to British Railways' completed identity programme.[35] This high-profile outcome of a working group of industrial designers and British Railways staff, chaired by Milner Gray, was planned to roll out across all operational aspects of the now snappily titled British Rail [3.53]. Although approved by its internal steering committee, economic considerations limited its speedy adoption. The most striking and enduring graphic element of the new identity programme was the double-arrow logo designed by Gerald Barney of the DRU. Jock Kinneir and Margaret Calvert's new Rail Alphabet font was also adopted, replacing the Gill Sans that had been widely used since nationalization in 1948.[36] This modernizing ethos was widely evident elsewhere, ranging from the clean lines at Coventry's new station (1962), designed by W.R. Headley, to cutlery and station furniture designed by David Mellor and others.

● 1.69 [OPPOSITE] Model of Eveline Lowe School, Southwark, London, David and Mary Medd, 1967 | Plastic, painted card, paper and wood RIBA Library Drawings Collection ● 1.70 [RIGHT] 'Children crossing' sign, Jock Kinneir and Margaret Calvert, 1964

State-owned London Transport also explored the social and organizational potential of design, establishing its London Transport Design Panel in 1963. Its most significant contemporary initiative was the building of the Victoria Underground Line, approved by government in 1962 and completed in 1971. Almost inevitably, the DRU and Misha Black (London Transport's design consultant) were involved with this new enterprise, working closely with senior London Transport architectural and engineering staff.

The rapid development of air-passenger transport systems was also an important dimension of national and international design in the post-war years and an essential economic building block. In January 1946 London Airport (later Heathrow) was designated as the capital's civil airport, under the Ministry of Aviation. Passenger numbers rose rapidly, reaching almost 800,000 annually by the early 1950s, by which time the airport's temporary buildings were inadequate for the purpose, resulting in the commissioning of Gibberd to design a series of permanent terminal buildings (1950–69) [1.71]. Executed in brick, concrete and glass with an aura of muted Modernism, these included the Europa Building (1955), Oceanic Terminal (1961) and Terminal 1 (1968). Typographer Matthew Carter designed a typeface for the airport in the early 1960s, working with Gibberd, who took a keen interest in the siting of signage. In this period of public ownership the airport's internal spaces were not overwhelmed by competing commercial retail outlets and were principally designed for passenger comfort and convenience.

Gatwick emerged as another of Britain's leading airports, the Conservative government having approved its development in 1952 in order to relieve pressure on Heathrow. Yorke, Rosenberg & Mardall were awarded the airport commission (1955–8); Allford and Henderson were responsible, under Yorke, for designing the passenger terminal with its glass walls, marble floor and crisp detailing, as well as the integration of air, road and rail transport systems, in which Gatwick was a pioneer [1.72]. Queen Elizabeth II opened the terminal in 1958, which was erected very swiftly following the temporary closure of the airport in 1956. The design enabled all passengers to wait in a single space until they were called to the departure gate, which they could reach without buses or a long walk. The typographer Kinneir was commissioned to design the airport's signage in 1957, marking his first collaboration with Calvert.

Alongside the development of airport design in post-war decades, the publicly owned airlines – the British Overseas Airways Corporation (BOAC) and British European Airways (BEA) – demonstrated a keen interest in the benefits of design. BOAC established a Design Committee in 1945, with Kenneth Holmes as Design Consultant and F.H.K. Henrion as Art Director.[37] Early attention was paid to the tableware design for in-flight service, to military-inspired uniforms and to interior design and, in order to compete effectively with the American airline industry on transatlantic routes, a publicity department was established. Comfort was important in attracting passengers, and a BOAC aircraft-interiors committee was set up in 1958, in which Gaby Schreiber played a significant part, working on colours, finishes and textiles.[38] Not being seen merely as a cosmetic matter or skin-deep, design was applied equally to non-public areas of company activity: Misha Black and Kenneth Bayes of the DRU worked with the BOAC technicians' committee on the interior and efficient layout of their engineering hall at the company's Heathrow headquarters.

As is clear from the discussion of railway and airport design, a striking characteristic of British transport design was the importance of clearly legible and high-quality aesthetic signage. Brief mention must be made of its place in the road and motorway systems throughout Britain, having become a source of increasing public debate in the 1950s and '60s, whether in editorials in the broadsheet press or among the design community itself. Kinneir and Calvert's crisply articulated signage at Gatwick airport had been favourably noted by Sir Colin Anderson, chair of the 1957 Ministry of Transport Advisory Committee on Traffic Signs for Motorways, resulting in Kinneir's appointment (in partnership with Calvert) as design consultant. The subsequent Worboys Committee on Traffic Signs for All-Purpose Roads reported in 1964, and Kinneir once again became design consultant.[39] The design outcomes – including the celebrated Transport font and a coordinated set of highly legible symbols and colours – proved to be successful and enduring and have been adopted in many countries worldwide [1.70, 1.73].

● 1.71 [OPPOSITE] Buffet bar at London Airport (later Heathrow), Frederick Gibberd, 1953

● 1.72 [ABOVE] Concourse at Gatwick Airport, Yorke, Rosenberg & Mardall, 1958

Crowland
B 1040

Peterboro'
A 47
Wisbech
A 47

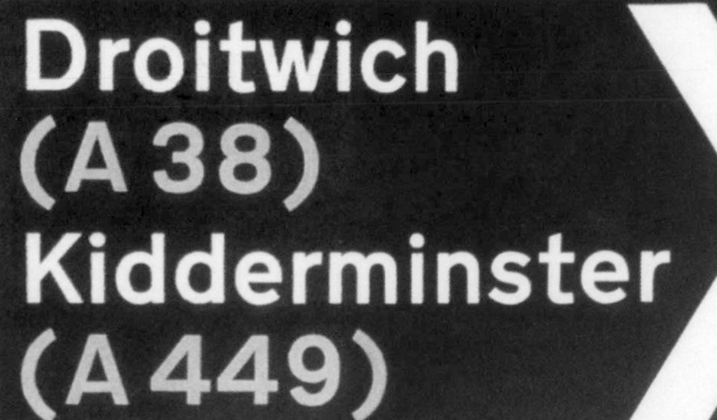
Droitwich
(A 38)
Kidderminster
(A 449)
Peterborough
A 47
Nottingham A 606
Leicester
A 46
Newark
A 46

Northchurch 1
Wiggington 4
Chesham 5
Potten End 2
Gaddesden 3
Ashridge 4

CONCLUSION: FROM WELFARISM TO INDIVIDUALISM

The post-war decades showed a gradual shift away from what was essentially a shared vision of a well-planned, democratic and material embodiment of the values of the Welfare State, the principles of which largely continued under the 1950s Conservative governments of Churchill, Eden and Macmillan and under succeeding Labour and Conservative governments during the 1960s and '70s. However, Prime Minister Thatcher, three years after her Conservative government had been elected in 1979, extolled the benefits of free enterprise and the primacy of the individual, in her opening speech to an information-technology conference at the Barbican Centre, London. She declared:

> The first ingredient of our approach is a passionate belief in the virtues of free enterprise and individual endeavour. Innovation and initiative cannot flourish if they are smothered by a state that wants to control everything. We shall not blaze again the trail that Brunel, Morris and Marconi found, if we consign their successors to the consensus of committees and excessive and irksome regulation.[40]

Discernible moves away from the dictates of the establishment and authority had also been emerging in the design world, which by the 1960s had experienced increasing criticism of what was seen as the restrictive 'official' taste of the state-funded CoID. From its origins in the 1940s to the mid-1960s the Council had pursued an aesthetic that essentially derived from a Modernist belief in fitness for function and truth to materials. Such an outlook had come under increasing pressure from a younger generation of designers and consumers in what had become a more affluent society, where, sustained by higher levels of disposable income, choice and individual taste were becoming the hallmarks of contemporary consumer life. The CoID's Director, Paul Reilly, acknowledged this in 1967 in his seminal article on 'The Challenge of Pop', in which he wrote that 'to ignore or reject the ephemeral *per se* is to ignore a fact of life' and conceded that there was a narrowness of choice in design circles.[41]

The CoID's shift away from consumer design towards capital goods was underlined by its amalgamation with the Engineering Council and its change of title to the Design Council in 1972. Similar concerns had arisen in relation to a wide range of other social and cultural structures, including what was seen as the restrictive outlook of the wider art, architectural and design establishment. This was a key factor in the art-school revolutions of 1968 in Hornsey, Guildford, Brighton and many other places nationally, resulting in subsequent radical revisions of the curriculum, the opening up of fresh horizons and the adoption of a more pluralistic outlook. Notions of 'alternative' lifestyles had also emerged, despite the dilution of their social potency through commoditization in the high street.

Furthermore, as has already been seen, increasingly bitter controversies surrounded the social acceptability and design of local-authority tower-block housing, following the partial collapse of Ronan Point in 1968 and widespread critiques of buildings such as Goldfinger's Trellick and Balfron Towers. By then the post-war consensual urban vision shared by designers, architects and planners in their quest to build a new, well-planned and modern Britain, sustained by the social and egalitarian ambitions of the post-war Welfare State, had largely ground to a halt. The optimism of the immediate post-war years – when designers, architects and planners strongly believed that they knew what people wanted or needed – was no longer acceptable to the wider British public, who had become increasingly resistant to what was viewed as unwanted paternalism, accompanied by a mistrust of authority, the establishment and notions of cultural leadership. From this period onwards the centrality of the Welfare State – or, more quintessentially, state control – was increasingly challenged in political circles, particularly by Margaret Thatcher during the 1980s and, more recently and with greater intensity, by David Cameron's 'Big Society' in the 2010s.

● 1.73 [OPPOSITE] Directional road signs, Jock Kinneir and Margaret Calvert, 1957–67

Coventry Cathedral
— Lily Crowther

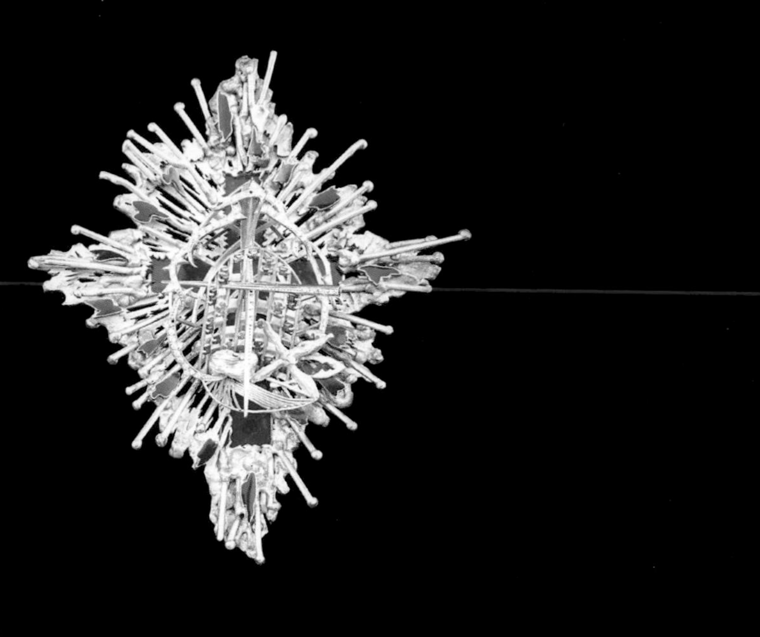

● 1.74 [OPPOSITE] The new Coventry Cathedral under construction, with the ruins of the old cathedral in the foreground, 1959 ● 1.75 [TOP LEFT] Ciborium and chalices, Gerald Benney, 1962 | Silver | Coventry Cathedral ● 1.76 [TOP RIGHT] Bishop's Jewel, Thomas Durant, 1963 | Gold, silver, diamonds and enamel, the outer part representing the destruction of the old cathedral, with symbols of the new cathedral at the centre, including the Baptistery window and cross of nails Coventry Cathedral ● 1.77 [LEFT] Model for the Baptistery window at Coventry Cathedral, John Piper and Patrick Reyntiens, 1958–9 Wood and stained glass | V&A: C.63–1976

As a centre for munitions manufacturing, Coventry was a major target for German bombing during the Second World War. The medieval Cathedral Church of St Michael was hit on the first night of raids, 14 November 1940; only its outer walls and tower survived. John Piper was serving as a war artist at the time, with a commission to paint bombed churches. He went to Coventry the morning after the raid and described the ruins: 'Outline of the walls against the steamy sky a series of ragged loops. Windows empty, but for oddly poised fragments of tracery, with spikes of blackened glass embedded in them. Walls flaked and pitted, as if they had been under water for a hundred years.'[1]

The scale of the damage at Coventry gave the city a symbolic status in post-war reconstruction. The Gothic Revivalist Sir Giles Gilbert Scott was initially appointed to design a new cathedral in 1941, but resigned in 1947 under pressure from critics such as J.M. Richards of *The Times* and Nikolaus Pevsner, then Editor of the *Architectural Review*, who felt that the project ought to be stylistically forward-looking. A competition was launched to choose a new architect. There were 219 entries, some of them extremely daring: Peter and Alison Smithson designed a glass-walled building with a square plan and sail-like roof, while Colin St John Wilson and Peter Carter proposed a simple space-frame.

The winner was Basil Spence, with a much less shocking basilica design [1.78]. Spence used the same pinkish sandstone as the old cathedral, and took the spacing of its bays as the basic module for his plan. The new building sits at right-angles to the old, with a monumental porch linking the two [1.74]. The liturgical west wall is glass, so that the high altar is visible from the ruins.[2] This underscores the theme of sacrifice and resurrection, symbolized by the progress from old cathedral to new. A second main axis runs across the nave, from the baptistery to the inter-denominational Chapel of Unity, reflecting the universal Christian belief in baptism.

The most dramatic features of Coventry Cathedral are Spence's many commissions from an extraordinary range of artists and designers. These included young innovators such as Elisabeth Frink, who sculpted the lectern eagle, and Hans Coper, who made the monumental candlesticks. But perhaps the defining sculptural commission for the project was Jacob Epstein's *St Michael and the Devil*, one of his final major works, mounted beside the porch steps.

The cathedral's windows form an especially strong aspect of the design. Entering from the porch, one passes through John Hutton's engraved glass screen, with its alternating rows of stately saints and energetic angels breaking through the grid of mullions. At the western end of the south wall is the abstract baptistery window by John Piper and Patrick Reyntiens. Piper began by sketching colour studies, which Reyntiens used to make a scale model of the window, testing the balance of colours for the final design [1.77]. The windows that line the nave are the last to be revealed to the visitor, because they face towards the high altar. Their colours and motifs represent the progress from baptism through life to death and resurrection. These windows were designed by Lawrence Lee, then head of stained glass at the Royal College of Art, and his former students Keith New and Geoffrey Clarke.

Clarke's many designs for the cathedral also include the silver-gilt altar cross, as well as the innovative cast-aluminium cross on the *flèche*, and an illuminated cross for the chapel in the undercroft, which was used for services while the cathedral was being built [1.79]. Leading goldsmith Gerald Benney was commissioned to make a set of liturgical silver for the cathedral, including chalices whose stems are decorated with his signature bands of texture, and a ciborium topped by a stylized version of the cross of nails, a symbol of Coventry's rise from the ruins [1.75].

In the niches beside the nave windows are a series of stone panels by Ralph Beyer, carved with passages from the New Testament. These are known as the Tablets of the Word, and Beyer based their lettering style on early Christian inscriptions in the Roman catacombs. He also designed a related typeface for cathedral signage and publications, giving the institution a consistent graphic identity. Beyer's interest in historical styles of Christian art was shared by many of the cathedral's designers, including Hutton, who had studied French Romanesque statuary, and Spence himself, who was inspired by the Gothic fortress-cathedral at Albi. Perhaps the most striking example of this type of influence is Graham Sutherland's immense Byzantinesque tapestry of *Christ in Glory*, which dominates the east end of the cathedral [1.80]. It was woven near Aubusson by Pinton Frères, the only firm with a loom large enough to make it in one piece. Spence had first seen a tapestry by Sutherland at around the time of the Coventry competition, and was so impressed that he appointed him very early in the project. However, due to the practical and design challenges of working on such a scale, the tapestry was only completed a few months before the consecration, which took place on 25 May 1962.

Critical reactions to the cathedral changed hugely during the period of its construction. The result of the competition was announced on 15 August 1951, during the Festival of Britain. Spence's design was inevitably judged in the light of his playful 'Sea and Ships' Pavilion at the Festival. The proposed cathedral was seen by many as lacking in grandeur; defending it, Pevsner praised its 'honesty and vitality', saying that 'what it may lack in monumentality, it will gain in life'.[3] Yet just after its completion in 1962, Reyner Banham dismissed it as 'the worst set-back to English church architecture for a very long time' and the competition assessors 'as square as could be found without going grave-robbing'.[4] In the intervening years Spence had joined the establishment – he became President of the RIBA in 1958, was knighted and elected a Royal Academician in 1960 and appointed Professor of Architecture at the Royal Academy in 1961. His building can now be seen as a late flourish of the Contemporary style, perhaps already somewhat dated when it opened, but nevertheless a tour de force of artistic collaboration on the model of the great medieval cathedrals.

● 1.78 [BELOW] Elevation drawing of Coventry Cathedral from the east, Basil Spence, June 1952 Graphite on transparent paper | RCAHMS: Sir Basil Spence Archive ● 1.79 [BOTTOM LEFT] Altar cross, Geoffrey Clarke, 1958 | Cast silver, commissioned in relation to Clarke's altar cross for Coventry Cathedral | The Worshipful Company of Goldsmiths ● 1.80 [BOTTOM RIGHT] Trial section of the tapestry *Christ in Glory*, showing the Eagle of St John, Graham Sutherland, 1958–9 Woven by Pinton Frères, Aubusson, France, wool | Herbert Art Gallery and Museum, Coventry

3 Nation, Land and Heritage

— Maurice Howard

The story of heritage and the land throughout the twentieth century in Britain is one punctuated by frequent expressions of alarm over threatened buildings, landscapes and local traditions. The foundation of conservation and amenity societies sought to make representation for and conserve every aspect of the past's material remains.[1] The promotion of the past on the assumption that its traditional values were worth preserving has often led to accusations that this implies an uncritical acceptance of a world static, unreconstructed and genteel. Wealthy classes who already enjoyed comfort and privilege were thereby protected, and the presentation of the past at heritage sites inevitably sanitized.[2] However, twentieth-century British artists have used the past for new ideas, and historic styles have proved flexible to new approaches. This chapter examines three major threads during the 40 years or so after 1945: the country house and its influence on film and interior design; book illustration and photography, and the celebration of a peculiarly British school of fantasy and evocation of childhood; and, finally, the land itself and its support and inspiration for traditional practices such as the art of ceramic.

The *Recording Britain* project of 1939–43 helped in important ways to define pathways that were followed after the end of the Second World War [1.81].[3] This was not because the project itself was enormously influential on the actual organization of heritage management, but rather because it offered distinctive categories of buildings and contexts thought worthy of preservation. The scheme was quite different in origin from the impetus behind much government legislation and the foundation of pressure groups to preserve the past. The latter often moved into action in response to a recent event, such as the loss of a structure like the famous case of the Euston Arch in 1962.[4] *Recording Britain* actually chose and sought to predict forms of culture that could be obliterated by the devastation of war. It identified four major themes: landscape, towns and villages, ancient churches and country houses. The very activity of recording supported a key British artistic practice, since it encouraged the revival of the tradition of watercolour, redolent of the great age of the early nineteenth-century Romantics and their evocative record of landscapes and buildings. *Recording Britain* was not to be an exact record of each chosen site or every building stone; places were depicted with an eye to the magic or mythology of place and of picturesque ordinariness that somehow fed into the image of both the deep rural landscape and an 'edge-of-town' quality, which many people were later to identify as key to understanding the continuities of British tradition. Nor did the project lay down a prescribed style; images included some with a meticulous depiction and others using a broader brushstroke to summon up a sense of place and mood, such as the work of John Piper.

Whilst *Recording Britain* was not without some surprise choices, it is true to say that some of its products envisaged a past cherished and faded – rather like, as one commentator has noted, an old family photograph album. Its legacy proved to be less about the destruction of war than about what the nation allowed to decay in the post-war period. In drama, film, literature and music, Modernist styles challenged the past to face its darker side. In a series of operas Benjamin Britten both celebrated and cautioned about the interface between the seemingly calm physical infrastructure of the traditional British community and those who suffered within it. *Peter Grimes*, which premiered in 1945, presented a dark portrayal of community prejudice against the unconventional individual; the traditional heritage buildings of moot hall, public house and fishing hut providing the settings, and the unchanging sea opening and concluding the piece as if sweeping over the cruelty that pervades this East Anglian fishing village. The social hierarchy and order of the fictive Suffolk village of Loxford in *Albert Herring* (1947) is upturned, this time to comic effect, when the annual ceremony of crowning the May Queen is cross-gendered to allow a male to play the role. And in *Gloriana*, composed for the coronation of 1953, the public face and painful private life of the first Queen Elizabeth are played out both in the elite setting of a Renaissance court and in the local revelry of the city of Norwich, where the Queen goes on progress. Two of Britten's operas make a particular feature of the country house. In *The Turn of the Screw* (1954), adapted from the short story by Henry James, the house at Bly becomes the setting for an ambiguous ghost story. In the later *Owen Wingrave* (transmitted for television in 1971) Britten explores the stultifying effect of skeletons in family cupboards and the oppressive nature of family duty. *Owen Wingrave* has only been rarely produced, but *The Turn of the Screw* has enjoyed many productions all over the world. Sometimes Bly is a period-specific house, emphasizing the enclosed world in which the imaginings of the protagonists are played out. In other productions the physical setting of the house is dematerialized, as if to underline the ambivalence of the story. In both streams of interpretation, however, the house has a character of its own and becomes a protagonist in the story.[5] The country house as an individual 'character' that needed to be defined and cherished was to feature prominently in the narratives of country-house history in the post-war world.

● 1.81 [OPPOSITE] *Disused Tin Mine, St Agnes, Cornwall*, Olive Cook, *c.*1940 | Pen and ink, watercolour and bodycolour on paper, from the *Recording Britain* series | V&A: E.1219–1949

The decline of the country house in the twentieth century is usually thought to begin with the agricultural depression of the 1870s.[6] By the beginning of the Second World War many people viewed country houses as dinosaurs of the past; indeed, Kenneth Clark, in setting the agenda for *Recording Britain*, opined that 'these will be largely abandoned after the war and will either fall into disrepair or be converted into lunatic sanitaria'.[7] But since that time these buildings have proved extraordinarily durable in different guises. A number of owners who chose to face the challenge famously made successful businesses of their ancestral seats; from the end of the 1940s the Marquess of Bath at Longleat, followed by the Duke of Bedford at Woburn Abbey and Lord Montagu at Beaulieu, attracted ever-increasing numbers until well into the 1960s. These stately homes played a significant role in British popular culture because they provided new places of resort to rival the traditional seaside and offered a different menu of attractions for family education and entertainment.[8]

However, after 1945 some house owners did not wish to return to houses requisitioned during the war, and the following 20 years saw the passing of a number of great and middle-sized houses to the National Trust, transforming that organization from one which, since its inception in 1895, had principally cared for its landholdings into one that for a generation and more fronted its buildings as major heritage assets.[9] The place of the country house in the national story was given a serious, academic significance through a number of key publications that became the 'textbooks' of architectural history, notably the Oxford *History of English Art* series and Penguin Press's *Pelican History of Art* series. Among the latter, John Summerson's *Architecture in Britain 1530–1830* (1953) made one thing emphatically clear. Thanks to the Reformation (hence no consistent programme of church-rebuilding thereafter), the evolution of a monarchy disrupted by civil war and increasingly constrained by Parliament (hence no royal palace on the scale of Versailles) and the overwhelming supremacy of London (which meant few grand civic buildings in towns and cities up and down the country), the story of great building from the 1530s until the early nineteenth century was effectively the evolution of the country house.

This sense of country houses changing from a private world of the elite into places of mass tourism had an impact on the image of these great houses as portrayed in the newest outlet for expressions of heritage: the world of film. In the critical appraisal of film and its depiction of the past, much attention has been given to the matter of historical costume, associated as it is with leading actors, but less to the architectural setting of historical films and their dependence on specific sources.[10] During the war the patriotic consensus of the need to celebrate a sense of community largely banished the very biggest houses from all depictions of contemporary troubles. In two films celebrating the nation's mythology and its resistance to external menace, Powell and Pressburger's *A Canterbury Tale* and Ealing Studios' *Went the Day Well*, the great house at the edge of the village is not a vast mansion, but a large comfortable house whose owner is part of the community.[11]

For historical dramas set in the past, large houses were more glamorous, and often film-makers used those made famous by recent sale or transfer, just as they explored the national collections for evidence of interiors and furnishings. At this period, while location on film was suggested by a real building in a single shot, all interiors were re-created in the studio. Here, therefore, was the chance for artistic directors to be inventive, and they used this freedom for narrative clarity. For the exteriors of Gainsborough Studios' *The Wicked Lady* (1945) and *Jassy* (1946), the recent National Trust acquisition of Blickling Hall, in Norfolk, was used as the exterior of the great house at the centre of the drama.[12] Within the house, however, in *The Wicked Lady* the Jacobean staircase was modified in the studio reconstruction to provide extra landings to facilitate dialogue [1.82]. In Ealing Studios' *Kind Hearts and Coronets* (1949) the exterior of Leeds Castle, in Kent, served as the ducal pile, which the protagonist seeks to succeed to in revenge for the family's mistreatment of his disgraced mother. However, an interior shot of its dining room used elements from at least two interiors at Bolsover Castle, Derbyshire, which was given to the nation in 1945.

The artistic director of the Powell and Pressburger films from 1940 to 1947, Alfred Junge, was especially creative with historical resources. When in *A Canterbury Tale* (1944) a young American officer stays at an inn at the imagined village of Chillingbourne near Canterbury, he sleeps in a bed derived from (though not an exact replica of) the Great Bed of Ware in the V&A (usually thought to have been created for an inn at Ware, in Hertfordshire) beneath an Elizabethan plasterwork ceiling. In *A Matter of Life and Death* (1946) a British airman goes to a temporary American base in a country house where they are rehearsing Shakespeare's *A Midsummer Night's Dream*. The great stair of the house, with its wide stone steps, tapestried walls and turn to the right at the summit, is patently based on the famous stair at Hardwick Hall, Derbyshire (this was to pass to the National Trust in 1957). When Junge won the Oscar for art direction for *Black Narcissus* (a studio creation of a different kind of British heritage and responsibility, an imagined building in Himalayan India) he left the Powell and Pressburger team just at the point when a different visual imaginative impulse was called for: the dream scenarios based on Surrealist painting in *The Red Shoes* (1948) and *The Tales of Hoffmann* (1953), created by his successor, Hein Heckroth.[13]

By the 1960s mainstream British film's treatment of historical subjects was turning towards a more realistic approach, and this reflected to some extent recent achievements in theatre and, increasingly, television. It would be wrong to label historical drama on film of this period as 'kitchen-sink', but it certainly began to engage with the stuff and smells of the past as never before. In Stanley Kubrick's *Barry Lyndon* (1975) the emphasis on the underside of eighteenth-century life – the Hogarthian bordering on the grotesque – was paramount. In John Schlesinger's *Far from the Madding Crowd* (1967) the mud and odour of the farmyard sought to bring the viewer close to the harsh daily life of the rural nineteenth century [1.83]. Authenticity is, however, always perceived through the filter of the contemporary; the characters of the Schlesinger film sported long hair, beards and clothes distinctly influenced by the 'hippy' mores of contemporary London.

● 1.82 [ABOVE] Still from *The Wicked Lady*, directed by Leslie Arliss, 1945

Critics have been quick to claim popular films and television adaptations as manifesting the political colour of the age, so that the series of adaptations from James Ivory and Ismail Merchant of the novels of E.M. Forster, as well as the television rendition of Evelyn Waugh's *Brideshead Revisited* (1981), have come to be branded as products of the conservative 1980s. These are often portrayed as journeys into nostalgia that revel in past differences of class and gender, of contrasting lives among the literary middle classes between the idle well-off and penurious companions, clergymen and clerks, and impoverished aristocracy living in faded splendour.[14]

In *Brideshead* the greater technical freedom, compared with the 1940s, to use the whole country house, inside and out, as film set meant that Castle Howard itself became a 'character' in the drama. However, in both the 1981 adaptation and the 2008 reshooting of the novel (also for television), interiors needed to look old and dilapidated. This was facilitated at this particular house by the fact that, since a fire in 1940, Castle Howard has – alongside surviving Georgian state rooms – empty spaces for temporary decor, so that both authentic period detail and something of the creative possibilities of 1940s films were possible.

If there was one period that had been most favoured to represent something of the continuity and tradition in film across the period of war and its aftermath, it was one that can be characterized as late medieval–Tudor. In the Powell and Pressburger film *One of Our Aircraft is Missing* (1941) the billet used by the army is a comfortable, familiar world of oak furniture, low ceilings, leaded windows, huge and simple smoking fireplaces and pewter. In the burgeoning world of heritage in the half-century since, this is the period served by the continual reinvention of central and powerful narratives: the plays of Shakespeare on the one hand, and the marital affairs of Henry VIII and the romance and heroics of the reign of Elizabeth I on the other, have ensured that. But this was not the distinctive style that engendered the most creative and influential offshoot of country-house culture in the wider story of design history; in the world of interior design and furnishing it was the clever elision of the late Georgian and Regency periods that became the most powerful message of the British style past, both for new interiors and for restoration of the old. The dominant figure in this achievement was the decorator John Fowler [1.84].[15]

The essence of this most powerful twentieth-century revival lay in its rich antecedents in both the material legacy of the past and its rich bibliography. Setting its face against a revivalism that was too slavish or archaeological, post-war designers who looked to the Georgian past made certain books the touchstones of their freewheeling inventiveness; James Ackerman's *Repository of the Arts* (1809–15), for example, was much favoured because it showed a range of taste from the Regency period across interiors and furnishings, fashion and textiles, down to their trimmings and ornament. The need to turn to such sources of invention was abetted by twentieth-century disruption; the loss of so much original furniture from Britain to the American market meant that the 'doing up' of Georgian and Regency interiors required the making of new things in the old style. Wartime austerity also led to invention, for the lack of access to high-quality finishing materials – *passementerie* – in the 1940s meant that designers had to be creative with materials to hand from discarded uniforms, canvas, ruched and stressed cotton in place of pure silk.

John Fowler (1906–77) emerged from a background of genteel poverty following his father's death when he was nine. He had no higher education, but made his way working for decorating and antique businesses, so that by his late twenties he was living on the King's Road in Chelsea and from that base came, in 1938, to join with one of the prominent women decorators of that part of London, Sybil, Lady Colefax, at her firm in Bruton Street. This business was later acquired by the American Nancy Lancaster (wife of the MP Ronald Tree), who added Fowler's name to the masthead and provided the money for the redecoration of three of her great Georgian houses, Kelmarsh, Ditchley and Haseley; photographic images of their interiors changed the aspect and quality of revivalist taste. The so-called 'humble elegance' of Fowler's achievements set standards because it was amenable to all manner of houses, from the very grandest country house to the town house, and beyond to the smallest cottage. He proved that the grandest classicism could be scaled down and made fit for site.

The key to Fowler's success lay in his willingness to improvise as he worked, though this means that his working processes are not well recorded in drawings, sketches or procedural photographs. His courage lay in sometimes using judiciously a strong depth of colour, his ability to turn pattern from Georgian or Regency fabrics originally designed for one piece of furniture towards others, and his fondness for informal pairings of objects rather than following the slavish tyranny of the set of furniture. He scrutinized very carefully those houses where old paint surfaces survived; his favourite house of this kind was Uppark, in Sussex. He would purchase for the client the most expensive materials, but have them made up by craftsmen local to the house, to ensure that an individual character overrode impeccable, cold, exact quality finish.

● 1.83 [OPPOSITE] Still from *Far from the Madding Crowd*, directed by John Schlesinger, 1967

● 1.84 [ABOVE] The drawing room, Hambleden Manor, Buckinghamshire, decorated by Colefax & Fowler, 1955
● 1.85 [OPPOSITE TOP] The drawing room, Hinton Ampner, Hampshire, decorated by Ronald Fleming, 1960s
● 1.86 [OPPOSITE BOTTOM] Design for 'Pot Pourri' wallpaper, Antony Little for Osborne & Little Ltd, 1978
Gouache, pencil and dyeline print on paper | V&A: E.3640–1983

At his own country house, a Gothick folly made out of an earlier house – 'King Henry's Hunting Lodge' at Odiham, Hampshire – Fowler formed a rustic style out of Regency-inspired fabrics and furniture using a light touch, bringing the sense of garden room and conservatory to living spaces as had been first explored in the early nineteenth century. In his many private commissions he was a keen collector of fragments of wallpaper, which he would copy, often adjusting the scale. He gave these papers a sense of their own 'belonging' to tradition by naming them after their place of origin, such as the 'Berkeley sprig' from a design of the 1740s at 44 Berkeley Square. He set the fashion for a range of tone within a single colour, such as the four shades of white that he used in the restoration of the great hall at Robert Adam's interior of Syon House, Middlesex. In the last decade or so of his life Fowler was much occupied with such restorations, especially for the National Trust. Though many of these interiors were also famously influential, his sure sense of 'making a room work' (as he put it) never left him, although restorative tasks proved less congenial to him and allowed him less inventiveness than his earlier work for private clients. The most substantial of these National Trust commissions was Clandon Park, Surrey, where between 1968 and 1972 he brought to life a grand Palladian interior of 17 rooms.

An especially evocative set of interiors in the Georgian–Regency taste is found at Hinton Ampner, Hampshire [1.85].[16] In the 1930s the owner, Ralph Dutton, author of books on the English interior and aspects of style, restored the house back to its Georgian core by removing its Victorian additions. A disastrous fire in 1960 led to a new restoration, and for this his designer was Ronald Fleming (1896–1968), who, like Fowler, developed an early taste for Georgian–Regency and freelanced in the world of decoration, in his case through work for the theatre. Fleming successfully created Modernist rooms, in terms of design and bold character, which nevertheless had the comfort of an earlier age of upholstery. He had designed such an interior for the actress and film star Gertrude Lawrence at her flat in Portland Place in 1933. At Hinton Ampner much was preserved from the fire and the contents rescued, so that the architectural salvage of fireplaces from the Adelphi and the Robert Adam ceiling from Berkeley Square were worked into new solutions. Fleming's decorator's eye meant that in the drawing room, for example, the colours of the Savonnerie carpet are picked up in a Boulle cabinet and in the choice of Old Master paintings for the walls. As in Fowler's brave improvisation, historical objects are given new appearances, new roles; a wine cooler is in use as a container for plants, and *torchères* for fruit. Upstairs there is a strong reminder of the early passion of Dutton's and Fleming's generation for the mixing of Modernist pieces and unadorned surfaces in the ensemble – so there is a bathroom with the panels around the bath in black, contrasting with a warm rose colour on the other walls.

The legacy of the work of a handful of key inspirational figures like John Fowler into the last quarter of the twentieth century is found in the widespread popularity of ranges of products that offer a continually changing selection of wall coverings and fabrics based on traditional design. These changed the scale of motif, colour, edging and finish in the way Fowler did, though the range of period for source materials has extended through the nineteenth century, including especially the work of A.W.N. Pugin and William Morris, and through now-classic twentieth-century styles such as Art Deco. Alongside the well-established firm of Sanderson (founded originally in 1860 as an importer of French wallpaper), firms such as Osborne & Little now command the market in hand-finished products [1.86, 1.87]. For the mass market, the idea of cross-matching key design elements across many objects was often taken to extremes. The same coordinated small-flower pattern covering bed linen, curtains, cushions and upholstered chairs filled the showrooms of leading chain stores from the 1960s, peaking through the following two decades. Yet something of Fowler's 'humble elegance', and the sense that sophisticated traditional design is equally at home in the country as in the town house, pervades tourist outlets beyond the metropolitan areas, such as National Trust shops.

Just as country houses evoked the past, so did literature. Book illustration drew on a timeless past in new stories created for children, and adult fiction and fantasy literature encouraged adults to revisit their fear and excitement through the lens of childhood experience. Generations of adults today can still recall the events of the national story through the images in successive editions of H.E. Marshall's *Our Island Story* (first published in 1905); these drew on nineteenth-century historical paintings on the walls of the Palace of Westminster and in waxwork tableaux. Odhams Press's *British History in Strip Pictures* (1953, by James Mainwaring) – with its portraits of sovereigns from William the Conqueror to the present on the flyleaf, and key events told in continuous illustration with legends beneath – brought the world of history book and comic together for young readers.

Key illustrators were formed by their experiences of war and by their ability to imagine and articulate worlds beyond the realm of everyday experience. Robin Jacques (1920–95) carried war injuries from which he essentially never recovered. Some of his most radical work came with his post-war years at *The Strand Magazine*: in 1962 he illustrated an edition of Kipling's *Kim* without having been to India; and one of his most celebrated illustrations was for a classic text demanding variations of scale, when he did the scene of Gulliver tied down by the people of Lilliput for an edition of Swift's *Gulliver's Travels*. Jacques's appeal to the child-like rested on his attention to character type, never slipping into the grotesque, and on his ability to express a moment of stillness worth examining carefully, amid a scene of violent action.[17]

● 1.87 [ABOVE AND LEFT] Design for 'Glade' furnishing textile, Kenneth Truman for Arthur Sanderson & Sons, 1950s | Gouache on paper | Arthur Sanderson & Sons (Abaris Holdings Ltd)

At the age of 17, Susan Einzig (1922–2009) was among the young people to escape from Germany in 1939 on the *Kindertransport*. She later worked for the War Office as a technical draughtsman and was then taught by (and in turn herself taught) a number of distinguished artists and illustrators. She gained the Carnegie Medal for illustrations to *Tom's Midnight Garden* (1958); this and other books evoked a childhood past of country vicarages, vintage toys, hoops, Eton jackets and four-poster beds [1.88].[18] Pauline Baynes (1922–2008) spent part of her childhood in India, then worked for the camouflage unit and subsequently map-making for the Ministry of Defence during the war – skills that she was to use to great effect in her most successful output. She was especially proud of her achievements in rich, coloured documentary illustration, notably for Grant Uden's *Dictionary of Chivalry* (1968), and rather regretted that she would be most remembered for work conceiving the visual image of imagined worlds: book covers for Richard Adams's *Watership Down* (1972) and, most notably, for J.R.R. Tolkien's *The Lord of the Rings* (1971); and, earlier, illustrations and maps for *The Chronicles of Narnia* (1950–56) [1.90].[19]

Flights of the imagination are never possible without recognition by the beholder of the ingredients of depiction that are familiar from everyday experience. The wood-engraver Monica Poole (1921–2003) was on two counts pigeonholed as someone whose contribution flourished and then faded; her association in the critical view with the so-called 'neo-Romantics' among the painters (Sutherland, Richards, Piper, Craxton and Minton), and the technique of woodblock, which she learned at the Central School from 1945 to 1949 [1.89].[20] By 1975 one reviewer commented that 'the sensation persists that wood-engravers live in the past, still waiting for the second coming'.[21] It was a verdict that she was to outlive, with exhibitions in the 1980s, culminating in a retrospective at the Ashmolean Museum, Oxford, in 1993. Her works of the organic nature of the natural world, the roots of gnarled trees, the composition of shells and stones, are akin to Leonardo da Vinci's thirst for intimate knowledge of the workings of the natural world, in whose power she stood in awe; she was traumatized by the hurricane that hit the south of England in the autumn of 1987. Her work also takes us back to the key essential of the identity of place, through her contribution to another strand of heritage, the post-war guidebook. In 1950 she contributed illustrations to Reginald Turner's *Kent* (the county of her birth and most of her later life) in the Paul Elek *Vision of England* series.[22]

● 1.88 [OPPOSITE TOP] Design for the cover of *Tom's Midnight Garden* by Philippa Pearce, Susan Einzig, 1958 | Gouache and pen and ink on card | The Susan Einzig estate ● 1.89 [LEFT] *Root*, Monica Poole, 1977 | Wood engraving | V&A: E.1687–1991 ● 1.90 [ABOVE] Design for a poster map of J.R.R. Tolkien's Middle-earth for *The Lord of the Rings*, Pauline Baynes, 1971 Watercolour and pencil on paper | The Bodleian Libraries, University of Oxford

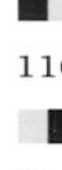

● 1.91 [OPPOSITE] *Path and Reservoir from above Lumbutts, Yorkshire*, Fay Godwin, 1977 | Gelatin silver print, from the *Calder Valley* series, published in *Remains of Elmet*, Ted Hughes, 1979 V&A: PH.15–1981 ● 1.92 [ABOVE] *Striding Arches*, Cairnhead, Scotland, Andy Goldsworthy, 2008 | Hand-dressed red sandstone ● 1.93 [BELOW] *Hidcote, Gloucestershire, England*, Edwin Smith, 1962 | Gelatin silver print | V&A: PH.844–1987

Documenting the country in the post-war period required evocative images in the photographic medium that would encapsulate both the stillness and silence of the unchanging natural world and the exact referencing of the built heritage. The first three volumes in the series of Nikolaus Pevsner's *The Buildings of England* were published in 1951, the beginning of a 23-year campaign to cover England county by county. This has continued to the present day through updated, enlarged editions and the extension of the project to the entire United Kingdom and Ireland. The work of major photographers in publications and archives contributed to the support for endeavours such as these. Edwin Smith (1912–71) photographed unsurpassable images, especially of the parish church, the garden and the English landscape [1.93].[23] Trained as an architect, Smith always considered himself an artist, yet some 60,000 photographs have left an indelible mark on our perception of buildings and landscape, the catching of light at the appropriate time of day as skilful as John Fowler's pools of light in room spaces. Smith's second wife and collaborator Olive Cook (1912–2002) contributed to *Recording Britain* and also collaborated with writers of guidebooks.

A particular success in evoking the land also came about through the collaboration of photographers and writers, most notably in the work of Fay Godwin (1931–2005) alongside novelists, playwrights and poets, sometimes with her images reflecting on their texts, as with Ted Hughes's lament for the Calder Valley in *Remains of Elmet* (1979) [1.91]; at other times inspiring the writing itself through her photography, as with John Fowles's portrait of the Scillies, *Islands* (1978). Like Edwin Smith, Godwin had a view of the world that celebrated the unchanging at particular times of the day. While human activity had no place in her work, somehow the narrative of the human past is never absent. We feel strongly the sense in many of Godwin's works that these are places where momentous things have happened, and will happen again, because we bring to them the knowledge of myth and legend in experiencing, for example, the landscape between the Mendip Hills and the Tor at Glastonbury – a terrain that has been the setting both for the Arthurian story and for the upheaval of the Reformation. Godwin's work culminated in the exhibition 'Land' of 1985 and has continued to be influential; 'Land Revisited' was staged at Bradford in 2011.[24]

The idea of the 'place-specific' that set the agenda for *Recording Britain* has remained the inspiration for artists, who have continued to be creative with the raw material of landscape experience. The artists who are usually gathered under the notion of 'Land Art' form no school as such, precisely because their interventions in the landscape are determined by the specific site – whether that of the brownfield wasteland with its evocation of a vanished populace or workforce, or the coastline with its clash of natural elements. The edges of the British Isles have proved especially fruitful as sites of intervention and installation. Andy Goldsworthy's most recent project, on Alderney in the Channel Islands, brings together the magic of natural scenery with the rusting and rotting remains of German occupation during the Second World War. Just as the concrete bunker decays, so will Goldsworthy's earth ball – some five feet in diameter – within it, to reveal its inner composition of the island's natural and human debris: found, discarded objects that will be found again and recycled as time passes.[25]

Alongside the creation of a body of images evoking the landscape, objects crafted with traditional skills have also paid respect to the natural world. A few leading figures showed a talent for multi-design, multi-skilled accomplishments, and no one more so than Edward Bawden (1903–89), whose work encompassed landscape watercolours, murals (he conceived the mural of the 'Lion and Unicorn' press pavilion at the Festival of Britain), linocuts and the making of cast-iron garden seats [1.96].[26] But it is with the work of potters that we find the clearest evocation of both landscape themes and the continuity of basic human activities, through the very materials of manufacture and the colours they use. The dominant figure in this area was Bernard Leach (1887–1979), whose example of a regional base of operation was followed by many, though his espousal of oriental forms, techniques and principles was not followed by everyone.[27] Michael Cardew (1901–83) revived lead-glazed slipware to create objects of emphatically everyday use, such as cooking and eating utensils. He worked and taught in the Gold Coast (now Ghana) and Nigeria, and was once described as the guardian of the English slipware tradition, 'a Gauguin manqué living in poverty in Gloucestershire' [1.95].[28] And the work of Michael Casson (1925–2003) – expressed through a variety of succeeding technical processes of earthenware and stoneware fired variously through wood, salt or soda – is especially redolent of landscape form and pattern, with undulating lines and the shapes of trees decorating bowls and dishes [1.97]. In the 1950s and '60s he made an imaginative excursion into ceramics in the shapes of human figures and fish, which became part of the popularity (through cheaper, mass-produced materials) of such things as ornaments and ashtrays in the homes and coffee bars of the period.[29]

Bernard Leach is an especially interesting figure, not only for his technical processes and his embrace of principles from another civilization, but for his very lifestyle, being faithful to the traditional image of the artist as someone who cannot handle money and who keeps a distance from established ways of teaching, buying and selling. Leach was highly critical of his son, David (1911–2005), when he trained for two years at the heart of industrial ceramic production at Stoke-on-Trent, though it was David Leach who brought the business side of his father's work under control and accepted more of a responsibility for teaching and the committee work of the artistic establishment [1.94].

As with all creative activity, British design since the Second World War has sometimes thrived through a business mentality and the seizure of new technology to its advantage, at other times through adopting an alternative lifestyle. Olive Cook devoted much energy for a time in her later years to resisting the development of Stansted Airport, near the home at Saffron Walden where she and Edwin Smith had settled. Fay Godwin was a champion of organic farming and the freedoms of the individual to roam in the landscape; she became President of the Ramblers' Association in 1987. Many of the figures discussed in this chapter lived extraordinarily long lives, some of them into their late seventies and eighties – a situation common in 2011, but considerably less so just 20 or 30 years ago. They often, as in the case of Monica Poole cited above, lived long enough to survive their own unfashionability. But their link with the world today is especially strong with the Green movement, whose efforts at conservation and preservation reach from the physical remains of the past to its cultural and performative practices. However, both the organic and historical pasts are alive and well in the second decade of the twenty-first century – the first through the celebration of organic materials, and the second through the revival of interest in art that juxtaposes old and disturbing objects in interiors, a re-emergence of the 'period room' in a new guise. The past, it seems, is always with us.

● 1.94 [TOP] Plate, David Leach, 1980 | Stoneware with wax-resist decoration in white over a tenmoku glaze | V&A: C.173–1980 ● 1.95 [ABOVE] Flask, Michael Cardew, 1950 | Stoneware with painted decoration on a grey glaze | V&A: Circ.426–1950 ● 1.96 [OPPOSITE TOP] Outdoor seat, Edward Bawden, 1955 | Manufactured by Bilston Cast iron, designed for his own garden | V&A: W.8–1986 ● 1.97 [OPPOSITE BOTTOM] Bowl, Michael Casson, 1975 | Stoneware with inlaid decoration in porcelain on a ground of clay-ash glaze, and a tenmoku glazed interior | V&A: Circ.9–1976

Ecology and Furniture Design

— John Makepeace

When I wanted to train as a furniture-maker in the late 1950s I paid £2 a week to work for Keith Cooper. As there was little prospect of earning a living, I did a distance-learning course in teaching during the evenings. That included topics such as the philosophy and history of design, the Bauhaus and the search for a machine aesthetic for the New Age. But I was also fortunate to spend time in Denmark when there were still a dozen workshops around Copenhagen making one-of-a-kind furniture of the most extraordinary beauty, with finely sculpted, humane forms. As a designer and craftsman I was not limited by machines, so why would I want to adopt an industrial aesthetic? Machines basically extrude timber – they produce linear forms, which seem to me to have nothing to do with our use of furniture. I want a desk to fulfil the needs of the user, rather than being a rectangle because that is the simplest shape to make by machine.

I have always felt that humans and wood are compatible. Wood is so diverse; no two pieces are the same. A tree is a historical record; it records its own biography. The landscape itself is also important to me, and I am excited by the whole cycle from tree-planting and nurturing them through to becoming woodland, and then using timber that relates to a specific place. I just love the idea of our woods providing the material for making things we need. What an amazing lesson for us – nature has designed the tree to be lean, efficient and beautiful. In a sense, a designer is devising forms and structures that fulfil their role both functionally and in terms of meaning. I love that sense of an object having a resonance, like a musical instrument. That implies a kind of inner tension where all the elements are working in harmony.

In the early 1960s I made products in batches for Heal's, Liberty's and Harrods, and subsequently for Habitat, but I found myself being compromised by that. If you are going to sell a table for £3, then you may get something that is functional, but I was much more interested in pushing myself to the limit of what is possible. That is not what the retail market wants, so I moved away from doing batch products. I did a number of university interiors, then office and domestic interiors, and subsequently moved towards one-of-a-kind furniture. I had started my career at the bench, and gradually came to realize the importance of design concepts. While it is not essential for a designer to have practical skills, it is hugely advantageous, and I probably design quite differently as a consequence. For example, I frequently design things that are more challenging to make, in the knowledge that they are possible and that the extra effort will yield some advantage.

One of the university furnishing projects I worked on was the Oxford Centre for Management Studies (now Green Templeton College). It was extraordinary to me that this college was solely for senior managers of our biggest companies. They were learning all the things that furniture-makers need to know. In British education, we separate subjects for study rather than cluster them into groups, which is what entrepreneurs need. When in 1972 Lord Eccles formed the Crafts Advisory Committee (later the Crafts Council) he gave us the brief to promote and improve the work of artist craftsmen. That led me to visit a number of design colleges, and they all had the same attitude: design is a superior skill, making is purely technical, and business is 'dirty' – we don't want to have anything to do with it! That is just so sad, because actually it is what makes things achievable. Further, it seems to me that creativity permeates the best of all human endeavour.

I saw myself as a kind of exemplar in that I had learned by accident the several disciplines required, while realizing how poorly equipped graduates were, so I was quietly confident about the need for a different kind of education. The furniture school at Parnham House, in Dorset, opened in 1977. It was a risk to buy a house of 80 rooms and set up an independent college, but the demand was immediate. It caused quite a stir in state education, and the better colleges looked to extend their business provision. Several students went on to the Royal College of Art and now design for industry. For example, it is very apparent in the work of people like Konstantin Grcic just how significant the broad understanding of design, manufacture and business gained at Parnham has been to his international influence as a designer.

In the 1980s and '90s I worked with several architects and European universities on a series of buildings for the new campus in woodland at Hooke Park, near Parnham. The inspiration behind the architecture at Hooke really comes from research into using small trees in the round. There was no scientific knowledge about what these 'thinnings' could do, because we normally use timber sawn from mature trees. But even thinnings have some excellent structural properties, such as their flexibility and their strength in tension. The award-winning buildings at Hooke are about exploiting the properties of a material that had no commercial value beforehand. They turn conventional wisdom on its head, and that is always exciting. There were no building regulations that could have permitted them previously; they would have been totally unacceptable. We had to prove the science, to understand what was actually going on, and as a result of the research the buildings have become models of sustainable construction for the future.

After running the Parnham Trust for 25 years I passed the reins to a new director, who with the Trustees decided to amalgamate the Trust with the Architectural Association, the international school of architecture, which uses the campus at Hooke Park for the practical elements of its programme.

This has enabled me to pursue my career as a designer making one-of-a-kind furniture to commission. It was encouraging to be nominated for the Prince Philip Designers Prize 2010 alongside Zaha Hadid, Bill Moggridge and Vivienne Westwood, in the same year as my Arts Council-sponsored touring exhibition.

● 1.98 [OPPOSITE] *Sylvan* chairs, John Makepeace, 1984 | English oak | Private collection

● 1.99 [OPPOSITE] 'Block Seat', Jim Partridge and Liz Walmsley, 2004 | Burr oak, hewn and charred; Partridge trained at Parnham from 1977 to 1979 | V&A: W.1–2005 ● 1.100 [BELOW] Parnham House, Dorset | John Makepeace's home, gallery, workshops and furniture school from 1976 to 2001 ● 1.101 [BOTTOM] *Storm* chair, Stephen Richards, 2000 | Various woods, including ash, oak, walnut, Douglas fir, sycamore, maple, elm and cherry, glued and jointed; Richards trained at Parnham from 1998 to 2000 | V&A: W.1–2003

4 At Home with Modernity: The New Domestic Scene

— Penny Sparke

In spite of the rhetoric of 'Swinging London', which depicted a city dominated by a young, classless society liberated by 'Pop' culture, class distinctions were still firmly in place in 1960s Britain. Nowhere was this more apparent than in the gulf that divided the domestic interior style of the sophisticated, upper-middle-class, metropolitan inhabitants of central London from that of their lower-middle-class near-neighbours in the suburbs. Only a few people succeeded in straddling the taste gap that divided them from each other. In her 2009 memoir *An Education*,[1] the journalist Lynn Barber, for example, explained that she was one of those few, but that it was only because she was young, attractive, intelligent, could speak French and knew how to wear fashionable clothes.[2]

Barber had benefited from the intensive programme of reforms that had taken place in 1940s Britain, among them the 1944 Education Act and the democratizing work of the state-funded cultural bodies, the Arts Council (the charter for which was created in 1946) and, most significantly for this essay, the Council of Industrial Design (CoID), which was formed in 1944.[3] Communicating its messages through popular magazines, television programmes and exhibitions, the CoID had set out to raise the level of the taste of the British population, in terms of what it took into its homes.[4] Barber was also a member of a generation for whom Europe provided models of sophistication and taste – a cultural tendency that had emerged in the 1950s, manifested in the popularity of Elizabeth David's recipe books and in the evocative images of Mediterranean seascapes on ceramic teasets [1.102, 1.103]. Taken to an Italian restaurant in Marylebone by a sophisticated older man called Danny, for instance, Barber remarked on the 'big pepper grinders, heavy cutlery… and crepes suzettes' that she encountered there for the first time.[5]

The sophisticated visual, material and spatial world of domesticity that Barber discovered with Danny embraced both tradition and modernity and, most importantly, a subtle, finely balanced juxtaposition of the two: its luxurious settings combined antiques (sometimes inherited, sometimes newly purchased) with modern decorative schemes and were usually the result of the interventions of interior decorators and designers. The look thus created was described in an advertisement in a 1967 copy of the upmarket Condé Nast publication *House & Garden* as 'classic yet contemporary'.[6]

That upper-class image of home was not the only one visible in post-war Britain, however. Indeed, a range of models of modern domesticity existed side by side, determined both by class and geography. The elite, urban model encountered by Barber was very different, for example, from that of the more traditional suburban home in which she had been brought up. That suburban model was different again, however, from the one that characterized the new British housing of the era. Built in the two decades following the end of the Second World War, the new homes – which were aimed, for the most part, at those members of the working-class and lower-middle-class population who wanted to, and could afford to, make a new start – represented a dramatic shift in the British public's engagement with modernity. They were built in new developments, such as Harlow and Cumbernauld New Towns, and, following the example of the United States and of Scandinavian countries, incorporated such progressive features as open-plan living and dining areas divided by open shelving, providing convenient display areas for exotic plants and ceramic and glass bibelots in the 'contemporary' style;[7] expansive picture windows that brought the outside inside; and large kitchens, which provided stages on which the new housewife hostesses could show off their new electric appliances. Interior decoration was as important to the New Town dwellers as it was to the metropolitan inhabitants of central London, but, as very few of the former could afford to employ interior decorators, they had to resort to 'doing-it-themselves'. The show houses that were created to encourage buyers, often furnished with the assistance of the CoID, helped them to see the stylistic possibilities open to them.

The widespread practice of upward emulation of those years created bridges between the different models of domestic modernity, which also shared many individual features. The existence of a clear social (and taste) hierarchy in the 1950s and early '60s made it possible for home-makers to aspire towards the style of the social group immediately above them. The continuing expansion of consumption – made possible by the increased affluence experienced by most levels of society during the two decades after the end of the war – the widespread desire for self-improvement and the growing social mobility of the era were fuelled by that sense of aspiration. While it had clear sociocultural effects, the roots of the phenomenon were political and economic. Both the British government and British manufacturing industry understood that, in order to sustain growth in home consumption (and, as a consequence, in international trade), the capacity for consumers' tastes to continually improve had to expand; and, for that to happen, the quality of the design of products in the marketplace had to be enhanced.[8] That realization underpinned the efforts of the CoID to raise the standards of what it dubbed 'good design'; the push by manufacturers to employ professionally trained designers to create ever more innovative modern items; the reorganization of British art and design education so that it could supply manufacturing industry with a generation of talented designers;[9] and the professionalization of design, especially 'interior design', so that it became increasingly hard for amateurs to achieve results by themselves, thereby ensuring their engagement with consumption.

● 1.102 [OPPOSITE TOP] Coffee pot, sweetmeat stand and plate from the 'Cannes' tableware range, Hugh Casson, 1954 | Manufactured by W.R. Midwinter Ltd, earthenware with printed and hand-coloured underglaze decoration, on the 'Fashion' shape designed by Roy Midwinter, *c.*1953 V&A: C.94&A, 98&102–1985 ● 1.103 [OPPOSITE BOTTOM] Frontispiece to *A Book of Mediterranean Food* by Elizabeth David, John Minton, 1950 Published by John Lehmann Ltd | NAL: 38041800427502

A Book of
Mediterranean
FOOD
by
Elizabeth David
Decorated by
John Minton
John Lehmann Ltd
London

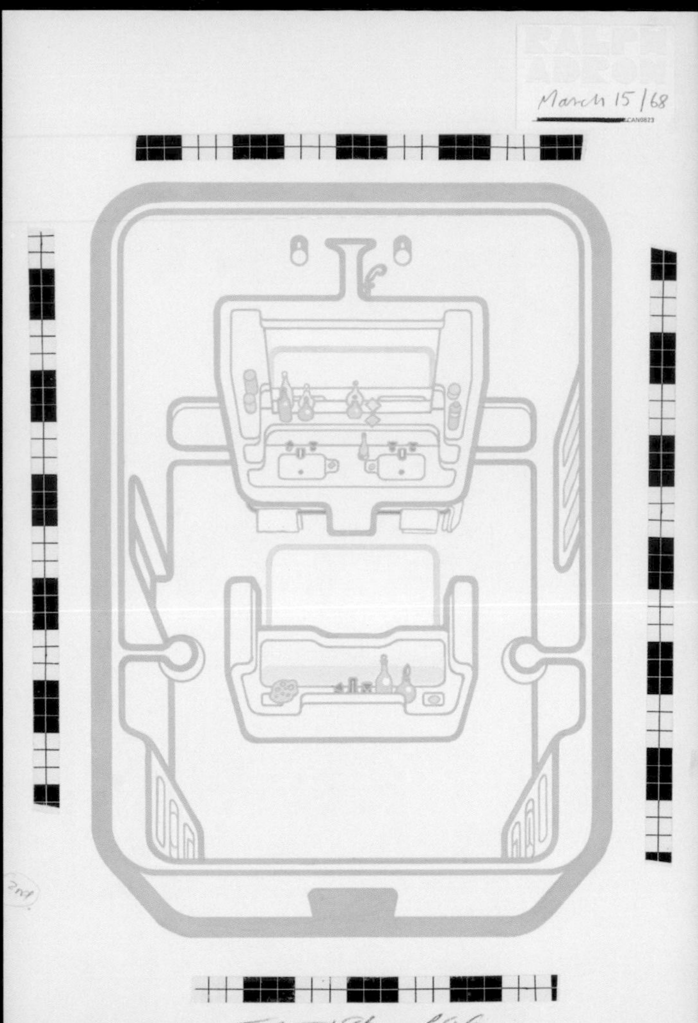
March 15/68

David Hicks '68
Living room for Mike Griggs.

Emulating developments across the Atlantic, the concept of 'interior design' emerged in Britain in the post-war years, reaching its full realization in the mid-1960s. The new, architecturally oriented profession defined itself in opposition to the perceived amateurism exhibited by the usually untrained 'interior decorator', who was linked with wealthy clients, was mostly associated with the domestic arena and worked for the most part outside the Modernist aesthetic. By the 1960s the term 'interior decoration' had also become associated with suburban amateurism and the 'do-it-yourself' movement.[10] In contrast, 'interior design' blurred the boundary between the private and the public spheres; was associated with the work of architects; and was aggressively modern in the revived spirit of interwar, international architectural and design Modernism.

In her 1964 book *Interior Design*, Diana Rowntree communicated that message very lucidly. She also made it clear that the feminine model of amateur interior decoration that had been prevalent through the first half of the century was a thing of the past and that interior design, as it had been within Modernism, had become re-masculinized. 'Space,' she contended, 'is the interior designer's main concern. His aim is to create a place with an identity of its own, rather than to assemble a fascinating collection of materials and objects.'[11] She went on to explain that interior design was strongly focused on the neo-Modernist themes of functionality, planning and scale (and thus, by implication, not on superficial decoration, pattern and colour). By linking the design of the home to the work of the professional architect, and by crossing the boundary between domestic and non-domestic spaces, Rowntree's book reinforced the disempowerment of the amateur home-maker, the victory of the metropolitan over the suburban and, where taste was concerned, of the British middle class over the working and lower-middle classes.

Notable interior designs created by architects in the period included, in the 1940s, work by the Hungarian émigré Modernist architect Ernö Goldfinger, who was involved in an exhibition organized by the Royal Institute of British Architects, entitled 'Planning Your Home' [1.3]; in the 1950s, by John Prizeman, an architect who devoted much of his time to the design of kitchens and other interior spaces, and who adopted an overtly modern approach while maintaining a respect for traditional materials [1.5]; and, in the 1960s, by Max Clendinning, who embraced the Pop ethos and aesthetic [1.104, 1.108, 1.109]. In spite of the profession's dominance by male architects, two very successful women were also active at the time. Gaby Schreiber and Jo Pattrick both contributed to the design of the *QE2* liner, launched in 1969, one of the largest interior commissions of the 1960s. Schreiber created the on-board theatre, while Pattrick was responsible for the design of the officers' wardroom and the crew's mess room. The project also provided work for many of the period's leading architect-designers, among them Dennis Lennon (who coordinated all the interiors), Stefan Buzas, Alan Irvine, Michael Inchbald and Jon Bannenberg [1.105].

In the early twenty-first century very few architect-designed and furnished homes and interiors in the metropolitan modern style from the period remain intact. A rare example is the Stanley Picker Trust's 'Stanley Picker House', located on Kingston Hill, Kingston-upon-Thames, which was completed in 1967. It was designed by the architect Kenneth Wood, and furnished by Conran Contracts, in collaboration with Wood.[12] It bears witness to the elite, idealistic design and lifestyle values that underpinned the revival of architectural and design Modernism that occurred in the 1960s on British soil.[13] It also represents the exportation of the metropolitan modern domestic style out of the city – not, in this instance, as part of suburbia's or the New Town's engagement with popular Modernism, but rather as a more modern and efficient version of the traditional, upper-class country house.[14]

The creator of many of the period's most notable elite modern domestic interiors, David Hicks – who made a huge impact in the period, and who designed the Q4 nightclub/lounge bar in the *QE2* – was closer to the interior-decorator end of the spectrum, however. Characteristically lacking a formal education, Hicks first made his mark in 1954 through the decoration of his own home, images of which found their way into the upmarket interiors magazine *House & Garden*.[15] He received commissions from wealthy private patrons – members, for the most part, of what was still referred to as 'society' at that time, and rich thirty-year-olds leading cosmopolitan lifestyles – to create a luxury, contemporary look. He decorated their homes in vivid colours – scarlet, pink and orange were favourites – which (perhaps surprisingly) blended with the family heirlooms that were already there [1.14]. Examples of his work included a 1967 dining room for the film director Richard Lester, featuring chairs with bright-red upholstery, and a living room for the banker and antiquarian bookseller Milo Cripps (Lord Parmoor) in 1968 [1.106].

● 1.104 [OPPOSITE TOP LEFT] Design for a bathroom, Max Clendinning, 1968 | Drawn by Ralph Adron, published in the *Daily Telegraph* colour supplement series 'Take a Room', 15 March 1968, poster-colour on paper | V&A: E.827–1979 ● 1.105 [OPPOSITE TOP RIGHT] The Double Room of the Cunard liner *Queen Elizabeth II*, Jon Bannenberg, 1969 ● 1.106 [OPPOSITE BOTTOM] Design for a living room for Milo Cripps, David Hicks, 1968 | Pencil, ink, felt and paint on paper | AAD: 1986/4

● 1.107 [ABOVE] Room divider, Robin Day, 1950–51 Manufactured by Hille International Ltd, steel frame, with mahogany and ebony storage units, one decorated with an engraving by Geoffrey Clarke bonded in plastic | V&A: Circ.384-T–1974 ● 1.108 [RIGHT] Cabinet and chair, Max Clendinning, 1965 | Manufactured by Liberty, painted plywood with tweed upholstery, the cabinet repainted by Clendinning for use in his dining room, *c*.1968 | V&A: W.19:1 & 2–2011, and private collection ● 1.109 [OPPOSITE] The dining room, 3 Alwyne Road, London, furniture by Max Clendinning and mural painting by Ralph Adron, 1969

DESIGN FOR INDUSTRY

Architect-designed, neo-Modernist interiors of the period frequently contained modern furnishings and artefacts – furniture items, lighting fixtures, furnishing fabrics, wall-papers, and ceramic, glass and metal objects among them. They were often imported from the Scandinavian countries, the United States or Italy, but products of British design and manufacturing were also included. So innovative were the last, in fact, that it is possible to talk about a British modern domestic design movement that began to emerge in the late 1940s and reached its peak in the mid to late 1960s. Stimulated by economic and political exigency, it was the result of a final burst of energy on the part of British manufacturing industry in those sectors that had been in gradual decline over the twentieth century and which, by the 1970s, were on a rapid downward spiral.

A significant expansion in British furniture manufacturing, design, retailing and consumption occurred during the period in question, for example. It began in the 1940s and '50s when a new generation of furniture designers, including Ernest Race and Robin Day, extended the Modernist programme by incorporating new materials – extruded aluminium, bent and moulded plywood, and steel rod among them, in their cases – into furniture designs [1.25, 1.107]. A striking design of 1950–51 – the 'Jason' chair – was, for example, created by the designer Carl Jacobs working with Kandya Ltd [1.110]. Its moulded plywood seat, containing two holes to create both a sensation and a reality of lightness, was reminiscent of early experiments by the American Charles Eames. Day's most lasting design was created more than a decade later, however. The moulded seat of his brightly coloured, little steel-rod-legged stacking chair, manufactured by Hille, was made of low-cost polyethylene [3.14]. The chair was cheap, cheerful and ubiquitous, and it heralded the Pop revolution that was just around the corner. Indeed, many of the furniture designers who embraced that ethos were to make extensive use of plastics, seeing them as materials with a capacity to redefine the furniture object and its meaning for all time.[16]

● 1.110 [OPPOSITE TOP LEFT] 'Jason' chair, Carl Jacobs, 1951 Manufactured by Kandya Ltd, beech frame, beech-faced plywood seat and back | V&A: Circ.305–1970 ● 1.111 [OPPOSITE TOP RIGHT] 'T5' stacking chairs, Rodney Kinsman, 1969 | Manufactured by OMK Designs Ltd, chromium-plated steel-tube frames with upholstered plywood seats | V&A: Circ.359-361–1970 ● 1.112 [OPPOSITE BOTTOM LEFT] 'Torsion' prototype chair, Brian Long, 1970 | Vacuum-formed ABS plastic shell, upholstered | V&A: W.15–2011 ● 1.113 [OPPOSITE BOTTOM RIGHT] 'Chair Thing', self-assembly children's chair, Peter Murdoch, 1964–5 | Manufactured by Persepective Designs, polyurethane-coated laminated paper | V&A: Circ.17–1970

The 1950s and early 1960s witnessed the appearance of a vast number of elegant, neo-Modernist furniture pieces that were created by British designers – among them Terence Conran, Alan Turville, Robert Heritage, and John and Sylvia Reid – and manufactured by firms such as Hille Ltd, Ercol, G-Plan, HK Furniture, Race Ltd and Archie Shine. However, by the mid-1960s it was becoming clear that, despite furniture's traditional function as a symbol of domestic stability, it too was succumbing to the 'Challenge of Pop'.[17] A new generation of designers – including Max Clendinning, Jon Bannenberg, Peter Murdoch, William Plunkett, Bernard Holdaway, Nicholas Frewing and the team of Jean Schofield and John Wright – embraced the novel concepts of 'knock-down', 'inflate' and 'throwaway' and spawned such lasting classics as Clendinning's 'Maxima' range for Hille – a set of self-assembly, flatpack chairs with frames made from lacquered plywood – and a side chair for Liberty's, which featured a painted plywood frame; Murdoch's so-called 'paper' chair for Perspective Designs, which in reality was made of robust cardboard strengthened with resin (a spotted version appeared in 1964, followed by one with a more complex pattern four years later) [1.113]; and Holdaway's 'Tom-o-Tom' range for Hull Traders.[18]

This new vision for furniture was linked to the general shift in design thinking that had been anticipated by the graphic designer Michael Wolff, when he had written in the *Journal of the Society of Industrial Artists* in 1965, 'It will be a great day when furniture and cutlery design, to name but two, swing like the Supremes.'[19] By the end of the decade the new, increasingly youth-focused concept of lifestyle, and the prioritization (in the context of mass consumption) of images over objects, had led in two distinct new directions: one to a new flexible form of seating that had abandoned the long-standing dependency upon chairs in favour of seating systems, and the other to a new emphasis on surface pattern that encouraged (especially young) people to take control away from designers once again, by adding their own images of flags and targets and brightly coloured stripes to the surfaces of their furniture items, both old and new.[20]

By the early 1970s the number of British furniture innovations had declined dramatically, however (exceptions included Brian Long's extravagantly shaped plastic 'Torsion' chair, created for a competition held by Dunlopillo in 1970) [1.112]. A few furniture retailers – Aram's among them – focused on importing European classics and progressive Italian pieces, while a handful of designers reinterpreted furniture items from the heroic era of European Modernism.[21] OMK's 'T5' tubular-steel-framed stacking chair of 1969 was just one example of many [1.111]. In spite of the fact that the radical British furniture movement had grown up on the back of an upsurge of popular taste, and apart from the effect it had on students' flats – which experienced a proliferation of beanbags and blow-up chairs – there was little evidence to show that it had made a significant impact on the average British home.

Furniture was not the only industrially manufactured material component of the home to receive the modern treatment in the post-war years, however. In the immediate post-war era the British textile industry had been challenged, and several manufacturers of furnishing fabrics – Heal's Fabrics, Edinburgh Weavers and David Whitehead Fabrics among them – had realized that to keep production going and to stimulate new markets they were going to have to work with designers and develop novel, innovative products. A new generation of textile designers – which, during the two decades after the war, included Lucienne Day, Jacqueline Groag, Marian Mahler, Barbara Brown, Eddie Squires, Terence Conran, Shirley Craven and Althea McNish (many of them graduating from the Royal College of Art/RCA) – manifested to service the needs of the re-emerging industry.

The textile manufacturers and designers worked closely with the CoID through the 1940s and '50s, and an influential modern textile-design movement emerged that took much of its visual stimulus from fine art, especially Surrealism. As such, while the work of the designers named above did not impact directly on the mass market, the idea of using modern, patterned textiles (and wallpaper) to offset splayed-legged furniture pieces and organically shaped coffee-tables filtered through into the public consciousness and into the homes of both the New Towns and suburbia. The work of the 1951 Festival Pattern Group, which demonstrated the influence of molecular structures on the abstract motifs used for textiles and wallpapers, played a mediating role in that process of taste dissemination and emulation [1.27, 1.30, 1.58].[22] The fact that Lucienne Day's famous, Surrealist-inspired 'Calyx' textile design, manufactured by Heal's Fabrics, was selected by the CoID to be displayed in the 'Homes and Gardens' Pavilion at the Festival undoubtedly helped in that process [1.114].

Jacqueline Groag and Marian Mahler both produced designs for David Whitehead Fabrics. Like Day's, their fabrics were characterized by abstract patterns and strong colours. The former's 'Café' textile, designed for Gerald Holtom in 1951 for use in the popular Kardomah cafés, helped to establish Groag's credentials as a leading figure in the field [1.115]. By the 1960s Barbara Brown's work for Heal's Fabrics – among them her 'Galleria' fabric of 1969 [1.116], which featured an Op Art pattern in vibrant colours – introduced an interest in large-scale abstraction, a new visual language that also featured in many of Shirley Craven's designs for Hull Traders. The latter's 'Simple Solar' furnishing fabric of 1967 boasted a complex graphic pattern that was more typical of designs from the end of that decade, however [1.118]. The psychedelic theme, visible in popular graphics and posters at the time, was developed by Eddie Squires in his fabrics for Warner & Sons, among them 'Colourtron' of 1967, which combined pink and scarlet with a bright green to dramatic effect [1.117]. Although textiles were produced in smaller quantities in the 1960s than had previously been the case, Britain still maintained an international reputation for its designs. Within another half-decade, however, the oil crisis had all but destroyed the industry and, as the economic and political situations became increasingly unstable, and the need for escape and comfort increased, a return to traditional patterns became the norm for domestic textiles.

A similar story can be told about the domestic ceramic, glass and metal items that were designed in Britain in the 1950s and '60s and featured in the most progressive homes, as well as influencing taste across a wider social spectrum. The 1940s had seen a short-lived revival of energy in these industries after the inactivity of the war years and, like producers in the other sections, manufacturers realized that, to maintain their positions, they were going to have to employ designers to create high-quality pieces that would earn them an international reputation for tasteful production. Some of the most widely acknowledged work emerged from this area as a direct result of the fact that, from the mid-1950s onwards, a number of companies employed a small group of distinguished RCA graduates: David Queensberry, Professor of Ceramics and Glass at the RCA from 1959, and recipient of the Design Council's Duke of Edinburgh Award for Elegant Design in 1964, who worked for W.R. Midwinter Ltd and Webb Corbett Glass, among others; David Mellor, who collaborated with the Ministry of Public Building in 1959 on his 'Pride' cutlery range [1.119]; Robert Welch, who worked with J. & J. Wiggin Ltd, for whom he created a highly sculptural three-legged candelabrum named 'Campden' in 1957, and with Old Hall Tableware Ltd, for whom he designed the Scandinavian-looking 'Alveston' teaset in 1962 and a simple and elegant cutlery set three years later [1.123]; and the silversmith Gerald Benney, who created many elegant and highly regarded metal designs, including water containers for the tables of the RCA's senior common room [1.75].

Several seminal ceramic designs also emerged in these years, notable among them the extremely popular and long-lasting 'Homemaker' tea service designed by Enid Seeney (who created the pattern) and Tom Arnold (who designed the form) for Ridgway Potteries in 1957 [1.120]. Jessie Tait's pieces for Midwinter, among them 'Cuban Fantasy' from 1957, also received much praise and were hugely influential [1.121]. Glass design also responded to the spirit of the age: Geoffrey Baxter's 'Unica' and 'Brick' vases from 1965 and 1966 respectively, for instance, abandoned the delicacy of 1950s designs in favour of the solid forms and bright colours of 1960s British Pop design, a shift that pushed glass to its technical limits [1.122].

Ceramic, glass and metal artefacts were also created by hand in those years as part of the burgeoning British craft movement, which was to reach its peak during the 1970s. The primitive aesthetic of the ceramic objects created by potters Ruth Duckworth, Lucie Rie and Hans Coper, for example, provided a perfect counterpoint to the slick look of the industrially manufactured pieces [1.124].

● 1.114 [OPPOSITE LEFT] 'Calyx', furnishing textile, Lucienne Day, 1951 | Manufactured by Heal & Son Ltd, screen-printed linen V&A: T.161–1995 ● 1.115 [OPPOSITE RIGHT] 'Café', furnishing textile, Jacqueline Groag, 1951 | Manufactured by Gerald Holtom for use in Kardomah cafés, screen-printed linen | V&A: Circ.222–1951

Made in United Kingdom
Made in United Kingdom
Made in United Kingdom

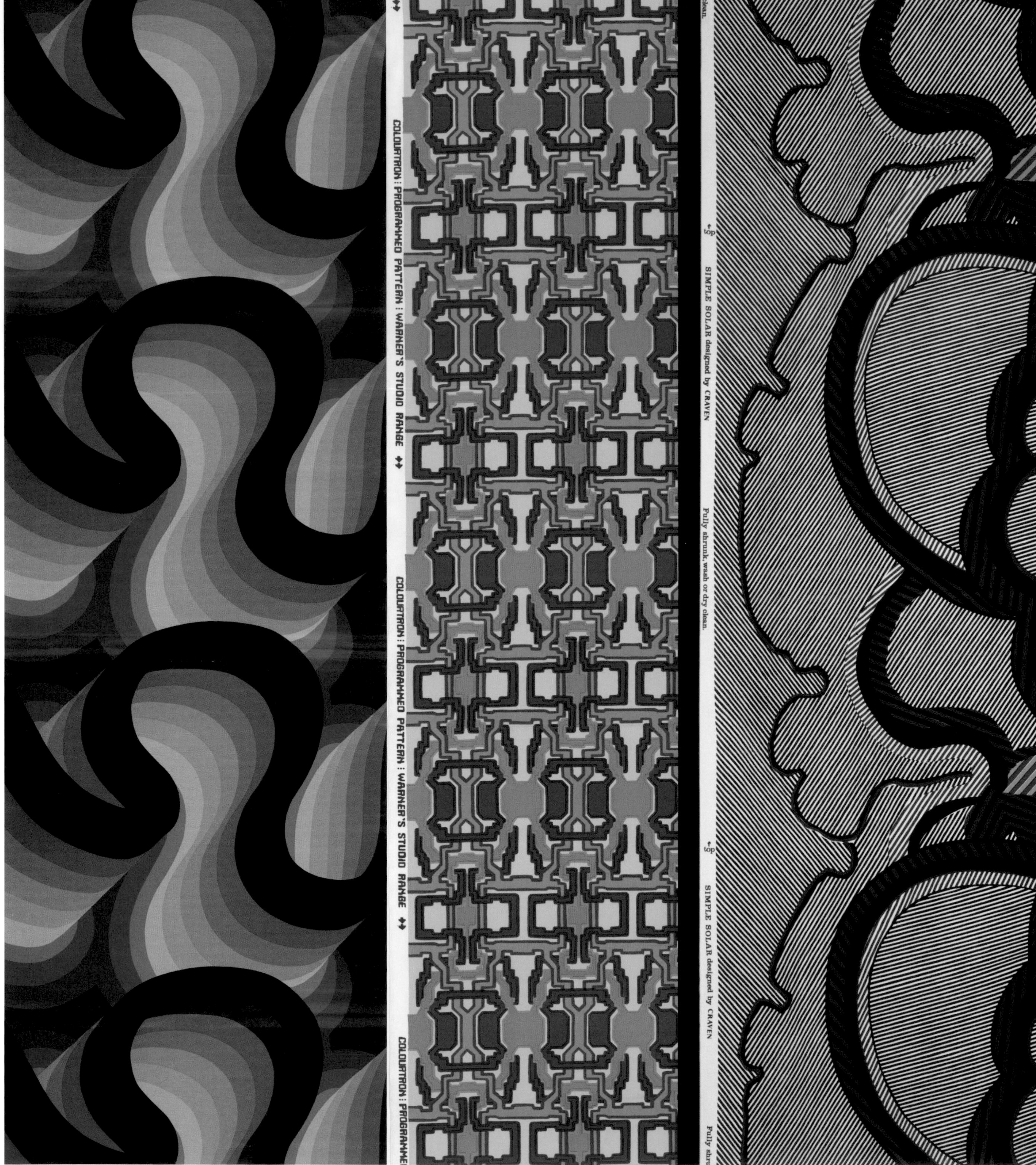
COLOURTRON : PROGRAMMED PATTERN : WARNER'S STUDIO RANGE
top
SIMPLE SOLAR designed by CRAVEN
Fully shrunk, wash or dry clean.

● 1.116 [OPPOSITE LEFT] 'Galleria', furnishing textile, Barbara Brown, 1969 | Manufactured by Heal & Son Ltd, printed cotton V&A: Circ.35–1969 ● 1.117 [CENTRE] 'Colourtron', furnishing fabric, Eddie Squires, 1968 | Manufactured by Warner & Sons, printed cotton | V&A: Circ.801–1968 ● 1.118 [LEFT] 'Simple Solar', furnishing fabric, Shirley Craven, 1967 | Manufactured by Hull Traders Ltd, printed cotton | V&A: Circ.791–1968

LIFESTYLE

In line with the expansion of consumption in the post-war years, the idea of 'lifestyle' – that is, of the belief that designed artefacts and spaces both facilitate and represent the activities (from domestic family rituals to sports, travelling and eating outside the home) that constitute people's modern lives – was democratized during the period in question. Manufacturers needed to employ designers who could differentiate artefacts from each other and input a level of taste into the products in the marketplace, to which consumers could aspire, but which they could not create for themselves. In turn, as they were increasingly confronted by desirable goods in the shops they frequented, and by seductive images in the newspapers and magazines they read on a daily basis, consumers began to see these artefacts as lifestyle accessories.

By the early 1960s it was clear that a mass market for lifestyle retailing and journalism had emerged, and the furniture and textile designer Terence Conran, who opened his first Habitat store on London's Fulham Road in 1964, was quick to exploit the fact. Although a number of other progressive retailers – Dunn's of Bromley, Heal's, Liberty's and others – had already branded themselves as 'design-led' through the 1950s, they had retained an exclusive appeal and had not played a direct part in the expansion of consumption. Habitat targeted a social group just below those who had shopped in those elite stores, and a younger, more fashion-conscious audience. As well as making available a new range of objects imported from overseas (Vico Magistretti's bright-red 'Carimate' chair was a special favourite), the key message that Conran communicated to his customers was that, as the interior decorators already knew well, it was possible to mix old furniture pieces with new items.[23] Rather than empowering his customers to do that for themselves, however, he offered them a ready-made set of choices. In effect they were being asked to trust his taste decisions and to purchase whole interior settings from his shop. That might have meant combining a Magistretti item with a reproduction Thonet chair or Chesterfield sofa, both of which could be also purchased at Habitat. Only a designer could be trusted to make such courageous decisions and Habitat thrived on that basis, subsequently opening a number of other stores around Britain.

Paralleling the unprecedented success of Habitat in the area of lifestyle retailing were the new mass-market publications, linked to popular newspapers, which adopted the lifestyle approach to winning over their audiences. Women's magazines had addressed the subject of design throughout the 1950s (*Woman* – whose Home Editor, Edith Blair, had been on the board of the CoID – *Woman's Own* and *Woman's Realm* were among the best-known), and a number of mass-market, home-related magazines (*Ideal Home* and *Homes & Gardens* among them) had addressed the same theme, but they had all embraced the 'good design' programme and had adopted the same paternalistic attitude to their readers as the CoID had towards its audience. The newspaper supplements that appeared in the early 1960s – the *Sunday Times* colour supplement first hit the news-stands in February 1962, the *Daily Telegraph* colour supplement followed in 1964 and the *Observer Magazine* a year later – adopted a radically different tone of voice. They set out to celebrate, and make available to as many people as possible, the whole range of lifestyle activities – from designer-inspired home-making to exotic travelling and eating out in smart restaurants. Their aim was to bring what had hitherto been seen as a design/style-led elite taste to a mass audience and, through that strategy, expand their readership.

Four months after its arrival on the scene the *Sunday Times* colour supplement featured an article in its 'Design for Living' section that contained the prophetic words: 'There are times when one longs to buy something plumb ugly and utterly unfunctional.'[24] What was being said (albeit obliquely) was that, although designed goods claimed to be universal and timeless, they were in fact simply messengers of a particular, fashionable lifestyle, which, like all other lifestyles, would eventually be replaced by new ones when its appeal had worn out. The article was responding to the growing sense that popular values were becoming more important than (what had believed to have been) the lasting ones of interwar architectural and design Modernism. As the zeitgeist changed, so – with the new emphasis on the values of mass consumption – a greater dependency on fast-moving images than on material objects became apparent. Not only did the mass-market publications play a role in consolidating that dramatic shift, but they also helped to create it.

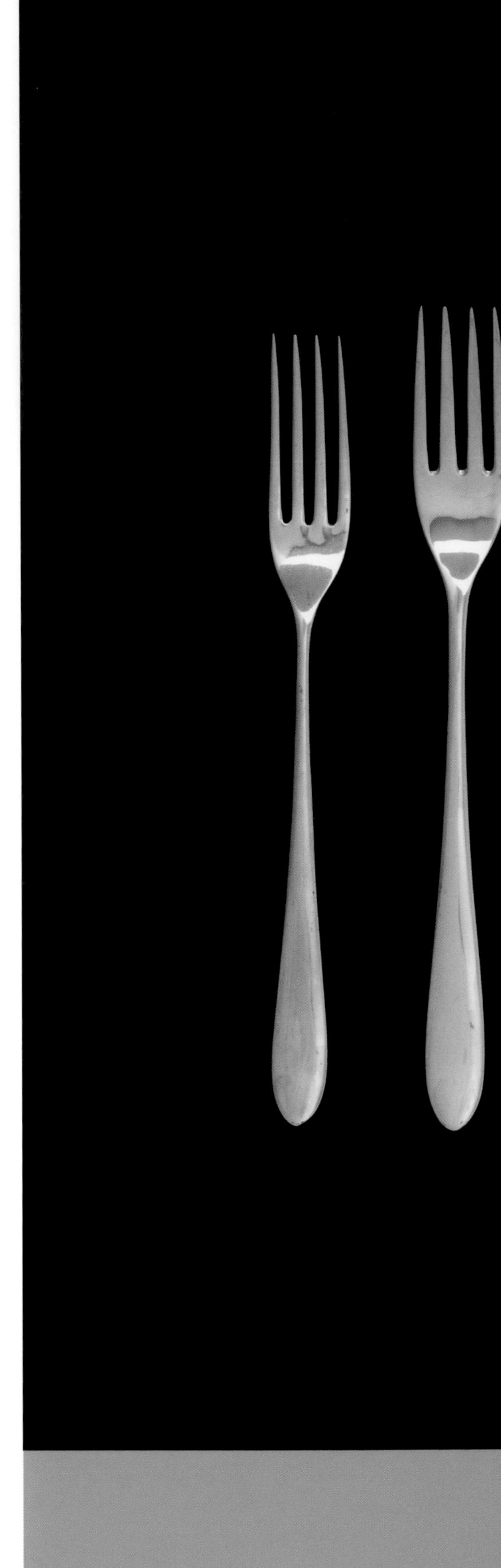

● 1.119 [ABOVE] ‘Pride’, cutlery, David Mellor, 1953 | Manufactured by Walker & Hall Ltd, 1959, electroplated nickel silver, with stainless-steel knife blades and composition handles | V&A: Circ.292-H–1959

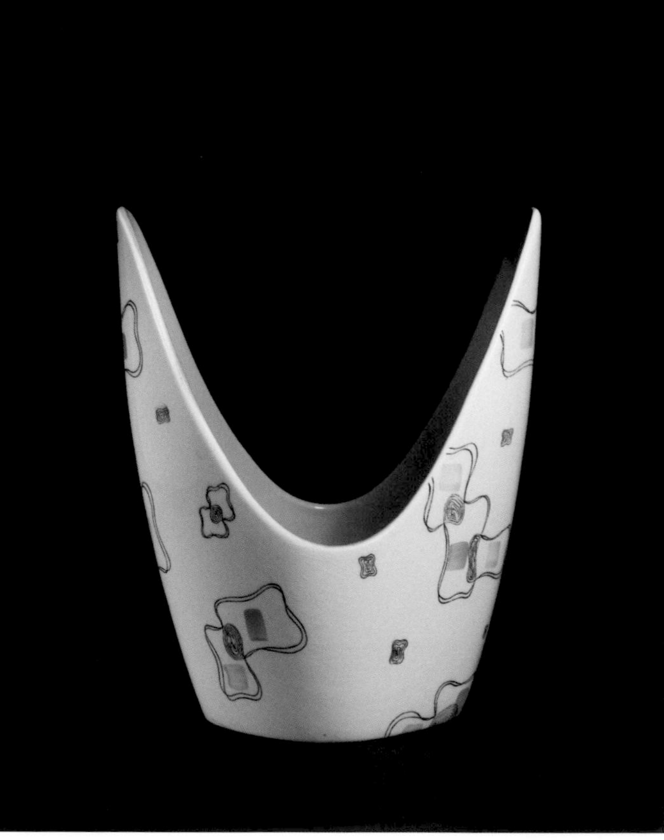

● 1.120 [ABOVE] 'Homemaker', ceramic service, Enid Seeney, 1956–7 Manufactured by Ridgway Potteries Ltd, 1957–68, earthenware, glazed and printed, on 'Metro' shape designed by Tom Arnold | V&A: C.67–1982, C.18:1 & 2–1996, C.50–1991, C.205–1991, C.237–1991

● 1.121 [LEFT] 'Cuban Fantasy', vase, Jessie Tait, 1957 | Manufactured by W.R. Midwinter Ltd, earthenware, glazed and printed | V&A: C.65–1988

● 1.122 [OPPOSITE] 'Bricks' and 'Unica' vases, Geoffrey Baxter, 1965–6 Manufactured by James Powell & Son (Whitefriars Glassworks), 1965–74, mould-blown glass | V&A: C.240 & 241–1991, C.175–1996

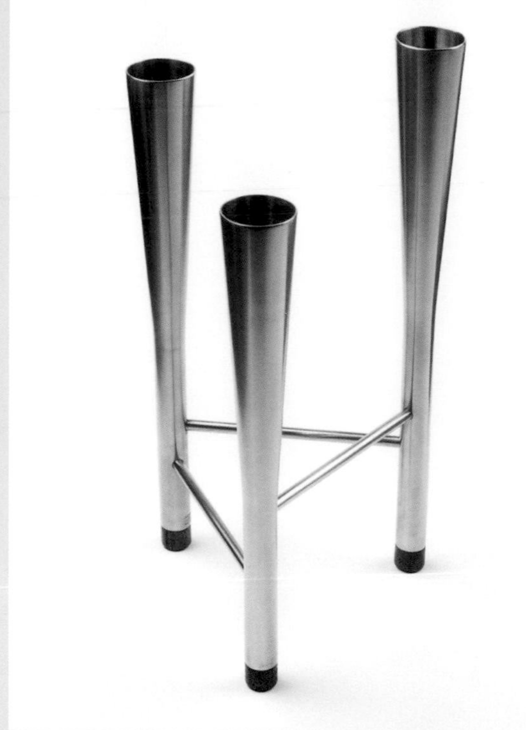

By the middle of the 1960s the new disseminators of 'lifestyle' had, arguably, over-popularized their message and, in so doing, had begun to undermine its strength. The gap that existed between the views of the CoID and the public's perception of the meaning of 'good modern design' had also become increasingly apparent. The architectural historian, design critic and Independent Group member Reyner Banham, who had defended popular values from the 1950s onwards, dubbed the Council 'Her Majesty's Fashion House', thereby showing his disdain for the elitist taste that it both represented and embraced.[25] The full impact of the crisis came in 1967 when the Council's director, Paul Reilly, wrote in his article 'The Challenge of Pop', 'We may have to learn to enjoy a completely new palette as gaudy colours have long been linked with expendable ephemera.'[26] By the late 1960s what had come, to many people, to look like the controlling, paternalistic approach of the CoID had become less and less relevant as it continued to address a public that had been democratized through consumption. Also, it came into conflict with the expanding power of the media, which had taken upon itself the task of disseminating the concept of 'lifestyle' – understood as a form of public emancipation and empowerment. With that emancipation came a surge of popular values that served to challenge the hitherto fixed social hierarchy upon which the Council had depended.

By the early 1970s, as a result of the downturn in the economy and the final demise of Britain's manufacturing industry, the British modern domestic design movement – which, through the 1950s and '60s, had created a new, elite image of domestic modernity that, in turn, had influenced mass taste – had all but vanished from view. And while the products of those industries had come together in the context of consumption to create a unified modern domestic style, so medium- and production-focused (and so strongly linked to the past and to specific geographies) were the manufacturers that they had made very few efforts to collaborate. Instead it had been left to retailers to undertake that task. Given their ability to import high-quality foreign goods, they had thrived where the manufacturers had failed.

For a little over a decade, in the aftermath of the international influence of Scandinavian design, and immediately before that created by the Italian modern design marketing machine, Britain was leading the way in the creation of an innovative modern domestic design movement. Its influence was short-lived, however, due to several factors: first, the impact of the Pop revolution and the cultural influence of youth were manifested predominantly in the mainly 'public sphere' fields of music and fashion and not in the home; and, second, the shift within progressive British architectural and interior design circles at the time, from the home to the public sphere, meant that the earlier focus on domesticity disappeared. Other reasons are linked, ironically, to the success of the democratization of lifestyle and the growing power of popular culture; to the rejection, in the 1970s, by a large sector of society of elite culture in all its forms; and to the re-emergence of the idea that you could 'do-it-yourself'.

In the early 1970s, for all these reasons and more, British society began to feel less at home than it had during the more optimistic climate of the 1940s, '50s and early '60s, and a sudden retreat to the safety of the past took place. The stripped-pine, Laura Ashley-led Victorian revival engulfed the popular British home, while, for the social elite, the country house replaced the sophisticated metropolitan home as a domestic idyll. In essence the modern style, created by interior designers and a generation of highly skilled designers for industry, had lost its potency and was replaced by an escape to the past and to the country. In the process, the engagement of the British public with modernity, and the subtle balance between tradition and modernity that had manifested itself in a number of different ways in post-war British homes, was irreparably disturbed.

● 1.123 [OPPOSITE] 'Campden', candelabrum, Robert Welch, *c.*1957 | Manufactured by J. & J. Wiggin Ltd, stainless steel with wooden feet | V&A: Circ.345–1959 ● 1.124 [ABOVE] Bottle, Lucie Rie, 1959 | Stoneware, with a flecked white glaze | Vase, Hans Coper, 1958 | Stoneware, with black and white matt glazes | Bowl, Ruth Duckworth, 1959 Stoneware, painted in black pigment on a green glaze | V&A: Circ.126–1959, Circ.154–1958 and Circ.241–1959

The Legacy of the Festival of Britain

— Terence Conran

● 1.125 [ABOVE] 'Chequers', furnishing textile, Terence Conran, 1951
Manufactured by David Whitehead Ltd, screen-printed cotton | V&A: Circ.283–1951
● 1.126 [OPPOSITE] Design for a dining room furnished with flatpack furniture, Conran Associates, 1976 | Drawn by Chris Williams, felt-tip pen on paper | V&A: E.1544–1976

The Festival of Britain was really the beginning of the British public's understanding that design added to their enjoyment and quality of life. It was amazing to see all those people on the South Bank in their mackintoshes, with their gas-mask cases filled with sandwiches. It was very emotional. It was the first time they had seen colour and all those exciting architectural shapes, like the Dome of Discovery and the Skylon [1.21, 1.22]. It really was an extraordinary period in London. Everything had been grey, with rubble everywhere. The only jolly thing was the purple loosestrife that grew on the bomb sites. But the Festival demonstrated that there was an alternative to the rather sad repro furniture that was available on the British high street.

I remember there was a great atmosphere of cooperation among those involved in planning the Festival. There must have been only around 50 of us, and we were still called industrial artists. I made the sign for F.H.K. Henrion's interior in 'The Country' Pavilion. It was an absolute disaster, because I made it out of cast plastic resin and I filled it with beetles, butterflies and all sorts of insects – unfortunately, when the sun shone on it, a terrible smell came out of those letters! I had a workshop in Bethnal Green at the time, which I shared with Eduardo Paolozzi. Eduardo had been my tutor at the Central School of Art and Design. I knew how to weld and cut metal with oxyacetylene, and this excited him because he wanted to make metal pieces. You could say I taught Paolozzi how to weld!

After the Festival the next big shift in British culture was the publication of Elizabeth David's cookery books [1.103]. They had an immense impact on food in this country, inspiring many people to go into the restaurant business. Once Habitat opened in 1964, I wanted to stock the kitchen department with Elizabeth David-inspired equipment. In fact I was in Paris one day and somebody said, 'Oh, you should go and see Dehillerin – it's where all the French chefs buy their equipment.' It was a wonderful warehouse shop in Les Halles, and we bought a truckload of the stuff. We were particularly excited one day when Elizabeth David came into Habitat and went round collecting various utensils. One of the knives was rather damaged, and the sales assistant said to her, 'I'll find a replacement for that one, it's not in good condition'; 'No, no,' she said, 'I like this', and the reason she did was because it had the French maker's name on it. And so when she did her own shop, she was looking for the same French items, and I thought it wonderful that it had gone full circle.

After Bethnal Green I had a workshop in Donne Place, Chelsea. Then we found an old forage merchant's in the North End Road. There were still horses and carts coming to pick up foodstuffs from this place, run by a charming couple called the Lavender brothers, and we moved in and established metalworking, woodworking and exhibition building out of the premises. As we expanded we moved our woodworking unit to a place called Cock Yard in Camberwell, but at about this time – the time of the New Towns – the London County Council started to try and move industry out of London. So we took 80 families from London to Thetford in Norfolk and built a new factory there. Suddenly we had to become more efficient. It was such an exciting moment. Most of the furniture we made was contract furniture, specified by architects for the new university buildings of the 1960s. Paul Reilly, who was the head of the Design Council at the time, opened the Thetford factory. We had an idea that instead of cutting a ribbon, Paul should use an electric circular saw to cut a plank, and it got stuck as he was cutting it and I thought, 'Oh, my God, it's going to cut his leg off!' Yes, it was an interesting time! I think it was very much a reflection of what had started at the Festival of Britain, but it took all those years to flow through.

It's also important to remember that the British taxpayer has invested in art and design schools ever since the war, and that's why we have such a reputation in this country for creative excellence in music, as well as design and art. Most of the good pop music came out of the art schools. It was often a case of innovating because you had to – to survive! I remember I designed a place called the Soup Kitchen, in Chandos Place, just off Trafalgar Square. I had sat with my partner, who was a doctor just back from Korea, in the kitchen in the house in which we both had a room, and we discussed what on earth we could do to make some money, and the Soup Kitchen came out of that. You know, people were really resourceful then; I mean, I've often been asked by students from the Royal College of Art today, 'What were the parties like when you were a student?' I say, 'There weren't any. We didn't have any money. It wasn't like it is now, constant partying!'

Still, the real problem now is British manufacturing. There's hardly a British furniture manufacturer left and, unless you're attached to a factory and understand how it all works – what machinery it's got, what skills and materials are available – you can't really design properly. Of course you can go offshore and study the factory there, but it's a very great problem. However, I think there is a perceptible change at the moment. I know of a British retailer who wanted to make ceramic shades recently, so he went to a factory in Stoke-on-Trent and got the shades made, then the factory phoned him up and said, 'We're going out of business', so he bought the factory. And, you know, he now makes all of these very good ceramic shades in Britain. It is still possible. The spirit of 1951 does still survive.

habitat mail order catalogue

● 1.127 [OPPOSITE TOP] Habitat catalogue, 1965 | Printed paper | AAD: 1995/12/5/3 ● 1.128 [OPPOSITE BOTTOM] Designs for the 'Viking' range of seating, Conran Associates, for Dual Furniture Ltd, 2 May 1977 | Drawn by G.P. Wood, felt-tip pen and watercolour on paper | V&A: E.1127–1979 ● 1.129 [ABOVE] 'Input', range of containers, Conran Associates, 1974 | Manufactured by Crayonne Ltd, ABS plastic | V&A: Circ.105, 111 & 114–1977

Section Two

Subversion 1955–97

Subversion 1955–97

— Christopher Breward & Ghislaine Wood

● 2.1 [BELOW] Poster for the exhibition 'This is Tomorrow' at the Whitechapel Art Gallery, Nigel Henderson, 1956 | Screen print, with photograph showing Henderson, Eduardo Paolozzi and Alison and Peter Smithson | V&A: E.179–1994 ● 2.2 [OPPOSITE] 'Pogo' chair, Peter and Alison Smithson, 1956 | Designed for the 'House of the Future' display at the Ideal Home Exhibition, manufactured by V.E. Edwards and Thermo Plastics Ltd, tubular steel with Perspex panels | V&A: Circ.81–1975

If the 1940s and '50s saw a generation of designers, architects and planners who had experienced military service in the war, or the trauma of emigration, building a new Britain informed both by a radical welfarism and a paternalistic instinct to conserve traditional values, then a rising generation born in the war years inevitably came to challenge what they viewed as the complacent and cosy consensus of their elders during the late 1950s and '60s.

Across Western Europe and America the so-called baby-boomers tested previous assumptions about racial and sexual identity, social class and gender roles in a manner that changed the cultural landscape for ever. In Britain, as elsewhere, much of this was expressed materially, especially through the media of fashion, magazines, music, interiors and film. The focus of design shifted from the infrastructure of cities and transport networks to the more mobile surfaces of the body and the exciting spaces of pleasure: homes, shops, restaurants and clubs. To adapt some common phrases of the time, the personal became political – and visible; and the medium was the message. Yet while these changes occurred on an international scale – in New York, San Francisco, Paris, Rome and Milan – in Britain's metropolitan centres the visual, aural and tactile intensity of the attack took on a special character and informed assumptions about the subversive nature of British design, from the phenomenon of 'Swinging London' in the mid-1960s, through the nihilism of punk in the 1970s to the public-relations 'speak' of 'Cool Britannia' in the 1990s.

A great deal of the impetus for this challenge emerged out of changes occurring in the British art-school system. The Royal College of Art, Central and St Martins, Camberwell, Chelsea, the Bartlett and Hornsey in London, and Newcastle, Manchester, Glasgow, Edinburgh, Brighton and Norwich, enjoyed long traditions as bastions of a hierarchical academic training in painting, architecture and to a lesser extent design, which by the late 1950s were coming under question from restive students and the industries that relied on the art colleges to provide trained workers. In 1968, at Hornsey and other art colleges, continuing dissatisfaction erupted in student action, to be followed by rapid reform. Essentially nineteenth-century training practices based on the primacy of drawing were increasingly coming to be seen as anachronistic, and in fields including graphics, textiles, ceramics and fashion the demand was increasing for graduates who understood the mood of the new British consumer and the rapid technical advances that were revolutionizing materials and production techniques.

Furthermore a radical, questioning attitude informed by new philosophical and aesthetic ideas and embracing the world of popular culture (particularly Situationism and early Postmodernism) – typified in the work of the Independent Group and British Pop Art, and finding institutional expression through organizations including the Institute of Contemporary Arts and The Architectural Association – inevitably blurred the boundaries between art and design disciplines, and encouraged students and designers to take greater risks in their work [2.1–2.4]. By the mid-1970s British art schools were increasingly coming to be seen, internationally, as seedbeds for a searing sense of creativity, not just in their core disciplines, but also in the worlds of music, performance and literature. As commentators including Michael Bracewell, John A. Walker and Simon Reynolds have remarked, a whole substratum of British music – from the Beatles, through the Rolling Stones, T-Rex, Roxy Music and David Bowie to Ian Dury, the Sex Pistols, ABC and Pulp – has been nurtured in an art-school context, or has at least benefited from a visual image informed by art-school networks [2.5, 2.8].

Beyond art education, the subversive spirit also made an impact in everyday life. Indeed, in some respects one of the strengths of late twentieth-century British design was its roots in the culture of the street. This was highly evident both in the innovative fashion boutique scene that grew up around Carnaby Street and the King's Road in London from the mid-1950s, spreading to other cities including Nottingham, Liverpool and Manchester by the 1960s, and in the raw working-class energy associated with British fashion photography in the same period [2.6, 2.7]. While many of the key personalities, including Foale and Tuffin, Zandra Rhodes and Ossie Clark, were trained in the art schools (particularly the new Fashion School of the RCA), others such as Mary Quant, Barbara Hulanicki and, in a later generation, Vivienne Westwood had enjoyed a more fleeting connection to a formal design education, falling back instead on a pioneering attitude and a strong empathy for independent retailing. As various observers have remarked, a stand-out quality of British design has been the skill exhibited by many of its practitioners in creating extraordinarily eclectic shop premises that capture avant-garde and underground tendencies in art, fashion, interiors and music, and that create both cult and popular followings. This continued to be as true in the 1980s and '90s as it was in the 1960s, and is demonstrated clearly by the career of Paul Smith.

● 2.3 [ABOVE] 12 Cubes, Glenys Barton, 1971 | Bone china, slip-cast, with silk-screened decoration | V&A: Circ.277-279–1973 ● 2.4 [OPPOSITE] *Large Pendant Body Piece*, David Watkins, 1975 | Acrylic, gold, aluminium | V&A: LOAN:WATKINS.1–2011

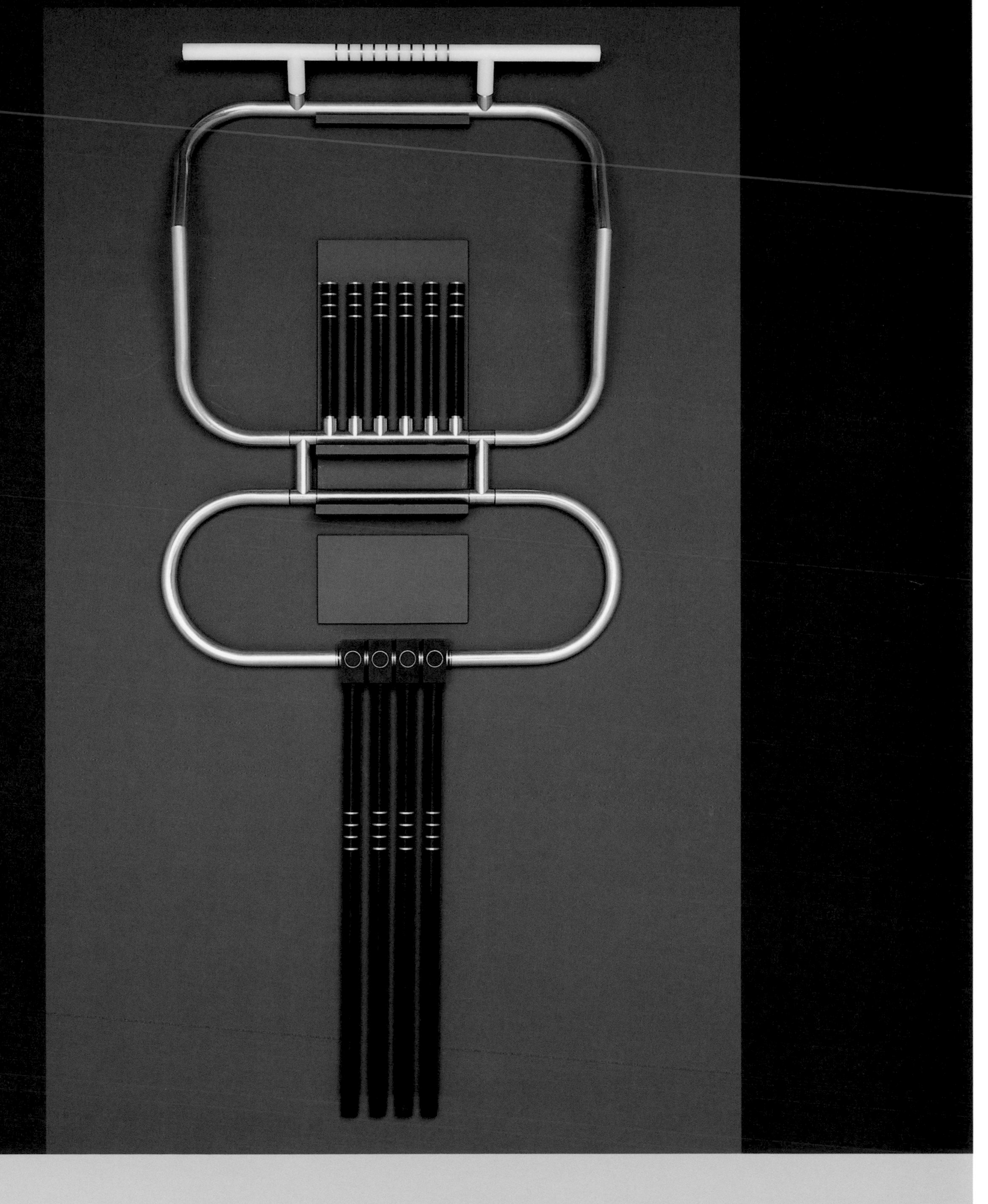

19
50
Terry O'Neill

● 2.5 [OPPOSITE] *David Bowie,* Terry O'Neill, 1974 | Promotional photograph for the album *Diamond Dogs*, gelatin silver print, printed 2009 | V&A: E.315–2011 ● 2.6 [BELOW LEFT] *Julie Christie,* Terence Donovan, 1962 | Published in *Women Throooo the Eyes of Smudger Terence Donovan*, 1964, gelatin silver print mounted on card | V&A: E.332–2011 ● 2.7 [BELOW RIGHT] *Jean Shrimpton*, Terry O'Neill, 1965 | Gelatin silver print, printed 2009 | V&A: E.314–2011

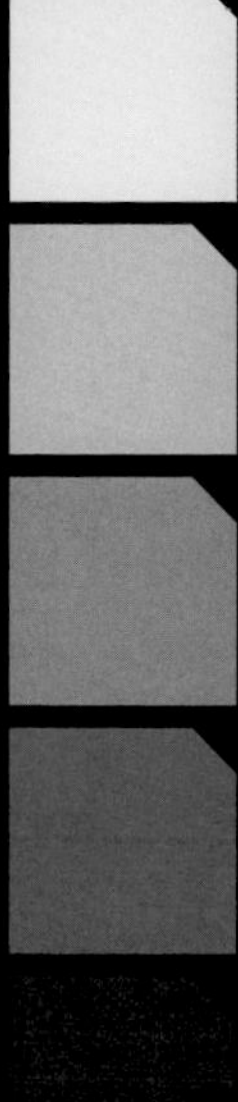

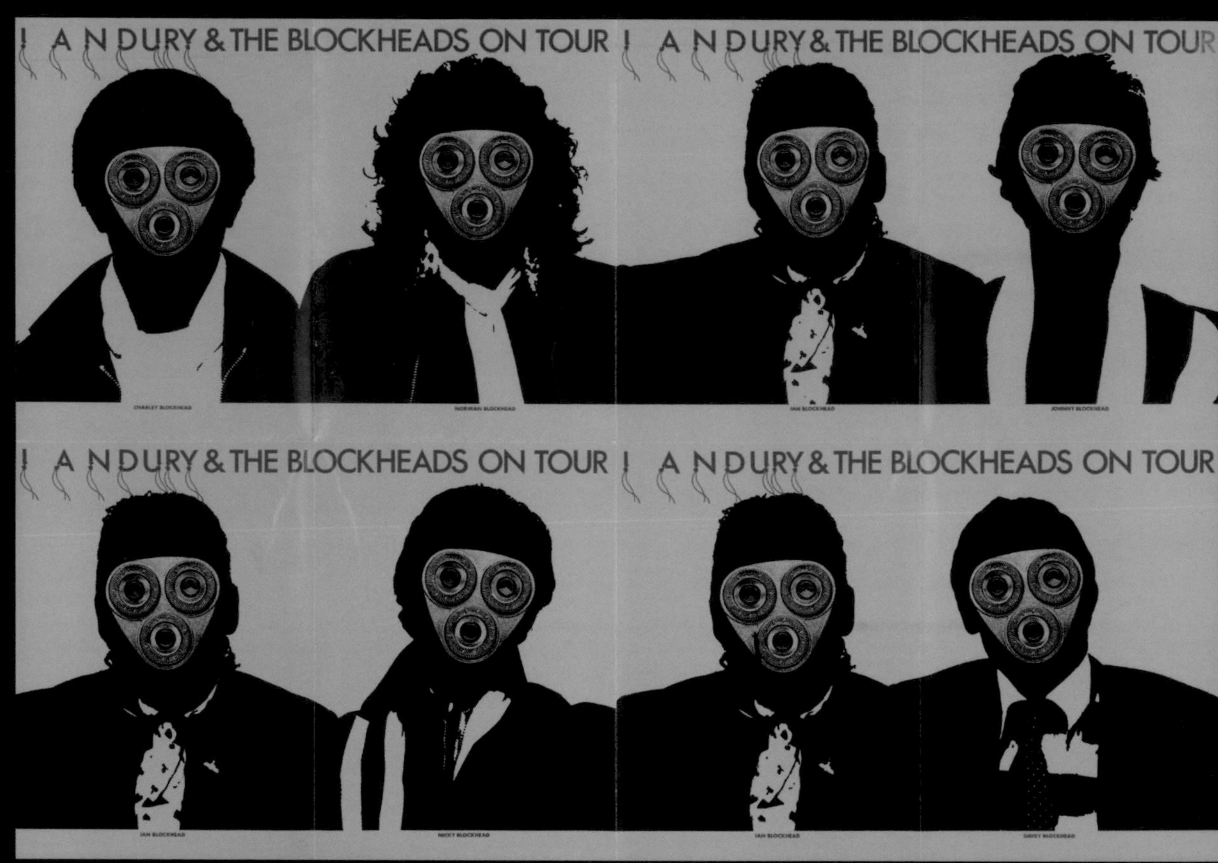
I A N DURY & THE BLOCKHEADS ON TOUR
I A N DURY & THE BLOCKHEADS ON TOUR
CHARLEY BLOCKHEAD
NORMAN BLOCKHEAD
IAN BLOCKHEAD
JOHNNY BLOCKHEAD
I A N DURY & THE BLOCKHEADS ON TOUR
I A N DURY & THE BLOCKHEADS ON TOUR
IAN BLOCKHEAD
MICKY BLOCKHEAD
IAN BLOCKHEAD
DAVEY BLOCKHEAD

Beyond the world of fashion, the design and promotion of British furniture, textile and interior design in the late 1970s and '80s was also inflected by the subversive attitude displayed on the high street, and particularly by the rough, bricolaged aesthetic of punk. Tom Dixon, André Dubreuil, Ron Arad and Mark Brazier-Jones (whose neo-Victorian, welded and rusted 'creative salvage' one-off pieces came to denote a sense of radical high style in the cutting-edge hotels, shops, hairdressing salons, clubs and boutiques of early 1980s London, Paris, Los Angeles and New York) postured like rock-stars with welding torches [2.10]. Their grand baroque sensibility was similarly revealed in the fascination with ruins, fragments and decay displayed in the woven and printed fabrics of Scott Crolla and Georgina Godley, Timney Fowler and English Eccentrics, Nigel Coates's evocative shop architecture in Japan and London, or the fantastical, sometimes morbid jewellery and accessories of Simon Costin, Judy Blame, Christopher Nemeth and Slim Barrett [2.14, 2.16, 2.17]. In Manchester and Sheffield the empty factories of the ruined textile and steel industries formed the backdrop for a similar interest in loss and memory that inspired Ben Kelly's spaces and Peter Saville's graphics for Factory, though here the aesthetic was aggressively post-industrial and Modernist rather than overtly romantic. What linked both northern and London-based examples were their roots in economic recession. A lack of backing and commercial opportunities for graduating designers resulted in a greater degree of creative resourcefulness and a lack of respect for the establishment (by the mid-1980s the Design Council was in a particularly moribund state) that was, counter-intuitively, to the benefit of the international reputation of British design 'plc'.

In the 1990s the process that had started with a generational shift and the reinvention of the British art school perhaps came full circle. The increasing prosperity of the nation, fuelled by an obsession with property and the effects of financial deregulation and globalization, inevitably ushered in a gradual waning of subversive intent alongside a growing interest in slick surfaces and aspirational lifestyles. This can be seen in the regeneration of post-industrial regions such as Docklands in London and Salford in the North-East; in the rising popularity of 'loft living' in UK cities; and in the evolution of work by Dixon and Arad: its transformation from rough-hewn statement of refusal to polished symbol of success [2.12]. It is also evidenced through the rise of upscale furniture retailers such as SCP and ARAM in the 1980s and '90s, whose choice of glamorous neo-Modernist forms by designers including Jasper Morrison and Michael Young graced the pages of British design magazines, including *Blueprint* and *Wallpaper*, and invited the attention of curators at the newly formed Design Museum (and, further afield, at the Museum of Modern Art in New York) [2.13, 2.15].

At Goldsmiths Art College and Central St Martins College of Art, in particular, graduates of the early and mid-1990s had also become skilled market-players, adept at combining critical commentary on a money- and status-obsessed society with highly desirable products. The provocative language of the Pharmacy bar and restaurant and the domination of the Paris couture industry by British fashion graduates at the end of the twentieth century were, arguably, both the ripened fruits of the 1960s and the apotheosis of British design's period of 'street-cred' [2.18, 2.19].

● 2.8 [OPPOSITE TOP] Concert programme for Ian Dury & the Blockheads, Barney Bubbles, late 1970s to early 1980s | Colour offset lithograph | V&A: E.312–2011 ● 2.9 [OPPOSITE BOTTOM LEFT] Mr Freedom, King's Road, Electric Colour Company, 1969 ● 2.10 [OPPOSITE BOTTOM RIGHT] Mark Brazier-Jones in front of his studio, with doors painted in *trompe-l'oeil* verdigris, 1993 ● 2.11 [ABOVE] Mini dress, John Bates, 1966–8 Manufactured by Jean Varon, viscose/nylon blend with rayon lining | V&A: T.262–2009

● 2.12 [ABOVE] 'Little Heavy' chair, Ron Arad, 1989 | Manufactured by One Off Ltd, 1991, beaten and welded stainless steel | V&A: W.17–1993 ● 2.13 [OPPOSITE TOP LEFT] 'Magazine Sofa', prototype, Michael Young, 1994 | Aluminium frame, foam seat and arms, upholstered in vinyl | V&A: W.11–2011 ● 2.14 [OPPOSITE TOP RIGHT] 'Not in Arcadia', furnishing textile, English Eccentrics, 1987 | Printed cotton | V&A: T.303–1988 ● 2.15 [OPPOSITE BOTTOM LEFT] 'Antelope Table', Matthew Hilton, 1987 | Manufactured by SCP Ltd, stained MDF top with a stainless-steel insert, turned sycamore and cast aluminium legs | V&A: W.17–1990 ● 2.16 [OPPOSITE BOTTOM RIGHT] Caffè Bongo, Tokyo, Nigel Coates, 1986

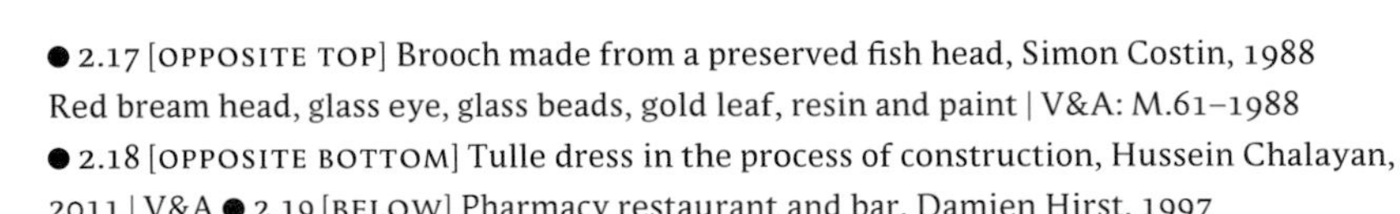

● 2.17 [OPPOSITE TOP] Brooch made from a preserved fish head, Simon Costin, 1988
Red bream head, glass eye, glass beads, gold leaf, resin and paint | V&A: M.61–1988
● 2.18 [OPPOSITE BOTTOM] Tulle dress in the process of construction, Hussein Chalayan, 2011 | V&A ● 2.19 [BELOW] Pharmacy restaurant and bar, Damien Hirst, 1997

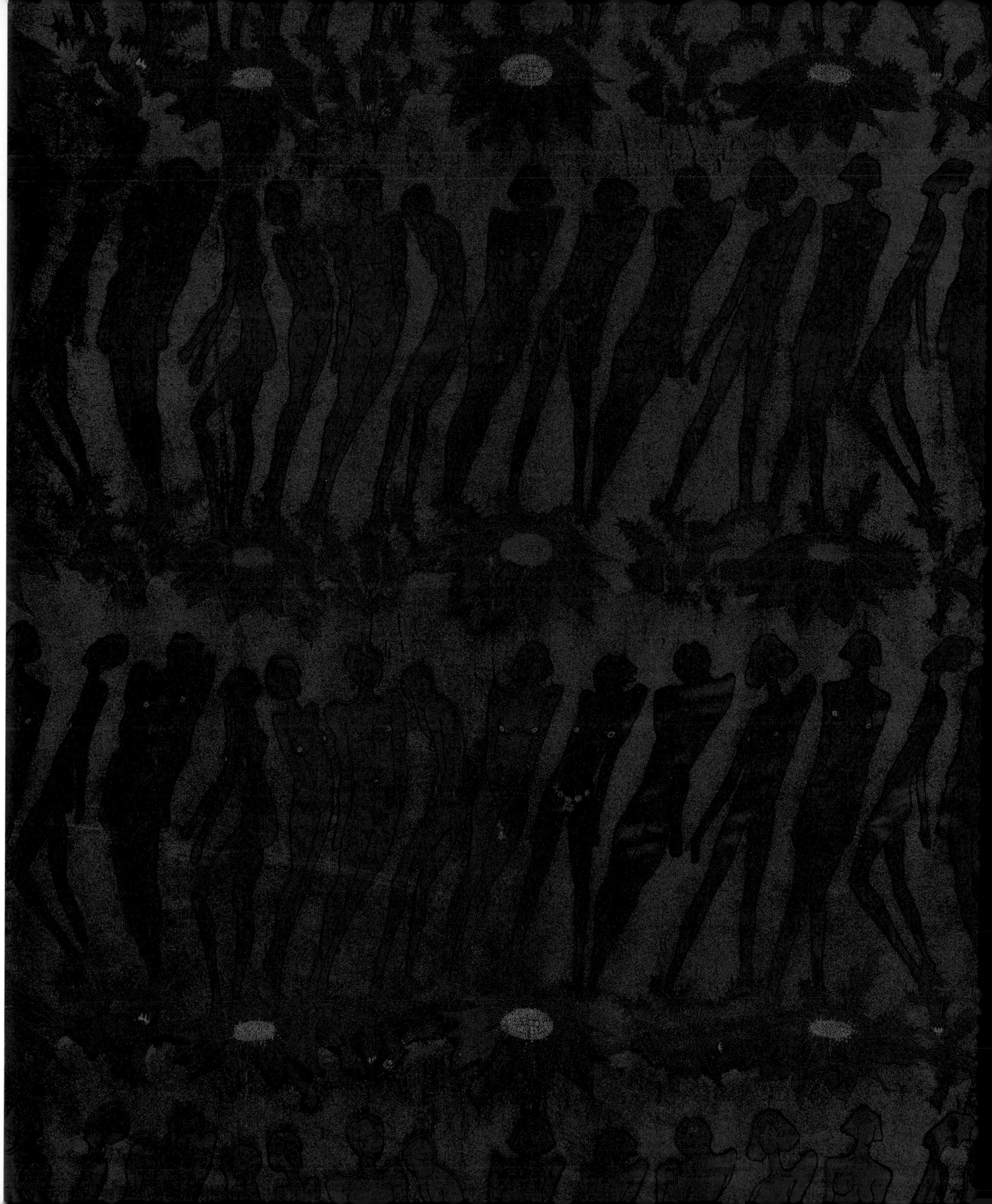

5 Pop Goes the Art School: Design and Education

— Simon Martin

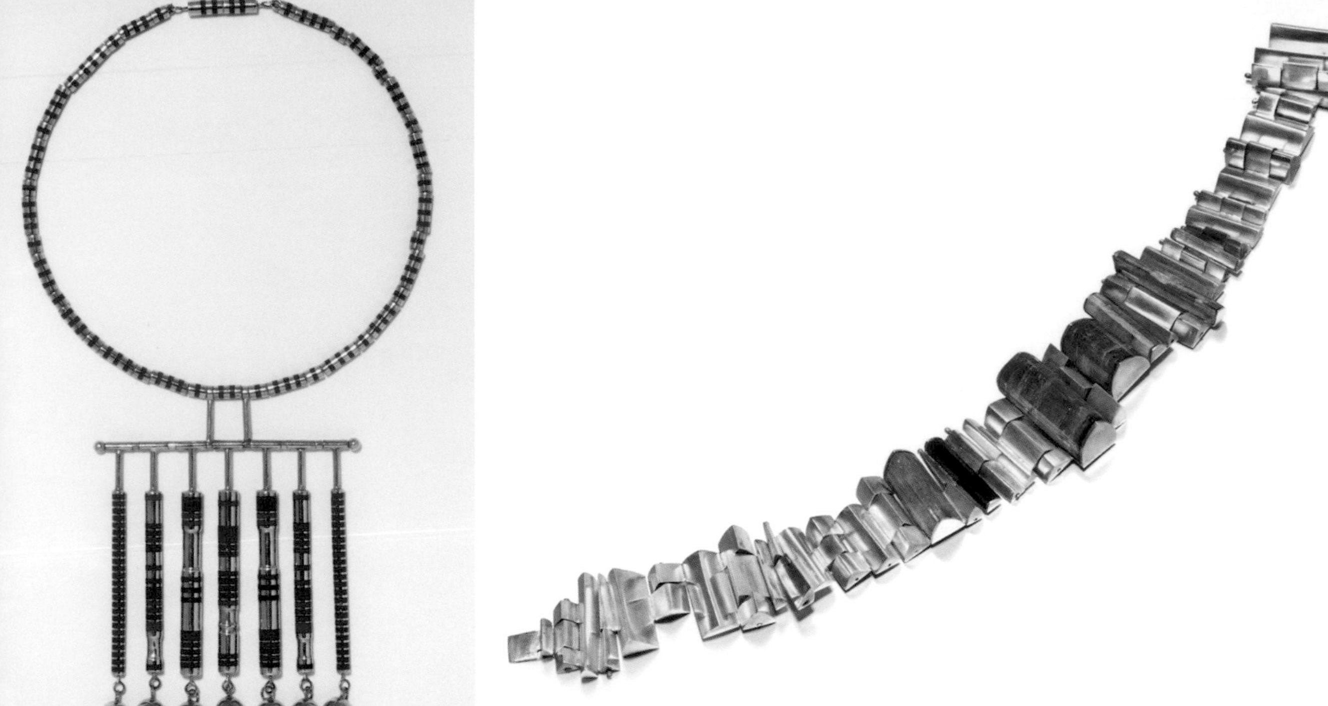

In the 1950s and '60s the British art and design education system underwent radical upheaval as both art schools and students faced the question of how to respond to the rapidly changing social climate of post-war Britain. Following the Second World War, during which the principal London art schools had undergone the disruption of being relocated to regional centres, these organizations had distinguished reputations, but were often underfunded, demoralized and still teaching according to a syllabus that had changed little since the nineteenth century.[1] An influx of students from a range of social backgrounds and ages entering into art education after active military wartime service or National Service radically altered the genteel atmosphere and structured curricula that had predominated in pre-war art schools, as they led iconoclastic and rebellious experimentation.[2]

From 1946 the main art-school qualification was the centrally examined National Diploma in Design (NDD), which was intended to provide all students with grounding in technical skills. Students would begin the NDD on leaving school at 16 and, after two years, would take the Intermediate Examination, which included tests in traditional skills areas of Life Drawing, Costume Life Drawing, Anatomy, Architecture, Creative Design for Craft, Drawing and Painting from Memory, Modelling and General Knowledge, before undertaking a further two years of specialization in a major and minor subject from an approved list of craft and design options. The NDD became increasingly unpopular, not only among staff and students, but also at the Ministry of Education, as it was seen as restrictive, and complaints were made that it produced 'neither good industrial designers nor satisfactory art teachers'.[3]

The *Report on the Training of the Industrial Designer*, written in 1946 for the newly formed Council of Industrial Design, stated:

> Many of the art schools, without the interest in their work and the demands upon their contributions which they have a right to expect from industry, have become somewhat remote from reality and, with the initial impetus given by the Morris movement, have tended to concentrate too exclusively on handicraft subjects and upon the fine arts. In these circumstances a number of industrialists tend to look askance of them.[4]

It is significant that two years later, in January 1948, the author of this report, the artist Robin Darwin, was appointed Rector of the Royal College of Art (RCA). Around the same time new principals were appointed at the other leading art schools in London, including William Johnstone at the Central School of Arts and Design in 1947 and William Coldstream at the Slade School of Art in 1949. In their respective institutions these new principals set about modernizing and restructuring the way in which art and design were taught, initiating changes that were to influence art schools across Britain in the subsequent decades. At the RCA Darwin set about forming a new independent governing body and severing direct connection with the Ministry of Education, with the aim that the RCA would provide facilities for the study of fine art, not purely as an end in itself, but as a means of enlarging and enriching the background of design students: 'the promotion of *art* in design'.[5] Aiming to integrate the RCA with the aims of industry and provide an 'essential buttress' to the CoID, he appointed numerous new professors, including Madge Garland as the first-ever Professor of Fashion in Britain (to be succeeded by Janey Ironside in 1956), Dick Russell as Professor of Light Engineering and Furniture, Rodrigo Moynihan as Professor of Painting[6] and Richard Guyatt as Professor of Publicity Design – which was subsequently renamed 'Graphic Design', a term invented by Guyatt to avoid the taint of vulgarity associated with publicity. Guyatt observed how:

> Inherent in the reorganization of the College was the tenet that the fine arts are the inspiration of the applied arts. Hence the importance, within the School of Graphic Design, of the Printmaking Department which deals with graphic media as a fine art. It is through the fine arts, the 'useless arts', that the 'useful' arts of design are invigorated, in much the same way as researchers in 'pure science' affect the work of 'applied' science.[7]

Darwin insisted that all staff members should be professional designers rather than professional teachers, and established a Diploma of Design RCA to sit alongside the diploma awarded to fine-art graduates, which would be awarded after the final examination and a monitored period of time in the appropriate Industry. As early as 1952, the year in which the first Des RCA students graduated, the RCA reported that out of the 59 students, 44 had gone on to posts 'in industry', either as consultants or as in-house designers. That year the RCA held an exhibition in the Imperial Institute entitled 'Art for the Factory', which was its first exhibition devoted entirely to industrial design, and featured the work of former students, including the silversmiths David Mellor, Robert Welch and Gerald Benney, the textile designers Pat Albeck and Audrey Levy, the ceramic designers Hazel Thumpston and Peter Cave and the furniture designers Ronald Carter and Robert Heritage.

● 2.20 [OPPOSITE TOP LEFT] Necklace, Wendy Ramshaw, 1971 Gold and enamel | V&A: M.169–1976 ● 2.21 [OPPOSITE TOP RIGHT] Necklace, Charlotte de Syllas, 1965 | Silver and tourmaline | The Worshipful Company of Goldsmiths ● 2.22 [OPPOSITE BOTTOM] Necklace, Gerda Flöckinger, 1963 | Gold, blister pearls, smoky quartz and aquamarine | The Worshipful Company of Goldsmiths

The Royal College student magazine *ARK* became a barometer for the changes in the college and beyond. First published in October 1950, it operated from within the School of Graphic Design, and was edited by students, with the Art Director and Advertising Manager being overseen by the school, and with early Art Editors including Len Deighton, Alan Fletcher and Raymond Hawkey. The album format of early issues was based on the *Penguin Modern Painters* series, with a focus on illustration, encouraging the depiction of everyday subjects as a continuation of a national tradition. Illustration flourished at the college under the tutelage of John Minton, whose images for literary magazines such as *Penguin New Writing*, *Horizon* and Elizabeth David's cookery books represented the pinnacle of neo-Romantic book illustration in the late 1940s and early '50s [1.103]. The content of *ARK* was largely drawn from staff and visitors to the Senior Common Room, including in the early 1950s contributions from John Nash on illustration, Herbert Read on De Stijl, Ronald Searle on his experience as a prisoner of war, Len Deighton on English chapbooks and new American comics, Spike Milligan on *The Goons* and Robin Day on Swedish furniture, as well as various articles on English popular art by the likes of Barbara Jones. By the end of 1950 the circulation had reached 2,000, and by the mid-1950s this included the libraries of every art school in Britain. The graphic designer Ken Garland recalled, 'Whether they liked *ARK* or not students at other schools looked at it with great envy because it was a magazine put together by students with ads designed by students for real clients. It had a real professional feel to it. It even had a professional business manager.'[8]

The approach at the RCA differed from that of its main rival, the Slade School, which was characterized by an intellectual and individualistic form of fine art that was based on respect for tradition. Its principal, William Coldstream, a founder of the Euston Road School of painting, encouraged the continuation of figurative painting and the study of art history through the appointment of academics such as Rudolf Wittkower and E.H. Gombrich.

At the Central School of Art and Design, William Johnstone fostered a different approach to pedagogy by bringing artists into technical departments, 'so that sparks would fly off to give a new life-enhancing environment'.[9] Thus, in the decade after 1948, the tutors in the department of industrial design under A.R. Halliwell included the ex-Bauhaus jewellery designer Naum Slutzky, the abstract painter Victor Pasmore, the design theorist Bruce Archer, the photographer Nigel Henderson, the sculptor William Turnbull, the designer Douglas Scott, and the artist and textile designer Eduardo Paolozzi. The creative crossover between the staff and the departments of the Central School was to enrich and expand the conceptual and design possibilities of the craft-based subject areas they were teaching. For example, the abstract painter Alan Davie, whose work was profoundly influenced by the American Abstract Expressionists and the notion of the subconscious, taught in the silversmithing department.

The possibilities of this situation encouraged Gerda Flöckinger to enrol at Central, after seeing an exhibition of American jewellery at the school while studying painting at St Martins. With a belief in the abstract nature of applied art and the necessity of art-school training for jewellers in order to evolve their own personal style, she subsequently established the experimental Modern Jewellery course at the Hornsey College of Art (1962–8), which marked a watershed in British jewellery design due to its interplay between design and technique [2.22]. One of her principles was to encourage her students' familiarity with materials, rather than designing in the abstract, so that design and process were always welded together. Flöckinger was to lead the way for a younger generation of women jewellery designers, such as Charlotte de Syllas, Caroline Broadhead and Wendy Ramshaw [2.20, 2.21].

BASIC DESIGN

The system of teaching at the Central School helped to nurture the 'Basic Design' movement, which was loosely inspired by the principles of the Bauhaus, the writings of Herbert Read and European Constructivism.[10] In 1959, Roger Coleman stated that, 'most of the subsequent basic design courses in British art schools owe something of their character to the work done at the Central'.[11] Victor Pasmore and Richard Hamilton were to become key figures in the introduction of the celebrated Basic Design course at King's College, Newcastle (later to become part of Newcastle University) after moving there from the Central School in 1953. The Basic Design course that they developed was a loose pedagogical approach that sought to strip away art and design students' preconceived ideas through exercises in the use of colour, establishment of form and construction of space. It was a move from technique-based teaching to an open-ended experimental and critical approach. Pasmore's original idea of devising a visual grammar that would provide the objective basis for abstract art was different from, but complementary to, that of Hamilton, who was interested in developing new ways of analysing the visual world. The course evolved into a foundation year that was common to all first-year students, who would subsequently specialize in painting, sculpture, textiles or stained glass, and in the 1960s influenced the general introduction of foundation courses for all art students. From 1954 Pasmore, together with Tom Hudson and Harry Thubron (who were to become tutors at Leeds School of Art), led a series of summer schools for teachers at Scarborough, where the principles of Basic Design evolved.[12] An exhibition about 'basic form' for art education was shown at the Hatton Gallery in Newcastle and at the Institute of Contemporary Arts (ICA) in London in 1959 and further publicized the approach.

● 2.23 [OPPOSITE] *Hers is a Lush Situation*, Richard Hamilton, 1958
Oil, cellulose, metal foil and collage on panel | Pallant House Gallery (Colin St John Wilson through the Art Fund)

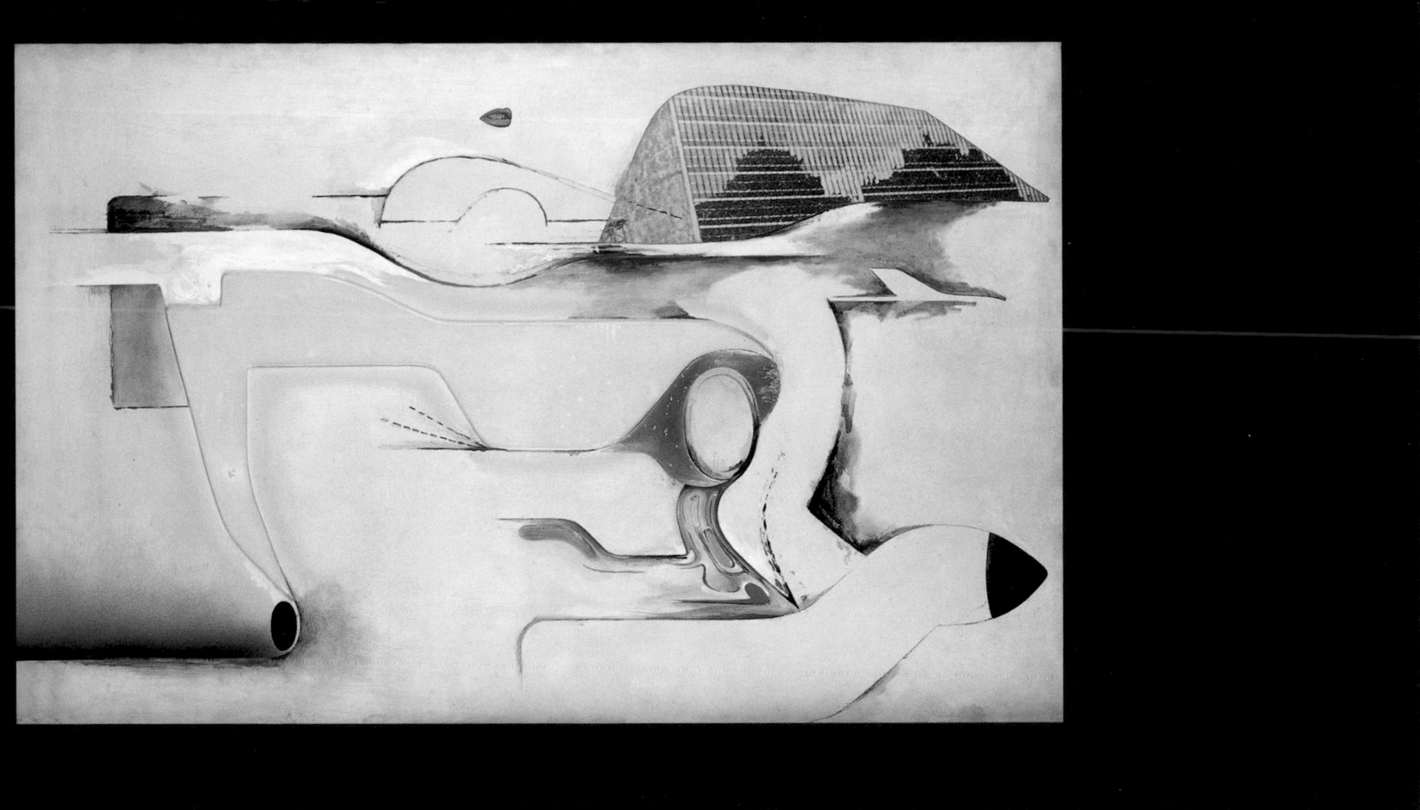

THE INDEPENDENT GROUP AND THE ROOTS OF POP ART

Basic Design was closely related in its methods and intentions with the activities of the Independent Group, whose members were well represented on the staff of the Central School, including Hamilton, Henderson, Paolozzi, Turnbull and the architect Peter Smithson and theorist Reyner Banham (who both taught in the School of Interior Design). The Independent Group was an unofficial discussion group that met at the ICA, made up of young artists, architects and writers, and also included the artists John McHale, Magda and Frank Cordell, the architects Alison Smithson, Colin St John Wilson and James Stirling, and the writers Lawrence Alloway and Toni del Renzio. It took Modernism as the starting point for its analysis of culture, but an alternative Modernism to that of the utopian, universalizing aesthetic of the ICA's first chairman Herbert Read, instead exploring the semiotics of contemporary popular culture and technology in an inclusive way. The Group developed a positive analysis of mass-media imagery, celebrating the 'knowing consumer' and discussing topics ranging from science fiction, fashion, American advertising and car design to popular music, western films, architecture and Abstract Expressionism. At one of the first meetings in spring 1952, Paolozzi used an epidiascope to present a rapid-fire lecture on his 'Bunk' collages, which were witty juxtapositions of disparate images of modern domesticity, cartoons and superheroes, glamour models, car and food adverts [2.40].

Much of the art produced at this time by Paolozzi and the other artist-members was influenced by the Surrealist and Dadaist strategies of European artists whom they had met, such as Jean Arp, Marcel Duchamp, Max Ernst and Tristan Tzara,[13] and their key texts suggested new forms of perception and sources for art, including Amédée Ozenfant's *Foundations of Modern Art*, D'Arcy Wentworth Thompson's *On Growth and Form*, Sigfried Giedion's *Mechanisation Takes Command*, László Moholy-Nagy's *Vision in Motion* and Alexander Dorner's *The Way Beyond 'Art'.* But it was the exhibitions organized by the members of the Independent Group at the ICA and other venues that were to be the main vehicle for disseminating their ideas. These included 'Growth and Form' and 'Parallel of Life and Art': total environments that engulfed the viewer with blown-up photographs to demonstrate the underlying unity of art and life, thus challenging the viewer's perception of what was beautiful and worthy of inclusion in a gallery.

The aim of breaking down the barriers between the artist, scientist and technician was endorsed by the 'Man, Machine and Motion' exhibition, which reflected Hamilton's admiration for Duchamp. Its theme was 'a visual survey of man's relationship with the machinery of movement', and within a modular grid were displayed blown-up photographs of aerial, aquatic, interplanetary and terrestrial imagery – space-travel imagery on the ceiling, underwater imagery on the floor. This relationship between man and machine was to be explored in subsequent works by Hamilton, such as *Hers is a Lush Situation* (1958), which articulated what Reyner Banham described as the 'rhetoric of consumer persuasion' written into car design, advertising and marketing through the erotic conflation of Sophia Loren's collaged lips and mechanical forms suggestive of a 1957 Buick [2.23].

this is tomorrow whitechapel art gallery

aug. 9 - sept 9 1956

Hamilton's exploration of visual signs and of people's interaction with their environment was encapsulated in his iconic collage *Just what is it that makes today's homes so different, so appealing* (1956), in which a semi-naked woman and the bodybuilder Charles Atlas holding a lollipop with the word 'POP' are presented within a domestic interior constructed from contemporary advertising: the latest appliances, a view of the moon, a cinema façade and tinned ham. It was created to be reproduced as a screen-printed poster for the exhibition 'This is Tomorrow' at the Whitechapel Art Gallery in 1956, which featured 12 environments that were each created by a team of artists, architects, designers and critical thinkers in the spirit of 'antagonistic cooperation' [2.24]. This revolutionary exhibition was dominated by two groups – the Constructionists, including Pasmore, Kenneth Martin and Adrian Heath, and members of the Independent Group – and has been celebrated as a summation of their diverse ideas. While the *Patio and Pavilion* installation by Group 6 (Paolozzi, Henderson and the Smithsons) presented a Brutalist habitat symbolic of human needs in the Cold War age, the exhibit by Group 2 (Hamilton, John McHale and John Voelcker) seemed to be dedicated to sensory pleasure and heralded the Pop Art of the 1960s [2.25]. Featuring cardboard cut outs of Marilyn Monroe, Robbie the Robot from the film *Return to the Forbidden Planet*, television advertisements for Pepsi-Cola, a group of Duchamp's *Rotary Discs* and a reproduction of Van Gogh's *Sunflowers*, the exhibit obscured the distinctions between popular and fine art. Musing on the exhibition in a letter to the Smithsons in 1957, Hamilton drew up a list of the characteristics that have come to define 'Pop Art':

Popular (designed for a mass audience)
Transient (short-term solution)
Expendable (aimed at youth)
Low cost
Mass produced
Young (aimed at youth)
Witty
Sexy
Gimmicky
Glamorous
Big business[14]

The iconic typography and layout of the 'This is Tomorrow' catalogue were designed by Edward Wright, who had joined the graphic-design department of the RCA in 1955.[15] The influence of the Independent Group became apparent in the design and content of *ARK* magazine from the mid-1950s [2.26]. Len Deighton and Raymond Hawkey had (controversially for Guyatt and Darwin) introduced articles on experimental typography, and photography began to edge out illustration inside the magazine. At the same time the content began to reflect an interest in American culture, featuring articles by Alloway on mass communication and by John McHale on 'technology and the home'.

● 2.24 [OPPOSITE] Poster for the exhibition 'This is Tomorrow' at the Whitechapel Art Gallery, Richard Hamilton, 1956 | Screenprint | V&A: E.176–1994
● 2.25 [LEFT] 'This is Tomorrow' at the Whitechapel Art Gallery, 1956 | Installation by Group 2 (Richard Hamilton, John Voelcker and John McHale), including an advertising billboard for *The Forbidden Planet*

BRITISH POP ART AND THE ROYAL COLLEGE OF ART

In the words of Christopher Frayling, '*ARK* became the bridge between the first generation of "Pop" artists, their discussions, and the studios of the RCA.'[16] The close relationship between the Graphic Design and Fine Art Schools at the Royal College enabled a particular merging of ideas that was manifested in the work that emerged in the late 1950s and early '60s. The Editor of *ARK*, Alan Fletcher, commented that 'Curiously the crossover came in the litho room, because we all used to meet in there. There was Joe Tilson doing his stencilled paintings with stencilled letters and Peter Blake used to be in there too.'[17]

The majority of the British artists associated with the Pop Art movement emerged from the RCA, including Peter Blake, the American R.B. Kitaj (who had studied in Britain under the GI Bill) and Joe Tilson, who graduated in the late 1950s, followed by Derek Boshier, Pauline Boty, Patrick Caulfield, David Hockney and Peter Phillips in the early 1960s.[18] They were given a public platform by a series of juried exhibitions entitled 'Young Contemporaries' that were held at the Royal Society of British Artists' Galleries between 1961 and 1963. Lawrence Alloway was one of the jurors, and observed of the RCA students' work, which was hung together in the 1961 show, that it was:

> connect[ed] with the city ... by using typical products and objects, including the techniques of graffiti and the imagery of mass communications... The impact of popular art is present, but checked by puzzles and paradoxes ... their work ... combines real objects, same-size representation, sketchy notation, and writing.[19]

● 2.26 [ABOVE] *ARK*, the magazine of the Royal College of Art, summer 1960 and summer 1963 | Printed paper and metal foil | NAL: 38041800727679 and 3804180072768
● 2.27 [OPPOSITE] *The Beatles 1962*, Peter Blake, 1963–8 | Acrylic emulsion on hardboard Pallant House Gallery (Colin St John Wilson through the Art Fund)

In 1962 the BBC arts programme *Monitor* showed a film by Ken Russell entitled *Pop Goes the Easel*, which was greeted with widespread controversy for its then cutting-edge content and form. It focused on four recent graduates from the RCA: Blake, Boshier, Boty and Phillips, exploring the contemporary influences on their art through a rich collage of images of film and pop stars, fashion magazines and even the artists themselves enjoying a fairground and a wrestling match. Critics spoke of a 'Royal College style', but in reality the unity of their approach represented more a shared interest in source material drawn from popular culture than a stylistic unity, and Kitaj, Hockney and Caulfield were all uncomfortable with the label. Although Hockney was to make allusions to consumer packaging in paintings such as *Tea Painting in an Illusionistic Style* (1961), on the advice of Kitaj he sought a personal subject matter in paintings such as *We Two Boys Together Clinging* (1961), expressing his interest in the poetry of Walt Whitman and Constantine Cavafy and his identity as a young homosexual male [2.28]. When Hockney was threatened with not being awarded his diploma for not complying with the requirements of the RCA's general-studies department in 1961, he defiantly etched a satirical diploma, depicting Robin Darwin supported by a half-moon (a reference to the Registrar, Mr Moon) upholding Michael Kullman of the general-studies department, while at the foot of the Principal five of Hockney's fellow students were seen with heads bowed. In the event, Hockney's abilities were recognized when he was awarded his diploma, as well as the Gold Medal for Painting that year.[20]

However, 'excessive independence' led to Allen Jones's expulsion in 1960, and Peter Phillips was thrown out of the Painting School due to his experimental approach and moved to the School of Television Design. Jones went on to produce an iconic series of forniphiliac sculptures of female figures as fetishistic domestic furniture, such as *Chair* (1969) [2.29]. These were cast in fibreglass by commercial sculptors, and questioned the boundaries between art and design. In a similarly suggestive way the Slade graduate Colin Self created a series of sculptures of *Leopardskin Nuclear Bombers* in 1963, which used assemblages of fake leopard-skin fabric, machine parts and other materials to convey connotations of battle armour and predatory sexual behaviour as a comment on Cold War politics.

The use of non-traditional and industrial materials characterized the work of several of the Pop artists, including utilizing commercial silkscreen printing processes for fine-art purposes by Caulfield, Kitaj and Paolozzi, who collaborated with the Kelpra Studios run by Chris Prater, overturning established ideas about originality and collaboration in printmaking. Caulfield purposefully used decorator's gloss paint to achieve the flatness and impersonality of a commercial sign-painter in his paintings, while in works such as *The Beatles 1962* (1963–8) Peter Blake mimicked the design of pop-record sleeves and fan magazines and the idiosyncrasies of the printing process, such as mis-registration [2.27].[21] Blake was later to collaborate with his first wife, the American sculptor Jann Haworth, on the iconic album cover for The Beatles' *Sgt Pepper's Lonely Hearts Club Band*, with its line-up of celebrities from history. Its quirky Victoriana was in stark contrast to Hamilton's later minimal design for The Beatles' *White Album*, which consisted of a plain white sleeve discreetly embossed with the band's name and a unique stamped serial number, creating the ironic situation of a numbered edition of something like five million copies [2.30].

During the 1960s there was a two-way traffic between the music and art worlds. Openings at the Robert Fraser Gallery in London's Duke Street, which represented the likes of Blake, Hamilton, Haworth, Paolozzi, Riley, Self and the Americans Jim Dine, Claes Oldenburg, Ed Ruscha and Andy Warhol, were frequently attended by singers such as Marianne Faithfull and members of The Beatles and The Rolling Stones. When Fraser and Mick Jagger were arrested for drugs offences in 1967, Hamilton produced *Swingeing London '67* (1968), a relief with a screen-printed press photograph of Fraser and Jagger in the police van, a comment on the media attention and a protest at the 'swingeing sentence' declared by the judge. On another level, the British art schools formed a breeding ground for future pop musicians. Performers in groups such as The Beatles, The Kinks, The Rolling Stones, Pink Floyd and Roxy Music had attended art school, including Syd Barrett, Ray Brown, David Bowie, Ian Dury, Brian Eno, Bryan Ferry, Dave Gilmour, John Lennon, Keith Richards and Ronnie Wood.[22]

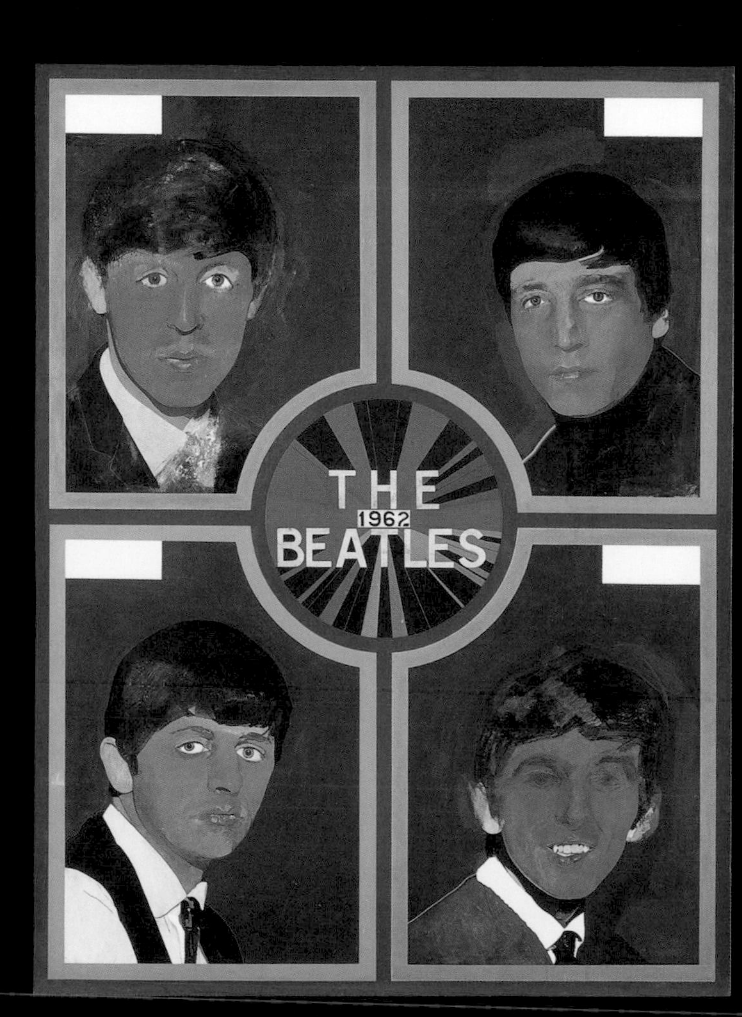

we 2 boys together clinging
never
boy
4.2.

● 2.28 [OPPOSITE TOP] *We Two Boys Together Clinging*, David Hockney, 1961
Oil on board | Arts Council Collection, Southbank Centre, London
● 2.29 [ABOVE] *Chair*, Allen Jones, 1969 | Painted plastic and mixed media | Tate

● 2.30 [ABOVE AND RIGHT] Sleeve for *Sgt Pepper's Lonely Hearts Club Band* by The Beatles, Peter Blake and Jann Haworth, 1967 | Art direction by The Apple and M.C. Productions, photographed by Michael Cooper, printed by Garrod & Lofthouse Ltd, colour offset lithograph on card | V&A: E.1803–1990 and sleeve for *The White Album* by The Beatles, Richard Hamilton, 1968 | Embossed card

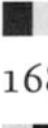

The BEATLES

№ 0486996

2.31 [OPPOSITE] *Mirror*, Frank Bowling, 1964–6
Oil on canvas | Tate: Lent from the artist, 2010

At the same time that the Pop artists emerged from the Royal College, a generation of young, broadly abstract artists also appeared, influenced by the first exhibitions of American Abstract Expressionism in Britain during the late 1950s. Frank Bowling, who had been born in British Guiana, navigated the boundaries between Pop and abstraction in paintings that radically addressed themes of post-colonialism rather than Western popular culture, while in 1960 the 'Situation' exhibition at the Royal Society of British Artists presented work that was defined as: 'abstract (that is, without specific reference to events outside the painting)...and not more than 30 square feet' [2.31].[23] These artists included Gillian Ayres, Bernard and Harold Cohen,[24] Robyn Denny, Gordon House, John Hoyland, Gwyther Irwin, Richard Smith and Marc Vaux. The title of the exhibition was taken from a quote by William Turnbull – 'the situation in London now' [25] – and the work demonstrated, in the words of Lawrence Alloway, 'an awareness of the world as something that contains both the work of art and the spectator (rather than the romantic notion of the work of art itself as the world) is at the core of recent developments in London'.[26]

Students who produced abstract work were restricted by the National Diploma in Design, which assessed students on the basis of figurative work. At St Martins School of Art this situation led Frank Martin, who from 1952 was head of the sculpture department, to develop the 'advanced sculpture course', which encouraged experimental abstract sculpture that did not 'fit into an existing art situation'.[27] Martin believed that 'abstraction was most important to the advancement of teaching art', and one of the studios was cleared of traditional tools and materials to create 'an area of study away from figuration completely'.[28]

Following his exposure to American abstract painting and the assemblages of David Smith, Anthony Caro (perhaps the most celebrated tutor on the course) had moved from working in cast bronze to steel, and a welding shop was introduced to the department. The need for larger working spaces and specialized equipment meant that students began to work independently in satellite spaces, meeting weekly at St Martins to discuss finished work, so that the department was 'an analogue of a sculptor's studio, in which discussion, criticism and experiment are actively pursued'.[29] The course remained 'vocational' because it was without official validation, and the school's application for accreditation as a postgraduate centre for sculpture was rejected, yet the course achieved a remarkable reputation.[30] Its impact was apparent in the second 'New Generation' exhibition at the Whitechapel Art Gallery in 1965, surveying emerging talent in British sculpture. Six of the nine exhibiting artists (David Annesley, Michael Bolus, Philip King, Tim Scott, William Tucker and Isaac Witkin) had studied at St Martins and had gone on to teach on the course. Instead of being carved and moulded, the sculptures in the exhibition were constructed in the synthetic materials of manufacturing: plastic, fibreglass and metal. Brightly coloured and presented directly on the floor without plinths, they demonstrated what the curator Bryan Robertson described as 'a radically new and different concept of sculpture'.[31]

THE FIRST COLDSTREAM REPORT

On 18 January 1958 an article had appeared in *The Times* entitled 'The Future of the Art Schools'. It discussed a specific issue: the proposed amalgamation of Chelsea School of Art and the Regent Street Polytechnic, but in doing so it reflected a wider concern about the relevance of the National Diploma and anxiety about the role and development of the art-school system, which it saw as 'part of a known Government intention to reduce the number of art schools throughout the country and, moreover, to slant them more in the direction of commercial and industrial art and design'.[32]

On the same page a letter by William Coldstream, the Principal of the Slade, was published, regretting the 'unfortunate proposal' and demanding that 'changes as drastic and far-reaching as those the Ministry has in mind should surely be preceded by informed public discussion'.[33] Coldstream's concerns related to the *Report of the National Advisory Committee on Art Examinations* that had been published by the Minister of Education in April 1957, recommending the formation of a new independent council for art education, abandoning the external assessment system and moving towards college autonomy. When the National Advisory Council of Art Education (NACAE)[34] was formed in January 1959, Coldstream was asked to be the chairman and his name was thus wedded to reforms of the British art-school system during the 1960s: the *First Report of the NACAE* was published in October 1960 and became popularly known as 'The First Coldstream Report'. Its recommendations for a complete restructuring of art education were to have significant implications over the coming decades, proposing the phasing out of the NDD and the introduction of a new Diploma in Art and Design (Dip.AD), before which all students were required to complete a one-year pre-diploma (subsequently to become the 'foundation' course). Through his position on the Coldstream committee, Victor Pasmore influenced the adoption of the Basic Design approach in the newly emerging foundation courses throughout Britain.[35] It included the agreement to have four main specialities: Fine Art, Graphic Design (including illustration), 3D Design (ceramics, glass and furniture) and Textiles and Fashion. One of the most far-reaching proposals was that history of art and 'Complementary Studies' should be studied throughout the course to 'strengthen or give breadth to the students' training'.[36]

A new independent body was formed in 1961 called the National Council for Diplomas in Art and Design (NCDAD), chaired by Sir John Summerson, which meant that each individual art school would have the autonomy to set its own curriculum and examinations, as long as they met approved national standards. Each college was required to present its syllabus based on its current teaching practices and future plans, and between February 1962 and March 1963 72 art colleges were assessed by visiting teams of specialists. However, when the Summerson Committee published its report in February 1964, of the 201 courses submitted by the 72 colleges visited, only 61 were approved, which led to widespread discontent. Coldstream proposed that colleges that failed to gain diploma accreditation could run vocational courses, or courses in design appreciation for the distributive trades. While the report did much to professionalize the teaching of art and design in Britain during the 1960s, it also sowed 'dragon's teeth' that were to lead to later problems.

THE HORNSEY REVOLUTION

On 28 May 1968 Hornsey College of Art was occupied by students in a dispute that was triggered over the control of Student Union funds, but which was ultimately about their frustration with the wider sweeping changes in national art education brought about by the Coldstream Report [2.32]. The students felt that the Diploma in Art and Design lacked relevance to contemporary society and was the 'assimilation of the bohemians into conventional higher education; and, beyond this, into the society which determines the form of this Higher Education'.[37] It was felt that the division between students on diploma courses and those on vocational courses reflected the social divisions outside the college. A letter from the students stated:

> The students of Hornsey College of Art have taken over direct control of the college, its buildings and facilities for the purpose of implementing a 'new' educational structure... We are demonstrating that it is entirely possible [to]...organize in co-operation with our tutors a curriculum in which individual needs are no longer subordinated to a predetermined system of training requiring a degree of specialization which precludes the broad development of the students' artistic and intellectual capabilities.[38]

Coinciding with the 1968 student revolutions in Paris, the planned 24-hour sit-in led to an occupation of several weeks, during which a student administration was set up with the support of sympathetic lecturers. The students printed newsletters and graphics using a Gestetner duplicating machine to promote a programme of films, lectures and debates critiquing all aspects of art education, and including high-profile speakers such as Tariq Ali, Buckminster Fuller, Nikolaus Pevsner and the psychiatrist R.D. Laing. The occupation led to the formation of the short-lived 'Movement for Rethinking Art and Design Education' (MORADE), a three-day national conference on art education at the Roundhouse at Camden Town, which concluded that the protest was 'of first importance to the future of art education in this country',[39] and to an exhibition at the ICA called 'Hornsey Strikes Again'.

● 2.32 [OPPOSITE] Handbill, Martin Walker of the Association of Members of Hornsey College of Art, 1968 | Linocut | V&A: E.139–2002

THE SECOND COLDSTREAM REPORT

On 24 June 1970 the Second Coldstream Report, entitled *The Structure of Art and Design Education in the Further Education Sector*, was submitted to Margaret Thatcher, then Secretary of State for Education and Science. Produced by a joint committee of the NACAE and NCDAD, it formed in part a response to the student protests about art education at Hornsey, Brighton, Croydon, Guildford and elsewhere. The report quietly dropped fine art as a core study, retaining the Dip.AD 'in a more flexible and comprehensive form' that allowed for experimentation and diversity, stating: '...we do not believe that studies in fine art can be adequately defined in terms of chief studies related to media. We believe that studies in fine art derive from an attitude which may be expressed in many ways.'[40]

This flexibility was not without opposition, and the report included a 'Note of Dissent' by Nikolaus Pevsner, who felt that while intellectual discipline might be unpopular with staff and students, that was too bad. However, the Coldstream Reforms acknowledged the development of conceptual art and avant-garde practices, and this was to allow for innovation and diversity. Even so, it coincided with an experiment in art education at Coventry College of Art, which was the 'Art Theory' course introduced by Terry Atkinson, Michael Baldwin and David Bainbridge, members of the conceptual Art & Language group, in October 1969. The course 'lived critically and thus precariously within the institutional framework of the Dip.AD',[41] as it neither sat within the 'complementary studies' required alongside the studio work, nor was it studio work in the traditional sense, as it critiqued the very art-object itself. Ultimately, the course was dismantled in 1971 after the Summerson Council stated that only studio work in 'its commonly accepted meaning, that is to say the production of tangible, visual art objects',[42] was acceptable for assessment.

By the 1970s the British art and design education system had altered enormously, not only reflecting the wider changes in British society, but as a result both of subversive students pushing the boundaries and of historic institutions accepting the need to evolve. The breakdown of the barriers between high and popular culture that had been fostered by the Independent Group and by the 1960s Pop artists, and the increasing acceptance of a conceptual approach, profoundly affected the art and design that emerged in the 1970s and '80s, particularly as the 1960s generation was by then teaching the next generation. For instance in the rich field of ceramics, a generation of art-school-trained makers, including Glenys Barton, Jacqueline Poncelet, Elizabeth Fritsch, Carol McNicoll, Alison Britton and Richard Slee, firmly shifted the discourse from utility and form towards a focus on concept and narrative [2.3, 2.33–2.36]. And a generation later, this was perhaps most explicitly manifested in the work of the Young British Artists who emerged from Goldsmiths College of Art in the late 1980s, such as Damien Hirst, Sarah Lucas, Michael Landy and Angus Fairhurst, by their contemporaries at the RCA, including Tracey Emin and Gavin Turk, and by the work of fashion designers emerging from Central St Martins, such as Hussein Chalayan, Giles Deacon and Alexander McQueen. British art schools have been one of the key generators of creative talent in an increasingly global context since the 1980s. As the progressive work emerging from degree courses and the 2010 student protests demonstrate, in the twenty-first century art schools continue to be a radical space for fostering creativity and questioning the status quo.[43]

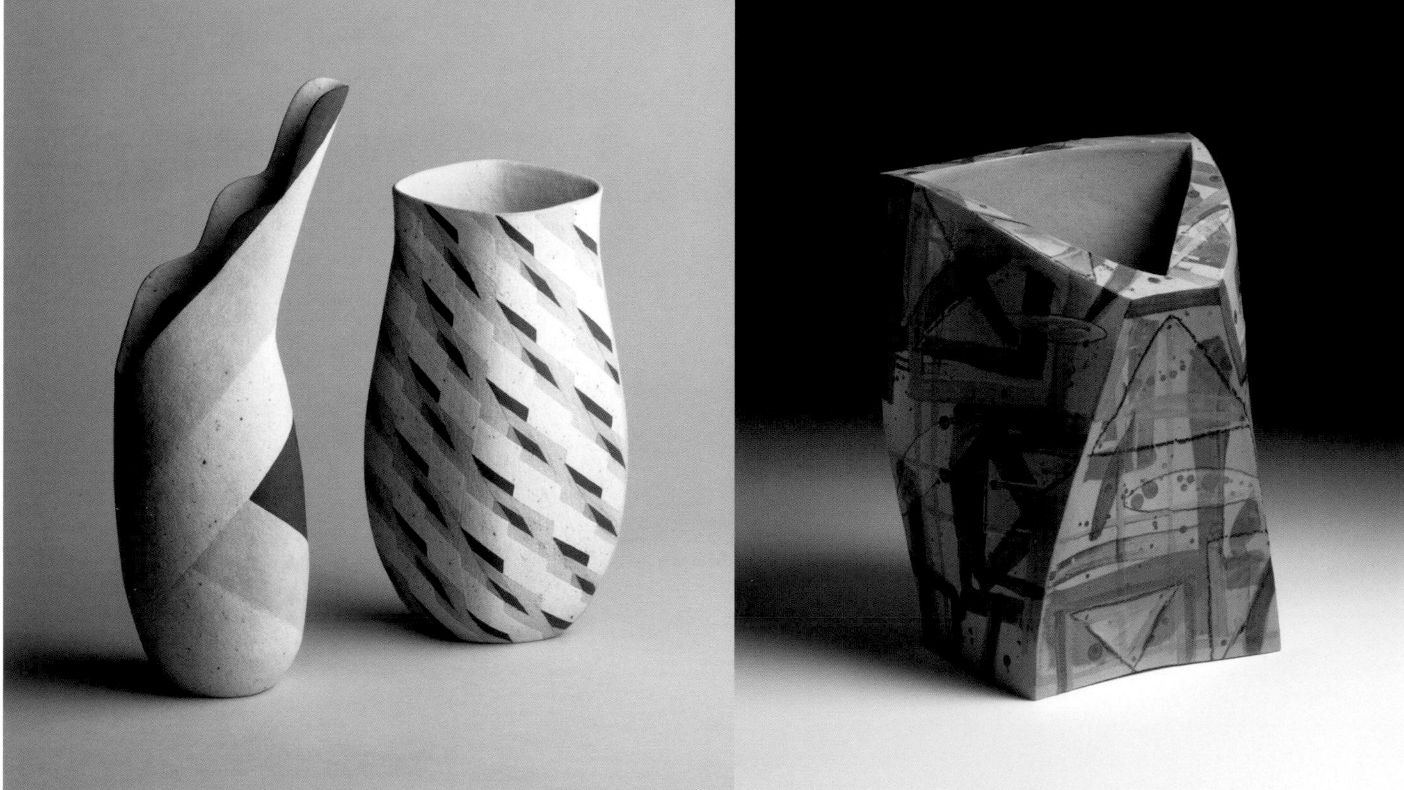

● 2.33 [OPPOSITE TOP] Two bowls, Jacqueline Poncelet, 1976 | Bone china, slip-cast and unglazed | V&A: Circ.255 & 256–1976

● 2.34 [OPPOSITE BOTTOM LEFT] *Saxophone and Piano Duo*, Elizabeth Fritsch, 1978 | Stoneware with matt glazes | V&A: C.160&A–1979

● 2.35 [OPPOSITE BOTTOM RIGHT] *Yellow Triangle*, Alison Britton, 1981 | Stoneware, slab-built with painted decoration | V&A: C.87–1981

● 2.36 [ABOVE] *Drunk Punch*, Richard Slee, 1991 | Earthenware, coiled, with coloured glazes | V&A: C.15:1-5–1992

Paolozzi and the Krazy Kat Arkive

— Anne Massey

The ephemeral and the everyday have long been a source of inspiration for the creative practitioner. But artists rarely amass the fragile traces of their inspiration, or store and archive this material for posterity. The British artist Eduardo Luigi Paolozzi (1924–2005) is an exception, and the V&A is the fortunate custodian of his important collection.

The Krazy Kat Arkive of Twentieth Century Popular Culture comprises some 20,000 files and objects, constituting the precious detritus of Paolozzi's career. Acquired in 1985 and added to by the artist in subsequent years, this unique deposit presents an important cross-section of the popular commodities consumed avidly by an enthusiast, from his boyhood in the 1930s until the pinnacle of his career in the mid-1990s.[1] Its content ranges from American science-fiction comic books, through moulded plastic gifts, to detailed images of technology and glorious Technicolor adverts for food. Just as mass-circulation magazines were passed around large circles of friends in the 1950s, so Paolozzi seems to offer us his own sample of prized possessions and images, sharing them for our delight.

As a collection of twentieth-century popular culture, the Arkive serves an important function as a wide-ranging sample of American and British ephemera that has normally been discarded rather than saved. Here we can reference back-runs of *The Beano*, *Beezer*, *Amazing Spiderman*, *Captain America*, *Picturegoer* and *Famous Monsters of Filmland*. Indeed, the Arkive contains some 4,200 comics in total: 255 titles from the United States, 157 from Britain, and a handful from Europe and Japan. In addition, Paolozzi collected tearsheets from mass-circulation magazines, which are now categorized by subject, from aircraft through films and film stars to smoking and world fairs. Objects – including toys, puzzles, games and souvenirs – also form an integral part of the collection, and many are on view in the V&A's Archive of Art and Design at Blythe Road in West Kensington, where the Arkive is installed in its own room. Plastic model kits of aeroplanes, metal cars and robots are carefully placed in the cabinets, like a scene from *Toy Story*.[2]

The Arkive also offers an insight into Paolozzi's working practices and imagination. The artist has roughly assembled a host of images and research references in a series of 10 volumes, utilizing material from commercially bought children's scrapbooks, through magazines and advertisements, to printed books. The cover of the first has a black-and-white checked background pasted with a telephone receiver, a sparkplug, a camera and an 'Air-o-Flap' by General Electric. Inside the volume we discover a visual feast of pages from *Time* magazine about Freud, juxtaposed with an image from the *Wizard of Oz* and a sticky frog. Further on, film star Lana Turner and jazz musician Duke Ellington are stuck next to a Mickey Mouse birthday card.

These images formed part of the inspiration for the Independent Group, and it was at its first meeting in 1952 that Paolozzi showed a cross-section of them, which were to be released later as a limited edition of prints entitled *BUNK* [2.40]. The Group was highly significant, as it advocated a unique approach to visual culture, which challenged accepted hierarchies and enjoyed popular art as much as high art. British artists Richard Hamilton and John McHale were stalwart members, as were architects Alison and Peter Smithson, Colin St John Wilson and James Stirling, art critic Lawrence Alloway and design writer Reyner Banham. Paolozzi's collage mentality informed the Group's understanding of the contemporary visual landscape at a time when Britain was still recovering from the ravages of the Second World War, consumer products were scarce and America was idolized by most as the land of plenty. The Group's creative output and valorization of American popular culture are partly due to Paolozzi's magpie habits and, many argue, led to the creation of Pop Art.

However, the Arkive also reveals a darker side to Paolozzi and his practice. Many images selected for inclusion in the scrapbooks feature the technology of war. Planes and battleships are frequently pasted next to images of Hollywood film stars and adverts for glamorous underwear. This visual dissonance may stem from the deaths of Paolozzi's father, grandfather and uncle in 1940 while they were on board the *Arandora Star*, being transported to Canada as enemy aliens. At the same time and for the same reason, Paolozzi was detained in Saughton prison in Edinburgh. His parents were Italian émigrés who ran a cafe in Leith, a relatively poor part of Edinburgh, so Paolozzi grew up with a distanced view of contemporary popular culture. The emotional impact of the Second World War on the sixteen-year-old surfaces in the way in which a naive image of a rainbow and village printed on the back of a scrapbook is torn and violated. The front cover is spattered with black paint, and a picture of a moth and a group of knives are clumsily pasted on top. Another scrapbook is based on a book entitled *People in China* by Ellen Thorbecke, but all the portraits have been torn out and replaced by images of Mussolini and Hitler, juxtaposed with an advert for Rice Krispies or glamour girls and aeroplanes.

Throughout his life Paolozzi continued to collect what the rest of us throw away, and reassembled them in his Arkive and in his head, resulting in a huge range of outputs, from wallpaper to mosaics, public sculptures to album covers. But all the time the small boy swapping comics in his bedroom in Leith was never far away.

● 2.37 [OPPOSITE] *Freda and Eduardo Paolozzi*, Nigel Henderson, 1949–52 | Bromide print | National Portrait Gallery

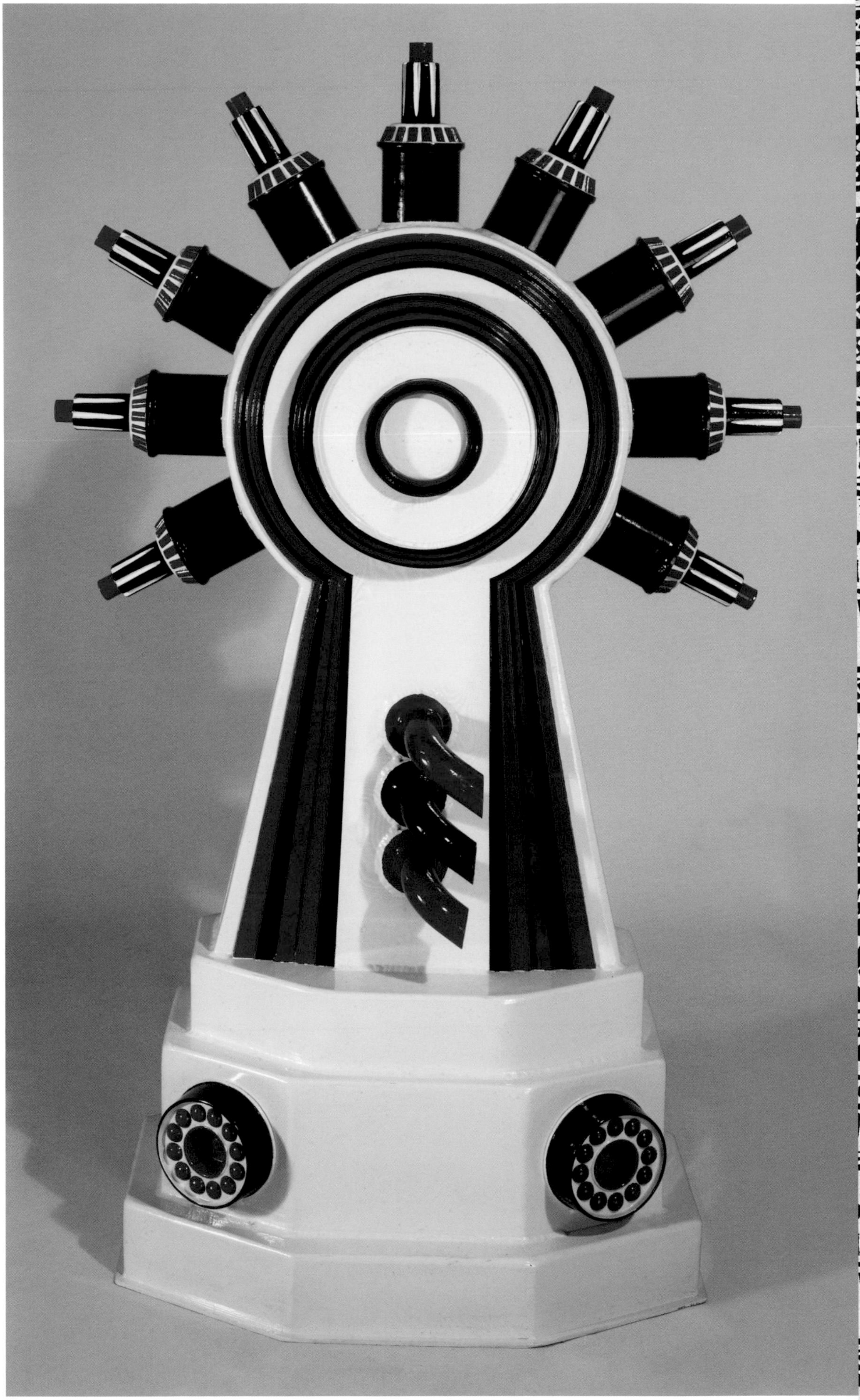

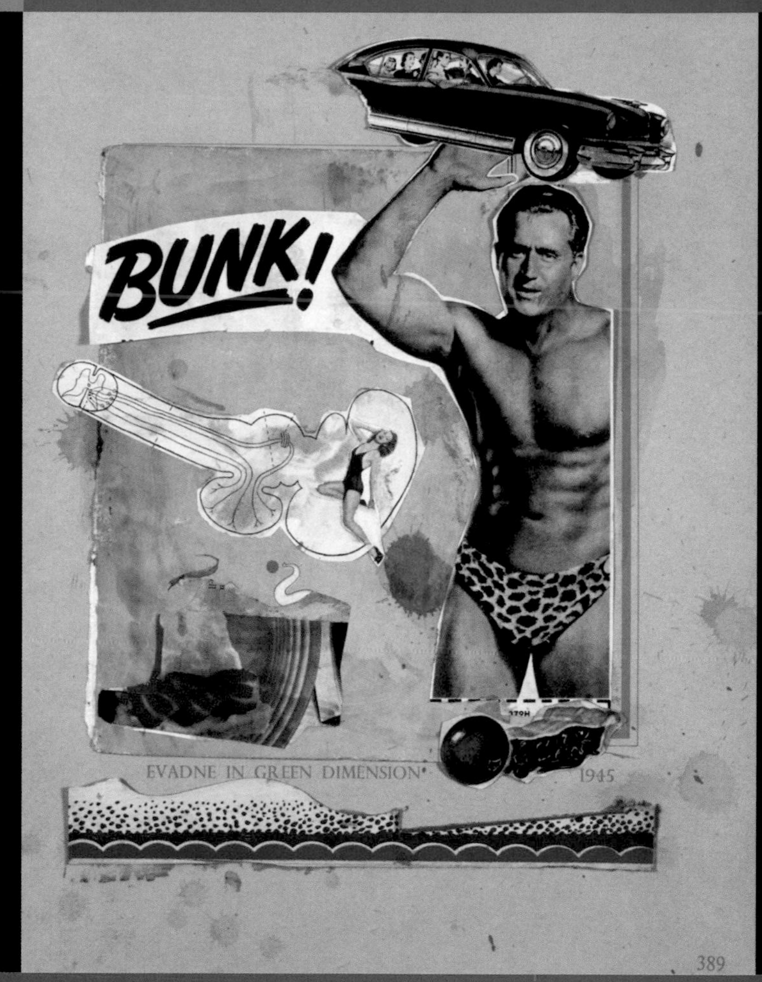

● 2.38 [OPPOSITE] *Diana as an Engine I*, Eduardo Paolozzi, 1963/6 Welded and painted aluminium | British Council ● 2.39 [CENTRE] 'Barkcloth', furnishing textile, Eduardo Paolozzi and Nigel Henderson, 1954 | Made by Hammer Prints for Penzance School of Art, screen-printed cotton | V&A: T.111–2011 ● 2.40 [TOP] *Bunk! Evadne in Green Dimension*, Eduardo Paolozzi, 1952 | Collage, paper, glue and string | V&A: Circ.708–1971 ● 2.41 [BOTTOM] Objects from the Krazy Kat Arkive of Twentieth Century Popular Culture | AAD: 1985/3

The RCA

— Zandra Rhodes

I went to the Royal College of Art (RCA) in 1960. It had been my ambition ever since going to Medway College of Art and studying printed textiles under Barbara Brown. She had carefully tutored me and another textile student, David Green. She ruled with a rod of iron, setting us wonderful projects. Our lives were organized with the sole purpose of getting into 'The College'.

The 'Royal', as it was then called, had become the most prestigious wholly postgraduate art college in the world. This was initially due to Sir Robin Darwin, who had taken over in 1948 after the war and put together an amazing team. He had been in the Camouflage Corps, together with some of the others he recruited. Not only did he put together the best painters and sculptors, but also the best tutors in ceramics, furniture, textiles and jewellery. Misha Black headed the new School of Industrial Design and Sir Hugh Casson the Interior Design School. The Textile School was headed by Roger Nicholson, with Margaret Leischner (from the Bauhaus). It already had some of the textile greats among its alumni, including Lucienne Day, whose revolutionary 'Calyx' textile for Heal & Son was a key image for the Festival of Britain; and Pat Albeck, who had created memorable textiles for Horrockses and John Lewis. Darwin also founded the Fashion School headed by Madge Garland (Lady Ashton). Her husband was one of the curators of the V&A, and their model was Parsons School of Design in New York. By the time I entered the Royal College, its fashion courses led the world.

To me, the RCA was the most overwhelming of places. At that time I was a little replica of Barbara Brown, dressed in purple Victoriana style with my black hair parted in the middle, sporting black jet jewellery and a paint-covered smock with purple-dyed lace around its hem. There were six of us in the printed-textile department; most made their subsequent mark in design. Julie Hodges went on to do all of the dramatic Biba imagery, especially its notable wallpaper, and Alex MacIntyre is still one of the foremost authorities on re-creating ancient fabrics in the most accurate detail.

● 2.42 [OPPOSITE] Oxana and Myroslava Prystay wearing dresses from the 'Knitted Circle' collection, Zandra Rhodes, 1969
Photograph by David Bailey, published in *Vogue*, December 1969

In my first term the Textile School was still in the galleries of the old Commonwealth Institute, and to get to it we went through wonderful Victorian dioramas of the wheat fields of Winnipeg, which lit up if we pressed the buttons (around this time I met Natalie Gibson, who had just left the college and has since built up the textile courses at St Martins [now Central St Martins] and developed her own highly colourful work). The school soon moved to the brand-new Cadbury Brown building opposite the Royal Albert Hall and the Albert Memorial, and I was a part of the first group of students to work there! Beyond textiles, the Royal College at this time was an inspirational mix of different talents. The pop movement was in full swing, with RCA students and alumni – including David Hockney, Derek Boshier, Peter Blake and Allen Jones – at its forefront. In the Sculpture School, Roland Piché was creating his living Bacon-like forms. Etchers like Norman Ackroyd (now a famed Royal Academician), photographers including Steve Hiett and Roy Giles, and of course fashion-design students Janice Wainwright and Ossie Clark all contributed to the buzz. It was very exciting!

These were the formative years of my own design style. I went to the RCA as a designer of furnishing textiles, wallpapers and carpets, and ended up becoming a designer of dress fabrics. I was influenced by the heady college mix of the painter David Hockney, with his 'Medalled Generals', the Pop Art movement and what was going on in the streets around London, with Mary Quant and Carnaby Street. My textile tutors put me in direct contact with the Fashion School, now under Janey Ironside and located in the same building. Janey transformed the school from being a part of the traditional fashion establishment, and moved it into the free, unconventional era of the Swinging Sixties. Grace Coddington (now with American *Vogue*) was the top catwalk model at the end-of-term show. The extremely glamorous fashion students I came into contact with were an inspiration. Also during this time the renowned furnishing fabric company of Heal's visited the Textile School and purchased my print 'Medals'. This was bright, madly colourful, but elegant: a sophisticated, yet childlike print design, and Heal's called it 'Top Brass'.

The Royal College gave me belief in myself. Together with its eclectic mix of staff and students, I was exposed to the best, and when amazing people came to London we were introduced to them. An appointment was made by the Textile School for me to show Emilio Pucci my folder when he was appearing at the Woollands store (at that time the most imaginative shop in London). There were also lectures in the V&A lecture theatre by Buckminster Fuller and others. The tutor Mary Oliver personally took me to Manchester to the textile-buying houses to sell my designs. Needless to say, they found them too extreme! When this did not work, the encouraging staff guided me to go directly to the hottest young designers of Swinging Sixties' Carnaby Street: Foale & Tuffin (the ex-RCA fashion students Marion Foale and Sally Tuffin).

The hands-on textile-printing experience that I had gained at the RCA, coupled with the caring advice from my tutors, guided me to become a 'converter' (someone who takes the original paper textile design and converts it to the printed textile product). In that way I no longer had to sell my designs in paper form, but delivered them as finished fabric to the designers themselves, thus cutting out the middle man. In the early 1960s this was a totally new approach (but I had stumbled on it by accident). It enabled my printed textile work to reach the shops as fashion in a very direct way. This practical experience in converting led me to set up my own textile studio with a print table in Porchester Road, Bayswater. I produced bright prints for Foale & Tuffin for five seasons, until my ideas became too strongly individual. I began to realize that my characterful designs did not easily lend themselves to the dress designs of others. I had always admired Pucci and Sonia Delaunay because their work and the resulting garments were textile-driven. Although I had not had official garment training, this led me to realize that the way forward for me was to create the print and the garment: Eureka! So in 1969 I put together my first dress collection.

For me, the Royal College represented growing up. The staff did not tell you what to do; they guided you. All of them were amazing achievers in their own right. Bernard Nevill, Dikky Chopin, Humphrey Spender and John Drummond: I thank them all.

● 2.43 [ABOVE] RCA students, John Hedgecoe, *c.*1968 | Published in *ARK*, the student magazine of the RCA, issue 41 ● 2.44 [BELOW] 'Diaghilev', dress fabric, Bernard Nevill, 1970 | Manufactured by Liberty, printed silk twill ● 2.45 [OPPOSITE] 'Gala', furnishing fabric, Zandra Rhodes, 1964 | Manufactured by Heal & Son Ltd, screen-printed cotton | V&A: Circ.746–1964

6 Staging Space: Design for Performance 1958–89

— Kate Dorney

A major shift in the role and perception of design and designers in British performance took place between the 1950s and 1980s: notably the growing influence of stage design courses, industry recognition (in the form of awards and associations) and the expansion of the discipline in theory and practice. A key factor in this was the introduction of state subsidy: via local authority grants to theatre design students; the donation of land and capital for new theatre spaces; and through the work of the Arts Council of Great Britain. As well as subsidizing theatre companies, the Arts Council was responsible for providing funds to build new theatres, refurbish existing venues and convert others. It also created a bursary scheme enabling newly qualified designers to work alongside established ones in regional repertory theatre. And, finally, the Arts Council purchased designs for exhibition purposes and, in doing so, created a market for theatre designers's work.[1]

The Second World War revolutionized British theatre practice: it gave professionals experience of touring non-theatre venues with minimal sets, provided the catalyst for introducing state subsidy for the arts and exposed the profession to European practice. War damage to theatres and urban centres led to a rolling programme of rebuilding, in which a new, purpose-built theatre was a badge of civic pride. Wartime research into the development of plastics and metals also provided a new range of materials for designers and architects to work with. Britain's existing theatrical stock was mostly Victorian and Edwardian with cramped foyers and large auditoria in which the audience was arranged in tiers (according to seat price) and faced a proscenium arch through which they watched the action on stage. The production style for this kind of theatre was necessarily one in which the actors faced forward, declaimed their lines and telegraphed their emotions in order to be seen and heard at the furthest points in the house. Performance design was largely picturesque: painted canvas backdrops and flats showing solidly upper-middle- and upper-class interiors or exotic locations to provide situation and decoration, but always striving for verisimilitude, so that things were depicted rather than suggested. There were exceptions to this style, particularly in university and experimental arts theatres, but the dominant mode was one in which the audience passively observed the actors from a distance.

This changed with the advent of war and the creation of the Entertainments National Service Association (ENSA), which provided professional and amateur entertainment for the armed forces, and the Council for the Encouragement of Music and Arts (CEMA). CEMA sent professional performers to theatre-less areas of the country to keep up the morale of local residents and provide work for the vast numbers of actors and theatre workers, who would otherwise be unemployed because of the bomb damage to theatres. It famously took Shakespeare and ballet to Welsh mining villages and other remote areas, setting up and performing in village halls, schools and factories. In doing so, it confirmed what amateur groups and the likes of Joan Littlewood's Theatre Workshop already knew: that there was an appetite for live performance that could transcend plush seats, velvet curtains and painted scenery.[2]

Exposing the general public to the live arts remained a key part of the council's mission after the war, with CEMA becoming the Arts Council of Great Britain in 1946. There was, however, a vast ideological gap between the agendas of the two organizations. CEMA believed that people could enjoy the arts by participating in them as well as by consuming them, and thus funded choirs, amateur painters, actors and writers alongside professionals. The Arts Council, particularly the drama department, was less convinced, and preferred the idea of providing a high-quality product for general consumption.

The most significant clash of ideals occurred over the Festival of Britain, described by Director General Gerald Barry as 'the people's show [...] not organized arbitrarily for them to enjoy, but put on largely by them'.[3] The Drama Department disagreed and rejected proposals for scores of innovative amateur events while searching for an elusive production that could deliver star quality. As a result, the performance attractions at the Festival on the South Bank were the individual elements – the exhibition; the fair; the fireworks; the Thames tightrope walker; the huskies in the Polar Theatre; the floodlit Festival site itself floating supernaturally on the river – and the people who interacted with them. Traditional theatre was upstaged by this interactive spectacle and, in this context, the foundation stone for the National Theatre, finally laid after a century-long campaign, looked like a tombstone: inert and flat in a world of light, colour and active enjoyment. It was another quarter of a century before traditional theatre matched this achievement with the opening of Denys Lasdun's National Theatre complex on the South Bank, fulfilling his vision for a building that functioned as a 'fourth theatre' (in addition to the three auditoriums within it) and in which 'the decorations will be people, carpet, concrete and light' [2.46].[4]

● 2.46 [ABOVE] National Theatre, Denys Lasdun, 1976

MAKING SPACE

Prior to 1950 entertainment was expensive to provide because Entertainment Tax ('temporarily' introduced in 1917 and persisting until 1950) took 10 per cent of gross profits. That changed with the 'Provision of Entertainments' (Clause 132) of the Local Government Act 1948 and the establishment of the Arts Council's 'Housing the Arts' scheme. Clause 132 encouraged councils to contribute to, or commission, theatres, dance and concert halls as well as arrange festivals and outdoor performances in their parks and open spaces. It empowered them to spend up to sixpence in the pound of their earnings from rates on providing 'entertainment', and crucially, also allowed them to borrow money to achieve these ends. In 1958 Harold Macmillan, then Chancellor of the Exchequer, commissioned the Arts Council to undertake the first-ever survey of existing entertainment venues and make recommendations for the future. The resulting report, published in two volumes in 1959 and 1961, recommended immediate government investment to improve existing stock (mostly inadequate and/or dilapidated) and to create new buildings. As a consequence the Arts Council established the Housing the Arts Scheme, through which they dispensed capital grants and encouragement to local authorities and other promoters to build or refurbish venues. Combined with Clause 132, this provided a significant incentive to build new theatre spaces and entertainment venues, and a building boom followed.

The Belgrade Theatre, Coventry (1958), although conceived too early to take advantage of the Housing the Arts Scheme, directly benefited from Clause 132. The first civic producing theatre to be built in Britain since the 1930s, it is a typical product of its time, reflecting the belief that the arts are integral to community living and civic pride (the building even included flats for theatre workers). It was built as part of the Coventry city-centre regeneration programme masterminded by Arthur Ling (1919–95) on land razed by the Luftwaffe. The theatre (named for the donation of beech wood from Belgrade that was used to line the auditorium) became a landmark in the new city centre, with its imposing glazed double-height foyer decorated by Arts Council commissions to Martin Froy (mosaics) and Bernard Schottlander (chandeliers). The latter's commission was part of the City Council's commitment to peace and reconciliation, which saw it commission a number of German artists to create public artworks for the city. The Belgrade embraced the new architectural style externally and in terms of its front-of-house space (in new builds the crush-bars of older theatres were replaced by spacious foyers with bars and cafés designed for patrons to use all day), but the auditorium was more traditional with a proscenium arch and tiered seating. In this respect it is atypical among municipal builds of the period, which tended to favour a more flexible space with an open stage (no proscenium) and moveable seats, which made venues more multi-purpose. The Belgrade came to represent post-war regeneration in Britain generally, and in the theatre industry in particular. It also contains the seeds of the post-war boom in theatre-building and scenography: the combination of local-government subsidy, Arts Council support and the marriage between teaching and practice (Froy taught at the Slade and Schottlander at St Martins).

More radical re-evaluations of the theatre space were taking place elsewhere in Britain, inspired by Tyrone Guthrie and Tanya Moiseiwitsch's experiments in thrust staging at Stratford, Ontario (1953), and the Guthrie Theater, Minneapolis (1963). The thrust stage reconfigured the actor–audience relationship by removing the proscenium and thrusting the stage out into the auditorium, thereby bringing the audience closer to the performers. Guthrie and Moiseiwitsch's experiment tried to re-create the conditions of the Shakespearean theatre, combining minimalist staging with immediacy. In an egalitarian gesture typical of the times, they also rejected tiered seating and placed the audience in a single sweep.

Their example inspired Bernard Miles, the actor, director and founder of the Mermaid Theatre, Blackfriars (1959), and Leslie Evershed-Martin, a local optician who founded Chichester Festival Theatre (1962). Miles and Martin raised the money to build their respective theatres via public subscription and commissioned open stages. The work done in these theatres on the plays of Shakespeare and his contemporaries and modern writers fed into the repertoire of the nascent National Theatre (NT) company. In his first year as Artistic Director at Chichester, Laurence Olivier was finally confirmed as Director of the NT and made no secret of his desire to work with a permanent company on a thrust stage, while the design of the NT's new home on the South Bank was still being debated.

Experimental staging was not solely the preserve of newly built theatres. In 1956 the Royal Court Theatre in Sloane Square, London (built in 1888), had found fame with its production of *Look Back in Anger*. Widely perceived as the first 'kitchen-sink' play, its set was a conventional representational one, albeit representing an unfamiliar environment, and by no means being typical of the Royal Court's design style. In 1958 the designer Jocelyn Herbert stripped the covers from its proscenium arch and exposed the lighting rig and back wall of the theatre. This allowed designers 'the luxury of designing a lighting grid to suit each play, i.e., the grid to echo the contours of the set … to light an acting area leaving darkness all around thus creating a surround out of light'.[5] Herbert cited Brecht:

> As a very large influence on all of us – my generation – visually and in general staging …the idea that you didn't have to hide anything, didn't pretend you were somewhere you weren't, and yet you created a visual image that was interesting and exciting, evocative of something.[6]

Across London in the East End, Joan Littlewood's Theatre Workshop was injecting new life into the equally Victorian Theatre Royal, Stratford East (1884). Littlewood relied on John Bury (fresh from the Fleet Air Arm and with no training in design) as her designer, lighting designer, rigger and carpenter, and on Sean Kenny (trained as an architect) to provide cheap and compelling sets. Limited by the grandeur of the proscenium, Bury and Kenny relied on rostra and simple three-dimensional constructions combined with lighting to produce spare sculptural forms. Within a decade, stage design shifted from a two-dimensional painted space to a three-dimensional one. Illusion gave way to real materials as Bury, Herbert and others experimented with new materials such as metal, plastic and fibreglass, creating a new orthodoxy. The next decade would see these changes ripple out from small spaces into mainstream practices, as these designers took their work to the new large subsidized companies: the Royal Shakespeare Company (RSC) and the National Theatre.

● 2.47 [OPPOSITE] Costume for Vendice in *The Revenger's Tragedy* by Cyril Tourneur, Christopher Morley, 1966 | Made for the Royal Shakespeare Company, black fabric with applied white and silver resins and glitter | V&A: S.2083-B–1986

THE ROYAL SHAKESPEARE COMPANY AND THE NATIONAL THEATRE

In 1960 Peter Hall became Director of the privately funded Shakespeare Memorial Theatre. By 1961 he had rebranded it as the RSC, expanded the operation to London and created a permanent company that combined leading lights of the West End stage with up-and-coming talent. By 1962 he had secured Arts Council funding and had transformed a major private enterprise into a public one.

The National Theatre had a more protracted birth, having been a gleam in the eye of philanthropists and theatre professionals since 1848, and having been proposed at various sites across London, but with neither a backer nor a home. By 1942 London County Council (LCC) had agreed to provide a site on the South Bank of the Thames, and Lutyens & Massey had produced a design for it. In 1946 a committee was established to oversee the promotion and building of the theatre, and on Lutyens's death it appointed a new architect, Brian O'Rorke. In 1949 the National Theatre Act was passed, in which the government pledged £1 million to the cost of building the theatre, albeit at the Chancellor's discretion. In 1951 the foundation stone was laid next to the newly built Festival Hall (paid for by the LCC, via Clause 132 of the Local Government Act); 15 years and many negotiations later, the government released its contribution to the project and increased it in line with inflation. During that time the site moved up and down the South Bank, reaching its final location in 1967, four years after Denys Lasdun replaced O'Rorke as the appointed architect.

Building work began in 1966, with an estimated completion date of 1972. In reality, industrial disputes and the challenges of building and installing state-of-the-art stage machinery, lighting and flying systems delayed the opening of the theatre until 1976. Hall's fleetness of foot in establishing the RSC as a state-funded theatre dedicated to the work of Shakespeare and his contemporaries was a major blow to the plans for the National Theatre, but would also turn out to be a valuable lesson in how to create a presence and an identity.

Heavily influenced by European subsidized companies, such as the Théâtre National Populaire and Brecht's Berliner Ensemble, Hall was keen to develop a house style of acting and presentation for his company. From the beginning he worked with established and innovative designers, including Lesley Hurry, Ralph Koltai (who was teaching theatre design at the Central School, now Central St Martins), Sean Kenny, Abd'elkader Farrah (the first designer in residence under Hall's aegis) and John Bury. In 1963, a year after the RSC was created, it produced *The Crucial Years*, a pamphlet outlining the achievements of the company to date and its vision for the future. There was a critical assessment of the work, manifestos from Hall,

Peter Brook and Michel St Denis (RSC Associate Directors) and a discussion of the inadequacy of subsidy between the NT and RSC by chairman Fordham Flower. It is clear from this document that the RSC aesthetic was already easily identifiable: 'light, air, space, the minimum of "scenery". Heavy, metallically gleaming objects are hung or planted in front of white screens, buff netting, or an uncluttered cyclorama. Furniture and clothes look lived-with, and texture is more sought after than colour.'[7]

This style is typified by *The Wars of the Roses* (1964), the amalgamation of *Henry VI Parts 1–3* and *Richard III*, adapted and directed by Hall, John Barton and Clifford Williams and designed by Bury [2.48]. Between them, Hall and Bury established an abstract visual style, described by the latter as 'unconventional realism', which focused on texture and form rather than the picturesque, heraldic Shakespearean tradition.[8] Inspired by a visit to the armoury of Warwick Castle, Hall envisaged a world of steel, and Bury a court that would change over time, but was recognizably the same throughout the three plays. To this end he created a set built on a huge scale and dominated by moveable walls of overlapping steel shapes (suggesting a mass of shields), that could shrink or enlarge the acting area or be swung off altogether for the epic battle scenes. To create the right texture for the walls and floor he experimented with thin sheets of iron and steel treated with chemicals. Dissatisfied with the 'romantic' spots of rust this produced, he drew on Ralph Koltai's experiments in tarnishing copper with sulphides and eventually bathed quantities of steel in an acid bath to create the walls and floors, then covered them in wire mesh. This created the steel world that he and Hall desired, but was rather less popular with the actors, who had to work on its treacherous and uncomfortable surface (the stage was steeply raked as well as highly textured). As one actor noted, 'you laid very carefully when you died'.[9] Bury lit the production himself, which was unusual at Stratford, but something he had become accustomed to on the road with the Theatre Workshop. Working on the principle that 'real materials need real light', he primarily used white lighting, which revealed the texture of the materials and illuminated the actors rather than spotlighting them.[10]

While Bury used traditional materials to achieve his sets, the techniques for achieving texture on the costumes relied on plastics. Ann Curtis, a ladies' cutter from the wardrobe department, worked alongside Bury to persuade the wardrobe department (which, like the paint shop, was used to a fine-art tradition) that the production required clothes rather than costumes. Mindful of Hall's dictum that 'Too rigid adherence to historical accuracy tends to create stuffed dummies', she designed garments 'worn enough to suggest the necessary period connotations; contemporary enough to free bodies of the actors and the minds of the audience'.[11] They conformed to a basic historical shape, with exaggerated, broad shoulders to suggest strength and power, but were made from cheap and robust fabric, principally calico, floor-cloth and leatherized suede cloth. Bury and Curtis wanted the people to be 'jewels in a metallic setting' and worked with the traditional colours of the rival houses to achieve this.[12] To give the costumes texture and metallic sheen, Bury and his team developed a liquid latex, which they called 'gunk' [2.47], coated the costumes with it and then threw a mixture of glue crystals, marble chippings, sand and gravel on the still-wet costume. When the fabric was shaken to remove the excess grit, impressions were left in the latex, giving the clothes a metallic lustre under the stage lights. Bury set up a production line of local people and art students from the Slade to treat the hundreds of costumes that were needed, while others (and members of the acting company) knitted thick butcher's string into long strips, which were then covered with silver lacquer, beaten flat and painted with a fibreglass compound. Although the principles of using cheap materials to create effects were not new (pre-war designers like Motley and Oliver Messel knew the value of painting canvas and using sweet wrappers for decoration), the intention was. Whereas Motley, Messel and their contemporaries had used these techniques to simulate reality, Koltai, Bury and others were using them to create a more abstract stage world. Once gunked, many of the costumes had to be broken down with paint in order to reflect Bury's concept that:

> the costumes corroded with the years. The once proud red rose of Lancaster became as a rusty scale on the soldiers' coats; the milk-white rose of York was no more than a pale blush on the tarnished steel of the Yorkist insurrection. Colour drained and drained from the stage until, among the drying patches of scarlet blood, the black night of England settled on the leather costumes of Richard's thugs.[13]

The experiments, textual and textural, paid off and the result was an era – and company-defining production, which established the RSC brand and a reputation for innovation. For Pamela Howard, who went on to run the Theatre Design course at Central St Martins, 'it was a definite landmark. And it did shock. Nobody expected raw materials in the theatre, it was the end of the illusionist theatre.'[14] Christopher Baugh, scenographer and theatre historian, sums up the impact of the work on his generation: 'as a theatre design student in 1966 my ambition was to design a setting that didn't use any paint but only used real materials'.[15]

Hall was certain that a clear style was essential to the company's success: '[it] started with a texture, a style of speaking, of presentation, a style of looking, which was all one'.[16] This attention to house style also extended to the RSC's marketing. Head of Press John Goodwin designed a distinctive RSC logo incorporating the Swan of Avon, and ensured consistent use of logo, graphics and typefaces across the company's proliferating range of products. Goodwin is widely credited as the pioneer of the modern theatre programme and, encouraged by Michael Kustow, who was heavily influenced by his time at the Théâtre National Populaire, produced programmes packed with information for eager students and actors, as well as free cast lists.[17] As the playwright Anthony Smith, who succeeded Kustow as programme producer, described it, the RSC made 'a new kind of programme which contained real, serious background on whatever play it was you were going to see'.[18]

The first of these new-style programmes was for *The Wars of the Roses*, containing an essay from Peter Hall about the theme of the plays, notes from John Bury summarizing the design scheme, a family tree and, in later reprints, letters from the public under the heading 'For and Against These New Programmes'. One, from John Davenport, a writer for *Queen* magazine, wrote: 'These programme notes are, quite frankly intolerable. I, for one, am not prepared to be lectured into insensibility by the comparatively illiterate'. He was in a minority.[19] At Kustow's instigation, the company also set up the RSC club, offering special rates, events and a free magazine, *Flourish*, providing interviews with the company, extracts from rehearsal and tour diaries (along with photographs), debates about contemporary issues such as censorship, and responses from readers. As Kustow announced in the first issue, the aim was to 'build a new relationship between our company's work and the public [...] it aims to be a forum and a meeting place'.[20] Through these initiatives the RSC became the leading purveyor of classical and modern drama, and the club opened with 12,637 members and exceeded 20,000 in the six months that followed. The club and magazine completed the feel of the RSC as a university. It had a faculty of directors, designers and performers, with Hall at its head, and an eager student body watching its shows in London and Stratford and following the company's work through *Flourish.*

When Hall departed from the company in 1968, he left it with a coherent identity and an identifiable house style. His success was both a blessing and a curse for the NT, for on the one hand it made it harder for the NT to establish itself as *the* national company; on the other, it provided a clear blueprint for success in terms of design and marketing. The NT ran a competition to find a designer to create a coherent visual identity for its print and promotional material, and appointed Ken Briggs who worked directly with Olivier and his Literary Manager, Kenneth Tynan. Briggs designed everything from the first seasons at the Old Vic through to the early 1970s (including the poster for *Equus*), and produced a clear and distinct graphic style that has changed very little over the years [2.56]. Olivier was careful to gather fresh talent around him, selecting associates from the new wave of theatre, such as the directors John Dexter and Bill Gaskill and actors from across the spectrum. He was hampered by his own success and institutionalization, as well as the expectations of the government, when it came to conceptualizing what a national theatre might be. The RSC had appropriated the national playwright and the Royal Court had dibs on the new writers, leaving Olivier with the 'best of world drama' as his speciality.

● 2.48 [BELOW] *Henry VI*, from *The Wars of the Roses* cycle, Royal Shakespeare Company, 1964

● 2.49 [LEFT] *The Royal Hunt of the Sun* by Peter Shaffer, designed by Michael Annals for the National Theatre Company, 1964
● 2.50 [RIGHT] Technical drawing for *The Royal Hunt of the Sun* by Peter Shaffer, Michael Annals, 1965 | Originally designed for the National Theatre Company, 1964, dyeline print | V&A: S.287–1991

In fact, the NT under Olivier produced a very balanced programme, including restoration comedy, Shakespeare, Feydeau and Strindberg, alongside Stoppard's debut, *Rosencrantz and Guildenstern Are Dead* (1967), and the extraordinary plays of Peter Shaffer, *The Royal Hunt of the Sun* (1964) and *Equus* (1973). Directed by John Dexter and designed by Michael Annals, *The Royal Hunt of the Sun* was a piece of total theatre, in which mime, movement and scenography were as important as the text. The play charted the invasion of Peru by Spanish conquistadors and featured memorable scenes, such as the Spaniards miming climbing the Andes, the 'rape of the sun' when the conquistadors stripped all the gold from it, leaving a vast black void, and the mime of the Great Massacre, which culminated in 'a vast bloodstained cloth billowing out over the stage'.[21] Like *The Wars of the Roses*, the design was sparse and sculptural, with the set dominated by a single object, in this case a vast golden sun (signifying the Inca empire and religion) made from an aluminium circle with hinged petals to which gold covers (constructed from bottle tops beaten flat) were fastened with magnets [2.49, 2.50].

A single sculptural image was also the key for Ralph Koltai's set for the all-male *As You Like It* staged at the Old Vic in 1967. Koltai, who had been a design associate at the RSC, and Head of Theatre Design at the Central School, took as his starting point 'the artificiality of the basic idea – an all male cast for no logical reason, thereby turning the forest of Arden into dream', which then released him from the demands of producing a realistic forest.[22] Koltai's Arden was represented by a chandelier-like structure of pierced metal panels interleaved with Perspex rods suspended above a reflective white floor [2.52, 2.53].

1973 also saw the first production of Shaffer's new play *Equus*, about a teenage boy who has invented a religion based on worshipping horses, and his relationship with the psychiatrist who treats him. It was directed by Dexter and designed by John Napier, who had trained with Koltai after studying at the Slade. Napier set the action in a lighted ring, which was part-showground and part-gladiatorial arena [2.54]. With the audience seated onstage, they became complicit in the voyeurism of Dysart (the psychiatrist), but were also close enough to appreciate the movement training of Claude Chagrin (the long-term choreographer at the National, also responsible for *The Royal Hunt of the Sun*), which – along with Napier's sculpted silver horse heads and feet – transformed actors into animals [2.55].

Equus was just one of the shows that had been conceived for the new theatre and had to make do with the Old Vic as project-creep and design by committee took their toll on the building process. When Hall arrived at the NT as co-director at the end of 1973, completion was delayed until 1975, largely due to the complex technical demands of the new auditoria and the stage mechanics commissioned for them. Olivier had been on the building committee for the NT since the 1950s, and along the way many distinguished practitioners had joined and fed into the process that resulted in the three auditoria, among them Devine, St Denis, Hall, Herbert, Kenny, Moiseiwitsch and lighting designer Richard Pilbrow, who was later employed by the NT to commission and oversee the lighting and stage mechanics. Olivier left at the end of 1973, exhausted by the continual pressure of the role, and Hall moved the company into the new complex literally stage by stage, as the builders relinquished the completed sections of the building.

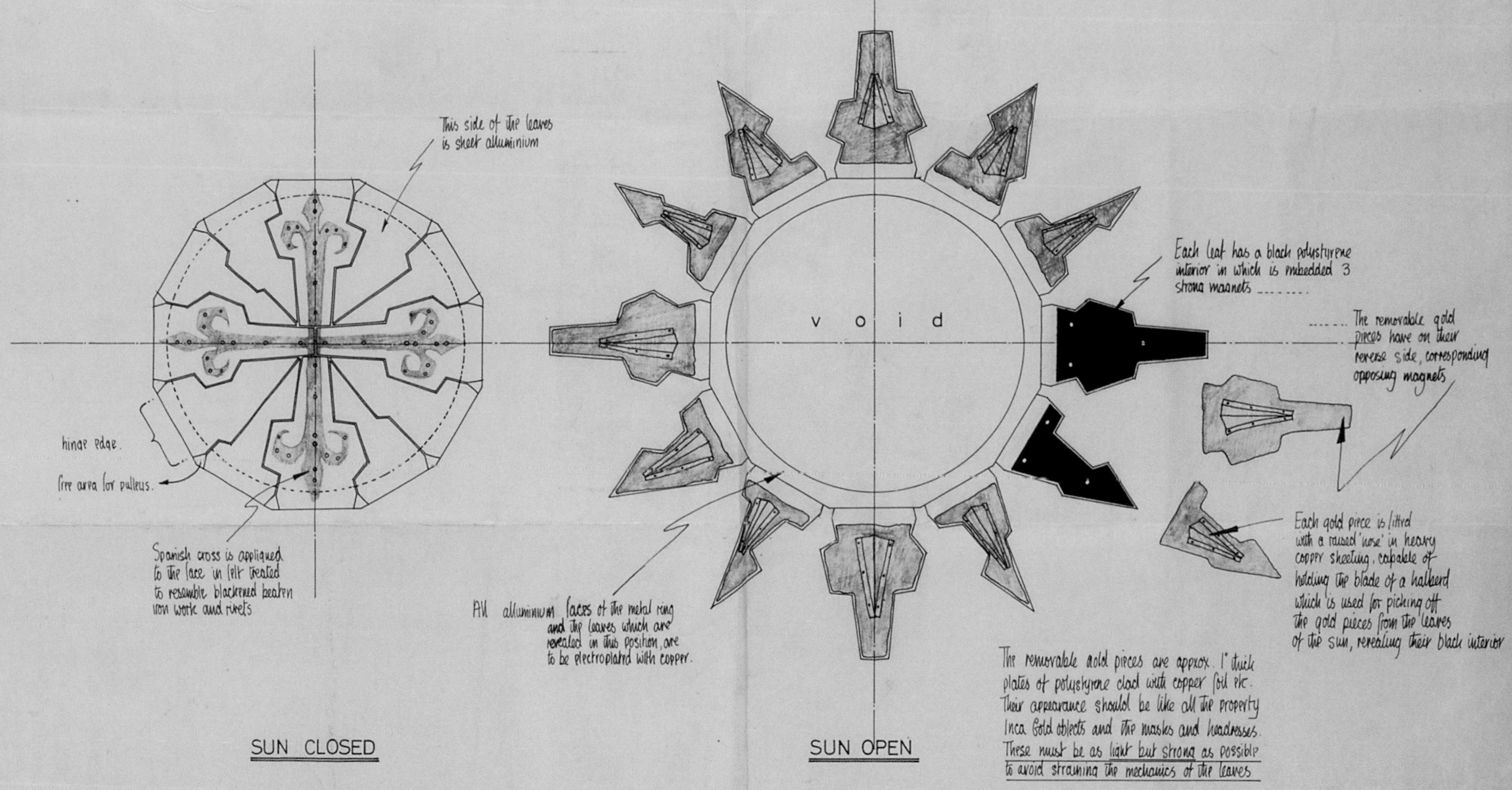

principle

The 'Sun' has three positions during the action of the play.

1) Sun closed showing the Spanish cross.
   The leaves are mechanically opened by a system of leves and pulleys concealed in the basic ring. to form position ....
2) Sun open with gold pieces intact.
   These are then plucked off one by one, by actors standing on the floor of the sun's interior by means of halberds, to form ....
3) Sun open with all gold pieces removed leaving the sun de-nuded symbolising the collapse of the Empire.

N.B. special note

This drawing represents to scale ½" = 1'0" the basic principle only. For the London production the National Theatre commissioned the services of a consultant mechanic to design its workings. The copyright of these drawings and their possesion are rested with the National Theatre and the use of them must be negociated with its production department.

'THE ROYAL HUNT OF THE SUN' U.S.A. THE SUN scale $\frac{1}{2}''=1'\ 0''$

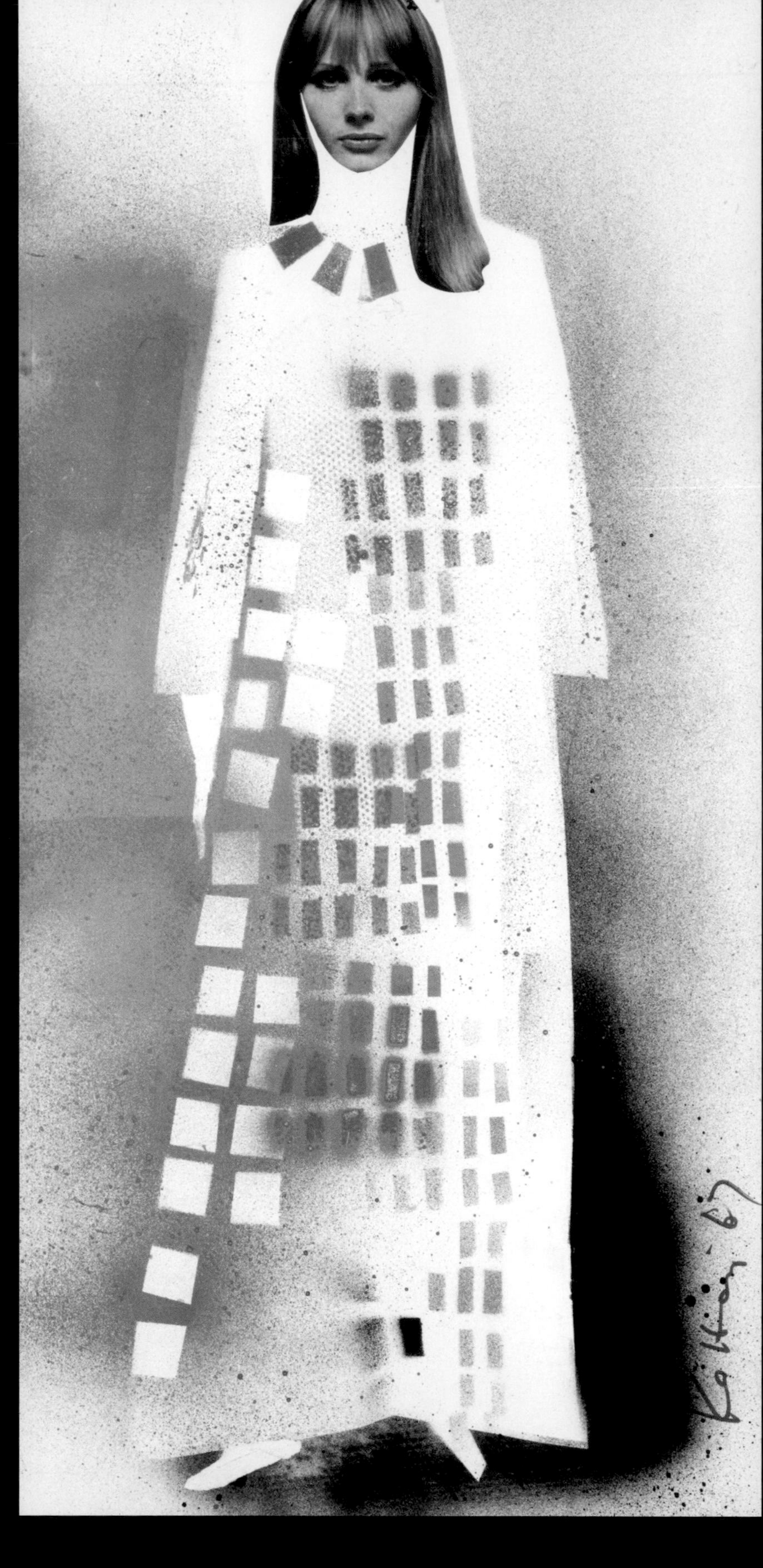

● 2.51 [OPPOSITE] Costume design for Rosalind in *As You Like It* by William Shakespeare, Ralph Koltai, 1967 Designed for the National Theatre Company, paint and collage on paper | V&A: S.1927–1986 ● 2.52 [LEFT] *As You Like It* by William Shakespeare, designed by Ralph Koltai for the National Theatre Company, 1967 ● 2.53 [BELOW] Set model for *As You Like It* by William Shakespeare, Ralph Koltai, 1967 | Designed for the National Theatre Company, Perspex, acetate, paint, plastic and wood | V&A: S.474–1980

When the NT finally opened in 1976 it combined under one roof the three most popular stage shapes: the open stage of the Olivier, the proscenium of the Lyttleton, plus the Cottesloe, the smallest auditorium whose default configuration is that of a Georgian playhouse (stage at the narrow end of a rectangle with the audience in front of the stage and ranged around the sides at the upper levels) engendering intimacy. Its size and flexibility (the floor and seating can be changed to create theatre-in-the round, traverse, promenade, thrust or a totally bare space) made it the natural home for experimental work. Having listened to the Building Committee debate the merits of the open stage, Lasdun finally modelled the Olivier on the open-air theatre at Epidaurus, designing an open stage with the audience ranged around it in a fan shape [2.60]. The audience and actors are then in one room and sharing the action between them – what Lasdun described as 'having a conversation'.

The Olivier combines a shallow thrust stage with a space stage behind it, so it can be used to support a full scenic environment or a bare stage. It also has a five-storey drum-revolve extending eight metres under the stage, designed to achieve dramatic effects and fluid set changes (taking one set down and bringing another up at the touch of a button), as well as operating as a basic revolve. It was the revolve and the spotline flying system that caused many of the delays to the building, as the systems required extensive testing and fine-tuning. For many years neither worked properly, and they became the butt of many jokes in the profession and in the media as a whole, but once the difficulties were resolved, the Olivier proved itself capable of anything and everything, from Greek drama to musicals and physical theatre.

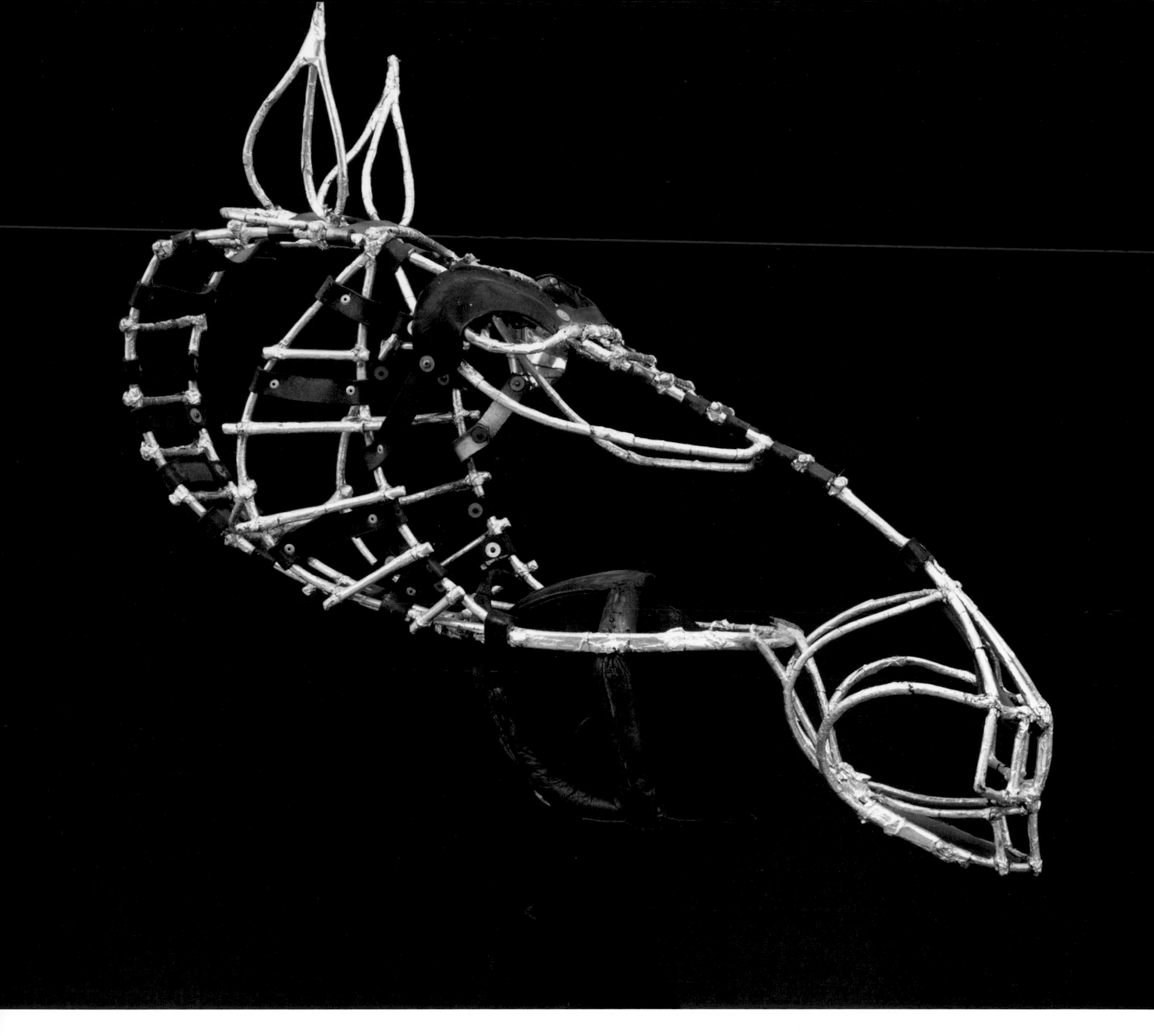

● 2.54 [OPPOSITE] *Equus* by Peter Shaffer, designed by John Napier for the National Theatre Company, 1974 ● 2.55 [ABOVE] Horse's head costume for *Equus* by Peter Shaffer, designed by John Napier for the National Theatre Company, 1974 | Cane, foil, leather and wire | V&A: S.43:1–1993

THE NATIONAL THEATRE
AT THE OLD VIC
EQUUS
PETER SHAFFER
DAI BRADLEY/MEL CHURCHER/MICHAEL JAYSTON
EDWARD JEWESBURY/MARY MACLEOD/PIP MILLER
LOUIE RAMSAY/PETER SCHOFIELD/JANE WENHAM
DIRECTED BY JOHN DEXTER/DESIGN JOHN NAPIER
LIGHTING ANDY PHILLIPS/MUSIC MARC WILKINSON
MOVEMENT CLAUDE CHAGRIN
IN REPERTOIRE PERFORMANCE DETAILS AVAILABLE FROM
THE NATIONAL THEATRE BOX OFFICE 76 THE CUT LONDON SE1 8LP
THE NATIONAL THEATRE RECEIVES FINANCIAL ASSISTANCE FROM
THE ARTS COUNCIL OF GREAT BRITAIN AND THE GREATER LONDON COUNCIL
GILBERT LESSER

The Barbican (1982) was designed to RSC specifications and originally planned by Hall and Bury, with input from Brook and St Denis. The brief was for an open stage auditorium with a seating capacity of 1,000 and, as at the Olivier, the desire was to create the feeling that actors and audience were sharing the same space. Like the NT, its opening was endlessly deferred and, by time it was completed, Hall had long since departed. In the meantime artistic director Trevor Nunn had developed an intimate performance style for the small found spaces he had converted (the [Donmar] Warehouse in London and The Other Place in Stratford), working with Christopher Morley and John Napier to reconfigure the actor–audience relationship. Faced with a 1,000-seat auditorium at the Barbican, and mindful of Hall's struggles with the Olivier, Nunn decided on a complete change of style.

A visit to the United States convinced him that a purpose-built theatre with up-to-date technical facilities 'should have productions to match the ambition of the building',[23] and he decided to enhance the physical presentation of the company's work so that it was more in keeping with the development of scenographic practice on the continent. The stripped-back aesthetic was replaced, quite literally in some cases, by an all-singing, all-dancing one as Nunn's commercial career – introduced to the world of the West End musical via his work on *Cats* – leaked into the RSC repertoire. In the long term this proved to be a tremendous success, with large-scale presentations such as *Les Misérables* (1985) providing the company with much-needed income, thanks to its West End transfer and global syndication. In the short term designers struggled with budgets, actors with the realities of the stage (like the Olivier, the Barbican's open stage and enormous fly-tower caused acoustic problems) and the company as a whole with a state-of the-art building and its inevitable teething problems. Chief among these was the difficulty that the centre as a whole presented to visitors. The RSC's poster may have claimed that the transition from Aldwych to Barbican was as easy as going from A to B, but the reality was very different, and the problems of way-finding in the Barbican became a recurring joke in the 1980s and '90s [2.58].

● 2.56 [OPPOSITE] Poster for *Equus* by Peter Shaffer, Moura George/Briggs, 1974 | Designed for the National Theatre Company, illustration by Gilbert Lesser, printed paper | V&A: S.651–1996 ● 2.57 [ABOVE RIGHT] Poster advertising the opening of the National Theatre, Tom Phillips, 1976 | Printed paper | V&A: S.35–1994 ● 2.58 [RIGHT] Poster advertising the Royal Shakespeare Company's move from the Aldwych Theatre to the Barbican, Paton-Walker Associates, 1982 | Printed by G&B Arts Ltd, printed paper | V&A: S.579–1995

These huge, purpose-built new theatres were only part of the picture of theatre space and practice in the 1960s and '70s. The end of theatre censorship in 1968 made it possible for the fringe to develop and for them to create new performance spaces of all shapes and sizes with the help of Arts Council funding. From the conversion of a railway turning shed (Roundhouse, 1964) to a banana-ripening warehouse (Donmar, 1977), from large spaces to intimate ones, the old and the new combined to provide fresh opportunities for architects, designers and theatre consultants as well as actors and directors. Visionary and influential teachers – such as Negri at Wimbledon, Koltai at Central, Georgiadis at Slade and Margaret Harris at Motley – encouraged their students to experiment with shape and form, and state subsidy provided an increase in productions and facilities in which they could practise their art on almost any scale. It was the period in which theatre design achieved institutional status and recognition: designers contributed to the planning of a number of important and innovative theatre buildings – Bury at the Barbican; Richard Negri at the Royal Exchange; Moiseiwitsch at the Crucible; the Arts Council established a Designers' Working Group and Design bursary scheme; and the Society of Theatre Consultants and Society of British Theatre Designers were formed. It was also the decade in which Britain entered work at the Prague Quadrennial for the first time, when Bury, Koltai, Tazeena Firth and Timothy O'Brien exhibited and won the Gold Medal (PQ75), before winning the Golden Triga four years later.

By the end of the 1980s sets were getting a round of applause as a boat floated across a moonlit stage (*Phantom of the Opera*, 1986) and a helicopter landed on stage (*Miss Saigon*, 1989). British theatre design was no longer a decorative backdrop to the main event, but an integral part of it.

● 2.59 [ABOVE] National Theatre logo, Ian Dennis at HDA International, 1974 ● 2.60 [OPPOSITE] Auditorium of the Olivier Theatre, National Theatre, South Bank, London, Denys Lasdun, 1976

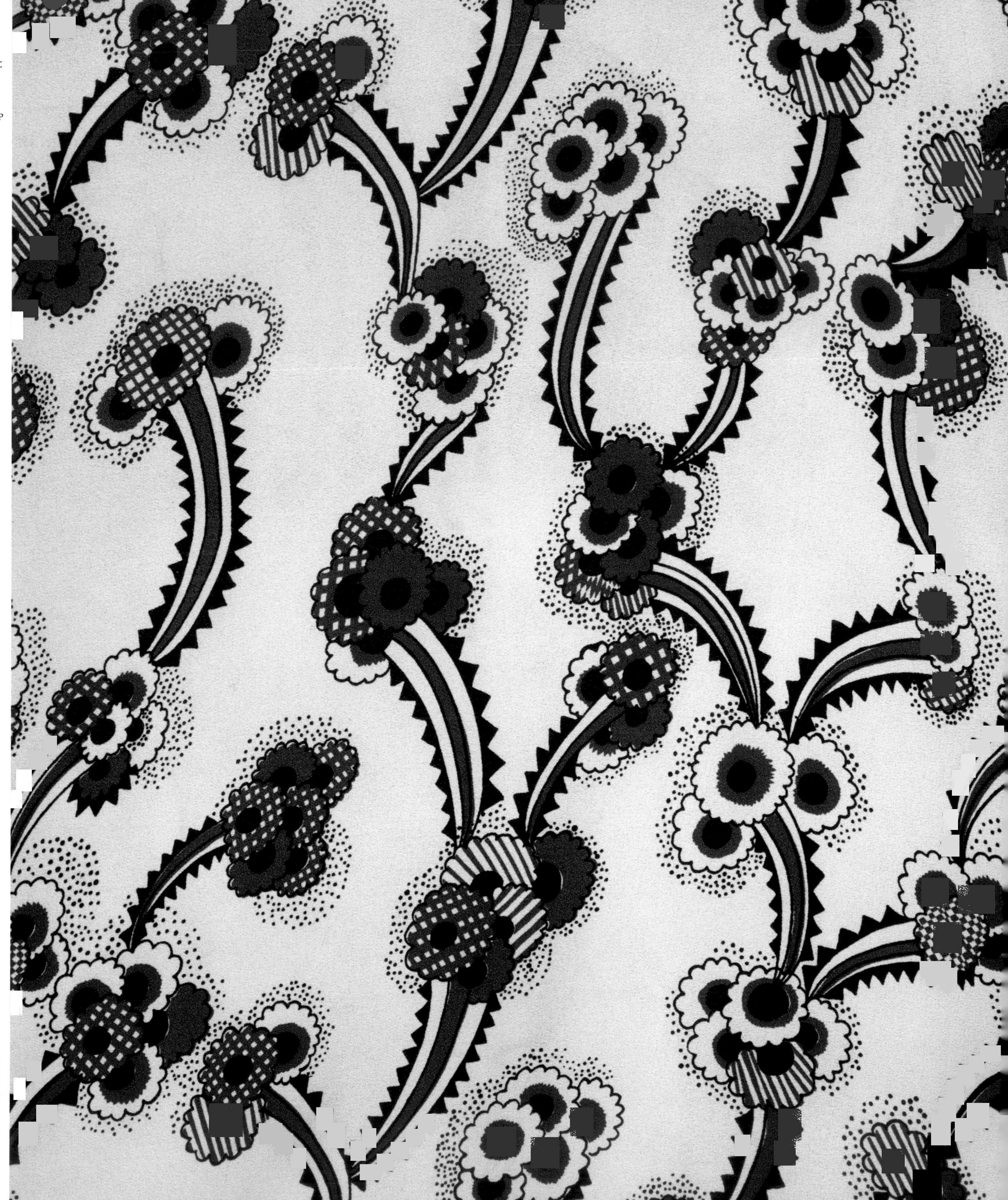

7 Boutiques and Beyond: The Rise of British Fashion

— Christopher Breward

developed recently is *Biba*, a 'pocket store' that sets out to provide cheap, well designed clothes and accessories which are often worn for a short time and then discarded. The owners, Barbara Hulanicki and her husband Stephen Fitz-Simon, achieve this by ordering relatively large quantities (up to 2,000) and introducing three or four new designs a week. *Biba* started as a mail order business, expanded to include a small boutique and now consists of a large shop in Kensington which is organised like a supermarket (but has quite a different atmosphere), and a shop in Brighton.

It is only recently that the success of these and other young designers, each with a distinctive approach, has become representative of the creative core of British fashion. Significantly, the big stores are now opening special departments for clothes which attempt to echo the boutique scale and the selling methods that were originally used. This development is probably more important for the future than the small boutiques which have sprung up everywhere on the crest of the wave.

It indicates that the movement has reached a commercial maturity; like most revolutions it has become institutionalised, complete with the paraphernalia of business methods.

Shops and graphics

It is particularly encouraging that the link between mass production and high design standards that exists in the best of the clothes has been carried over into the environment where they are sold and the graphic design and packaging that goes with them.

There are two main reasons for this. First, some of the designers concerned have felt strongly about it; and second, they have realised that their young customers will respond to surroundings which are as colourful and modern as the clothes. The whole emphasis of the boutique approach is to make shopping enjoyable, and to replace what Mary Quant calls "grey striped wallpaper and chandeliers" with entertainment. Myles Antony of John Stephen says "We like to amuse."

Of course the intended effect is to provide an environment in which it is easy to sell clothes, but the amusement and entertainment are none the less genuine. As with the *Golden Egg* restaurants, the starting point is a desire to escape from the dreariness of predominantly drab and depressing surroundings into something that comes much nearer to the dream world promised by twentieth century technology.

Inevitably with this kind of aim, standards vary enormously. There is a great difference between Foale and Tuffin's sophisticated shop and beautifully detailed graphics and the only half successful results achieved in Carnaby Street itself by the John Stephen boutiques.

Carnaby Street is stuffed with original and influential ideas, but they are often tattily carried out; and the same goes for a large number of the more amateur boutiques which are generally decorated on a shoestring. In fact, there are three main categories of shop where these clothes are sold. Those owned by the successful designer-manufacturers who use their shops as show

text continued on page 26

Photograph by Tim Quallington

"The whole emphasis of the boutique approach is to make shopping enjoyable" – some witty examples of boutique graphics and packaging are shown here. 1 *Price tag for Foale and Tuffin Ltd designed by David Cripps.* 2 and 5 *Price tag and bag for Gladrags Ltd designed by Max Robinson.* 3 and 6 *Bags for Biba designed by Anthony Little.* 4 *Carrier bag for Bazaar designed by Alexander Plunket Greene.* 7 and 8 *Packs for cosmetics by Mary Quant Cosmetics Ltd designed by Tom Wolsey.* 10 *Carrier bag for Top Gear designed by Harri Peccinotti.* 9 and 11 *Carrier bags for Clobber designed by Jeff Banks.* 12 *Price tag for Mary Quant's Ginger Group Ltd designed by Maureen Roffey, art director Tom Wolsey.*

● 2.61 [ABOVE] 'Behind the Scene', packaging and retail graphics, published in *Design*, August 1966
● 2.62 [OPPOSITE TOP] A young woman shopping for shoes in London, 1966
● 2.63 [OPPOSITE BOTTOM] Cover artwork for *Queen*, Rod Springett, 1967
Designed for a special issue edited by RCA students, published 21 June 1967

In March 1966 Reyner Banham, Independent Group veteran and pioneer of a fresh 'hip' architectural criticism, celebrated the ways in which recent commercial architecture styles had responded to the changed context of an increasingly youthful British population. Under the provocative heading 'Zoom Wave Hits Architecture', his *New Society* article set down the characteristics of a nascent design movement:

> What matters, overall, about the movement is its insistence on relevance ... the rounded corners, the hip, gay, synthetic colours, pop-culture props, all combine to suggest an architecture of plastic, steel and aluminium, the juke box and the neon-lit street, the way a city environment should be... The movement is right in insisting that architecture ... must also be relevant to what this week's dolly-girls are wearing, to ergonomics, inflatable air homes, the voice of God as revealed by his one true prophet Bob Dylan, what's going on in Bradford and Hammersmith, the side-elevation of the Ford GT-40, napalm down the neck, the Royal College of Art, caravan homes... Admittedly, the level of relevance is often only that of form-fondling, round corner styling, art-work and paint-jobs. It is often more than that, but even if it were purely visual and superficial that would not in itself be contemptible. It does still matter to people what buildings look like.[1]

A year later, in the more conservative pages of *The Listener*, resident architectural critic Nikolaus Pevsner gave short shrift to Banham's revolutionary call to arms:

> What is happening in architecture today is in the line of descent of the High Victorian style, of Art Nouveau and of Expressionism, not of the International Modern of Gropius and Mies. It is ill-suited for most architecture now because the majority of buildings are built of industrially produced, i.e. impersonal, materials ... for large numbers of anonymous clients and because the first concern of the architect must therefore be with their practical and emotional needs, and not with the expression of his own personality. And finally, the style of today is unlikely to last... Because phases of so excessively high a pitch of stimulation can't last. We cannot in the long run, live our day-to-day lives in the midst of explosions.[2]

This was more than a replaying of the 'battle of the styles' (that mid-nineteenth-century argument between classicists and goths about the appropriate architectural language for modern times). In this mid-1960s showdown the New Left's embracing of a grammar of 'Pop' that threatened to topple the vested interests of an ageing design and architectural establishment wedded to high-Modernist principles had repercussions beyond the pages of the literate press. In its appropriation of the language of style, this debate about taste, urban design and the creative challenges of contemporary popular culture revealed the ways in which youth fashion and its retailing had come to play a much more prominent role in the British design landscape, and set the context in which its production would continue to evolve through the remainder of the century.

BAZAAR

To some extent the repositioning of fashion as all-pervasive symbol of modernity in mid-twentieth-century design criticism should come as no surprise. As design historian Nigel Whiteley pointed out, the key provocation of the British 'Pop' movement was its rejection of elitist abstract theorizing and its embracing of the superficiality of style culture for its own sake. The world of teenage fashion was a natural fulcrum for actions of this nature, and its vigorous promotion by designers, artists and critics during the 1960s and '70s helps to explain what some writers have remarked upon as 'Pop's [seemingly] anti-articulate and often anti-literate character'. George Melly noted the bias in Pop towards the visual and musical, and described the 'deliberate impoverishment of vocabulary in spoken and written utterances'. Mick Farren (author of the supremely vernacular-sounding alternative culture tracts *Watch Out Kids* of 1972 and *Get On Down* of 1976) wrote about Pop's 'non-literal culture dependent on style, mannerisms and emotional response for its expression'. And Theodore Roszak in *The Making of a Counter Culture* (1969) claimed that much that is best in Pop culture 'does not find its way into literal expression ... one is apt to find out more about youth's ways by paying attention to posters, buttons, fashions of dress and dance – and especially to the pop music'.[3]

'Paying attention to posters, buttons, fashions of dress and dance' was certainly a central concern of the academics Stuart Hall and Paddy Whannel in 1964. In their influential book *The Popular Arts* they argued that:

> because of its high emotional content teenage culture is essentially non-verbal. It is more naturally expressed in music ... in dress, in certain habits of walking and standing, in certain facial expressions and 'looks' or in idiomatic slang... This teenage look can be partly attributed to the designers of mass-produced fashions and off-the-peg clothes... But these styles have a deeper social basis. The very preoccupation with the image of the self is important – pleasing, though often taken to extremes. Dress has become, for the teenager, a kind of minor popular art, and is used to express certain contemporary attitudes.[4]

This energetic expressiveness ran in tandem with a strong critical assertion that 'Pop had resulted in a major education of visual awareness.' In an article on 'The Style of the Sixties' that appeared in *The Spectator* in July 1967, the critic Mario Amaya claimed that the 'conscious awareness of style in the Sixties, the preoccupation with the way things look, has come to mean that more people are more aware than ever before of their visual environment'. This represented, he continued, 'an upgrading of taste, a keener awareness of the things around us as they infiltrate our lives and our art'.[5]

KENSINGTON AND CHELSEA: FROM SCHOOL TO STREET

Sentiments such as Amaya's had, as Simon Martin's essay in this book suggests, clearly begun to influence the curricula and student expectations within a rapidly changing British art-school scene. In a special 'Fine Artz' edition of the Royal College of Art (RCA) student journal *ARK* of 1964 the editors concluded (in an echo of Hall and Whannel):

> It is our opinion that the world of the teenager could well provide vital information for the new generation of professional culture propagators. What impressed us most about the kids was the way in which they seem to understand modern styling, fashion and expendability so much better than the professionals. The reason for the inadequacy of modern artists and designers lies, we feel, in the anachronistic training they are subjected to in Art Schools. The admen and Wimpey Bar designers don't do badly in supplying the sort of thing that is required nowadays, sometimes even quite imaginatively, but why should they have what amounts to a virtual monopoly in the manipulation of our visual environments?[6]

Such sentiments would inspire the transforming student protests of 1968, but had already been partially addressed by the introduction in 1962, under the professorship of Janey Ironside, of a Royal College fashion-diploma course that was more responsive to contemporary conditions in manufacturing and the marketplace than had been the case under the previous regime of Madge Garland, whose focus had been set squarely on the concerns of the London couture industry alone. Over the course of the decade the school (which was housed in the Faculty of Industrial Design) retained the central aim of training:

> students interested in fashion to develop their taste, knowledge and skill in such a manner as to fit them for important positions in the industry. Fashion [was] understood in its widest possible sense, as including everything connected with women's clothing which is influenced by the changing demands of contemporary life [and] in relation to the varying demands of haute couture, medium priced goods and mass production.[7]

● 2.64 [OPPOSITE] Bazaar, King's Road, London, 1959

In 1967, at the height of the boutique phenomenon, the course offered students the opportunity 'to gain some experience of buying and selling in retail stores'.[8] And by 1969 the Royal College had upgraded the diploma in fashion to a Master's degree in design and had broadened the syllabus to offer instruction in menswear or womenswear, focusing on 'the design of clothing and accessories, functional, social and technical aspects; materials, including those newly developed in relation to clothing; industrial methods, including experimental techniques in clothing manufacture; professional practice and marketing methods; and the evolution of fashion and costume and critical analysis of contemporary clothing design'.[9]

This level of symbiosis between educational theory, industrial need and the pervading cultural context was unique and explains the dominance of Royal College fashion graduates in the British design scene during the 1960s and '70s. That Ironside and her team conceived of their school as a launchpad for subversive, headline-grabbing talent was clearly recognized in critiques of the resulting collections that regularly appeared in the popular press. In June 1966 tabloid columnist Jean Rook voiced her protest at that summer's final degree show, 'not only as a fashion editor but as a rate payer', commenting disapprovingly on the 'X-certificate sinister circus of girls in plastic Bermuda shorts and hats made of sheets of wrapping paper... Mickey Mouse trouser suits... [and] tape-recorded Arab music that sounded like a Learner driver changing gear'. Ironside defended her students, explaining that 'They are sick of Courrèges ... of mini skirts ... of everything but colour and movement.'[10]

Ken Baynes, Ironside's colleague in the RCA School of Industrial Design, agreed with her analysis of the changing times. In 1967 he identified:

> a fresh impetus ... from the world of fashion ... a new interest in surface, colour and pattern based on young people's concern with gay, exciting clothes. Increasingly the environment which young people want in shops and restaurants is entertaining... The purism of the early days has been overtaken by events in which the joint forces of commercialization and mass taste have thrown up criteria which are themselves strong and valid.[11]

In the same publication Baynes cited Michael Wolff, of design consultancy Wolff Olins, who, in an article in the *Journal of the Society of Industrial Artists and Designers* of 1965, had proclaimed:

> The sort of designers in Britain who have really given people a bang in the past two years are Ken Adam, as Art Director of the James Bond films, Frederick Starke, with his clothes for Cathy Gale; and Ray Cusick, with his Daleks. People like Mary Quant and John Stephen have had the same impact on a more limited age range. It is their zing, their zest, and their vigorous understanding of what design is all about which should be one of the main

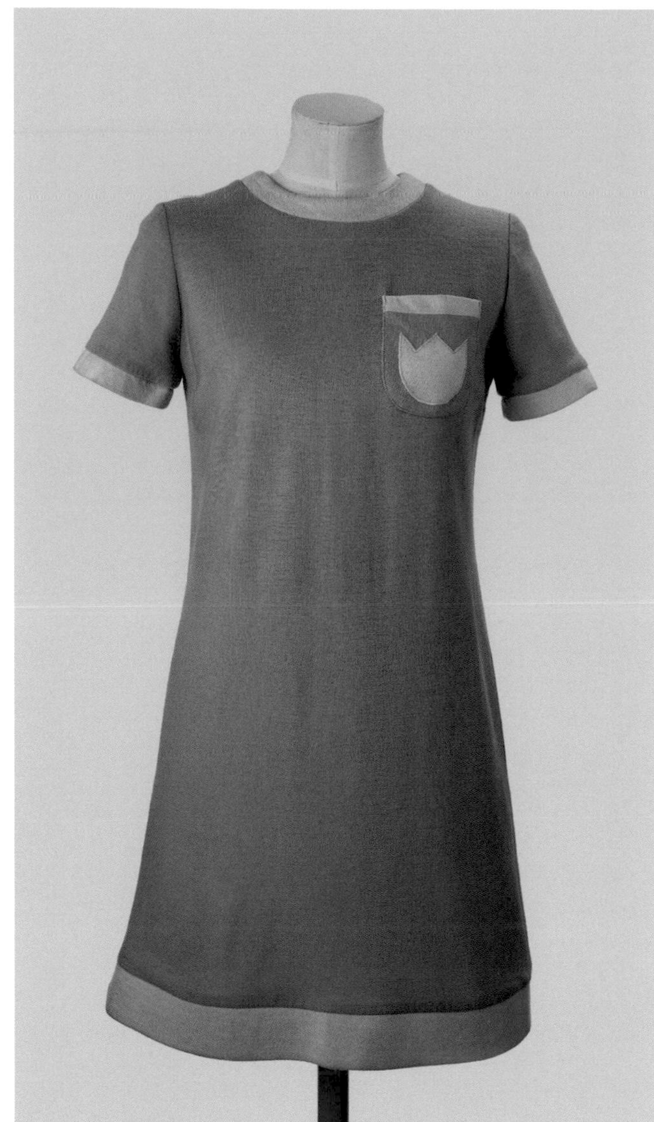

● 2.65 [TOP] Mini dress, Mary Quant, 1966 | Wool jersey | V&A: T.86–1982 ● 2.66 [ABOVE] Ankle boots, Mary Quant, 1967 | PVC lined with cotton jersey | V&A: T.59:1 & 2–1992 ● 2.67 [OPPOSITE TOP] *Queen*, 22 June 1966 | Cover photograph of Claudia Duxbury by Claude Virgin | NAL: 38041800727695 ● 2.68 [OPPOSITE MIDDLE] *Nova*, May 1971 | Cover photograph of Amanda Lear by Brian Duffy AAD: 1985/3/2/549/1 ● 2.69 [OPPOSITE BOTTOM] *Time*, 15 April 1966 | Cover designed by Geoffrey Dickinson

> contributions of … designers to modern society… [W]hat is happening is that ordinary people and the designer are moving towards one another – it is a rapprochement based on a re-awakening delight in gaiety, vulgarity and humour.[12]

Mary Quant, perhaps the most high-profile of the Swinging Sixties fashion generation, was certainly in touch with the new spirit, suggesting to the writer Jonathan Aitken that 'the secret of successful designing is to anticipate changes of mood before they happen… I get new ideas all the time … going to nightclubs, seeing colours in the streets. It's a sort of flair within me. I'll keep in alright.'[13] Though she was not a Royal College graduate, Quant certainly moved in progressive circles where discussions of a new subversive spirit in design and culture were taking place. She had met her creative partner, Archie McNair, when the two were studying together at Goldsmiths College, he in illustration, she as a trainee teacher. In 1955 they opened their boutique, Bazaar, in the bohemian backwater of London's King's Road [2.64]. In the early days its stock, sourced from fashion students' designs and eclectic choices from wholesalers, was (as Quant recalled) 'a bouillabaisse of clothes and accessories … sweaters, scarves, shifts, hats, jewellery and peculiar odds and ends'.[14] Gradually they gained confidence and made up their own characteristic designs using traditional British fabrics, but in modern iterations that caught the attention of journalists and earned Quant a reputation as a designer of a look variously described as 'dishy, grotty, geary, kinky, mod, poove and all the rest of it' [2.65, 2.66].[15] By 1962 Quant's innovative appeal had been recognized by the American company J.C. Penney, which ordered a series of ranges for its chain of stores, and the following year she launched 'Ginger Group', a diffusion label that made her designs available to a British mass market through 'in-store' boutiques in 160 department stores.[16]

Beyond international commercial success, it was Quant's talent at visual merchandising and publicity that placed her within the progressive context noted by architectural and design critics.[17] The boutique window as Pop Art installation was a familiar feature of the iconography of 'Swinging London', and as early as the late 1950s Bazaar was offering such Surrealist extravaganzas as 'figures in bathing suits … with madly wide stripes … all strumming away on white musical instruments … with bald heads and … wearing round goggle sun-specs which … were incredibly new'.[18] This approach, and the crowds of shoppers, tourists, journalists and television crews who converged on the King's Road to experience it, ensured that by the early 1960s 'Chelsea ceased to be a small part of London; it became international; its name interpreted a way of living and a way of dressing far more than a geographical area.'[19]

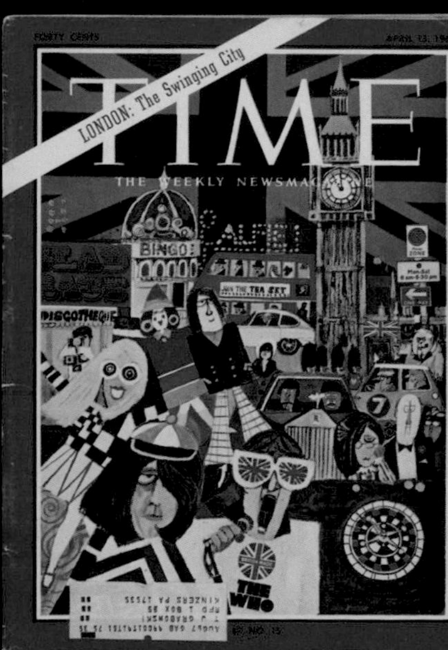

● 2.70 [ABOVE] *Marisa Berenson*, David Bailey, 1968 | Gelatin silver print, variant published in *Vogue*, August 1968 | V&A: PH.209–1983

CARNABY STREET, MAYFAIR AND BACK TO CHELSEA

By 1966 the whole of London appeared to dominate the fashion consciousness of the world. *Time* magazine's now-famous April issue devoted itself to an investigation of 'the swinging city', breathlessly suggesting that:

> this Spring, as never before in modern times, London is switched on. Ancient elegance and new opulence are all tangled up in a dazzling blur of op and pop. The city is alive with birds (girls) and beatles, buzzing with minicars and telly stars, pulsing with half a dozen separate veins of excitement [2.69].[20]

The enthusiasm of journalists should not be taken as proof of real change on the ground, beyond the narrow boundaries of metropolitan life. But articles and images such as those included in *Time*, and the recent proliferation of home-grown lifestyle publications, including the *Sunday Times* colour supplement, and fashion magazines *Queen*, *Town* and *Nova* (employing a new wave of working-class photographers, such as David Bailey, Terry O'Neill, Ronald Traeger, Brian Duffy and Terence Donovan – whose irreverent and sexy approach replaced the elegant reserve of their forebears, Cecil Beaton and Norman Parkinson) do suggest a shift in attitude and a growing recognition that the work of a generation of young British fashion creatives was worthy of constant exposure [2.68, 2.70, 2.71].

From the mid-1960s the centre of fashion gravity in London had also expanded out from Chelsea to incorporate the aristocratic streets of Mayfair and the more democratic environs of Carnaby Street. Mayfair witnessed the arrival of a more directional men's tailoring with the opening of Rupert Lycett-Green and Charley Hornby's firm Blades in 1963 and of Michael Fish's men's boutique, Mr Fish, in 1966. Savile Row, bastion of the traditional bespoke suit, finally caught up in 1969 with the opening of Tommy Nutter and Edward Sexton's 'Nutters of Savile Row', backed by the pop star Cilla Black (the precursor of a later 1990s generation of tailors, including Ozwald Boateng, Timothy Everest and Richard James) [2.72, 2.74, 2.75]. What linked the 1960s generation with their turn-of-the-millennium counterparts was an iconoclastic take on the conservative rules of aristocratic masculine elegance. While retaining the characteristic cut associated with British bespoke tailoring history, all these establishments experimented with outrageous textiles and exaggerated detailing, courting celebrity clients as a means of boosting their profile.[21]

Carnaby Street, on the other hand, had established itself since the opening of Bill Green's Vince boutique in 1955 as an edgier destination for gay and working-class male fashion consumers, selling trendy goods that revelled in their 'vulgar' associations. With an ethos closer to the commercial realism of the established rag-trade, exemplified by the local retail empire of John Stephen, its 'here today, gone tomorrow' atmosphere of rapidly changing trends nevertheless set a precedent for the youth-focused, music-influenced and market-led nature of British street fashion that would dominate for the remainder of the century [2.73].[22]

It was also in the locale of Carnaby Street, in Marlborough Court, that RCA graduates Marion Foale and Sally Tuffin established their more avant-garde and select boutique in 1965 [2.77]. Its sharp interior echoed the striking abstract qualities of their collections and was designed by the jeweller Tony Laws. Foale and Tuffin recall:

> to get the maximum out of the space we just put scaffolding poles right across widthways and then hung the hangers on those... And all around above those were the light bulbs, blue and red light bulbs... And minimal wooden floor and minimal white desk... Oh, and a model of Twiggy in the window. The window went straight to the floor and there would just be Twiggy standing in all sorts of poses.[23]

Like Quant, Foale and Tuffin pioneered the British version of the arty new boutique, aided by the contemporary mannequin designs of Adel Rootstein and a visual language borrowed from Pop Art. Throughout the 1960s this Carnaby Street concept inspired the high street. As early as 1959 the venerable menswear chain Austin Reed had employed RCA painter Robyn Denny to complete a large red, white and blue Pop mural for its flagship store in Regent Street. In 1966 Selfridges launched the Miss Selfridge 'in-store' boutique for women under 25, and in 1967 Harrods joined the bandwagon with 'Way In', an internal street of boutique-like concessions for men and women. And the Topshop boutique chain gradually replaced its parent Peter Robinson stores during the early 1970s.[24]

That most of these brand-names survived into the twenty-first century is testament to the continuing resilience of a British fashion retailing tradition invented in the era of 'Swinging London', though at the time the concept seemed in danger of burning itself out.[25] In a prescient article published in *Design* in 1968, Corinne Hughes-Stanton argued that in:

> a brief three years [the Carnaby Street style] has explored and exhausted every conceivable form of three-dimensional as well as graphic titillation. The race has been headlong, exhilarating, immense fun for protagonists and onlookers; but the last few months have seen a slowing down of pace and an ingrowing of ideas which suggest that Carnaby Street and all it stood for is no longer a spearhead of innovation.[26]

Nevertheless, in the movement's focus on novelty and liberation, Hughes-Stanton recognized the seeding of a revolution, in tandem with Ken Baynes's dictum that:

> today the pedantry and purism of functionalism seems irrelevant, a debased coinage in the riotous but cramped environment of the mid twentieth century. The direction for design should surely be related to the central theme of the present, to the growing concern with the ... expression ... of individuality in the context of society. If this means more decoration, more colour, more flamboyance, a closer link between entertainment and everyday life, design has no brief to impose its more limited morality.[27]

By 1973 Charles Jencks and Nathan Silver had utilized the term 'Adhocism' to describe subsequent developments in international design theory and practice that would eventually be identified through the term 'Postmodernism'.[28] Hughes-Stanton was perhaps correct to predict that 'the design possibilities sparked off by the Carnaby Street era', however naive and accidental their formation, 'are not going to be extinguished very easily'.[29]

Back in west London the step-change from the bright, futuristic fashion iconography of the early and mid-1960s to the more 'ad hoc' and eclectic fusion of retro and exotic styles favoured in the late 1960s was reflected in the work of Barbara Hulanicki at Biba and of Ossie Clark at Quorum. Hulanicki, who had trained as a fashion illustrator, was an early promoter of the sinuous aesthetics of glamorous decay that would become the signature of London's unique fashion style during the 1970s. In 1964 she had opened the first Biba shop in a dilapidated pharmacy on Abingdon Road, off Kensington High Street. In her published memoir she recalled:

There were lots of black and gold signs left and the windows were painted half way up with scratched black paint with gold leaf edges. The woodwork outside was covered in marvellous peeling blue grey paint... [Inside] a friend lent us two bronze lamps with huge black shades. We made long curtains in a plum and navy William Morris print with a plum dress fabric lining. I refused to have the flaking woodwork outside painted.[30]

The following year, having established a cult following and launched a profitable mail-order line, Biba moved into larger premises on Kensington Church Street. Here, 'amidst the Victorian splendour of a massive panoply of burgundy coloured wallpaper and heavy mahogany,' customers could buy 'everything from luminous pink socks to sombrero-sized felt hats and pop art jewellery'. Jonathan Aitken estimated that '3,000 dolly birds each week push[ed] through the heavy Victorian wood and brass doors, intent on dissipating their last shillings on the tempting ... baubles of the Aladdin's Cave ... within.'[31] Though Biba attracted famous customers, including Julie Christie, Sandy Shaw and Twiggy, the majority of its fans were 'working girls of slender ... incomes' who spent an average of £7 a week on Biba clothes and accessories, contributing to a cult success that financed subsequent moves to larger premises in Kensington High Street in 1969 and 1973. The latter shop, known as 'Big Biba' and taking over the old Derry & Toms department store from 1973 until the shop's closure in 1976, was a phantasmagoria of glamorous Art Deco styling, with a celebrated roof garden, the perfect environment for a look that announced a very different mood in British fashion for the coming decade [2.83]. As one devotee recalled:

As it moved from a back street to the main thoroughfare of Kensington, a certain lasciviousness, a sort of voluptuousness crept in. Crowded into dimly lit communal dressing rooms, now proud of the leanness that made every garment fit me better than those around me, I tried on clothes for the sinful and louche: slithery gowns in glowing satins, hats with black veils, shoes stacked for sirens. There were ... evening gowns to make Betty Grable sigh, make-up – chocolate and black – for vamps and vampires. And for real life there were raincoats to sweep the London pavements, tee-shirts the colour of old-maid's hats, dusky suede boots with long zippers.[32]

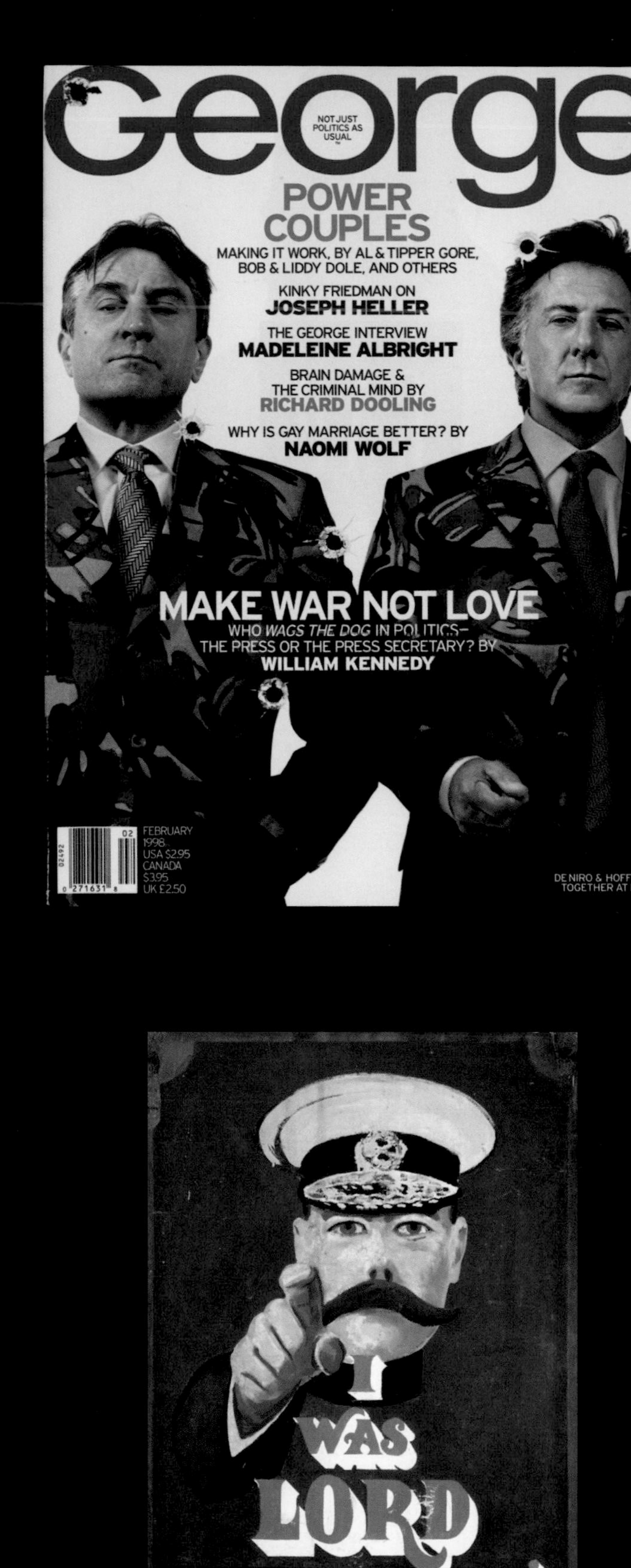

● 2.71 [OPPOSITE] *Thermodynamic*, Terence Donovan, October 1960 Gelatin silver print, printed 2011, originally published in *Man About Town*, January 1961 | V&A: E.329–2011 ● 2.72 [TOP RIGHT] *George*, February 1998 | Cover photograph shows Robert de Niro and Dustin Hoffman wearing suits by Richard James ● 2.73 [RIGHT] Signboard from I Was Lord Kitchener's Valet, Pat Hartnet, 1964 | Gloss paint on fibreboard | V&A: E.1428–2001

NEW WAVE

Close to Hulanicki's first Biba store, Quorum – a shop part-owned by designer Alice Pollock – offered a platform for Ossie Clark and printmaker Celia Birtwell, also RCA graduates, to develop the more sinuous, emphatically sexy line of the early 1970s [2.76]. Birtwell's exotic and nostalgic prints perfectly complemented Clark's slinky cut and provocative use of transparent fabrics and naked skin [p.202]. Throughout the late 1960s the Ossie and Celia 'look' garnered commercial success and press adulation, though it was Ossie's name that was increasingly picked out by the press. The buying out of Quorum by Radley Gowns provided a base from which Clark could produce both couture and accessible designs for a broader market, and by 1971 he had completed a ready-to-wear collection for the French manufacturer Mendes, which was launched at the Louvre to an international press. As *The Times* Fashion Editor Prudence Glynn noted, on choosing his chiffon trouser suit at Bath Museum of Costume's 'Dress of the Year' in 1969:

> Ossie Clark is, I believe, in the world class for talent; in fact I think that we should build a completely modern idea of British high fashion around him. We should stop being amazed by our creative talent and start capitalizing on it, as do the French and Italians.[33]

Clark's chaotic 'rockstar' lifestyle and lack of personal business sense meant that his success did not last beyond the mid-1970s, but his innovative work and uncompromising attitude did mark a change of spirit in the British fashion scene – one where the playful, bright naivety of the generation of Quant was replaced by a darker edge and a distinctive subversive intent.

The collaboration between Malcolm McLaren and Vivienne Westwood on the King's Road in the 1970s epitomizes this sea-change. Westwood's Derbyshire family arrived in London in the late 1950s and she enrolled for a short period on a jewellery course at Harrow Art School, before embarking on a secretarial course, marrying and seeming to settle down to suburban life. However, her growing acquaintance with art-school student McLaren and his 'dangerous' situationist ideas pre-empted divorce from her first husband and an almost complete self-reinvention. Adopting the confrontational fluorescent wardrobe of the revived Teddy Boy cult of the early 1970s, Westwood rejected what she saw as the mawkish romanticism of the King's Road retro-emporia and sought inspiration in the subcultural energy of the proletarian British teenager's wardrobe and in the seedy debauchery of life in the art-school underbelly as revealed to her by McLaren.

● 2.74 [OPPOSITE TOP] Suit, Ozwald Boateng, 1996 | Wool, polyester and kid mohair | V&A: T.22:1-6–1997 ● 2.75 [OPPOSITE BOTTOM] Suit, Tommy Nutter, 1983 | Wool, with a horizontal stripe | V&A: T.10-B–1983 ● 2.76 [LEFT TOP] Dress, Ossie Clark and Celia Birtwell, 1970–71 | Printed chiffon and silk satin | V&A: T.194–1997 ● 2.77 [LEFT] 'Double D', mini dress, Foale & Tuffin, 1966 | Linen with a partial cotton lining | V&A: T.29–2010 ● 2.78 [ABOVE] Chips with Everything, Chancery Lane, London, 1965

The first incarnation of this development was the opening of the shop Let It Rock at the grimy Fulham Road end of the King's Road in 1971. Here McLaren and Westwood sold mid-twentieth-century bric-a-brac and authentic 1950s clothing. Westwood gradually fell into renovating and copying drape coats and drainpipe trousers for the shop, under the guidance of East End tailor Sid Green. Following the demise of the Teddy Boy cult, the duo reopened as Too Fast to Live Too Young to Die in 1973. The vaudeville theatricality of Ted gear gave way to the denim and leather masochism of James Dean, and jeans and biker jackets were augmented by T-shirts printed up with McLaren's propagandist slogans. These were then customized by Westwood with overtly sexual and violent motifs, including nipple-revealing zips and chicken bones shaped to spell profanities.

A year later, as its sexual themes developed into a brazen celebration of the sadistic imagery of pornography, the shop changed its name to SEX and stocked a selection of rubber fetish items, customized lingerie and ever-more explicit T-shirts. It rapidly attracted a following from the edgier side of the pop, art and fashion worlds, as well as suburban and provincial outsiders whose anti-establishment energies would go on to fuel what would become known after 1976 as punk. Alongside McLaren's Svengali-like promotion of the Sex Pistols, Westwood and her assistants at SEX produced a sartorial language that would fix an understanding of London's avant-garde fashion sensibility in the public consciousness. Their pulling together of sadomasochistic bondage paraphernalia, Nazi memorabilia and garments associated with the asylum produced a look endowed with a fierce talismanic power.[34]

Ironically the commercial success of punk underwrote Westwood's emergence as a bona-fide fashion designer. In 1976 SEX evolved into Seditionaries, and its profitable promotion of mass-produced T-shirts, accessories and fanzines gradually distilled the home-made punk ethic into a viable business proposition [2.79]. By 1979 many of its core customers had themselves realized the marketing potential inherent in the punk philosophy and were restyling themselves at the centre of a glossy nightclub revival of glamour, popularly labelled New Romanticism. Westwood mirrored the aesthetic and political ramifications of these developments in her epochal 'Pirate' collection of 1981, the first time she had enjoyed the opportunity of presenting a coherent design statement under her own name. In its amalgamation of vivid African colours, seventeenth-century costume references, Hollywood high-seas bravura and innovative use of serpentine prints and ostentatious draping, the collection certainly suggested those daring elements of visual and intellectual piracy that McLaren was exploring in music. For Westwood, the debut marked her entry into the British fashion establishment. The clothes – whose covert romanticism shadowed and critiqued the ostentatious ceremonial of the 1981 marriage of HRH Prince Charles and Lady Diana Spencer – explored elements of masquerade that struck a chord among style editors, international buyers and museum curators (the V&A acquired an example for its permanent collection). They also laid the foundation for the development of Westwood's signature themes over the remainder of the twentieth century, though her research increasingly looked to the model of the traditional couture collection and the history of high fashion rather than to the theatre of the street.[35]

ART-SCHOOL POSTSCRIPT

The trajectory that links Westwood's inspirational iconoclasm with the longer history of subversive creativity (most of it focused around independent boutiques) and underpins the rise of British fashion over the last 50 years found its ultimate resolution back in the art school during the 1980s and '90s. In this context the fashion courses (undergraduate and postgraduate) at Saint Martins School of Art (to become Central Saint Martins College of Art and Design in 1988) have been particularly celebrated as hothouses for a generation of talent that would come to have global influence. The location of the Fashion School of Saint Martins in Charing Cross Road, close to the bohemian district of Soho, seemed to bind the powerful myth of the institution with its environment. As the school's prospectus suggested in the early 1980s:

> All [fashion] courses are highly fashion-orientated and aimed at developing to professional standards each individual student's potential ability... Saint Martins is traditionally a place where, even more than in most art schools, the development of the individual student's flair is very important. This tradition, of encouraging personal development and diversity, is still very strong in most areas of the School's work and perhaps is what gives Saint Martin's its special flavour. Some of the atmosphere of the surrounding area percolates through the School – the buzz, the energy, the feeling of competitiveness.[36]

Out of this unique context graduated John Galliano (BA) in 1984, Alexander McQueen (MA) in 1992 and Hussein Chalayan (BA) in 1993 (later graduates included Stella McCartney, Matthew Williamson and Gareth Pugh), all of whom pioneered a highly personal fashion vision and took on the most senior creative roles in the fashion industry outside the UK (Galliano at Dior and McQueen at Givenchy) [2.80–2.82, 2.18]. Fashion historian and professor at Central Saint Martins, Caroline Evans notes that:

> Fabio Piras called his generation of designers who graduated from London's Central Saint Martins in the early to mid 1990s 'fashion desperadoes'. Describing how arduous conditions were for newly graduated young designers, Piras said 'you had no money, and a certain synergy grows out of a recession. People said "fuck it, we're going to have a show".'[37]

Certainly it is possible to claim that the 1990s generation of successful British fashion graduates (who also studied at the RCA, London College of Fashion, Kingston University, Middlesex University and other institutions) put on the most spectacular show to date. Evans goes on to quote Stéphane Wagner of the Institut Français de la Mode, who said in 1997, 'if we accept that much of haute couture is about squeezing out maximum media coverage – good or bad – then the more spectacular the presentation and collection, the better. And from that point of view the English are the best by far.'[38] In this they were surely following a tradition stretching back at least to the Royal College of Art and the King's Road in the mid-1960s.

● 2.79 [OPPOSITE] Interior design for Seditionaries, 1976, Malcolm McLaren | Drawn by David Connor, Xerox collage, pencil, pen and crayon on paper, mounted on board | Private collection ● 2.80 [RIGHT] Dress from the Christian Dior haute couture Spring/Summer collection, John Galliano, 2000

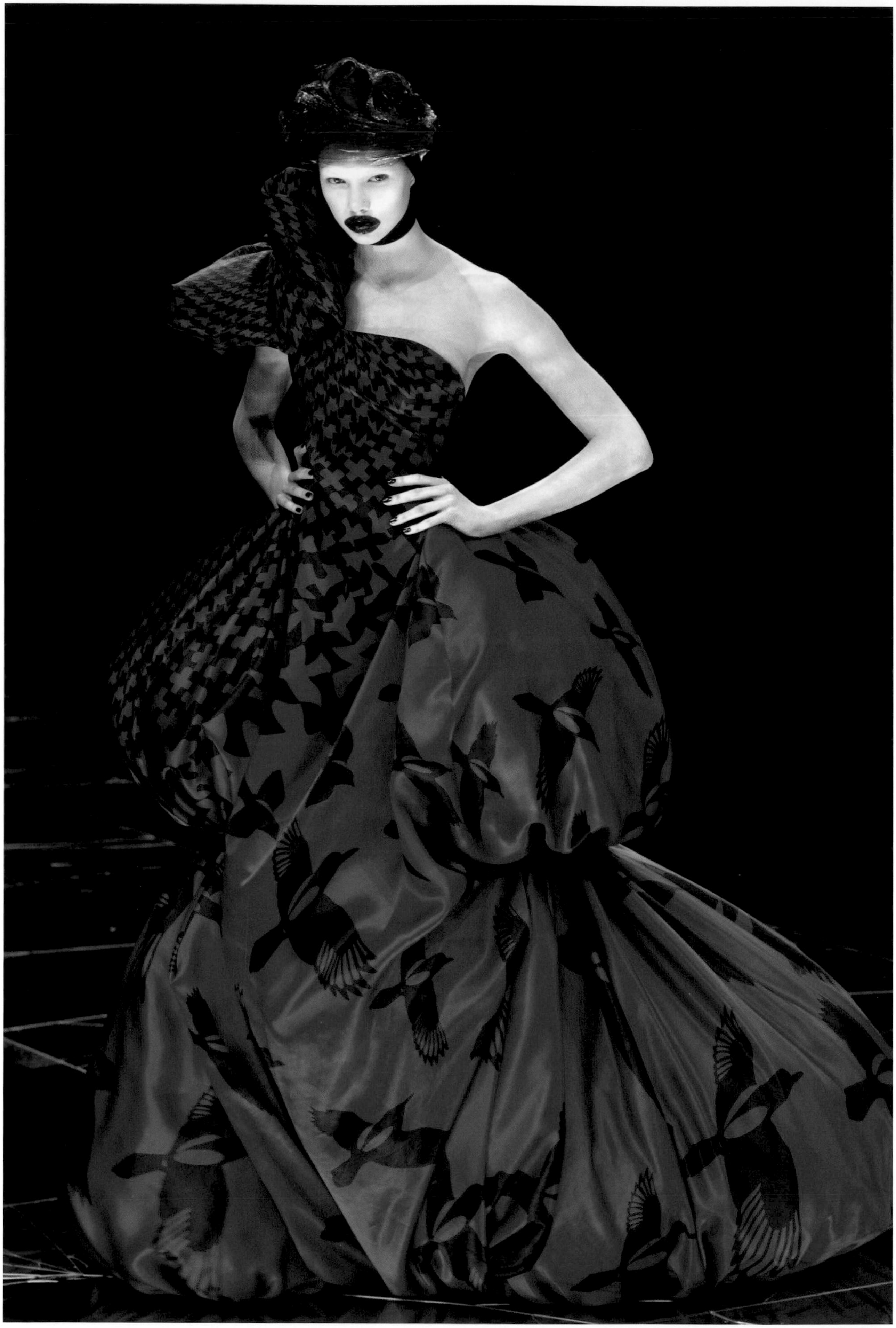

● 2.81 [OPPOSITE] Dress from the 'Horn of Plenty' collection, Alexander McQueen, 2009 | Digitally printed silk | V&A
● 2.82 [BELOW] Alexander McQueen working on the 'Horn of Plenty' collection, 2009 | Photograph by Nick Waplington

Biba

— Barbara Hulanicki

2.83 [ABOVE] Exotics (kasbah) unit, Big Biba, High Street Kensington, London, Whitmore Thomas, 1973

When we started Biba in 1964 there was no fashion retail scene at all. The clothes had basically been the same since the war. They were badly cut and the shapes were boring and formless. Everything was blue, brown or beige; there wasn't even black to be had. I think it's impossible to comprehend now what it was like to be a young woman at that time. Now we are inundated with choice at every price point. The retail scene is cut-throat and competitive, constantly chasing after the next look, which is wonderful for the consumer of today.

When we founded Biba, our customers were just like me. I had a good job paying me enough money, which meant I could live away from home and have enough left over at the end of the week to go out shopping. The problem was that there was nothing to buy. Everything was aimed at frumpy mums. Shops at the time were the sorts of places where the shop assistants would slide over to you when you came in and ask unctuously, 'May I help you, Madam?' It was incredibly frustrating. I was working as a fashion illustrator at the time, so I was well placed to see the entire scope of the awfulness that was out there. I would be sent these horrible dresses, which I would somehow have to make look good. I was in a constant state of despair. There was nothing I even wanted to buy. It was very much like that wonderful Mike Leigh movie, *Vera Drake*.

My husband, Fitz, and I saw an absolute void in the market and we thought we could do something different – something special that young women might respond to. The average weekly wage for a girl at the time would have been about £9 and her rent might have been about £3 per week. Most of the depressing brown sacks that were available to buy cost anywhere between £6 and £10, so even these were out of the reach of our potential customers. Fitz had the idea of keeping all our dresses at £3, a price point that was unheard of at the time. This meant that our girls could buy themselves a new dress every week and still have money left over.

I took my inspiration from all the old movies that I loved as a child. My icons were the great Hollywood stars: Marlene Dietrich, Greta Garbo and Rita Hayworth. The clothes I designed were clothes that I wanted to wear. They were form-fitting, with cleaner lines and very graphic shapes. They harkened back to another era before the misery and austerity of two world wars, but they were also looking forward to a world that was creeping back into the light of freedom and self-expression. Everything was in very strong colours: we used prunes, plums, blacks; we would have rich chocolates and poison purples. We had a palette of 24 colours that the entire line was based on, which we would change from season to season. The winter palette would be warmer and darker, whereas for summer we would lighten it up and introduce pastels. Everything was matchy-matchy, even the accessories and cosmetics. We knew we had got it right because everything sold and sold. Our first premises was an old apothecary's on Abingdon Road in Kensington. It had all the lovely original shop fittings. I was in the shop one day, before we had even opened for the first time, doing some work with music playing and a few rails of dresses strewn about the floor, when girls came in and started rummaging through the rails and buying things. We sold out before we had even opened. Everything always sold extremely well, especially the cosmetics. We had new styles in all the time, with everything changing every three or four weeks. This was unheard of anywhere else at the time. Deliveries came in and sold out and were replaced by something new and fresh. Dresses and coats were always the best-sellers. We had one mac, not unlike that Burberry style now, that we sold for 12 years. Separates were also very strong as a category, fashion-wise.

As the Sixties developed, I found there was no inspiration from what other people were designing at the time. I've always loved movies, even to this day, but most of the movies of the period got it completely wrong. I remember when *Blow-Up* by Antonioni came out. It angered everybody. It had nothing to do with London at all. It was all Italian style, which was very different. If anything, my inspiration was my own life and the lives of the girls who came to the shop. I wanted nice shoes, so we did shoes. I had my son, Witold, and we did baby clothes. We slowly educated our customers, introducing new categories one at a time. We did menswear, food, home – whatever was needed. The inexpensive furniture at the time was all vintage, the sort of thing that is now sold as pricey antiques. We made all our house-wares to work with that, sprucing them up and reinterpreting them for modern lives. The best fun of all was the mail-order catalogues. We were able to use wonderful photographers, Sarah Moon and Helmut Newton, to present a complete story to everyone. The actual catalogues themselves were things of beauty and became collector's items.

Creatively, the scene was very competitive. Everyone who came into the shop wanted to outdo everyone else with their look. It was a fabulous energy. The Biba girls were all dating the top musicians of the time, and they all came into the shop – The Stones, The Beatles, The Animals, everyone came in. If the guys weren't dating a Biba girl, they came into the shop to meet one. In terms of the business, the only competition we had at the time were the rag-trade copyists, but we were always three steps ahead of them and they got it all wrong anyway. The other fashiony labels that came around – Mary Quant and Ossie Clark and such – were much more expensive and didn't affect our girls.

'Designer' was a very bad word at the time. It had terrible connotations, usually associated with being expensive and difficult. Very few designers had any training. Before we started Biba I had worked for years as an illustrator, seeing every collection and having to translate it into something appealing to the readers. By the time Biba was rolling, I didn't have time to over-think anything. I pulled the ideas out of my head and we developed them into product. We would recruit girls from the shop floor. We would find the ones with the strongest sense of style and drive and assign them a category. We would send them out with my drawings and designs to see them through to samples and manufacturing. We did tons of research. There were no Pantone colour charts back then to pull out and mull over at your desk. So all the colours were mixed in the studio and the Biba prints coloured up. Samples of the designs were pattern-cut, sewn and filed in the studio before they were sent to local manufacturers.

● 2.84 [ABOVE] Biba logo, John McConnell, 1966
● 2.85 [OPPOSITE] Ingrid Boulting wearing Tiger Lily dress, Biba, 1970
Photograph by Norman Parkinson, published in *Vogue* July 1970

Although Biba came out of the unique needs and desires of girls in the British scene of the time, it was extremely well received abroad. Movie stars and musicians from Europe and America all understood what we were doing and flocked to us. French high-end fashion was much younger and stylish. Even the Americans, who were very staid, loved it. Our overseas success was really driven by the cosmetics. We had a 600-foot boutique inside Bergdorf Goodman's on Fifth Avenue in New York that did very well, but our cosmetics were everywhere: Bloomingdale's, Neiman Marcus and all the big chains, and Fiorucci in Italy. The clothing was a little more difficult to translate because of the manufacturing mark-ups. It was hard to bring in the clothes at the prices we wanted. Later, though, we did go to manufacturers in other countries for different categories. We had shoes made in Spain; some platform shoes, sweaters and bags in Italy. The yarns were often better overseas and the manufacturing more sophisticated. We had one holdall-style bag in 20 colours manufactured in Hong Kong, which was a strong seller for us for 12 years.

Towards the end of Biba, the nation was in a very different state. There was the three-day working week, which meant we only had power to light the store for three days. Fitz had to get in gas lamps so that we could stay open. It was all very dark and everyone was affected, but people still came in and bought.

Biba finally ended because the company fell into the hands of people who just did not understand what we were doing. They didn't see the point of being special and unique and wanted to buy everything else in. They saw Biba as a property to be exploited, and didn't get that it was driven by style and by the energy and atmosphere of the shop itself. We tried to buy it back from them twice, but they weren't interested. They put in fluorescent lights and tacky signs, and then dismantled and sold off the assets of the business like a butcher dismembering and processing a carcass. It was very sad. It is still treated as a commodity to this day.

I strongly believe that the legacy of Biba is not that particular look, that particular style, but rather what it stood for. Style can be a way of life, of self-expression, that is available to everyone. We started with our customers, with their needs and desires, and created a framework for them to discover themselves. We never told them what to do or wear, or how to live. We simply gave them an alternative to the mainstream and invited them in to play.

Out of Nottingham
— Paul Smith

I was born in the city of Nottingham, which was famous for the manufacturing of beautiful lace, created on machines that we in Britain had designed and invented. In nearby Leicester, the city and the area were famous for all forms of knitting, which included a machine that made the famous argyle diamond-shaped pattern. Again, the machine had been the invention of a local engineer. When starting my career, I visited many fabric mills in Yorkshire and Lancashire, and the design of the fabrics – along with the wonderful quality – was famous around the world.

After the horror of the two world wars we slowly found our feet and all the creative industries started to blossom, but also individual groups started to be able to express themselves. In the 1950s we got rock 'n' roll and Teddy Boys' clothing taking influence from the Edwardians, and then the Mods – they were amazing for the fact that they were often working-class guys and girls who were really taking care about how they looked and saving up their money to have suits custom-made to their own designs. All forms of creativity were exploding in the 1960s: music, graphic design, photography. We saw the hippies and then the punks, New Romantics, goths, and so on. With regard to fashion, I liked the fact that it was young people wanting to be different from the older generation and the establishment, but what I really admired in Britain was the fact that it was all about how they looked, and their expression was non-violent, non-political.

I started work at the age of 15 in a warehouse selling clothes and shoes. Not fashion, just clothes. But after a few years a hint of fashion appeared in this East Midlands city of Nottingham. I remember our first fashion suit, which was called a San Remo: a three-button jacket, very slim, very reminiscent of the clothes seen in the great films of the day, for instance *La Dolce Vita*. At the age of 18 I left the warehouse and helped a friend open Nottingham's first 'boutique'. She designed the clothes and I organized the shop, the window display and the general running. The shop was pioneering and started to establish itself after a few years.

Eventually I decided to open my own shop, which was a tiny 12-foot-square room with no windows [2.87]. It wasn't really a shop, just a room, but everything about it was so different and unique that eventually it started to draw attention to itself. This was quite a turning point for me, because I began to realize the importance of the customer; and because of the tiny space, the shop was very confrontational and you were immediately engaged with the customer. This made me try to understand how to make customers relax. I started to buy some antique objects and books, on my travels finding things such as old stationery or old posters, which I had in the shop; and this really helped me create an interest immediately the customer walked into the shop.

This idea is something that I have continued with today. And all my shops are approached in a very individual way – all different, always respecting the building or town where the shop is, and always full of photographs, paintings or objects to create this interesting environment [2.88, 2.89]. The key point about this that I learned – and it is something all designers need to bear in mind – is that the customer is the most important person. It is he or she who pays your wages. There is a real danger, as a designer, of being too self-indulgent, and it's also vital to be aware of what is already available in your field. Today's creators need to be more aware than ever of all aspects of their trade: not only of the ability to design, but to understand that the product is just part of the process and must be linked to price, delivery, quality, press, marketing, and much more. I have always tried to stay focused on the importance of the customer.

My first collections were always quite simple in design, but always beautifully made. This came from the insistence of my then-girlfriend (now wife), Pauline, who had studied at the Royal College of Art as a fashion designer during a period when the college was still teaching design and making based on couture, hand-made clothes, where quality and the understanding of how a garment was made and of the importance of cut and proportion were paramount [2.86]. She passed this knowledge on to me, so right from the beginning my clothes were well made. As Pauline was my teacher, because I never had any formal training, I learned my skills at home through conversation and practical experience. But I understood from my early collections that, along with simplicity, I needed some sort of special point in order to sell.

Bear in mind that the fabrics available to me were very basic: a white fabric for shirts or possibly a simple stripe. A jacket fabric would probably only be available from stock in navy blue, and so this led to me always adding a surprise of some sort. This might come in the form of a bright-coloured lining in a simple jacket, or a shirt with contrast button holes or buttons. The way I worked has been described as 'classic with a twist', and this slogan has stayed with me throughout my career, but it works. When I started, many fellow designers were far more creative than me, but were often let down by poorly made clothes, and this meant that many of them would fall by the wayside.

And so, to sum up, we British have got this long, great history of creativity, which I think comes from our openness and more inquisitive character, our feeling relaxed with individuality. Where possibly we have not done so well is in combining creativity with good organization. Our future designers need to be all-rounders, understanding every aspect of their discipline, and this should enable us to continue our great design tradition.

● 2.86 [OPPOSITE] Paul and Pauline Smith, 1970s

● 2.87 [BELOW LEFT] Paul Smith in his first shop, 10 Byard Lane, Nottingham, 1970s ● 2.88 [BELOW RIGHT] Paul Smith boutique, Westbourne Grove, London ● 2.89 [OPPOSITE TOP] Paul Smith boutique, Milan ● 2.90 [OPPOSITE BOTTOM] 'Bird' jacket, Paul Smith, Autumn/Winter collection 1998 | printed velvet | Paul Smith

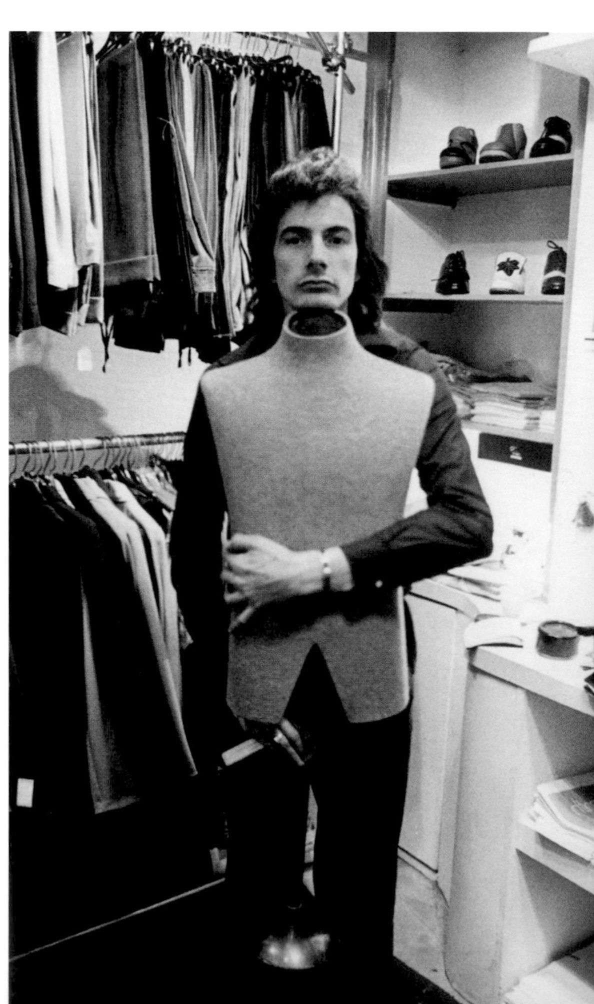

K·L

8 'A Danceable Solution to Teenage Revolution': Subcultural Lifestyles, 1973–86

— Michael Bracewell

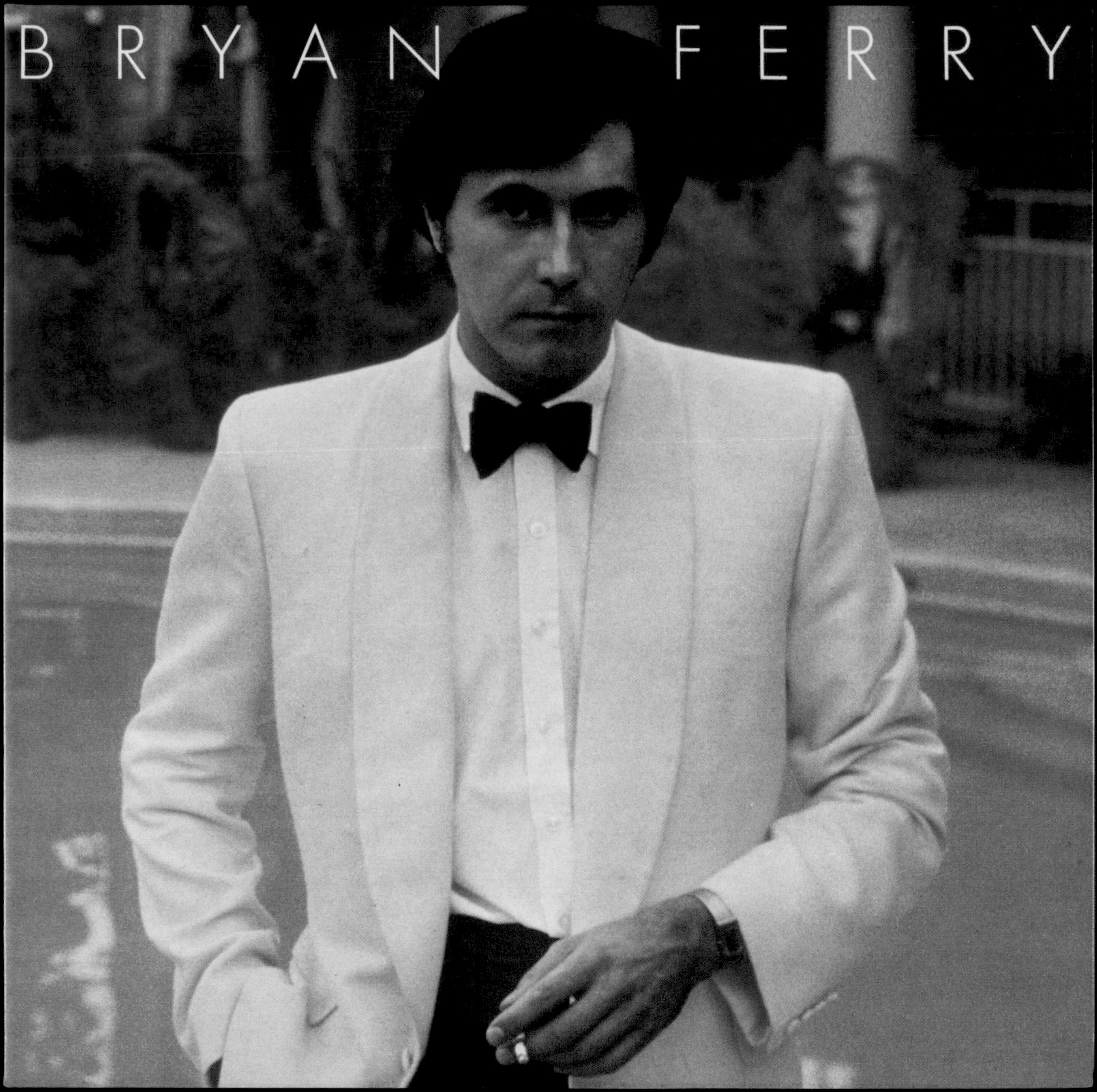

BRYAN FERRY

The second the house lights went down, the first 10 rows of the audience broke ranks and ran hell-for-leather to the front of the stage. Ran, that is, as best as their sheath skirts, antique fox stoles, bomber jackets, platform boots, dark glasses, meticulous coiffure and zealously upheld sense of self-possession would allow. They were all young, and their excited faces, red from the heat and the crush, seemed at odds with the mascara, powder, lipstick and lip gloss that were intended – in a key-chain code of associative ideas – to summon up some camp Americana sci-fi reclamation of Betty Boop or Humphrey Bogart by way of the Weimar Decadence.

Beneath a low, pale-blue cloud of cigarette smoke, Art Deco compacts – in the middle years of the 1970s still easily salvaged from suburban jumble sales – were produced from ancient mesh handbags that had once been the property of flappers who were the great-aunts and grandmothers of these pop children; and with fingers gloved in black or cream satin, rippling up to the elbow, a diamanté bracelet sitting on the wrist, over the glove, young women dabbed at their cheeks and cheekbones with rouge or fern-scented white power. They held amber cigarette-holders or wore tortoiseshell dark glasses with celluloid lenses of mill-pond green; here and there, one of their boyfriends was sporting a second-hand tuxedo, its satin lining the colour of vanilla ice-cream; spiffy net veils seemed to tumble from the front of home-made pill-box hats; and all around were young people – mostly suburban and provincial – dressed in vivacious home-created ensembles that pursued their own fantasies of modern artifice and synthetics, like stage clothes worn as street wear: outlandish styles and fabrics that were nearly all touched with sexual fetishism – lurex and vinyl, plastic, old air-hostess uniforms, scarlet high heels, greased-back hair, faux leopardskin, green nail polish...

By now, the drumbeat had taken up a military, marching rhythm, quickening the pulse, blowing a gale of rising excitement. In the darkness on the stage you could just make out the pinprick beam of a roadie's torch, guiding some shadowy figures; to the side, long banners hung ceremoniously beside banks of amps, each black monolith of which was topped with a winking red light, as though sentient, alert... The kids at the front had started stamping and clapping, their shining eyes fixed unwaveringly on centre-stage; then, from out of nowhere, a terrific double-crash on the drums was joined by the preposterous, haunting, uplifting sound of an electric oboe, conjuring up an implausibly pastoral melody – only to give way to what sounded like a reversed crescendo, deafening and yet still intact, whipped up into new frenzy by the screaming chords of an electric guitar, and the scything screech of an electric violin.

The roar from the audience was deafening: anyone down at the front who happened to glance around the packed auditorium, trying somehow to imprint the scene on their memory, would have seen nothing but entranced, ecstatic faces – in the stalls, the circle, the balcony, rising up as one mass into the dark corners of the old Edwardian theatre. And as the roar intensified, the tall, slick figure of the singer snaked seductively into the spotlight, centre-stage; he moved in curious, marionette movements, as if he were a film of himself that stopped and started; at the level of his hips, his hands chopped the air. Hitting the crest of the rising wave of sound, he crooned out a line that dropped down a scale with effortless finesse: 'All your cares now they seem, oh so far away...'

Such – more or less – was the scene at the beginning of the rally-like concerts performed by the British art rock group Roxy Music, on its UK tours during the middle and later years of the 1970s. The group was particularly popular – this retro-futurist-hard-rock-doo-wop-café-concerto ensemble, dedicated to a credo of richly amplified musical, sartorial and artistic style – in the big industrial cities of northern England and Scotland. Indeed, the audience 'dressed' so devoutly and imaginatively, in what they regarded as the band's spirit, that one music paper (with no small degree of editorial elegance) reviewed the fans' appearance rather than the group's set. As the group's singer and creator Bryan Ferry told *The New York Times*: 'In England, the kids with the most style and the ones most into our music come from places like Liverpool, Birmingham and Newcastle. In England you see kids at our concerts not only in glitter and platforms, but full black tie...'[1]

While pop and rock music had always created youth fashion cults, the ideas behind Roxy Music were a consciously determined confluence of 'high' and 'low' culture, in which the languages of fine art were knowingly mixed with the drama and eroticism of pop. Proposing their own aristocracy – a style elite – Roxy Music and their followers seemed most to echo Baudelaire's pronouncement on dandyism:

> Dandyism appears above all in periods of transition, when democracy is not yet all-powerful, and aristocracy is only just beginning to totter and fall. In the disorder of these times, certain men who are socially, politically, financially ill at ease, but are all rich in native energy, may conceive the idea of establishing a new kind of aristocracy, all the more difficult to shatter as it will be based upon the most precious, the most enduring faculties, and on the divine gift that work and money are unable to bestow. Dandyism is the last spark of heroism amid decadence...[2]

● 2.91 [OPPOSITE] Sleeve for the album *Another Time, Another Place* by Bryan Ferry | Photograph by Eric Boman, 1974

In Britain during the 1970s, for many young people, 'work and money' would be in thin supply; and yet a new concept of dandyism, of which Roxy Music was both the most spectacular pop manifestation and the house band, would begin to take hold and inaugurate a new set of attitudes towards trend, creativity and lifestyle. Peter York, in an iconic series of essays written for *Harpers & Queen* magazine during the latter half of the 1970s, subsequently published in book form under the title *Style Wars* (a pun on the title of the blockbuster movie of 1977, *Star Wars*), would monitor the ways in which pop styling – as originated in London – would mutate into a new mode of flamboyance, the temper and aesthetic codes of which were meticulously sourced and selected, as if by connoisseurs of cult iconography. 'In the Golden Age,' York would write later, 'that is the 1970s, the Phoney Wars were ... Style Wars... Style became a weapon to forge your own legend. Style started to be accessible in a quite unprecedented way...'[3]

The fashion designer Antony Price, whose styling of Roxy Music (long before 'styling' was a practice recognized anywhere, save in cinema) had made him an honorary member of the band, would later point out that this new revolt into style was the brainchild of some sharp thinkers: 'The world we are talking about was a world obsessed with things clever,' he pronounced, retrospectively, 'and with spotting things clever...'[4] Few were cleverer than Roxy Music's founding synthesizer and tape player, Brian Eno, who routed the group's sound through a series of filters and effects that created a ghostly, filmic sheen to the music. In interviews with astonished music journalists, for many of whom Roxy Music's brand of art-school artifice was a desecration of rock music's church of the blues (in which musical 'authenticity' was worshipped above all), Eno would occasionally claim to be an alien from the planet Xenon. So lateral and multi-allusive were his musical and cultural theories that many almost believed him. But vital to the development of subcultural style, as it would emerge in the 1970s and take distinct form in 1976, through punk, was Eno's observation that the founding members of Roxy Music regarded the band as 'a school of art set up in opposition to all prevailing trends'.[5] Likewise the group's singer, Bryan Ferry (a former student of Richard Hamilton at the University of Newcastle), would airily remark, 'I am a collagist...', adding, 'Roxy Music are, above all, a state of mind...' To the bewilderment of the US press he would later cite Marcel Duchamp and Smokey Robinson as equal musical inspirations.[6]

At the centre of Roxy Music's cult of 'clever' style (which is not to underplay the dexterity and passion of their music) lay the proto-Postmodernist notion that ideas from the world of fine art and 'high' culture could be transposed to the media of mass popular culture, without compromising the identity of either. The artist Carol McNicoll, who had created one of Eno's most memorable stage costumes – with a collar of protruding, rococo black feathers – would recall Roxy Music fans running to the front of the stage, and overhearing one girl screaming to her friend, 'He's wearing the feathers!' [2.92]. McNicoll later remarked:

> One of the other things that was important in the idea of the band was the notion that you could make things that were serious art, and they could also be 'popular' – that was the ideal. Not to make something obscure that only a few people would ever see or listen to. The same was true for me: that I had made this costume and hadn't compromised, but had been as far out as I wanted to be; and it had become really popular. One wanted to get away from being an artist in the art world sense – one wanted to move out of the art world. So you weren't making paintings or making a big splash at the ICA; you were actually out there in the 100 Club or wherever, in popular culture, and loads of people loving what you did. At the same time, it was all about elitism...[7]

Such ideas – treating art history and cultural history as part-dressing-up box, part-manifesto – would both lay the foundations for the subsequent development of punk and, in keeping with punk's flaunting of nihilism and negativity, be treated as the later movement's first target and victim. Peter York, in an essay entitled 'Them', would summarize the immediate pre-punk moment in London. 'Them' was a semi-satirical but highly detailed piece of social anthropology, and its importance lay in its identification of subcultural lifestyle being asserted as an art form, and vice versa – 'the art school bulge and the assimilation of Camp'.[8] Using the term 'Art Necro', York recounted the rise of a new class of 'creatives' whose ideas were based on merging camp, revivalism, Pop Art and pop music. Over all of this, like twin patron saints, hovered the enshrined presences of Andy Warhol and designer Ossie Clark; but the agents of mass culture who would take these ideas from Kensington and Earls Court to the high streets, factory towns and dormitory suburbs of the UK would be two pop stars: Roxy Music's Bryan Ferry, and former Mod, turned hippy, turned glam art rocker, David Bowie [2.93, 2.94]. Both of whom, York concluded, should hang side by side in the Tate Gallery as contemporary works of art.[9]

● 2.92 [OPPOSITE] Stage costume for Brian Eno, Carol McNicoll, 1972 | Rayon jacket with feathers, satin trousers embroidered with silver thread | V&A: S.156 & 157–1977

● 2.93 [ABOVE] *David Bowie*, Brian Duffy, 1973 | Photographed for the album *Aladdin Sane*, dye transfer print | Duffy Archive
● 2.94 [OPPOSITE] David Bowie wearing a stage costume by Kansai Yamamoto, 1973 | Knitted wool

To be young, bored and ravenous for glamour, in Britain in the mid-1970s, was to become a cultural archaeologist. In a youth culture that still had a deeply conservative and restricted media, ideas and influences were harder to research, but – once found – were embraced more fervently. As such, subcultural lifestyle became a key-chain code of reference points, recognized by fellow foot-soldiers in the style wars, and through which new iconographies were established. And for those whose tastes were inclined towards cool alienation, extreme aesthetics and cultural 'difference' – a stance that was simultaneously confrontational, elitist and deeply romantic – the cosmography of artificiality, decadence and doomed glamour appeared most relevant and inviting. Throughout the late 1970s and even beyond punk, Roxy and Bowie would remain the two imperial forces in British pop and rock culture to inspire subcultural club scenes (Pips in Manchester, for example, and Billie's and Blitz in London) devoted to self-reinvention. As an advert for Bowie's album *Heroes* in 1977 stated, 'There is Old Wave, There is New Wave, and there is David Bowie.'

Punk in the UK would become the psychic and cultural lightning conductor to which the energy and creativity of the disaffected or culturally enquiring youth of its core period from 1976 to 1977 would be drawn. In this, punk would hold up a mirror to the sensibilities of those for whom it became an engrossing catalyst of personal or creative experience. To some, the movement was political – actual class warfare, fought in terms of pop ideology; for others, punk might seem the reclamation of Zurich Dada or the Ballets Russes. In terms of creativity, however, and the continuing lineage of art made in the media of subcultural lifestyle (how you dressed, what you read, what reference points you followed and which style codes you acknowledged), its power lay on the one hand in its eclecticism, and on the other in its elitism.

An array of ideas and inspirations, from Surrealism (Malcolm McLaren and Vivienne Westwood creating a tie made out of feathers or an old rubber inner tube) to Situationism (Jamie Reid's graphics for the Sex Pistols) to science fiction (the desolate urban landscapes photographed by Jon Savage), were reprised and reshaped to express through music and fashion the idea of modernity itself having reached critical mass, and being set to self-destruct [2.95, 2.96]. The aesthetic and the mood of punk thus played games with auto-deconstruction: punk clothing appeared simultaneously derelict and fetishistic, often literally falling apart when one wore it, or impeding the wearer's movements; punk graphics – as demonstrated by Linder's 'domestic utensil/pornography' photomontages made between 1977 and 1978 – utilized the historically political medium of collage [2.98]; while punk music played games with acceleration and deceleration – turning a song into a blur or a dirge, in which the idea of musicality was debased or hyper-stylized into new and outlandish forms.

An ideology based on a code of cultural reference points, punk routed creativity back to the amateur and to the individual. If Style had become the weapon with which one created one's own mythology, as Peter York had suggested about the 'Them' generation immediately preceding punk, then punk itself became a process of self-reinvention for those who participated in its closed world. As evidenced by a photograph of punk model and SEX-boutique sales assistant Jordan – her make-up resembling a Cubist rearrangement of her features, while her clothing suggested the prim English style of an elderly suburban librarian – meeting a clearly amused Andy Warhol, the notion that you could turn yourself into a mythic work of art (and a 'star', in the Warholian sense) was encouraged by punk creativity [2.97].

For many young people in Britain during the latter years of the 1970s and the early years of the '80s the sensibility loosely defined as 'punk' would authorize this practice of self-reinvention. This often took hold in those suburban or provincial districts where there were fewer distractions on offer, and where the call of glamour and confrontational attitudes sounded loudest. As with the youth movements that preceded it, punk prompted its devotees to first rebel locally and then migrate to London – often in the (usually futile) hope that their subcultural lifestyle might lead to wider and financially rewarding recognition.

Many (but not all) punks rechristened themselves, as though to mark their commitment to self-reinvention. In suburban London, a group of teenagers and young adults known as the Bromley Contingent included the writer Bertie Marshall, whose own 'punk name' was Berlin. The title of Marshall's punk memoir, *Berlin Bromley*, neatly summarizes the collage-like punk formula of self-recreation; and singer Boy George, in his introduction to the book, describes the comic, yet intent manner in which suburban outsiders attempted to become subcultural aristocracy – risking all to pursue some dream of urban glamour by making auto-faction, in effect, the medium for the creativity. In this, sexuality and androgyny became a form of cultural metaphor, suggestive of wider notions of difference. As Boy George recounts, of the early punk scene of which the Bromley Contingent were founding 'stars':

> We were all Bowie freaks and who hadn't wondered what life was like in pre-war Germany (Berlin, in fact) after seeing the movie 'Cabaret' with its blatant and yet matter-of-fact bi-sexuality? For any young Space Oddity, it was a time of great hope and discovery; David Bowie might have laid Ziggy Stardust to rest but he was still flirting with camp, and, to quote Quentin Crisp, 'wearing the sort of make-up that would have killed a beginner.' Seeing John Hurt portraying Crisp in 'The Naked Civil Servant' was yet another chapter in the 'How To Be An Outsider' handbook.[10]

● 2.95 [OPPOSITE] Poster promoting the Sex Pistols, Jamie Reid, 1977 | Designed to advertise the single 'God Save the Queen', offset lithograph | V&A: S.759–1990

GOD Save THE QUEEN
SEX PISTOLS

THE
CLASH

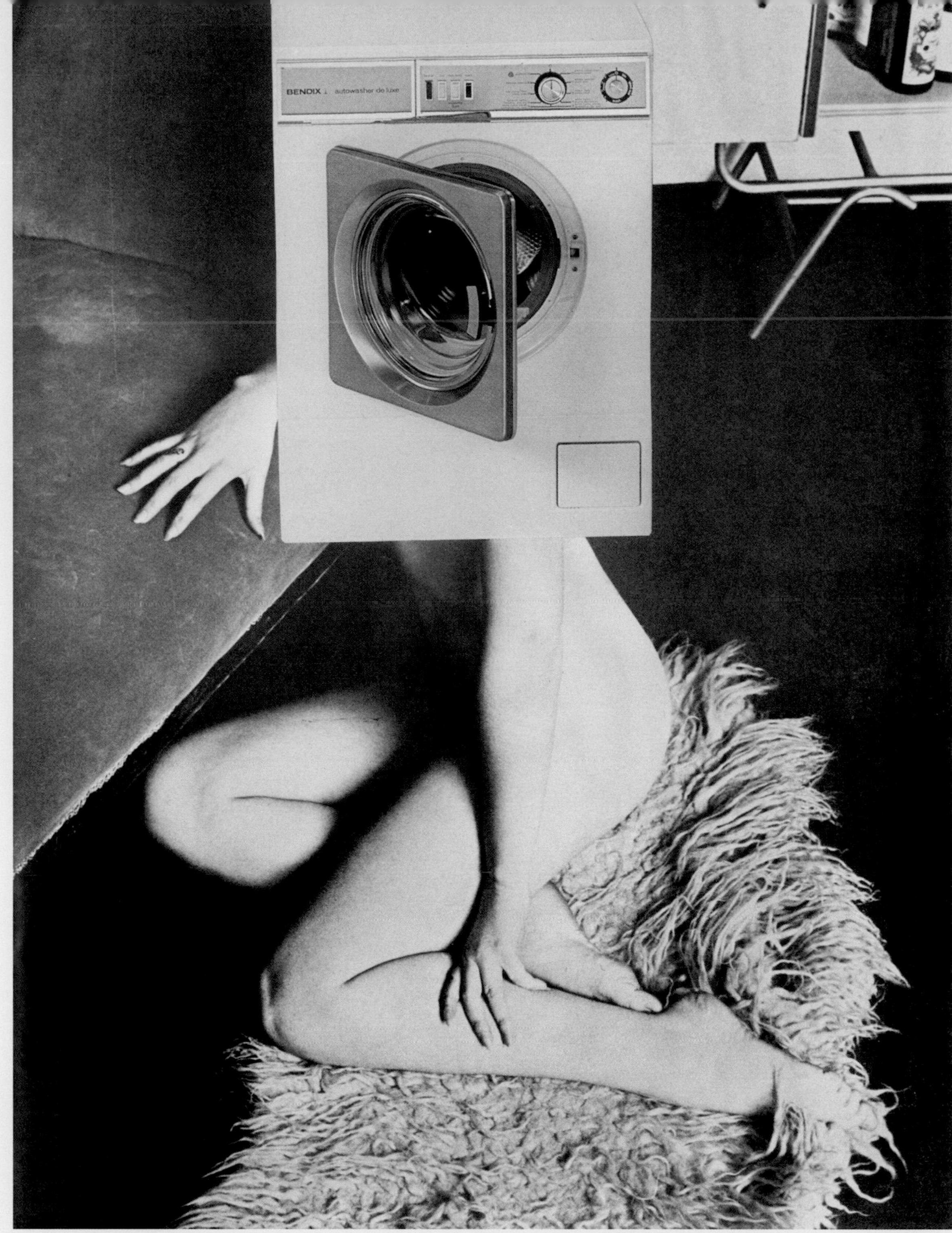

● 2.96 [OPPOSITE TOP] Photograph from the *Uninhabited London* series, Jon Savage, January 1977
● 2.97 [OPPOSITE BOTTOM] Jordan meeting Andy Warhol at his exhibition at the Institute of Contemporary Arts, 1978
● 2.98 [ABOVE] *Pretty Girl*, Linder Sterling, 1977 | Photomontage

● 2.99 [OPPOSITE] Sleeve for the album *Closer* by Joy Division, Peter Saville, 1980

Crisp, the suburban Sutton-born life-model and writer, whose first volume of autobiography, *The Naked Civil Servant*, was reprinted in 1977 to become one of punk's manuals, had experienced the direct consequences, in the 1930s and '40s, of outraging the British public by his very presence as an unashamed 'effeminate homosexual' (in his own words). His account of walking through the streets of London can be read as a precursor to the hostility with which his punk and post-punk descendants would be greeted beyond the confines of their own meeting places:

> As my appearance progressed from the effeminate to the bizarre, the reaction of strangers passed from startled contempt to outraged hatred. They began to take action. If I was compelled to stand still in the street in order to wait for a bus or on the platform of an Underground station, people would turn without a word and slap my face. If I was wearing sandals, passers-by took care to stamp on my toes; and once a crowd had started to follow me, it grew and grew until no traffic could pass down the road...[11]

The attraction during punk of Crisp as an icon, whose autobiography could be read as a fable of revolt, lay in his dedication to a form of extreme individualism that doubled as a negation of society and social rules. Crisp, by his own admission, had neither ambitions nor passionate desires; he wished simply to exist ('my occupation is breathing,' he quipped) on his own terms, unmolested. And in this seeming passivity lay his outrageousness and his unwavering sense of contrariness and protest. His dyed hair and touches of make-up asserted his right to non-conform, at the risk – in London during the 1930s and '40s – of constant and violent persecution. For many young people whose lives were shaped or informed by punk, the tenets of Crisp's determined stance struck an encouraging and exhilarating chord.

1977 would be regarded as punk's zenith – a Year Zero in which the movement's chaotic assertion of modern revolt within a derelict and deliquescent urban society would reach the peak of its notoriety. While contemporary British art seemed remote, insular and largely irrelevant to the significant number of punks attending art schools or interested in the arts, both Stephen Willats (who had been taught in the early 1960s by the controversial adherent of cybernetics, Roy Ascott) and Gilbert & George would make work that mirrored both the extremes and the aggression of the punk sensibility, and its surprising capacity for poetic insight.

The *Dirty Words Pictures* (1977) by Gilbert & George were richly atmospheric studies of the Brutalist and post-industrial urban landscape, the tension between their violence and melancholy further intensified by details of simultaneously frantic and child-like graffiti [2.102]. Their titles read like the titles of punk tracks: *Prostitute Poof*, *Are You Angry or Are You Boring?* In the same year Stephen Willats made works that combined photography and sculpture with research and anthropology into urban communities – specifically those groups or individuals who might be regarded as socially marginalized or culturally disaffected. His six-panel photo/text work *I Don't Want to Be Like Anyone Else* (1977) directly questioned the ways in which individual identity was both constructed and perceived (and therefore controlled) within modern society [2.100]. (A later work, *Living Like a Goya* [1983] explored the manner in which a woman who frequented the Cha Cha Cha sex club in west London had redefined herself and her life through her extreme clothes and make-up. The title of the work, like that of Bertie Marshall's memoirs, was both poetic and succinct in its description of self-re-creation as a subcultural art form.)

For the 'Them' generation of the mid-1970s the 'art directed lifestyle' (to coin York's phrase) and its expression within music, design and the arts had been leavened with camp, Pop Americana, Pop Art and a super-stylized nostalgia for *la vie deluxe* of the 1920s and '30s – the heightened romance summoned up by Roxy Music. By the close of the 1970s a new darkness had passed into the iconography of pop and rock subcultures: punk's concentration on ruins and dereliction had been joined by an identification with industrialism and sepulchral melancholy – rather as though, following punk's pronouncement of modernity's death ('Modernity Killed Every Night,' ran the slogan at McLaren's boutique at 430 King's Road), there was now a mood of requiem and stillness. Peter Saville's design for Joy Division's second and final studio release, *Closer*, released after the suicide of the group's singer, Ian Curtis, in 1980, would capture this mood precisely [2.99].

The election in Britain in 1979 of a Conservative government had added an increasingly political strain to the darkling, industrial-elegiac mood within subcultural creativity. Regarded as repressive and ill disposed towards the arts in general, as well as towards low-income and unemployed people, the Conservative regimen was swiftly perceived to endorse the dour, end-of-the-world mood that had risen amid the ruins of punk. The surreal and cartoon-like playfulness of punk – the folk devil pantomime of the Sex Pistols or X-Ray Spex, for example – gave way to a sensibility that was coldly post-industrial and drawn to the imagery of bleak and authoritarian landscapes. At its most creative – *Metal Box*, released by John Lydon's second group, Public Image Ltd, in the late autumn of 1979, for example – the music of post-punk deployed a coldly electronic style to express a lead-heavy sense of depression and urban alienation. In Manchester and Sheffield (as cities hard hit by the new Tory policies, and whose own post-industrial and '60s Brutalist landscapes had become worn out and unwelcoming) there would be an emergence of what Philip Oakey, singer of The Human League, from Sheffield, would describe as 'alienated synthesizer music'.[12]

·CLOSER·

● 2.100 [BELOW] *I Don't Want to be Like Anyone Else*, Stephen Willats, 1977 | Photographs, ink, text on card ● 2.101 [RIGHT] Sleeve for the 12" single 'The Dignity of Labour' by the Human League, 1979 ● 2.102 [OPPOSITE TOP] *Are You Angry or Are You Boring?*, Gilbert & George, 1977 | From *Dirty Words Pictures*, mixed-media ● 2.103 [OPPOSITE BOTTOM] Dress and stockings, Bodymap, 1985 | Hand-knitted cotton and rayon, nylon, polyester and Lycra | V&A: T.313-B–1985

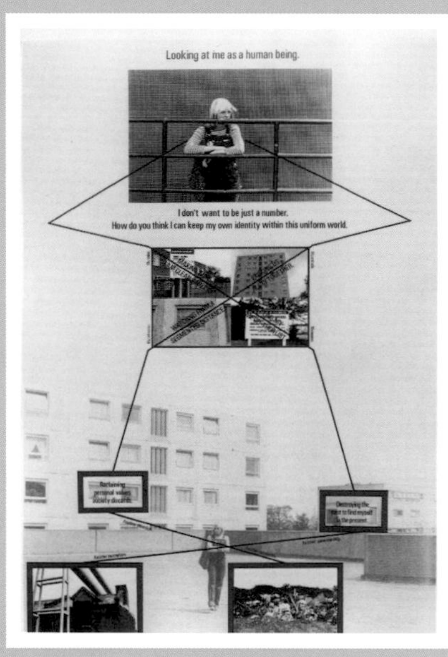

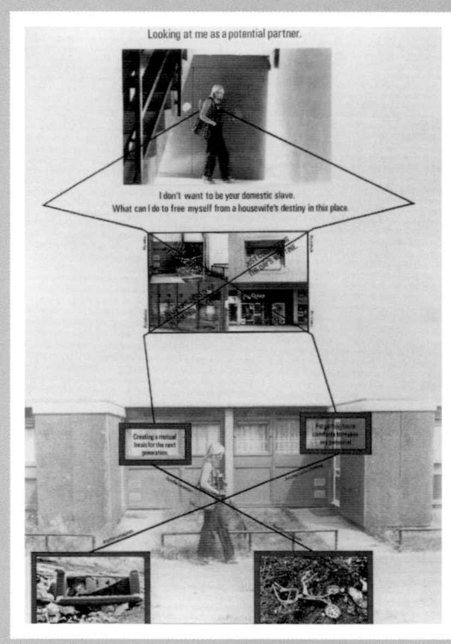

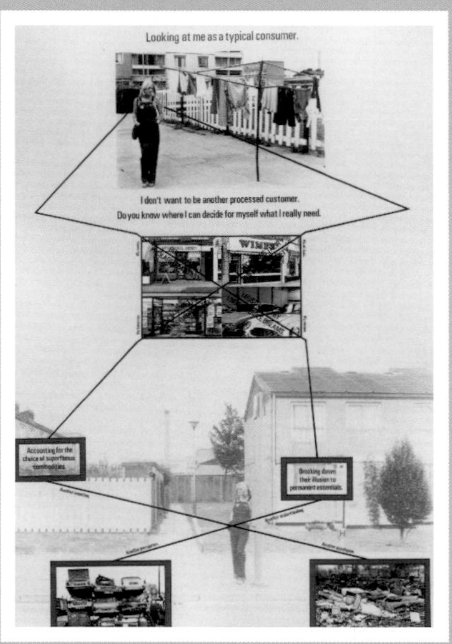

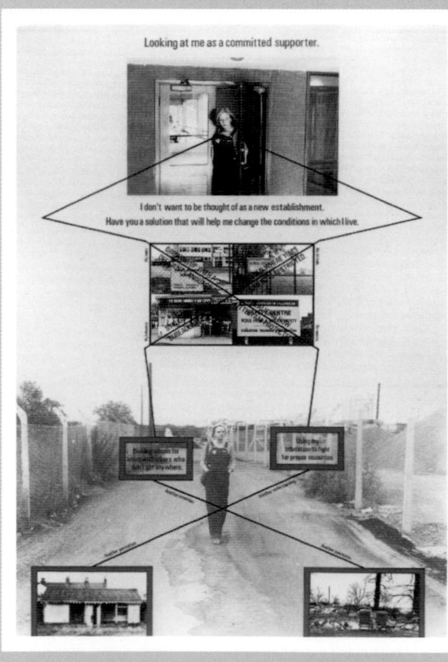

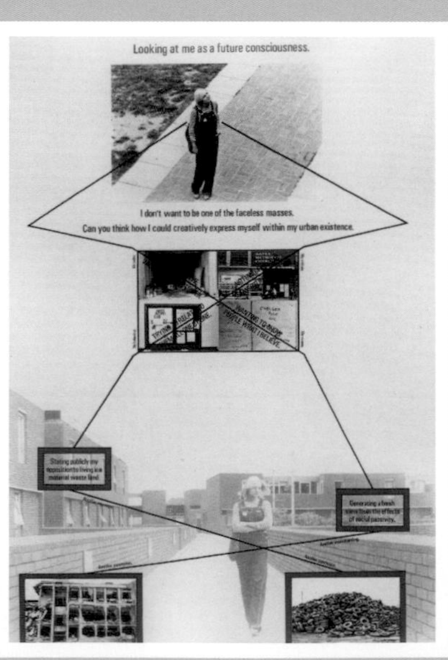

The bleak midwinter of post-punk in the UK was seen by its creators and participants as culturally related to an idea of Germany and Eastern Europe – an idea largely borrowed from David Bowie's residence in Berlin during the latter years of the 1970s and the electronically influenced trilogy of albums that he recorded there. If *Cabaret* had been an inspiration to an early and pre-punk notion of hedonistic and androgynous 'divine decadence' (to quote from the film), then this new engagement with a romantic projection of Berlin, Düsseldorf or even Warsaw was far darker. It was a sensibility of romantic disaffection that pursued, through an oddly refracted British subculture, both Bowie's new European/industrial aesthetic (on his albums *Low* [1977] and *Heroes* [1978]) 'give me steel, give me steel, give me pulsars unreal' and a grimmer and more questionable identification with the horrors and tragedies committed under Nazism and Eastern European totalitarianism.

Two of the most iconic British groups of this period would have the roots of their founding imagery and creative identity in this post-punk identification with phantasms of European and Eastern European totalitarianism. Manchester-based Joy Division (which remains perhaps the most-referenced rock group in contemporary art) would be notoriously named after the slang term for prostitutes frequented by Nazi officers, and had previously been entitled Warsaw. The group's subsequent incarnation, following Curtis's suicide, was entitled New Order – a name that also possessed Nazi references. In Sheffield, the first release by The Human League would be entitled 'The Dignity of Labour Parts 1–4' – a title that had authoritarian overtones that were emphasized by the 12-inch single's artwork, featuring a photograph of Russian cosmonaut Yuri Gagarin marching in full uniform to collect a medal of honour [2.101].

As with all pop cultural moments, there was a sense in which the cultural morbidity of early post-punk and new industrialism (as a musical genre, typified in the UK by groups such as Throbbing Gristle and Test Department) would swiftly dissipate into a lighter form and a pop fashion. Reaction followed action, and the darkness and intensity of British post-punk circa 1978–80 would almost inevitably give way to its opposite: a return to more upbeat pop glamour, in which so-called 'futurism' (meaning synthesizer pop) was mingled with a heavily stylized reprise of fashions from the 1950s and '60s. The 'time-travelling' aspect of pop subculture (initiated by Roxy Music as early as 1972) was taken into a new configuration – electronic pop running alongside nostalgia for earlier pop forms – the common denominator of which was the exchange of industrialism and alienation for the language and ethos of glamour.

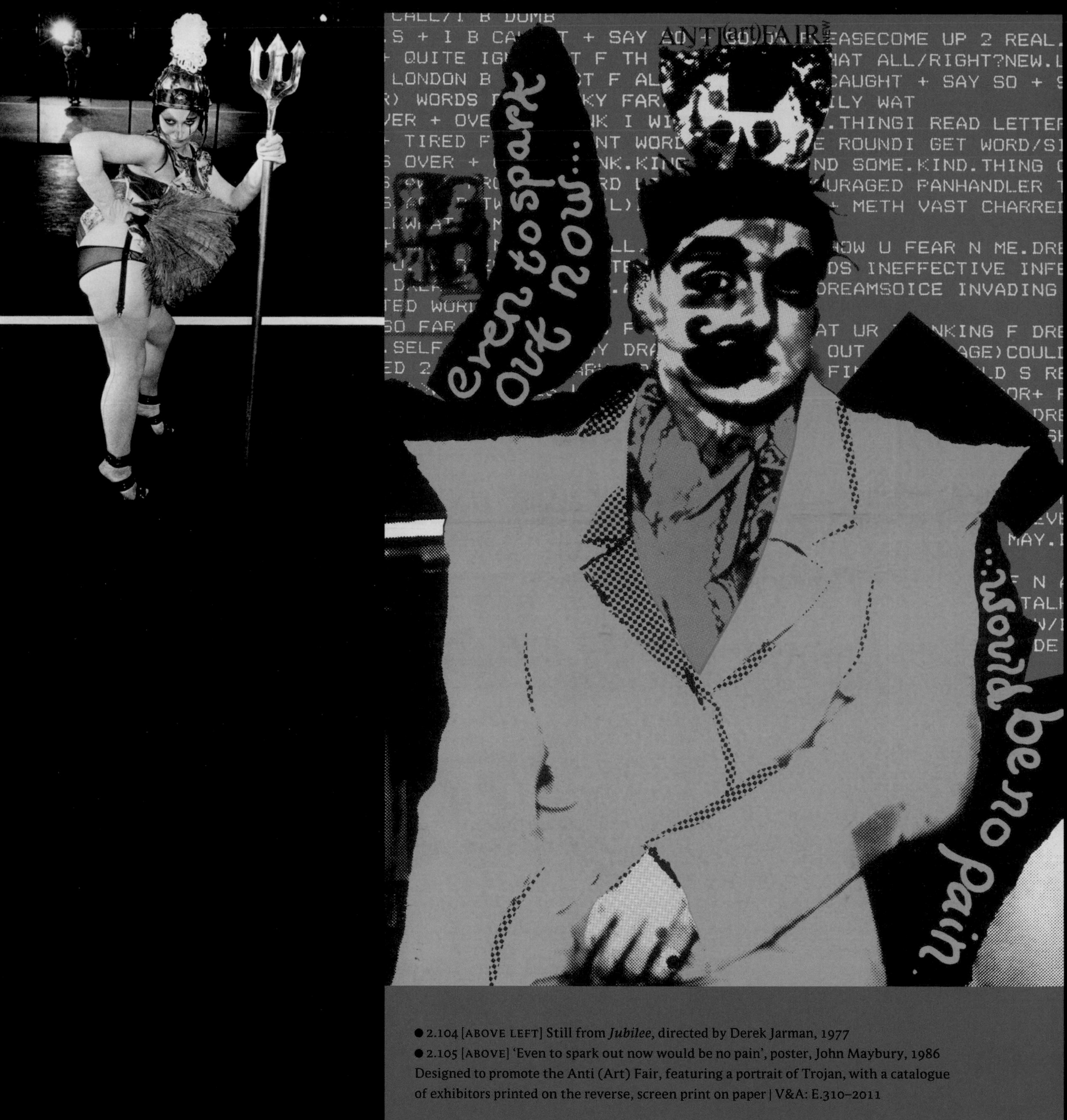

● 2.104 [ABOVE LEFT] Still from *Jubilee*, directed by Derek Jarman, 1977
● 2.105 [ABOVE] 'Even to spark out now would be no pain', poster, John Maybury, 1986
Designed to promote the Anti (Art) Fair, featuring a portrait of Trojan, with a catalogue of exhibitors printed on the reverse, screen print on paper | V&A: E.310–2011

This was best demonstrated by the shift in The Human League's image and artwork: from the Soviet grey and electronic sparseness of 'The Dignity of Labour Parts 1–4' to the dazzling whiteness of their multimillion-selling masterpiece *DARE* – its typography a direct and triumphant reference to that of *Vogue* magazine, and the somewhat pallid maleness of the original group now feminized by the presence of two young female singers.

Between 1973 and 1983 British pop music and its related subcultural fashions would experience a wave of intense and extraordinarily varied creativity. Coinciding with the end of the pre-computer and pre-digital period, the 'Them', punk, post-punk and New Romantic movements (although none of these sensibilities ever subscribed, within their own participants, to anything so definitive as a 'movement') would inspire intense and highly intelligent creativity – becoming for many of their adherents as artistically relevant as (or more so than) anything on offer within the institutional art world of galleries and art schools. Just as Roxy Music's Brian Eno had once quipped, 'I was a teenage art school', so for many of the young artists and designers who would emerge in the later 1980s the experience of punk or New Romanticism would be of fundamental importance to the development of their ideas.

In the decade between post-punk's beginnings in 1978 and Damien Hirst's 'Freeze' exhibition in London (the starting whistle for what would become known as Young British Art) the divide between the institutional art world and the art deriving from subculturally inspired creativity would be pronounced and almost impossible to bridge. But by way of a largely (but not exclusively) gay network of artists, designers and socialites, there would emerge during the first half of the 1980s a school of subculturally informed creativity that might be regarded as the last hurrah of the old 'underground' sensibility.

Figures such as performance artist and musician Genesis P. Orridge and film-maker Derek Jarman would provide generational links between the 'underground', 'transgressive' and experimental art scenes of the 1960s and '70s, and a new generation of London-based artists that would include Cerith Wyn Evans, John Maybury, Royal Ballet School protégé Michael Clark and others [2.104]. As important to this densely and intimately networked, subculturally informed creativity would be club personalities Trojan (Guy Barnes) and Leigh Bowery. Volatile and flamboyant, drug-using and often outrageously behaved, this was a group that existed beyond the furthest fringes of any pop or subcultures, and who exploded image and style into mesmeric and wildly audacious new languages. The fashion designers Bodymap – Stevie Stewart and David Holah, both graduates of Middlesex Polytechnic in 1982 – created vivacious and outlandish collections that restructured and reinvented conventional models of clothing in a manner at once avant-garde and daring [2.103]. More than this, Bodymap became a kind of sartorial livery for the punk-informed, metropolitan coterie of Maybury, Michael Clark, Boy George, Leigh Bowery et al. Highly acclaimed for their creativity, Bodymap would, however, go out of business in the late 1980s, thus confirming their somewhat mythic hold over the zeitgeist of a short-lived and perilously self-destructive era.

Aggressive modernity and almost child-like sexual flippancy were balanced within the art of these post-punk, often drug-using, predominantly gay outsiders – the primary medium and raw material for which were their own appearance and identity; thus derived, their 'work' was as unsettling and aesthetically jarring as it was meticulously conceived and precisely crafted. And, as such, their activities resembled the ultimate endorsement of Boy George's idea of a 'How to Be an Outsider' handbook.

A sale catalogue entry for John Maybury's poster for the Anti (Art) Fair, organized by art dealer David Dawson and film-maker Akiko Hada, held in Camden in 1986, does much to characterize and define the personnel and aesthetic of this particular milieu [2.105]. Trojan (quoted a close friend of Boy George) would die from a heroin overdose the following year – thus making his observation appear closer to a suicide note:

> Maybury (John). Even to spark out now would be no pain – Trojan. An Anti (Art) Fair – Original exhibition poster. 65.5 x 94 cm ... a montage portrait of the artist Trojan in five colours and oversized Benday dots on a white stock... A vivid image; the level of colour saturation is astonishing. Trojan is depicted as a semi-mustachioed, one-and-a-half-eared aesthete in an oversized jacket. A skull floats directly above his tousled hair.[13]

While several of these artists – notably Michael Clark, John Maybury and Cerith Wyn Evans – would become senior figures within contemporary dance, film and art respectively, others were killed off by drugs, alcohol or AIDS-related illnesses. In this much, the short springtime of their creativity during the first five years of the 1980s seems to close, historically, a 10-year period in British art and culture when an 'art beyond the gallery' and an art derived from subcultural and pop-cultural lifestyle seemed briefly to interpret and react to its times in ways that were as intelligent, poised and risk-taking as they were artistically and aesthetically innovative.

All of these artists, designers, socialites, misfits, fans, dilettantes, writers, dandies and activists were in one sense reworking the traditional soil of youthful romanticism; yet within their temper, wit, elegance and style, their yearning for heightened modes of expression and heartfelt assertions of individualism they asserted a mode of creativity as politically intent as it was artistically vertiginous, which still stands in direct opposition to the pasteurized vastness of the corporate consumer mono-environment that would be built over the cities where they had once lived and worked.

The Autonomous Opportunity
— Peter Saville

The post-war pop generations have been informed and characterized by their consumption of commodities – becoming collectors of culture initially through music, and subsequently through fashion and design. Enquiry, association, aspiration and, ultimately, the desire to participate in person have inspired individuals to embrace cultural activity and define their own identities creatively.

Factory Records was a case study in participation. Founded in 1978 in the vacuum of post-punk uncertainty, our independent collective was inexperienced, but idealistic and in pursuit of progress. In the context of Factory, progress meant doing things differently and – we believed – better, because we could. In the absence of any remit of profitability, each individual was at liberty to pursue their own own ideal of what could be...

As a co-founder and the 'art director' of Factory, I had the freedom to quote from the canon of art and design that I had begun to discover in the library at Manchester Polytechnic, rather than in the reality of my everyday experience. Such freedom is uncommon in the discipline of communication design. A largely adolescent audience was introduced to, familiarized with and, in some cases, inspired by this dissemination of 'cultured' aesthetics, which were endorsed through their association with music. Thus new standards of expectation were set and carried into adult life by this audience.

The concrete manifestation of this was to be Factory's club The Haçienda, which opened in 1982. Housed in one of Manchester's former warehouses, the club was really a site-specific statement by Ben Kelly – signing a new way of being in a former industrial city – a place where the DNA of industry was reconstituted for our post-industrial generation. Ben's way of working was one of free-association between the International Style and a particularly British type of industrial high-tech. And, as such, it quintessentially belonged in the first industrial city. This was the true beginning of the journey of regeneration for the city of Manchester.

As Factory artists, Ben and I were granted channels of self-expression to a mass audience through the subculture of pop. It was this autonomous opportunity, born out of Factory's idealism rather than any commercial objective, that allowed us to transport ideas, aesthetics and, ultimately, values that would advance the form of our everyday experience.

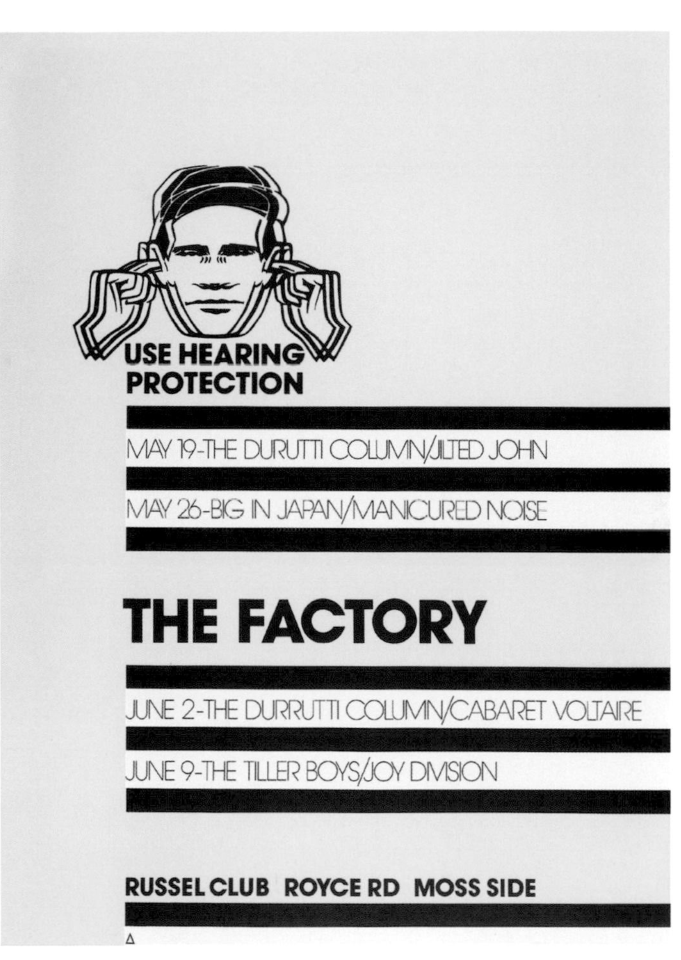

● 2.106 [OPPOSITE] Sleeve for the album *Unknown Pleasures* by Joy Division, Peter Saville, 1979 | Printed by Garrod & Lofthouse Ltd, offset lithograph on card | V&A: E.2274–1990 ● 2.107 [TOP] The Haçienda, Manchester, Ben Kelly, 1982 ● 2.108 [ABOVE] Poster for the Factory nightclub, Peter Saville, 1978 | Silkscreen

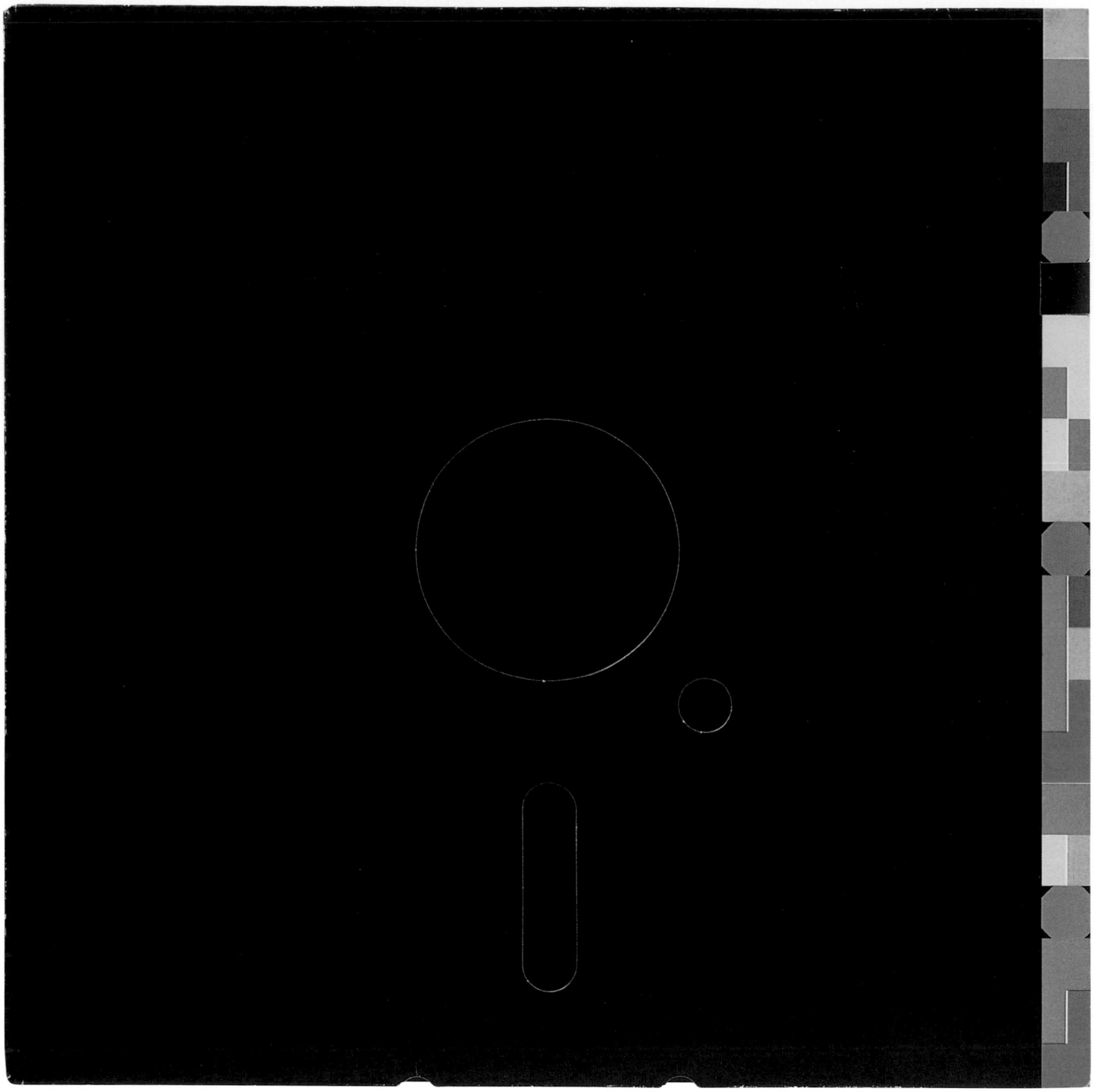

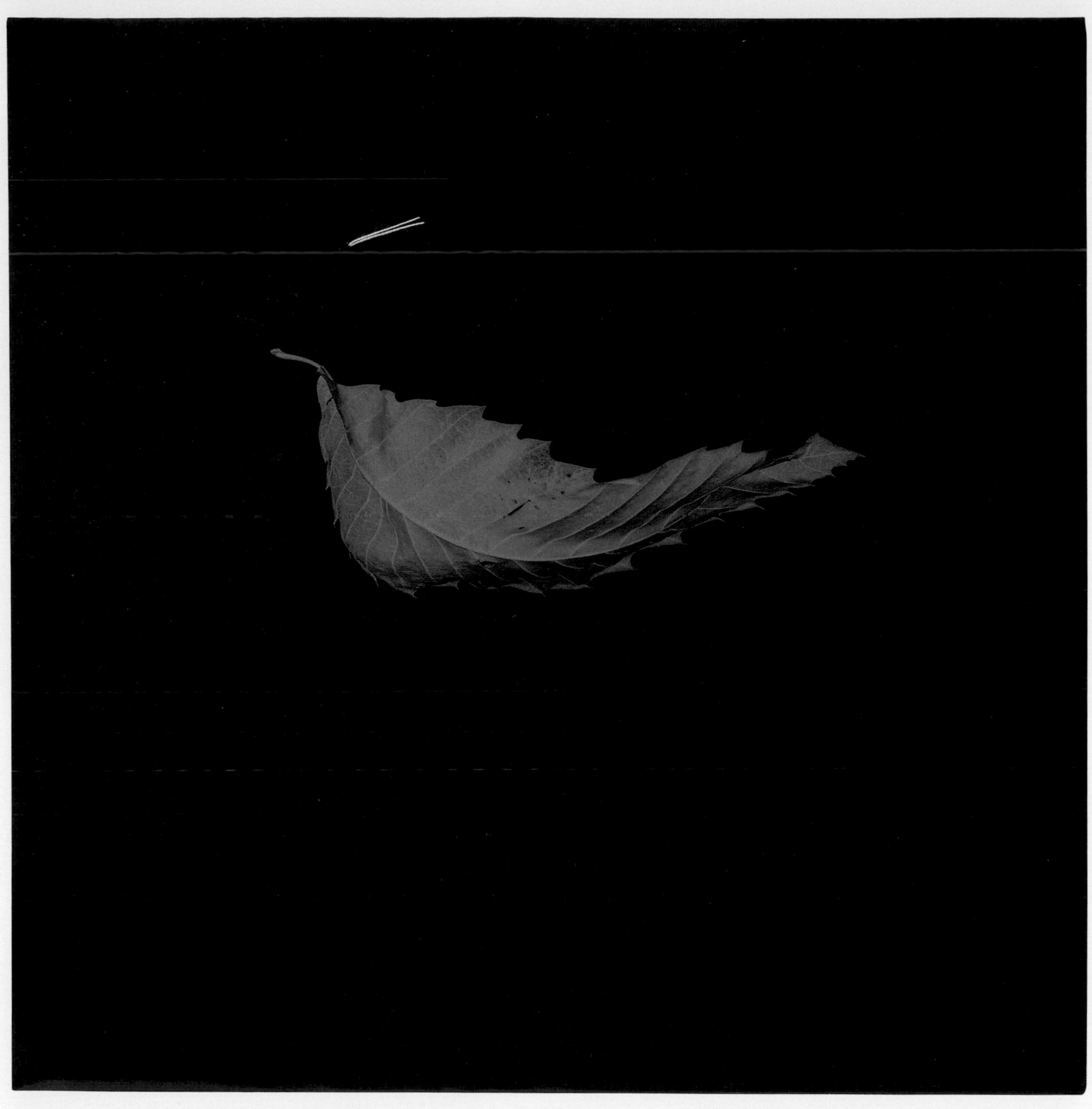

● 2.109 [OPPOSITE] Sleeve for the 12" single 'Blue Monday' by New Order, Peter Saville, 1983 | Offset lithograph on card ● 2.110 [ABOVE] Sleeve for the 12" single 'True Faith' by New Order, Peter Saville, 1987 | Dichromat image by Trevor Key and Peter Saville, offset lithograph on card

Eighties, Nineties, Noughties

— Tom Dixon

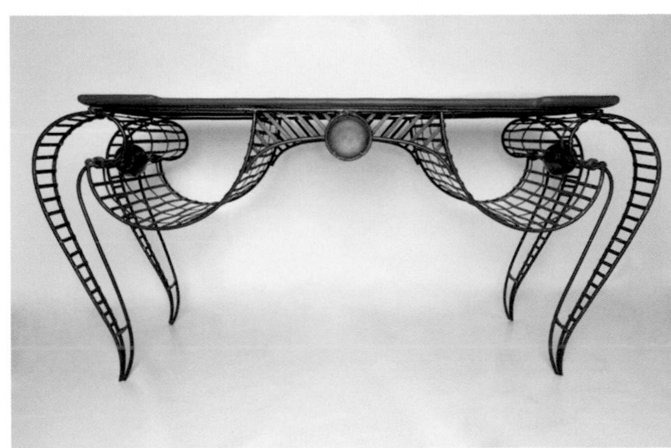

I wasn't really that conscious of a design scene and didn't think of myself as a designer when I started out – I was much more involved with the music business and the emerging club scene, which was where I was making my money.

There really were no design galleries, no Sunday supplements with style pages and no particular design establishment that I knew about. I vaguely knew about the Design Council and the Boilerhouse at the V&A, but they seemed only concerned with 'proper' industrial design: Instamatics and Kenwood Chefs, Concorde and disposable razors.

I had spent a couple of years running discotheques in the West End with a small group of friends, and when we finally ran out of luck and leases in proper nightclubs, we took to hiring warehouses and devising elaborate entertainment: kung fu and body-building demonstrations, crockery-smashing stalls and black-light art shows, and we had to make decors and structures for the entertainment. I learned to gas-weld in Paul Richman's garage in Brixton and fell in love with the molten metal and the speed at which I could stick things together. A small group of us started welding and devised a primitive manifesto – I can't for the life of me remember what it said, but we had been used to creating promotional material from being in bands and clubs. Anyhow, Mark Brazier-Jones, Nick Jones and I decided to buy a ton of scrap metal from the yard in Chelsea harbour, dump it in a vacant shop front in Kensington High Street and weld an exhibition together within a week [2.111]. We called that 'Creative Salvage', which seemed to be a sticky name, and when we sold a fair proportion of the output that weekend, it seemed like a fantastic way to make money: very chaotic and definitely influenced by the do-it-yourself attitude of the music business.

There were other people making things in a similar way – Judy Blame in jewellery and Christopher Nemeth in clothing, Andy the furniture-maker in wooden furniture – all in junk materials, but we all had different outputs and locations in London. I think Ron Arad was the only person who had a more established business, which had been going for a while. I taught André Dubreuil to weld, and he joined us and added a slightly more classical twist to the enterprise [2.112]. Jasper Morrison was making furniture out of bicycle handlebars and flowerpots at the Royal College of Art, but it really didn't feel like a cohesive scene. 'Creative Salvage' had a distinctive aesthetic [2.113, 2.114, 2.117]. It was very rusty. It was quite pointed, jagged and dangerous. It was highly impractical and bits would often fall off. It was irreverent, but had lots of character – it wasn't Postmodernism in crappy patterned Formica, or high-tech in super-serious matt black and chrome, or Laura Ashley ruched curtains and swags and pelmets, which dominated interior design at the time.

It was mid-Thatcherite Britain in a bitter recession when we started. Manufacturing was very grim, and people and companies didn't seem to really enjoy making things any more; it was incredibly difficult to get things made, so you just ended up doing it yourself. By the 1990s the Japanese and the Germans started using British designers, and we used to go and show work out there. The Italians started seeing our potential and we began having an international presence through them. It became fashionable to have a pet British designer...

For Habitat I had an extraordinary time learning about international sourcing and product development from Vietnam to Poland, Portugal to Latvia – I visited deepest Tanzania to find rare baskets and learned retail: what colours people like in Hamburg and Barcelona; how many doormats and tea-lights you can sell; what price you can sell a parasol for; how you mould melamine; how much a container costs from Delhi; and much, much more. I cooked up many hare-brained schemes, like 'Living Legends', which gave me the opportunity to work with Pierre Paulin, Achille Castiglioni, Verner Panton, Nanna Ditzel, Ettore Sottsass, Robin and Lucienne Day, and I was able to commission work from Tord Boontje and Marc Newson, Carla Bruni and Gilberto Gil, the Bouroullecs and Buzz Aldrin. I quite liked it.

The opportunities presented by the new digitalization of production are liberating for anybody involved in design and manufacture now – the availability and flexibility of industrial production techniques mean that anybody can manufacture and reach a global audience. For instance, with our Etch lamp, which uses photo acid-etching, I was able to design and produce a new lamp in three weeks and sell it live in Milan, when it would normally take me a year and a half to get a new design out [2.116].

Sticking out from the crowd is the main challenge for UK-based designers now – there are too many being badly trained up, and they could all merge into a massive computer-generated conceptual obsessed gloop, if they are not careful. The proximity to manufacturing remains a problem, and arrogance, laziness or even blinkeredness in the face of the rising tide of energetic talent from Australasia and South America.

● 2.111 [OPPOSITE] Nick Jones, Tom Dixon and Mark Brazier-Jones salvaging scrap metal, mid-1980s ● 2.112 [ABOVE] Desk, André Dubreuil, 1981 | Wrought iron, leather and glass | Private collection, France, courtesy of Themes & Variations, London

● 2.113 [ABOVE] Chair, Tom Dixon, 1986 | Welded cast iron | V&A: W.16–2011 ● 2.114 [OPPOSITE TOP LEFT] *Northern Fleet*, chandelier, Deborah Thomas, 1988 | Glass shards, wired to a metal armature, with halogen lights | V&A: C.49–2011 ● 2.115 [OPPOSITE TOP RIGHT] 'Jack' lights, Tom Dixon, 1996 | Manufactured by Eurolounge Ltd, 1997, low-density rotary-moulded polyethylene with electric light fitting | V&A: W.8-11–1997 ● 2.116 [OPPOSITE BOTTOM LEFT] 'Etch' light fitting, Tom Dixon, 2011 | Digitally acid-etched brass ● 2.117 [OPPOSITE BOTTOM RIGHT] 'Lyre' chair, Mark Brazier-Jones, mid-1980s | Steel | Courtesy of Liane Brazier

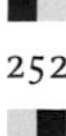

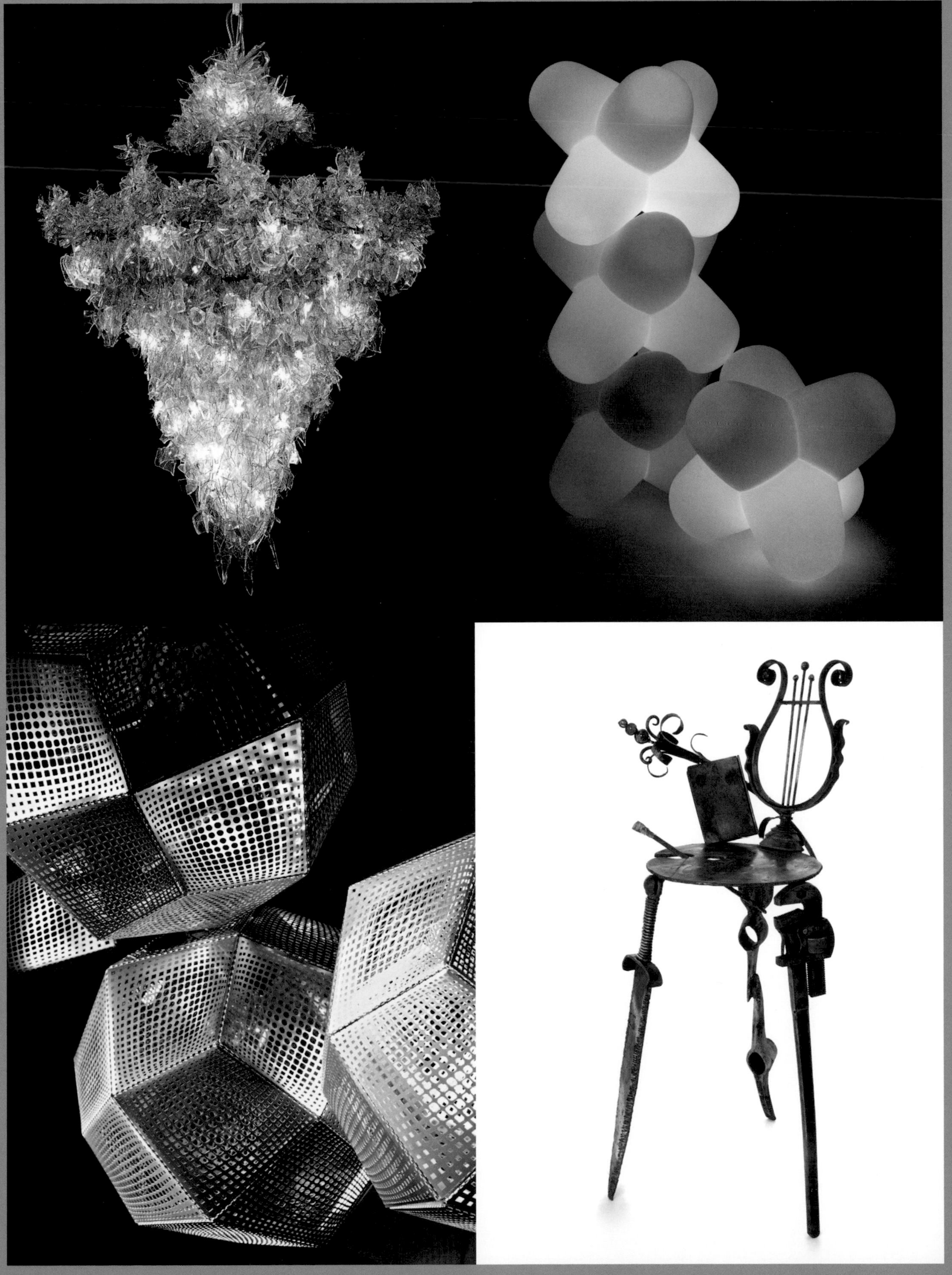

Section Three

Innovation and Creativity

1963–2012

Innovation and Creativity 1963–2012

— Christopher Breward & Ghislaine Wood

Britain has long been associated with the pioneering of new ideas and processes, particularly in the areas of engineering, industrial design and new technologies. Since the mid-eighteenth-century the concept of inventiveness has constantly been used to characterize British industrial and design culture, from the introduction of new spinning and weaving machines in the 1780s, through the launching of ships and opening of bridges in the 1840s, to the development of computer codes in the 1950s, '60s and '70s and the invention of the World Wide Web in the 1980s. However, over the last 40 years the rhetoric has undergone a radical change. Britain has most often been described in post-industrial terms, as moving further away from the status of being the world's first manufacturing nation ('the workshop of the world') towards becoming a state focused on the provision and consumption of innovative financial, retail and creative services.

The context for this shift was one of increasingly difficult economic conditions throughout the 1970s and '80s. In 1973 the OPEC countries doubled the price of oil, sparking a worldwide recession, and by the mid-1970s inflation in Britain had reached record levels. The election of a Conservative government in 1979, and the subsequent institution of Thatcherite policies promoting free enterprise and the autonomy of the market, saw a drop in spending on infrastructure in the public sector, denationalization of the coal, steel and rail industries (among others) and a decline in manufacturing in the private sector (for example, in the home production of cars). This move away from traditional 'production-line' industry during the 1980s, and towards the generation of profit in the service sectors of banking and financial services, law, consultancy, property and retail, was accompanied by new attitudes towards commodity culture and global connections, which fundamentally shifted the ways in which design was produced, consumed and understood.

British advertising and branding consultancies – such as Pentagram, Saatchi & Saatchi and Bartle Bogle Hegarty – thrived in this environment, becoming international players with the clout to challenge Madison Avenue. Growing competition from countries better able to mass-produce objects, especially in Asia, also led to increasing specialization of production in Britain, which has, by the twenty-first century, created a vibrant, highly skilled and technologically advanced design culture; but one that is localized in districts such as Hoxton and Shoreditch in London, Sheffield and Dundee (precisely those locales that had once been associated with 'heavy' manufacturing, but are now famous as centres for experimentation in and the promotion of digital design, especially computer-gaming).

● 3.1 [OPPOSITE] 'Rio TR70' transistor radio, Eric Marshall, 1961 | Manufactured by Ultra Radio & Television Ltd, polystyrene cabinet and aluminium grille | V&A: Circ.293–1963
● 3.2 [ABOVE RIGHT] 'Fish' and 'Bird' bath toys, Patrick Rylands, 1970 | Manufactured by Trendon Toys, ABS plastic with internal ballast weights | V&A: Misc.41 & 42–1970

● 3.3 [ABOVE] E-Type 3.8 FHC, 1961 | Manufactured by Jaguar ● 3.4 [LEFT] Concorde, on the 10th anniversary of commercial operations from Heathrow, 1986 | Manufactured by British Aircraft Corporation and Aérospatiale, first commercial flight 1976 ● 3.5 [OPPOSITE TOP LEFT] 'Topper' sailing dinghy, Ian Proctor, 1976 | Manufactured by J.V. Dunhill Boats Ltd, injection-moulded polypropylene ● 3.6 [OPPOSITE TOP RIGHT] 'Sovereign' calculator, John Pemberton, John Holland and Victor Thomas Manufactured by Sinclair Radionics Ltd, chrome-finished steel case and LED display | V&A: M.17–1991

Britain's manufacturing sector just before the moment of change, in the late 1950s, '60s and '70s, was marked by its range and inventiveness, but also by a certain sense of pragmatism. Alongside established industries such as textiles, motor-manufacture and aeronautics, Britain also began to specialize in products that utilized newer technologies, such as electronics and music equipment. The strength of this area can be seen in the many Design Council Awards (DCAs) for technical products, such as the Rio TR70 transistor radio, by Eric Marshall for Ultra Radio and TV (1961), and the Sovereign calculator by Sinclair Radionics (1977) [3.1, 3.6]. In the area of marine technology, for instance, awards were given not just for boat design, but also for new compasses, radars and auto-helm systems. This interest in technological innovation also led to the development of new production methods. When Ian Proctor's 'Topper' dinghy of 1976 won a DCA, *Design* magazine highlighted the use of injection-moulding machines to create a mass-produced 'Propathene' polypropylene hull; 5,000 boats were sold by the end of its first year, with exports all over the world [3.5]. Rolinx, which developed the technology and invested in the tooling for large-scale injection-moulding, had had the motor industry in mind, but the recession had forced it to look elsewhere. The 'Topper', which was made in two parts, required 'an exceptional advance in tooling technology ... and a lateral leap in mould making'.[1] Many British products of the 1960s and '70s reflected this innovative and pragmatic approach.

However, by 1978 *Design* magazine was commenting on the effects of the recession on the awards, noting:

> it is extraordinary that the judges could honour so few products this year; fabrics, wallcoverings and furniture are all conspicuously absent. This is not an indictment of British design capability, but just another symptom of the severe economic restraints and pressures of recent years... Though British manufacturers may not be able to compete with the countries that dominate world markets for mass-produced popular goods, some will achieve success by exploiting the most quality-conscious markets. This year's winners could prove the strength of high-quality, highly exportable product innovations in those markets.[2]

Some of Britain's most outstanding design and engineering achievements during this period required a huge scale of investment and risk. The Anglo-French supersonic airliner Concorde was arguably the most important development in aircraft design and technology of the century. The project combined the development and manufacturing capabilities of the French Aerospatiale and the British Aircraft Corporation, and built on the research of both countries into the delta wing and turbo-jet power. The aircraft's first flight was celebrated in 1969 and seemed to capture all the futuristic aspirations of the Space Age, but only 20 were eventually made, as orders for the new planes collapsed during the economic crisis of the 1970s. The British and French governments subsidized their national airlines in the purchase and operation of Concorde, and the project represented a considerable financial loss for both countries. However, it conveyed immense prestige and had an enormous cultural impact.

The sublime quality of Concorde's design was very clearly manifested in its astonishing shape, and its final flight in 2003 was a cause for national mourning.

Another icon of British engineering was the E-type Jaguar, manufactured from 1961 [3.3]. Described by Enzo Ferrari as the most beautiful car ever made, the E-type was extremely successful during the 1960s, with more than 70,000 sales completed. By the mid-1970s Jaguar, like many car manufacturers, was suffering the effects of the recession and finally stopped production on the E-type in 1975. The company was subsequently to be sold to Ford in the 1980s and is currently owned by the Indian conglomerate Tata – the trajectory of its ownership being indicative of wider trends within British industry and the creep of globalization.

● 3.7 [OPPOSITE] Chair, David David and Glass Hill, 2011 | White beech with individual hand-drawn pencil crayon design; and *Relay*, drawing, David David, 2011 | Pencil crayon on cold-pressed illustration paper | Collection of David David and Glass Hill
● 3.8 [ABOVE] 'Pyrenees' sofa, Fredrikson Stallard, 2007 | Flocked CNC-routed foam on an aluminium frame | V&A: W.25–2011

● 3.9 [TOP] British Pavilion, Shanghai Expo, Thomas Heatherwick, 2010
● 3.10 [ABOVE] Poole Harbour Second Crossing, Wilkinson Eyre, 2012

In recent years new technologies have also been changing the way objects are designed and made in Britain, and as techniques migrate from one area or discipline to another, the possibilities for development are ever expanding. For example, the 'Pyrenees' sofa by Fredrikson Stallard (2007) uses several production processes not usually associated with furniture design, and is typical of the practice's experimental approach, highlighting 'their unorthodox and adventurous use of materials and ... the practice's platform of combining technology, craft and concept' [3.8].[3] The sofa is made of a solid block of polyurethane foam, which is initially hand-carved to create a sculptural 'landscape'. A three-dimensional scan is taken and fed into a CNC (computer numerical control) router, which can automatically carve the delicate 'rocky' formations from a solid block of foam to create an edition from the original. The foam is then coated with a specially developed rubber to protect it, and finally covered with upholstery-grade flock fibres, giving the appearance of velvet. The piece combines hand-made and new technologies to create an object that brings to the fore an old technique – flocking – which is clearly associated with the traditional interior, but here completely reimagined. While the possibilities of new technologies are dramatically changing design practice, there is also a growing interest in the hand-made, allied with an intensifying concern around issues of sustainability. David David and Glass Hill's hand-made chair with its hand-drawn decoration, which at a distance looks like machine-made vinyl, typifies the interests of a younger generation in the authenticity of the object and its production processes [3.7].

Of all the high-tech industries, architecture is arguably the most visible, highly celebrated and fiercely debated field of British design to have emerged in the last 30 years, and one that is truly global in its reach. The innovative ideas of British architects – revealed both in the creation of new buildings across the world and in the planning and regeneration of cities such as Gateshead, Salford and Newcastle – continue to position Britain as a leading generator of new design solutions in the twenty-first century. The impetus for expansion resided both in the deregulation of the Stock Exchange (or 'Big Bang') in 1986 and in the consequent reinvention of banks, insurance firms, venture capitalism and the City in general; and in New Labour's programme of urban regeneration, school and hospital rebuilding, and the Heritage Lottery Fund-sponsored investment in capital projects in the cultural sector during the 1990s and early twenty-first century. While some critics have argued strongly against the social implications and aesthetic quality of the radically changed landscape of Britain's towns and cities that have resulted from these changes, it is hard not to acknowledge the continuing existence of a deep-rooted spirit of technical brilliance and visual elegance in the best examples of contemporary British building [3.9, 3.10]. The 2012 Olympic Games, which will see a number of important and stunning new venues and regeneration projects launched in London and beyond, is a case in point. As this book and the exhibition that it accompanies aim to suggest, British designers have created some of the most iconic objects, technologies and buildings of the last 60 years and continue to pioneer innovative solutions for the future. A simple story of manufacturing decline does not do the sector justice.

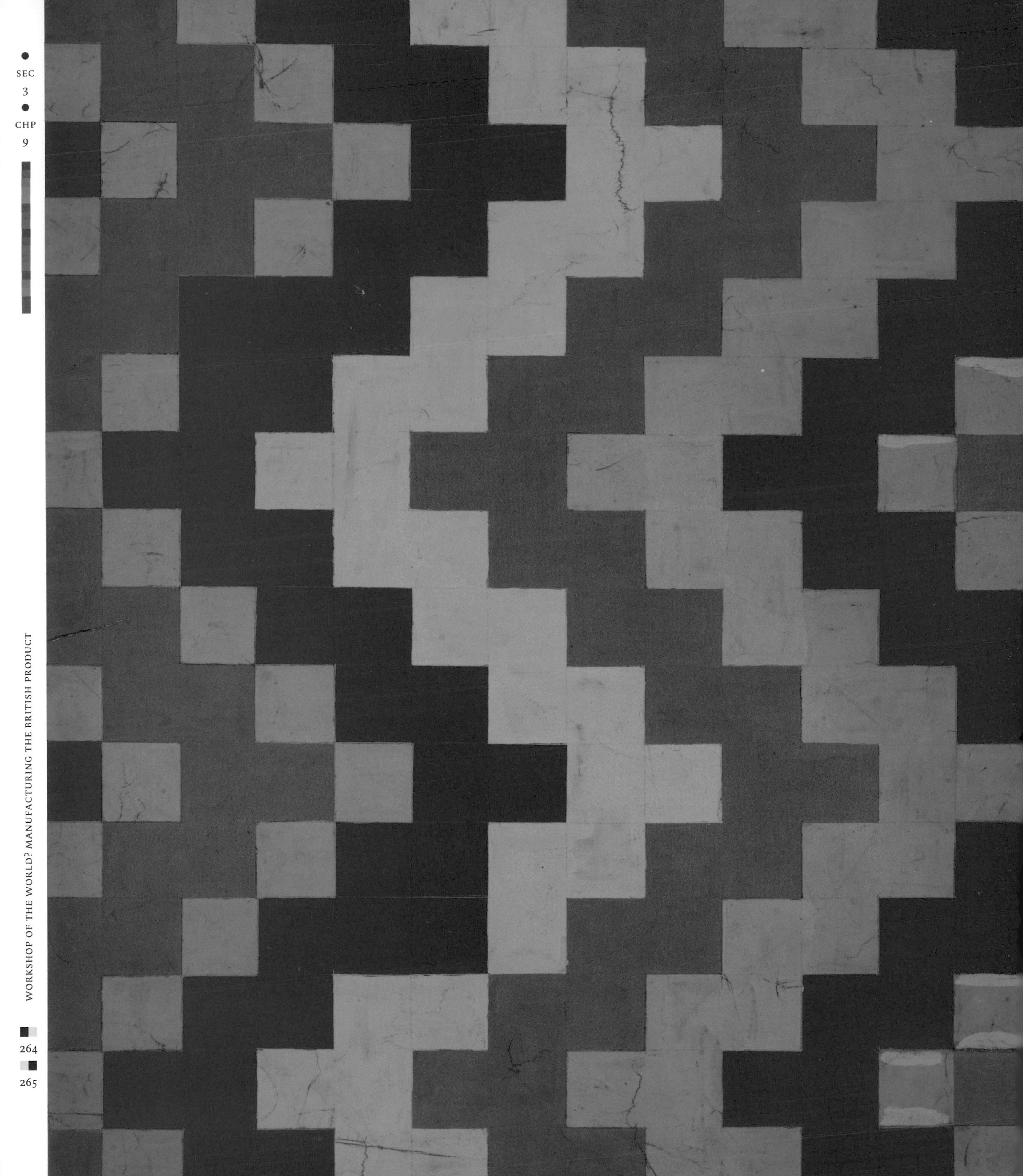

9 Workshop of the World? Manufacturing the British Product

— Deborah Sugg Ryan

It was once commonplace for authors of historical surveys to refer to Britain in the eighteenth and nineteenth centuries as the 'Workshop of the World'. Great national pride has been taken in British inventors and entrepreneurs, particularly those associated with developments in iron and steel manufacturing, machine tools, ship-building and the textiles industry. These developments occurred at the height of British imperial expansion, which provided both raw materials and guaranteed markets for British products that continued into the mid-twentieth century.

Conventional histories of British manufacturing and production have contrasted this rise with an equally dramatic fall-off in productivity, coinciding with the end of Empire and Britain's decline as a world power in the 1930s, '40s and '50s.[1] This was followed by the 1967 devaluation of sterling, the 1973 oil crisis, the 'winter of discontent', the introduction of VAT, bankruptcies, mergers and takeovers, and restrictive practices due to the enduring power of the trade unions. No wonder then that in his assessment of the state of the British design industry in 1987 Richard Stewart came to some 'hard to admit' conclusions:[2]

> The 'vicious circle' described by Owen Jones in 1852 survives almost complete. British manufacturers and retailers still propagate mediocrity for a large section of a visually illiterate community, while discriminating purchasers look to foreign designs for elegance at a price. Expensive furniture is imported from Scandinavia, sophisticated electrical goods from Japan and luxury cars from Germany. Of most concern is the apparent lack of innovative, entrepreneurial spirit possessed by the Victorians.[3]

But was the story of the British product from the 1960s onwards really a straightforward narrative of decline? To what extent could Britain still claim to be the Workshop of the World at the end of the twentieth century?

This chapter addresses these questions by considering how institutions, individuals and industries responded to new circumstances of manufacturing the British product from the 1960s onwards. New forms of education for industrial design resulted in the emergence of the consultant designer and in design consultancies that worked in partnership with industry in Britain and abroad. Research and Development (R&D) witnessed investment in some fields, but decline in others. As British manufacturing evolved within a changing world economy, a decline in R&D in some fields was matched by an equal (though less well-documented) investment in other areas. In the meantime, the tradition of the British inventor and design entrepreneur, contrary to fears of commentators like Stewart, was far from dead. More hidden was the role of women, but here too female designers and consumers played important roles. Britain also became a workshop in innovation and creativity, set against the backdrop of Swinging London, developing new technologies and exporting design expertise.

● 3.11 [ABOVE] 'Deltaphone', telephone, Martyn Rowlands, 1963
Manufactured by Standard Telephones and Cables Ltd, marketed as 'Trimphone', ABS plastic with polycarbonate switching bar and dial finger plate and rubber feet | V&A: W.65:1–2002

EDUCATION FOR INDUSTRIAL DESIGN

A new kind of consultant designer, who was trained to design for industrial production and the new consumer boom, emerged in the early 1960s. Some were graduates of industrial-design courses with a technical and professional base that had been established at the Central School of Arts and Crafts and at colleges in Glasgow and Leicester in the 1930s. In 1960 there were fewer than 1,500 industrial designers in Britain, compared to about 20,000 architects.[4] However, significant changes were made to British design education in the wake of the 1961 Coldstream Report. What Christopher Frayling has termed the 'expressive' tradition emerged, where the focus of education was on personal creativity, within the constraints of the design process and within a wider sense of visual culture and style.[5]

At the forefront was the Royal College of Art (RCA), which pioneered new and innovative forms of design education and produced a significant number of leading designers. In 1948 Robin Darwin, the new rector, organized the college into six separate materials-based design schools and introduced a new postgraduate qualification of Des.RCA to allow a greater degree of specialization. In 1959 the Department of Industrial Design (Engineering), headed by Misha Black, was formed. Two years later a design research unit was introduced in the school under the leadership of L. Bruce Archer, becoming the separate Department of Design Research six years later, offering courses in research techniques and continuing until 1988. Archer was an exponent of what became known as 'Design Methods',[6] and was heavily influenced by his experience at the successor to the Bauhaus, the Hochschule für Gestaltung at Ulm, Germany,[7] which contrasted with the creative and 'expressive' approach of some of his colleagues at the RCA.

Design education was not just found in art colleges. In 1963 the Robbins Report on Higher Education recommended that all Colleges of Advanced Technology should be given the status of universities. These new universities of technology transformed engineering and design, developing associated disciplines such as ergonomics, which had a big impact on product design.[8] The Society of Industrial Artists and Designers (SIAD) campaigned for designers to be afforded the professional status accorded to architects, and advised on the proposals for new university first-degree-equivalent Diplomas in Art and Design (Dip.AD), which were initially awarded in 1966. Polytechnics, established from 1968 onwards, incorporated both colleges of art and technology into new institutions. This alarmed those who thought they were less conducive to creativity than the old art schools. However, the large polytechnics had the advantage of forging

links with subjects outside art and design that were relevant to industry, such as computing, electrical engineering, physics, statistical sciences and foreign languages.[9]

As a result of these changes in design education, the consultant-design profession became established in Britain between the late 1950s and the end of the 1970s.[10] Inspired by American examples and following the precedent of the Design Research Unit (set up in 1942),[11] innovative multi-disciplinary design agencies emerged, offering a variety of services to industry, including graphics, corporate-identity schemes, exhibitions, packaging, products and product planning. For example, Oliver Hill established the Industrial Design Unit in 1965. Hill was previously Hotpoint's industrial-design manager and continued to work closely with the company, winning a Design Centre Award for the Automatic 1501 washing machine in 1966. And the influential design consultancy Pentagram originated in 1962, joined later by Kenneth Grange.

These new consultancies developed fruitful collaborations between designers and manufacturers in Britain. For example, Kenneth Grange developed a long working relationship with Kenwood after being referred to them by the Design Council, earning the epithet the 'British Braun', working along similar lines to the German industrial designer Dieter Rams.[12] Grange's 1966 redesign of Kenwood's Chefette hand mixer, in the same austere style he had used for the Chef Kitchen Machine in 1961, resulted in a 25 per cent increase in sales [3.25].[13] Kodak also retained Grange for more than 20 years from 1958, designing cameras and projectors as well as in-house non-consumer products such as film-processing machines, company exhibitions and packaging.

Despite these improvements in design education and the emergence of professional industrial designers, the Council of Industrial Design (CoID) and designers were frustrated that industry and consumers did not appreciate British design talent. Thus the Council attempted to educate both industry and consumers in 'good design'. The establishment of the Design Centre in 1956 led to several initiatives, including exhibitions, the Design Centre label (devised as a hallmark of quality) and the *Design Index*, which listed approved products and other publications. The CoID's Record of Designers listed British design talent, which led to several successful relationships between designers and industry.

There were also concerns about standards of engineering, particularly in cars, aircraft, ships and missiles, which was hugely important to a sense of British national identity. The 1963 Feilden Report on Engineering Design addressed concerns about a lack of interest in design in engineering. The 1968 Conway Report recommended a single body to promote industrial design and engineering standards, and consequently the remit of the newly formed Design Council in 1972 (which took over from the CoID) was expanded to promote both disciplines.[14]

Design Centre Awards were introduced in 1957, and the Duke of Edinburgh's Award for Elegant Design in 1959 (renamed the Prince Philip Designer's Prize in 1990). The awards were thought to be beneficial to designers and industry in recognizing their achievements as a guarantee to consumers of 'good design': innovation, fitness for purpose, ease of use and good appearance. However, awards did not ensure success and some winning products ultimately failed to remain in production for long. Kenneth Grange's 'Courier' cordless, portable battery shaver is a case in point [3.26]. It was an attempt by its manufacturer, Henry Milward & Sons – which specialized in knitting and surgical needles and fishing tackle – to diversify into other industries. The shaver was, in *Design*'s assessment, 'a total and elegant design of a product'.[15] Its technical innovations included a switch in the head that only worked when it was pressed against the face, to conserve battery power, and hollow-ground circular blades. Despite these technological and design features, sales were disappointing because of inadequate marketing, and the stake in the business was sold to a large competitor.

Many designers and manufacturers believed that, commercially, an award was a 'Fate worse than death'.[16] A common criticism of award-winning products was that they had not been sufficiently tested, had significant manufacturing difficulties or a short shelf life because they were superseded by new technology.[17] Some products even took such a long time to come to market that their technology ran the risk of becoming outmoded.[18] Despite the supposed high status of the awards, some winners found that retailers did not see their value as a promotional tool.[19] However, Sinclair Radionics boasted about their 1973 award for the 'Executive' pocket electronic calculator in an advertising campaign in the *TV Times* magazine.

Even if they won awards, manufacturers were not necessarily committed to 'good design'. Standard Telephones and Cables (STC) employed Martyn Rowlands for the design of the two-tone 'warbling' Quickstep 'Deltaphone' [3.11]. Launched in 1963, it was marketed by the Post Office as Trimphone. It had a lightweight body only slightly wider than the dial, and a handset that was about half the weight of previous phones. Its warbling electronic-tone caller replaced the bell of previous phones. However, STC hedged its bets in the modernity of consumer tastes; at the same time as it made the Deltaphone, it also produced a 'candlestick' telephone and the traditional 'Classic' gold and marble.[20] As Dominic Sandbrook has noted, many consumers' tastes owed more to the continuities of the pre-war years than to the radical shifts of the Swinging Sixties.[21]

Consumers were also given advice by commercial publications and exhibitions, which were arguably more influential than state-sponsored bodies like the CoID. The Consumers' Association's *Which?* magazine was founded in 1957.[22] The Daily Mail Ideal Home exhibition, which had acted as a three-dimensional household advice manual since 1908, endorsed British producers with its Blue Ribbon scheme founded in 1965, although not all its exhibitors would have been deemed representative of good design.[23] Newspapers and magazines, particularly the colour Sunday newspaper supplements, were also influential showcases of products. Women's magazines such as *Good Housekeeping*, with its Good Housekeeping Institute Seal of Approval, and *Woman's Journal* featured product-testing and comparison by the mid-1960s.[24] With the growth of 'lifestyle' retailers such as Biba and Habitat, consumers were increasingly educated by shop displays and catalogues.[25]

● 3.12 [OPPOSITE] Pendant lampshades, John and Sylvia Reid, 1956
Manufactured by Rotaflex (Great Britain) Ltd, cellulose acetate

RESEARCH AND DEVELOPMENT

Despite an increasingly professionalized design industry, one of the most common post-war anxieties about the quality of British product design was a lack of investment in R&D. The amount of research undertaken by British firms increased between 1945 and 1965, but was mostly concentrated in the areas of chemicals, aircraft and electrical engineering. In 1967 Britain was second only to the United States in the proportion of GDP devoted to R&D and also to R&D funded by industry, excluding military and civil prestige projects. However, this did not necessarily result in a better economic performance; both Germany and France overtook Britain in GDP before 1970, despite spending less on R&D.[26]

There were, however, some innovative design research projects. One of the most successful was the King's Fund hospital bed, which started in 1967 as a joint venture between the RCA, headed by L. Bruce Archer, the Nuffield Foundation and the Department of Health [3.13]. A team of professionals, including doctors, nurses, mechanical engineers, industrial designers and time-and-motion experts recruited from outside the college, worked on the project to design a bed of adjustable height, angle and profile for the comfort of patients and to ease the work of nursing staff. The final product was a great success with the NHS and many similar briefs followed, attracting significant external funding.[27]

The work of some product designers was grounded in their own research. Kenneth Grange's designs, for example, are not a mere restyling of a product, but often arose 'from a fundamental reassessment of the purpose, function and use of a product'.[28] His 'Brownie Vecta' camera for Kodak, for the British market [3.27], was inspired by his visits to the company's film-processing laboratories, where he noted:

> most pictures were of people, and many of those pictures were of one person or at the most two. So you have got this contradiction, you have a landscape format for a portrait, and I knew that if you turned it round the image on the film would be better.[29]

Consequently, Grange designed the camera in a vertical portrait format, reminiscent of Kodak's earlier Box Brownie design. Although it was one of Grange's favourite designs, and its moulded acrylic lens set a new standard, the Vecta was not a commercial success. It used 127 roll film and was made redundant overnight by the introduction of the new cassette-film system. However, its ergonomic finger recesses on the top and bottom, designed to reduce camera shake, were an innovation that continues to this day.

Some manufacturers, such as the furniture company Hille, were willing to invest significantly in R&D. Robin Day, who had been a consultant designer since the early 1950s, worked with Leslie Julius to develop a low-cost mass-production stacking side chair in the new mouldable polypropylene, a type of thermoplastic.[30] A crucial question was whether Hille could sell the chair in sufficient numbers to warrant the enormous investment in time and injection-moulding tooling. After nine months in development, Rosamind Julius sent the Mark I chair out to 600 architects, designers, journalists and other potential users with a questionnaire. Orders outstripped supply, but Hille also acted on feedback about comfort issues and invested in a second set of expensive tooling to produce the successful Mark II in 1963, which was given a Design Centre Award in 1965 [3.14]. In all, £20,000 was spent in development.[31] Genuinely democratic, Hille's chair is arguably the biggest-selling British design classic of all time and is still in production today.[32]

One area in which the state was prepared to invest in R&D was aeronautics. Developments in aircraft were thought to stimulate technological progress and to be in the nation's best interests. As the historian David Edgerton says, 'aircraft were an encapsulation of the technological prowess of a nation and an index of commitment to modernity. Aircraft became symbols of a nation's manufacturing prestige, the spearhead of its industrial might, a kind of flying advertisement for washing machines and motor-cars.'[33]

Concorde, a co-production between Britain and France, performed an important symbolic function in keeping Britain at the forefront of aviation [3.4]. It took more than 20 years to develop, from 1962; although the first test flight was in 1969, the first commercial flight did not take place until 1976. Flying at twice the speed of sound and with a long, thin shape with a delta wing (the result of physics and aerodynamics), Concorde had a design that was symbolic of futuristic twenty-first-century technology.

By 1990 Britain's investment in R&D had fallen to middle-ranking among industrial countries.[34] There were technological failures in rubber tyres, motorcycles, consumer electronics, motor-car manufacture and office machinery. However as the historian Alan Booth argues, 'periodic failure in some branches of manufacturing is an integral part of the fast-moving, competitive, unified world economy, not conclusive diagnostic proof of the British disease'.[35] Therefore it should be noted that there were continuing strengths in aerospace and rapidly emerging world-leading developments in the pharmaceutical and biotechnology industries.

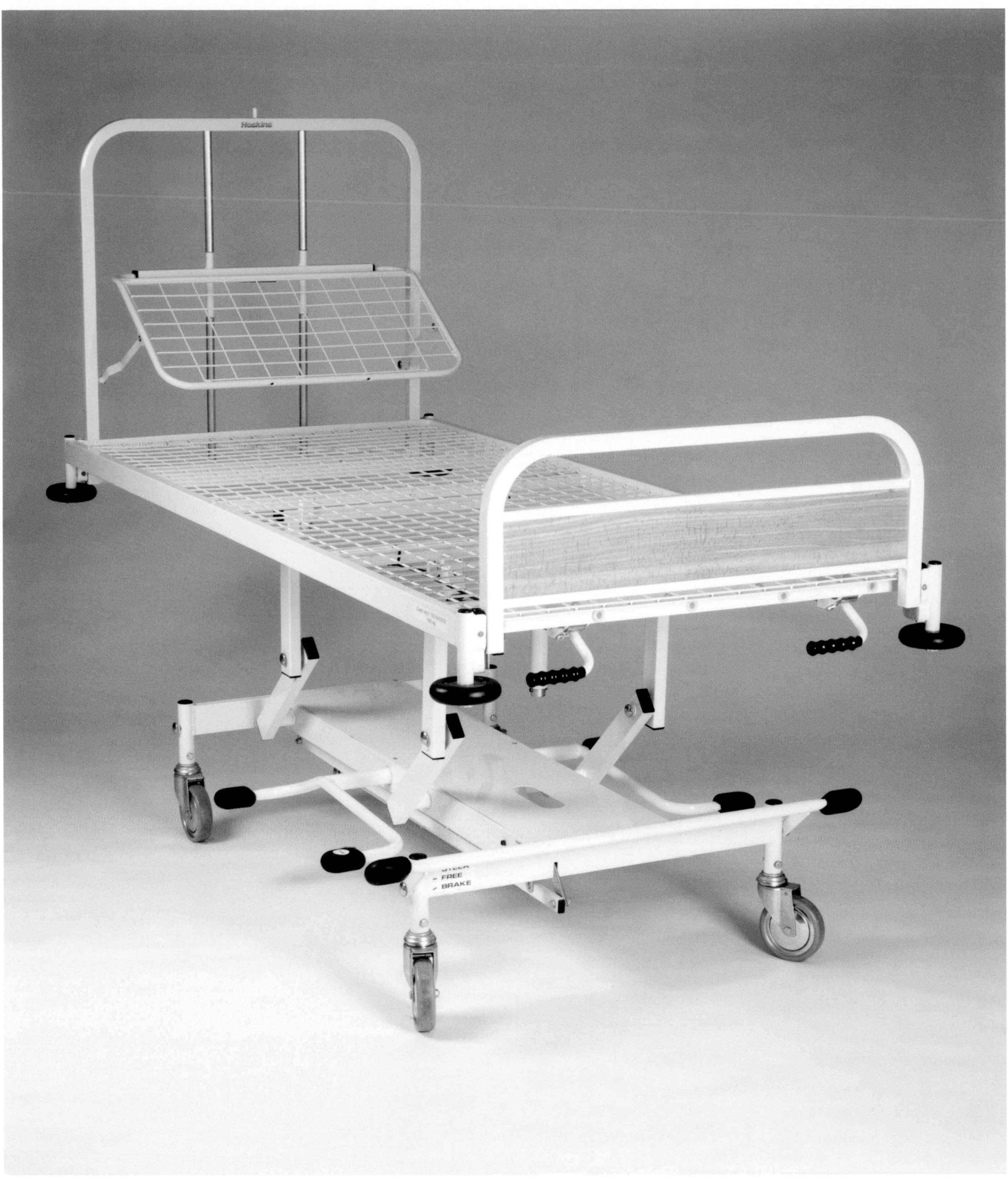

● 3.13 [ABOVE] King's Fund hospital bed, L. Bruce Archer and Kenneth Agnew, *c.*1967 | Manufactured by Hoskins Medical Equipment Ltd, 1994, steel with tilting and height adjustment mechanisms | Science Museum

● 3.14 [OPPOSITE] 'Mark II' chairs, Robin Day, 1963 | Manufactured by S. Hille & Co. Ltd, injection-moulded polypropylene shells on metal bases with a range of finishes | V&A: Circ.15-B–1966
● 3.15 [LEFT] Trevor Baylis with a Freeplay wind-up radio in his workshop at Eel Pie Island, London

MEN IN SHEDS? INVENTORS AND DESIGN ENTREPRENEURS

Despite the advances in design education and the growth of agencies and consultancies, it has been claimed that there is a peculiarly British tradition of the maverick inventor.[36] Inventors were promoted in the popular BBC TV series *Tomorrow's World*, which ran for 38 years from 1965. They are also personified in Heath Robinson's cartoons and the animator Nick Park's Wallace and Gromit characters. A number of products were the work of individual, independent inventors who set up their own manufacturing plants, including Alex Moulton's Standard bicycle, Owen Maclaren's B01 Buggy and James Dyson's vacuum cleaners [3.16, 3.18]. As Michael Evamy said in *Design Week*, 'It's time designers latched on to the public popularity shown towards inventors ... inventions and inventors capture the public imagination and designers don't'.[37]

As the scientific entrepreneur Gordon Edge declared in 1985, in Britain 'we are still preoccupied with the inventor rather than the process of innovation'.[38] For example, much of the popular publicity given to the Freeplay radio concentrated on its inventor Trevor Baylis – a large-moustached, pipe-smoking, former 'underwater escapologist' who valiantly experimented in his workshop on Eel Pie Island for years – and barely mentioned the role of the designers at TKO Product Design, without whom the product would not have been brought to market [3.15]. Baylis had no formal university-level design training, but had learned engineering skills in his father's shed. After a career as a stuntman and swimming-pool salesman, he made forays into design with a series of disabled aids in 1985. The clockwork radio was his response to a TV documentary about the problem of educating people in Africa about the spread of AIDS; radio was thought to be the ideal medium, but electricity supplies were sparse and erratic and batteries were expensive. Like James Dyson before him,[39] Baylis took his prototype to British manufacturers, but was met with indifference and even hostility. He even tried the Design Council, to no avail. Eventually, as a result of being featured on *Tomorrow's World* in 1994, he was approached by entrepreneurs who saw the radio's potential in Africa. However, it needed significant development in both its clockwork mechanism and design to bring it to market.[40]

TKO Product Design worked on the exterior styling to turn the invention into a manufacturable, functional and attractive product. Andy Davey's design took into account African preferences for a substantial rather than a miniaturized product. TKO's Anne Gardener commented, 'The invention was a quantifiable idea, but had to be handed on to someone else to communicate it. That's what happened between Trevor and Andy: the articulation of the idea. Andy was giving the idea life, like an actor does to a character.'[41]

The resulting model FPR1 Freeplay wind-up radio was first manufactured in 1996 by a new company in South Africa, employing disabled workers. In the same year Baylis and Davey were awarded BBC Designer of the Year and BBC Product of the Year. Despite the considerable success of the product, Baylis continued to be seen through the lens of a man in a shed, and he was invited to give advice to aspiring inventors in a humorous feature called 'From me shed, son' on Channel 4's *The Big Breakfast*. More seriously, his conviction that inventors needed help with ideas, inventions and products, patent applications, copyright and trademarks led him to set up Trevor Baylis Brands in 2003 to bring new products to market.

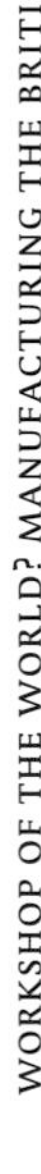

● 3.16 [OPPOSITE] 'Moulton Stowaway' bicycle, Alex Moulton, 1964 | Manufactured by Moulton Bicycles Ltd, mild steel frame and rubber suspension | V&A: Circ.125–1965
● 3.17 [ABOVE] Adjustable spotlights, John and Sylvia Reid, 1961 | Manufactured by Rotaflex (Great Britain) Ltd, anodized aluminium lamp housings with vitreous enamelled base-plates

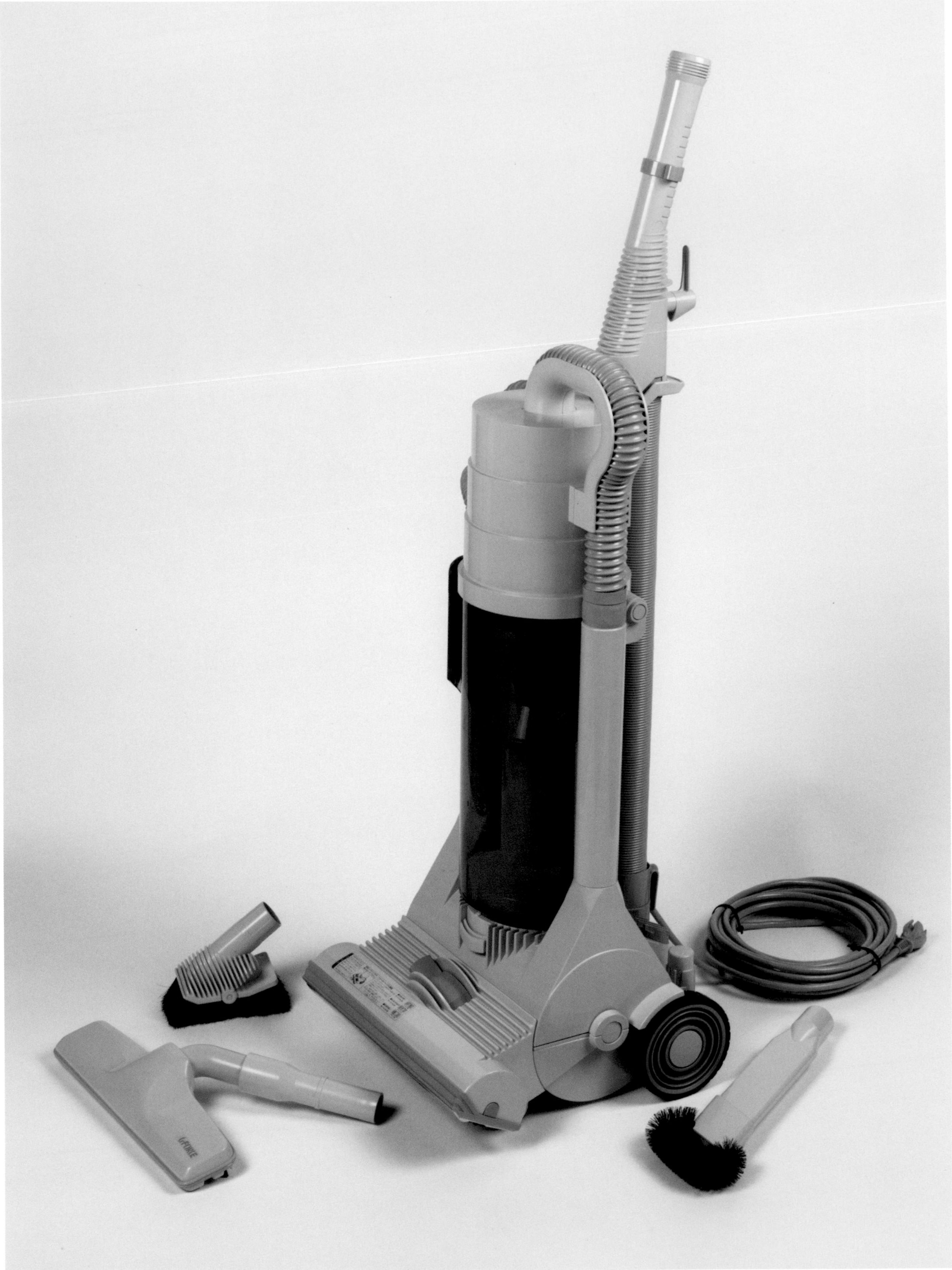

If male inventors were to be found in sheds, then where were women? Women designers tended to be concentrated in textiles, fashion and ceramics. The male image of the design profession disguised the achievements of award-winning women designers. For example, Sylvia Reid worked in partnership with her husband John on Stag furniture and their Lightplan Universal designs for Rotaflex won a Design Centre Award in 1961 [3.12, 3.17]. In ceramics, Helena Uglow designed ashbowls for JRM Design Sales, which won a Design Centre Award in 1970. Hille employed Ray Hille, Rosamind Julius and Cherrill Scheer, all women who were key to design and management in the company. Sometimes women's contributions to design teams went unrecognized because of the emphasis on the designer rather than the whole range of activities that went into developing a product and bringing it to market. For example, Anne Gardener had a key role in keeping the project on track in the team at TKO that designed the Freeplay radio, but went unacknowledged in the citation for the BBC's Designer of the Year Award.[42]

The role of women as designers was also obscured within the masculine aesthetics of the 'good design' of the 1960s, which has been described as a 'return to geometrical correctness', characterized by 'formalism, precision, balance, repetition and symmetry' in contrast to the Contemporary style of the 1950s.[43] This also chimed with Harold Wilson's 'white heat of technological change'. This masculine aesthetic was often contrasted with what was seen as the inherently feminine 'bad taste' of mass culture, particularly signified by unnecessary streamlining.[44] In the late 1970s and '80s there was a resurgence of interest in goods for gendered markets. One trend was a spate of Postmodern designs quoting the nostalgic femininity of pastel designs for the 1950s housewife – for example, James Dyson's pink-and-lilac G-Force vacuum cleaner for the Japanese market [3.18]. In contrast, Dyson's later grey-and-yellow Dual Dyson model for the British market was credited with being a vacuum cleaner with masculine styling, which men were happy to operate.

In the 1960s women were more visible as consumers of product design. They worked in offices with the new technologies of adding machines and telephone exchanges. They also worked in the home, aided by the promise of 'electric servants'. Although labour-saving appliances had long existed, the easily cleanable, smooth outlines and pared-down designs of, for instance, Grange's kitchen machines for Kenwood pandered to the idea that technology would liberate the housewife to pursue a career or leisure. Products like the Chefette, which came in a range of bright 'Pop' colours, even acted as fashionable accessories to style the kitchen [3.25]. However, this was something of a double bind, because for many women the aspiration for domestic consumer goods such as vacuum cleaners, televisions, refrigerators and washing machines became the reason they did paid work outside the home.[45]

A product that was genuinely liberating was the lightweight telescopic aluminium-framed folding Maclaren B01 Buggy, designed in 1965 by Owen Maclaren, a retired aeronautical engineer and test pilot who had worked on the Spitfire. The buggy was a practical solution to a problem that his daughter faced when travelling by plane with his grandchild. *Design* enthused:

> Erecting and collapsing the Baby Buggy is a very simple operation involving a foot and a hand, so that it can be done even when one is holding a child in the other arm. As the chair has crooked handles, it can be hung, when folded, on an arm, the back of a seat in a bus or even on a trolley in a supermarket, while the amount of space it requires is so small that it can be stowed quite easily on the rear window ledge of a Mini.[46]

With its deckchair-striped Tygan seat that nodded to Pop Art, the buggy's modernity represented a distinct break with the cumbersome and bulky baby carriages of the past. Also notable to audiences today, at a time when products aimed at children are almost always clearly gendered pink or blue, is the Maclaren buggy's unisex styling, a common feature of many products for children in the 1960s and '70s.

● 3.18 [OPPOSITE] 'G-Force' vacuum cleaner, James Dyson, 1986 | Manufactured by APEX Inc., Japan, plastic and electro-mechanical parts | V&A: M.64:1-5–1993

● 3.19 [ABOVE] 'Globoots', children's waterproof boots, Globoots Footwear, 1969
Manufactured by Plastic Coatings Ltd, PVC plastisol uppers and soles with removable sock

The early 1960s witnessed a confidence about the possibilities of technology. Thus Harold Wilson declared, 'We're living at a time of such rapid scientific change that our children are accepting as part of their everyday life things that could have been dismissed as science fiction a few years ago.'[47] There was mounting excitement about the *Apollo* moon landings, which were eventually realized in 1969, and a new 'Space Age', along with the possibilities of computers, transistors and miniaturized products. An enthusiasm for technology, innovation and the future was also evident in the Independent Group's fusion of art, design, architecture and popular culture during the 1950s.

Pop Art became absorbed into a popular design aesthetic, symbolized by Carnaby Street, the shopping mecca of Swinging London. In 1967 Paul Reilly, director of the CoID, wrote about 'The challenge of Pop', acknowledging the appeal of the ephemeral and recognizing the gulf between the young and 'ageing advocates' of the Modern Movement who promoted a recognizable Design Centre style.[48] *Design* magazine began to use 'Carnaby Street' as a descriptor for a design style, already dubbed 'Post-Modern' by Reyner Banham in 1968, that encompassed 'Pop, Op, and Surrealist fine art, cottage pinewood furniture, Buckminster Fullerism, amusement arcades, hot dog stands, and Archigram... as much influenced by close-up photographs of complex constructional engineering and models of moon vehicles as by American comics and ice cream vans outside the V and A'.[49] There were relatively few expressions of Pop in product design, although it did impact on furniture with cheap, 'throwaway' cardboard and plastic inflatable chairs.[50]

'Carnaby Street' lent itself more readily to graphics and surface pattern. One of the foremost exponents was JRM Design, a small print company set up in 1964 by John Stevens, an ex-Central student who did a lot of work for trendy fashion and interior companies, including Mary Quant, Jeff Banks and Biba. The textile designers Natalie Gibson and Ian Logan (also ex-Central) designed fabrics and other printed goods in brightly coloured psychedelic florals. Their tin-ware Salome range of trays, waste bins, storage tins, tablemats and coasters were enormously successful.

A colourful Pop sensibility informed a number of Duke of Edinburgh award-winning products. Many of these were made of plastics, with connotations of modernity and disposability, and produced in bright colours. Examples include Day's Polyprop stacking chair and David Harman Powell's 1968 stacking plastic Nova tableware for Ekco Plastics. The latter were commended for their development of forms, which were not just a copy of existing ceramic designs, but exploited their plastic material. A number of plastic products aimed at children drew on Pop's colourful and child-like sensibility, which was also a feature of Mary Quant's work. Plastic Coatings Ltd's double-dip moulded colourful Globoots, with bright translucent uppers and opaque soles, were launched in 1969, selling 320,000 within two years [3.19]. Patrick Rylands, who had trained in sculpture and worked at Hornsey, designed a range of toys for Trendon in 1970 [3.2]. Rylands's 'Playplax' consisted of squares and tubes of transparent coloured polystyrene that could be slotted together to learn about colour combinations as well as construction.[51] Martin Hunt and James Kirkwood's lamps and Helena Uglow's ashbowls for JRM Design Sales in 1970 were examples of ceramic Pop products [3.22].

Sound equipment benefited from a combination of Pop styling and technological innovation. In 1973 a Design Centre Award was given to Rank Radio's 'Wharfedale Isodynamic' headphones, developed in collaboration with Oliver Hill from the Industrial Design Unit [3.21]. Hailed as a 'headphone breakthrough', they were the first commercial orthodynamic headphones to be released and, at £19.95, had a sound quality associated with products four times as expensive. Their large white circum-aural cups combined comfort with a striking Space Age look, very different from Hill's restrained designs for Hotpoint a decade earlier.

Two of the most striking hi-fi products were Lecson Audio's AC1 pre-amplifier and AP1 power amplifier, by designer Allen Boothroyd and engineer Bob Stuart [3.20]. A contemporary reviewer described the appearance of the AC1 and AP3 (which succeeded the AP1, but was of a similar design) as 'unparalleled among amplifiers for sheer beauty – it's almost a work of art'.[52] *Design* enthused about the 'shallow preamplifier, fitted with colour-coded slide controls in place of conventional knobs, set between strips of glossy Perspex'.[53] Retailing at nearly £200, they were high-end products for 'a lunatic fringe of wealthy consumers who must have the most striking piece of design in the field, regardless of price'.[54] The Lecson Audio Company, founded in 1972 in St Ives near Cambridge, was one of a number of electronics companies that thrived in the area, including Sinclair Electronics, which drew on expertise from the university. Boothroyd and Stuart went on to found their own company, now known as Meridian Audio, in 1977. Specializing in low-volume and high-quality production, the company exemplifies a number of high-specification audio producers who represent an overlooked success story in the history of innovative British product design.[55]

There were also some innovative and creative developments in product design by designer-craftsmen moving between disciplines such as glass, metalwork, silver-smithing and industrial design, producing products for mass manufacture. For example, Brian McClelland, who trained in silversmithing and jewellery (which was undergoing a revival, with Andrew Grima winning the Duke of Edinburgh Award in 1966) at the RCA, worked on the ergonomics and product design for the first truly portable cardiac defibrillator. This innovative piece of medical equipment was invented and developed by Frank Pantridge in the second half of the 1960s, and engineered by John Anderson in Northern Ireland in the early 1970s. McClelland conceived its design with striking red metal casing and paddles, which owed something to Pop. He later recalled that 'the marketing people quickly quashed this colour in favour of a more "neutral" paintwork'.[56]

The combination of high-tech design and Pop styling would seem to be a distinctive feature of British product design in the late 1960s and the first half of the '70s. *Design* magazine enthused about the export successes of 'Carnaby Street' style. However, from the second half of the 1970s engineering began to dominate the Duke of Edinburgh Award, along with anxieties about the state of British manufacturing and exports.

● 3.20 [ABOVE] 'AC1' and 'AP1', pre-amplifier and power amplifier audio units, Robert Stuart and Allen Boothroyd,1973 | Manufactured by Lecson Audio Ltd, matt-black aluminium and Perspex | V&A: Circ.70 & A–1977 ● 3.21 [OPPOSITE LEFT] 'Wharfedale Isodynamic' headphones, Oliver Hill with the Rank Radio Industrial Design Unit, 1973 | Manufactured by Rank Radio International Ltd, ABS plastic moulded shell and stainless-steel headband | V&A: Circ.466–1973 ● 3.22 [OPPOSITE RIGHT] 'Neptune' lamp, Martin Hunt and James Kirkwood, 1970 | Manufactured by JRM Design Sales Ltd, ceramic, with electric light fitting | V&A: Circ.79–1977

DESIGNED IN BRITAIN – MADE ABROAD

By the late 1970s Britain was seen as an international centre for design expertise. Many of the new design consultancies, such as Wolff Olins, Minale Tattersfield and Conran Associates, worked with European and other international clients.[57] Seymour Powell designed the world's first cordless kettle for the French company Tefal in 1985. Although many bemoaned the decline of British exports, there were some notable export successes. Day's Polyprop was particularly prolific; the chair was licensed for manufacture in many countries to strict standards, with tools made in England. It was chosen for the main sports stadium at the Mexico Olympics in 1968. It also achieved less-predictable adaptation on a truly global scale; when Day visited Botswana in the 1980s he found that shells from the Polyprop chair had been appropriated and installed in canoes [3.23].[58]

Despite flourishing electronics, pharmaceutical and biotechnology industries there was a widespread feeling of decline in British manufacturing in the 1970s and '80s. For example, the motorcycle industry in Britain, which had been the world's largest in the 1950s, barely existed by 1975. Fears of a 'brain drain' of British talent at home heading abroad were well founded between 1976 and 1982, when only slightly over half of polytechnic design graduates found permanent employment at home and many sought work abroad. Some inventions made in Britain were exploited abroad, an issue addressed by the Design Council in their 1981 exhibition 'Designed in Britain – Made Abroad'. In 1983 Prime Minister Margaret Thatcher held a seminar with representatives from industry, education, government and the Design Council, which was followed by a number of initiatives to improve the links between education and industry and improve funding for the employment of consultant designers in companies. Despite these efforts, liquid-crystal displays, carbon fibres, the electron microscope and optical fibres are all examples of British inventions commercialized by non-UK companies.

This picture of declining manufacturing is also apparent in the UK motor industry. After the Second World War the majority of cars on the road were British-designed and made. The 1959 Mini broke new ground in engineering and design, and the 1961 E-type Jaguar was a sleek and powerful icon of quality and luxury [vii, 3.3]. There were some notable developments in the 1970s and '80s. The Range Rover, designed by David Bache, Gordon Bashford and Charles Spencer King for Austin Rover in 1970, established its own market [3.24]. With a permanent four-wheel drive and a high driving position, it was originally intended as a luxury vehicle for senior people in the army, constructors and farmers. The company certainly did not envisage it being used by women on the suburban school run. Its popular success was in part due to a wave of nostalgia for the countryside, found in retailers such as Laura Ashley and the 'country kitchen' look; the Range Rover's drivers could imagine they lived a rural life. Austin Rover was unable to meet demand and overseas competitors produced their own versions. The company had another critical success with their Austin Metro, intended to replace the Mini. However, the prevailing trend was of declining British manufacture and export and increasing foreign imports. Britain was nevertheless a successful exporter of automotive design talent. There are other recent engineering success stories in the automotive industry in Britain, particularly in specialist performance and sports cars such as Aston Martin, McLaren F1 and Lotus and low-volume micro-manufacturers, such as the long-established Morgan and the newer companies such as Noble.[59]

As we have already seen in the case of Moulton, Maclaren, Dyson and Baylis, some designers set up their own production. This tradition was continued by Tom Dixon in 1996, who designed and produced his stackable 'Jack' lights in Britain under his Eurolounge label to prove that it was still possible to manufacture in the country [2.115].[60] Matthew Hilton's 'Wait Chair' for Authentics in 1996 was similarly designed for manufacture at home. However, with increasing globalization in the late twentieth and early twenty-first centuries some British designers have moved production to countries that could offer lower labour costs and more adaptable suppliers of components. The rapidly growing consumer aspirations of the workers in product industries in these countries also offer new markets. Dyson, for instance, moved production to Malaysia in 2002 because it was no longer economically viable to manufacture in Britain, although his R&D operation remains in the UK. The much-loved icon of British engineering, the JCB digger, is now 80 per cent manufactured abroad.

CONCLUSION: BEYOND THE PRODUCT

In 1976 the 'Design for Needs' conference was held at the RCA, demonstrating a growing awareness of the social and environmental impact of design. In Victor Papanek's influential words from *Design for the Real World* (1971), designers were urged to 'design for needs, not wants'.[61] These issues were addressed by both the craft revival of the 1970s and the Design Methods movement, which put the focus on users' needs. After the designer decades of the 1980s and '90s, which were criticized for an emphasis on marketing rather than design *per se*, these issues have come to the fore again in recent years in the face of increasing globalization and the needs of developing countries. The Freeplay radio, for instance, is a brilliant example of a product designed for social purposes.

The wider context of sustainability, in a world with finite resources, has led to a renewed interest in ethnography, reminiscent of the Design Methods movement, employed as part of multidisciplinary teams in co-design, user-led, inclusive and service design, some of which posit design as a problem-solving methodology rather than something that produces three-dimensional, actual products.[62] Critical design and gallery design, by proponents such as Dunne & Raby, are prominent and influential in British design education [3.41].[63] CAD technology has not only offered new ways of problem-solving, but the possibility of infinitely customizable design and short product runs, while the internet offers sole practitioners and small and medium enterprises (SMEs) the possibilities of commissions and direct selling. For example, in 2004 Omlet, formed by a group of recent RCA graduates, produced their 'Eglu' chicken house for urbanites interested in growing their own 'slow' food, sold direct to the public via their website [xi]. Finally, a growing move towards 'slow' design, alongside a renewed interest in craft, has been accompanied by a call for what the designer Jonathan Chapman has called 'emotionally durable' design.[64] Young designers are addressing the challenge to design products that are not only made of sustainable materials that can be repaired, but are aesthetically desirable and make a personal connection with their user (for example, by customization) to ensure their longevity.

● 3.23 [OPPOSITE] Robin Day in a canoe fitted with 'Mark II' polypropylene seats, Botswana, 1980s ● 3.24 [ABOVE] Advertisement for Range Rover, originally designed 1970 Manufactured by Austin Rover

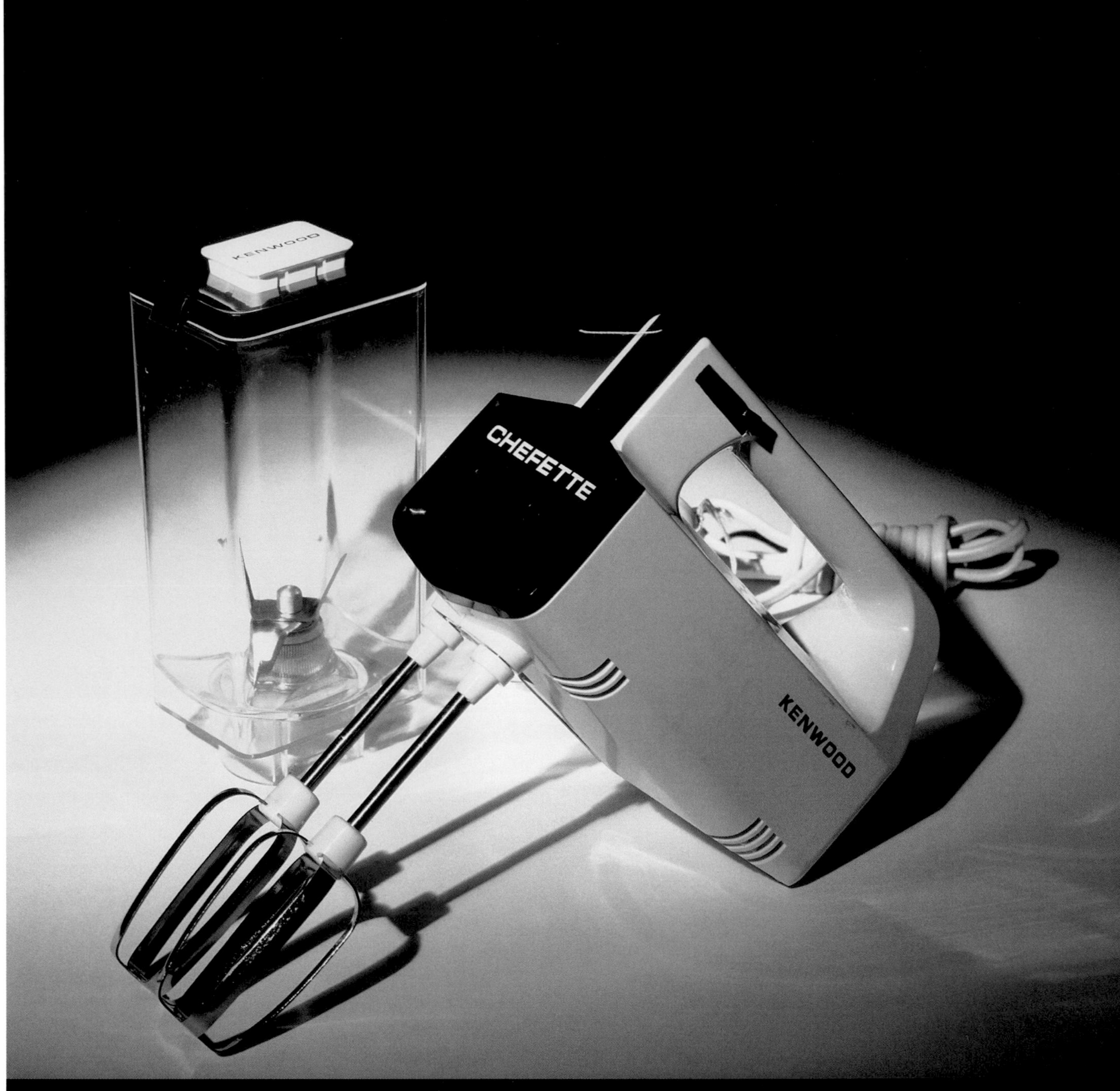

Sixty Years of Design: Reflections

— Kenneth Grange

● 3.25 [OPPOSITE] 'Chefette' food mixer, Kenneth Grange, 1966 | Manufactured by Kenwood, plastic with metal whisk attachments | V&A: Circ.731-F–1968
● 3.26 [ABOVE] 'Courier' electric shaver, Kenneth Grange, 1963 | Manufactured by Henry Milward & Sons, steel cutter screen mounted in chromium-plated brass with melamine casing and cellulose acetate carrying case | V&A: Circ.132–1965

● 3.27 [ABOVE] 'Brownie Vecta' camera, Kenneth Grange, 1964 | Manufactured by Kodak Ltd, plastic body with nickel-plated fittings | V&A: Circ.124–1965
● 3.28 [OPPOSITE] InterCity 125 high speed train, Kenneth Grange, 1975

My introduction to design and Modernism came more than 60 years ago. I was only 18, and had been drafted into the army for National Service. But first I was allowed through the door of an architect's office, where I worked for six months. It changed my life for ever. Here was the 1948 equivalent of Foster or Hopkins, although I was too ignorant to see it at the time. The offices were white with jolly colours – not like the brown and cream I had at home. The people were kind, spoke gently and designed prefab houses. They had the largest drawing boards I had even seen, and high skills with Bow pens and ink drawings on linen. I saw an Ernest Race table, folded paper lampshades and the first (and at that time very expensive) Biro pen. It was thrilling in a way that nobody can even imagine today.

By the time I set up my own little design office eight years later I had worked in four architectural practices. The modern architects' office shaped all my future expectations – indeed, my whole life. I cannot imagine a healthier, happier and more ethical place in which to learn and work.

By 1951 we'd seen 'Britain Can Make It' and the Festival of Britain. We'd got the Council of Industrial Design and we had a society of designers. In America talented designers, both men and women, were practising 'styling', but significantly the name was changing to 'industrial design'. Through magazines and travel we saw all the USA's new post-war products, though our own stagnated surroundings were largely unchanged since 1939. Yes, we'd had Utility furniture – which we later came to admire for its blend of simplicity and function. But any flourishes of light and colour were almost exclusively in women's clothes. The smallest of changes were big news: a street light, for example, or a newly opened shop; or the sleek, clear glass in a bus, which replaced anti-blast netting that had previously covered the windows. Although modest, these were important symbols of a new and lighter society. Then, all of a sudden – and mainly from Scandinavia and the USA – came Modernism. This we had only seen in magazines before. It was a heady extravagance, and it came in a rush. By the 1960s and '70s the tempting products of UK industry were shocking housewives and breadwinners into a new world – one that we now call modern. After 20 years of restraint it seemed that almost anything could happen. And if you were lucky, and were the right age in the right place, you too could be swept into the thrilling and dynamic enterprise that was Modern Britain.

In my career is an example. I was asked to make a new design for Morphy Richards – then the biggest UK maker of electric irons. I used moulded handles for an 'open' iron, which, very sensibly, enabled its nose to reach into sleeves and pockets. I was replacing a 1935 model, which Morphy had happily been making since the war to meet an insatiable demand. Indeed, my own mother was still heating her cast-iron 'iron' on a gas ring. My new design could not fail. And, in turn, it had a life of many years... And the same applied to radios, to lighting and to wallpapers and fabrics of all sorts. Some products were genuinely innovative. The icon of that age was surely the washing machine. Here was true Modernism, where fulfilling a function eased countless hours of household drudgery.

Modernism developed through the 1960s and '70s. We came to expect new versions of this and that. Further genuine innovations were the Walkman, car windscreen washers and tower cranes; even a new train and a bus shelter. From the 1970s to the '90s Modernism took root. But only occasionally was a genuine innovation a 'must-have'. There were not many, really. Some, however, truly did fulfil that timely modern maxim of 'less is more', and the human lot was bettered.

Sadly, in recent times, that stricture has been reversed. Now we have a glut of 'more is less'. Our affluent, but debt-laden society has spawned thousands of offers of wilful differences – but barely an improvement in sight. Much is claimed, of course, but very little achieved. Marketing has postured as Modernism, but the motive is clear: less for more profit. So it is truly ironic that this has brought about an exponential growth in the trade of design. There has been a huge increase in the numbers employed – vast design offices below every grand brand – with inevitably a parallel growth in the education business. Yes, design training is indeed a business. That original, primitive and truthful choice in an art school of fine or commercial art is no longer enough. Now hordes of graduates, with their thousands of redesigns of cars and irons and washing machines, are themselves the new products. Indeed, design has moved out of the shadows of manufacturing into a theatre where not only is making itself unworthy of attention, but the function is solely a token: chairs that are only seats by name, and utensils bought as symbols of affluence. Some are even made in so few numbers that they claim to pass as art. Design art is now a legitimate and madly valued branch of the art trade.

It has been an amazing 60-year journey for the designer – from a bit player in the emergence of designed products to a celebrity in the dodgy world of confidence conjurers.

10 The Cult of the Lab – A Nation of Inventors

— Louise Shannon

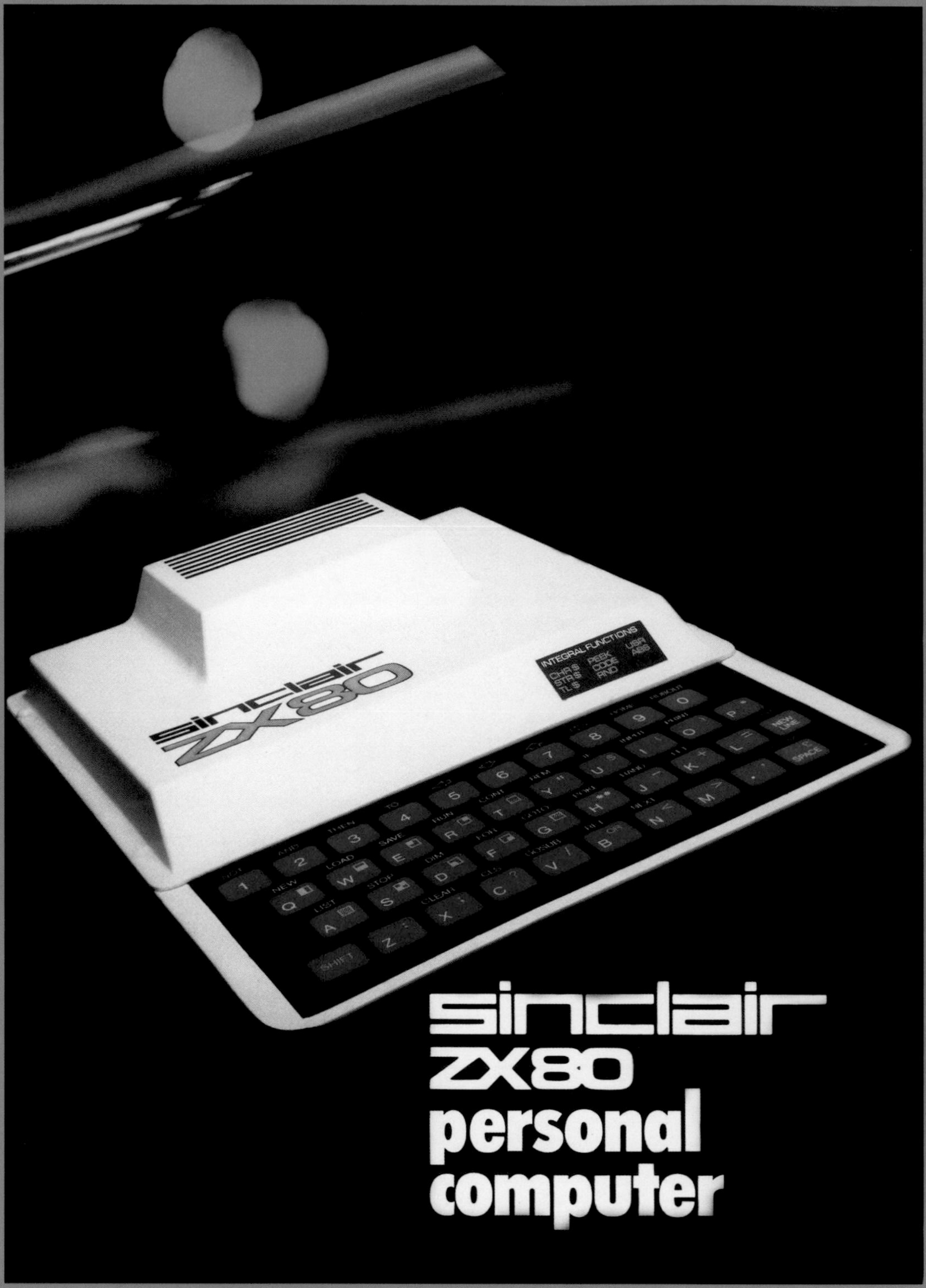

● 3.29 [ABOVE] 'Sinclair ZX80', Jim Westwood and Rick Dickinson, 1980 | Manufactured by Science of Cambridge Ltd, plastic shell with membrane keyboard, computer and electrical components

Over the last 30 years digital technologies have provided new tools for designers, ensuring a dynamic and entrepreneurial design landscape in the United Kingdom. New design industries have grown out of a technological revolution created by an increased availability of cheap hardware and the development of new software, together with the vast expansion and paradigm shift in the mode of production of digital goods and services. As Paola Antonelli remarked in the catalogue accompanying the influential 2008 Museum of Modern Art (MoMA) exhibition 'Design and the Elastic Mind', designers have helped us to navigate a 'technological revolution, grasping and converting momentous changes in technology, science and social mores to convert them into objects and ideas that people can understand and use'.[1]

At the beginning of the twenty-first century the UK has become one of the most experimental and influential centres for the development and production of digital-informed and -influenced design, nurturing an industry that balances commercial success and innovation alongside lively debates around the nature of design. These discussions take place across the country in digital-design studios, innovative design schools and experimental agencies, developed in commercial industry as well as educational contexts. These innovations can be seen across the field of computer hardware, the software industry and the design and manufacture of product, furniture and fashion.

FROM HARDWARE TO SOFTWARE

In the 1980s Britain developed a competitive and vibrant computer-hardware industry. The worldwide thirst for home computing was growing, and Britain's offering to the global market came from innovators such as Sinclair, Amstrad and Acorn. Sinclair, founded by the electronics entrepreneur Clive Sinclair in 1981 in Cambridge, enjoyed success with various computers. The Sinclair ZX80 was launched in home-assembly kit-form in 1980 to a relatively niche, amateur-enthusiast market [3.29]. This was followed by the ZX Spectrum in 1982; an eight-bit home computer that enabled users to play games, insert code, swap and share games. The Spectrum was incredibly successful, selling more than five million units worldwide.

By the late 1980s the Essex-based computer company Amstrad had gained a significant share of the UK computer-industry market, a position strengthened with the acquisition of Sinclair in 1986. Acorn Computing produced the BBC Microcomputer System in 1981, largely for schools. Linked to the BBC's Computer Literacy Project, it joined the host of successful computer companies in Britain in the 1980s. However, many of these computers operated on individual operating systems that found it hard to compete with the growing flexibility of an international new generation of PCs.

In a relatively short space of time, digital technologies became embedded within contemporary life. This mass social acceptability of technology is due in no small part to the British-born and -trained Jonathan Ive. In his role as Senior Vice President of Industrial Design at Apple Inc., Ive has been responsible for the iconic and desirable technology that has been omnipresent in the digital-design landscape for the last 15 years. Educated at the Northumbria School of Design (now known as Northumbria University), Ive is part of a diaspora that has shaped the global design economy in a significant way. The iMac G3 personal computer was launched in 1997 in a range of colours, the hard edges and drab colours of home PCs transformed by gentle curves and a rainbow palette [3.30]. The fixed covers and moulded coloured plastics were a world away from the kit computers of the 1980s that encouraged an experimental tinkering approach adopted by early amateur enthusiasts.[2] Under the moulded plastic casing was an operating system that appealed for both its usability and the innovative software programs that were being developed and refined. The combination of products including Illustrator, PostScript and LaserWriter enabled 'vibrant activity and widespread innovation in the field of visual design in the 1980s and 1990s'.[3] Adobe's Photoshop and InDesign became almost ubiquitous among graphic designers across the globe. Graphic design for the web was boosted by the growing prevalence of ActionScript which is now also owned by Adobe.

In 2010 Apple products accounted for 95 per cent of tablet computer sales until September, dipping to 75 per cent at the end of the year.[4] The iPad, Apple's tablet computer, joins Ive's portfolio of products, including the iPod and the iPhone. Each of these products has been groundbreaking, not only in changing the way we communicate with each other, but in changing the way we consume information.

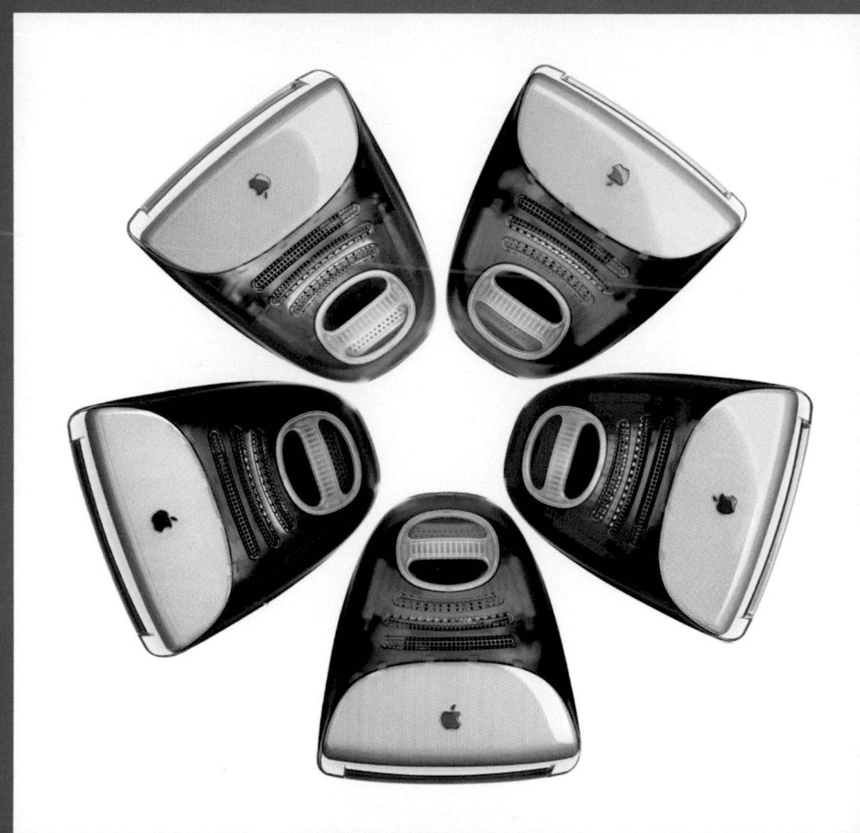

● 3.30 [OPPOSITE AND ABOVE] 'iMac G3', Jonathan Ive, 1998
Manufactured by Apple Inc., USA, moulded polycarbonate housing, computer and electrical components | V&A: W.29–2008

● 3.31 [ABOVE LEFT] *Elite*, David Braben and Ian Bell, 1984
● 3.32 [ABOVE RIGHT] *Tomb Raider*, Toby Gard at Core Design, 1996
● 3.33 [BELOW] *Grand Theft Auto IV*, Rockstar Games, 2008
● 3.34 [OPPOSITE] *LittleBigPlanet*, Media Molecule, 2007

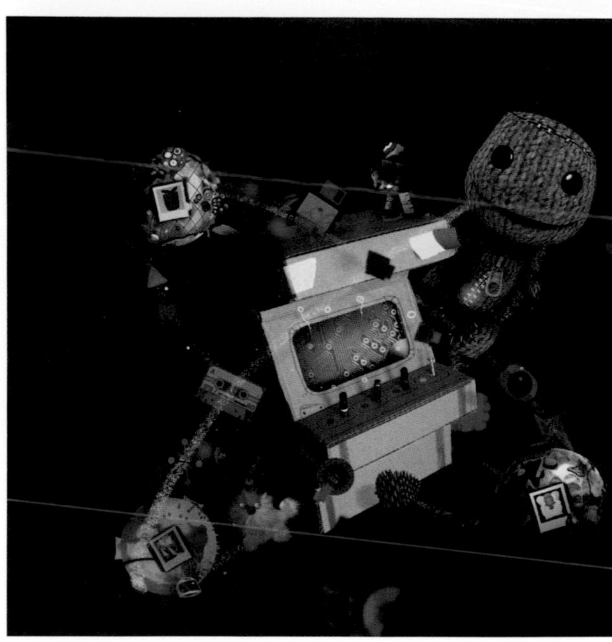

CREATIVE CODING

Computational code and programming languages have played their part in revolutionizing the design process. With the proliferation of home computers in the 1980s, programming reached a wider audience.[5] It moved beyond the confines of the aerospace and car industries and into the homes of amateur programmers. Many of these programmers became the protagonists in an entrepreneurial design industry that combined experimentation with innovation.

Innovative design studios have been fuelling and sustaining a successful digital-design sector in the UK that includes video-game design, website design, digital branding and marketing. Adopting a similar entrepreneurial attitude to that displayed in the hardware industry, design studios developed from small, start-up companies that capitalized on the developing market, and which 'lived and died'[6] through the dot.com booms and busts to create a dynamic and innovative digital-design centre in the UK.

Today Britain is renowned for designing and producing some of the most innovative and influential video games. Often based in post-industrial cities, the studios that develop the games are part of a global multibillion-pound industry. The UK has been credited with producing some of the most important games of recent times. *Elite*, launched in 1984, was the first video game to use wire-frame graphics on a home computer and went on to inspire a whole generation of games designers [3.31].[7] It was developed by two Cambridge University graduates, David Braben and Ian Bell. Working in their spare time (as was often the case in the development of early computer games), the pair conceived and built what was to become one of the most important titles in video-game history.

Tomb Raider (1996), designed by Toby Gard at Core Design in Derby, became one of the most iconic computer titles of the last century [3.32]. The original game combined the challenges associated with two-dimensional platform games (moving through a map to a goal) with a three-dimensional perspective that meant that the player (normally literally) follows the character Lara Croft through her adventure.[8] The game made the monumental leap from a specialist market into mass public consciousness as Lara Croft became part of fan culture when she appeared on the cover of *The Face* magazine, in comic books and novels, and was franchised to the movie series *Lara Croft: Tomb Raider* in 2001, in which she was played by Angelina Jolie. *Tomb Raider* helped to boost the British computer-game industry, showing that the characters it created could have the same commercial appeal of those of the gaming giants based in Japan and North America. The game sold in excess of 35 million units on a number of platforms worldwide.

The increasingly important place of gaming in mainstream culture is perhaps best demonstrated by Rockstar Games, developers of the hugely influential *Grand Theft Auto* series of games, in which players explore the underworlds of a range of wittily stylized cities [3.33]. The first *Grand Theft Auto* game was released by BMG in 1997; the following year, Rockstar was founded by a group of former BMG employees. The fledgling Rockstar studio took over the Edinburgh-based DMA Design, and after several top-down versions, released the groundbreaking *Grand Theft Auto III* for the Playstation 2 in 2001, a sprawling, living metropolis fully realised in three dimensions.[9] What made the *GTA* experience so new was its seamless combination of mission-based, linear plotting with so-called 'open world' play, in which players could discover their environment off-mission. Over the past decade, every new *GTA* game has become an international bestseller. The commercial and critical success of the series is due largely to its unprecedented depth of narrative detail and complexity, humour, and keen awareness of popular culture.

The UK is also a world leader in digital design education. Abertay University, Dundee, is one of the most important centres for the training and development of world-class games designers. Its 'Whitespace' centre is a hub for game-design development, mixing undergraduate and postgraduate study with commercial business residencies. This environment ensures a dynamic exchange between education and commerce, encouraging innovation in both sectors. The university was the first institution to provide a degree in computer-games design and has trained a number of influential designers. Dundee is home to some of the world's leading game studios, and continues to produce globally influential titles. UK studios such as Ruffian Games and Rare are increasingly influential, producing award-winning games for multi-platform consoles and hand-held mobile gaming devices.

The British computer-games industry continues to deliver influential titles such as *LittleBigPlanet* (2007) and its successor, *LittleBigPlanet 2* (2011) [3.34]. Developed by the Guildford-based games company Media Molecule, the *LittleBigPlanet* series is built on user-generated content. The platform video game revolutionized the games market by allowing users to effectively design their own games. Players can decide on the structure of the game and design the characters, levels and backgrounds. When accessed by online players, these games can be shared by gamers across the globe. The first *LittleBigPlanet* release accumulated more than three million levels, shared by an online community that had designed and developed them.

DIGITAL INDUSTRIES: THE SILICON ROUNDABOUT AND BEYOND

In the wake of the first dot.com bust, digital-design companies were realizing the growing potential of new digital service industries, developing projects that drove the sector with innovation and experimental design work. Advertising agencies looked beyond print, utilizing and exploiting the recovering markets, which had been damaged during the worldwide stock-market crashes of 2003.

Dubbed the UK's answer to California's Silicon Valley, the Silicon Roundabout originally comprised approximately 15 digital start-up companies.[10] The term, coined by Matt Biddulph in 2008, illustrated the high concentration of digital-design agencies and start-up companies working in this sector. This burgeoning sector of the creative industries, based around the Old Street area of east London, produced a vast range of digital products and services. As Biddulph has remarked, the emergence of these digital communities was built on experimentation, developing a 'culture of self-education and mutual support'.[11] The area was home to the internet radio station Last.fm (founded in 2002), which was sold to CSB Interactive for £140 million in 2007. They were joined by the likes of digital branding and advertising agency Poke London, and by Tinker, a design agency based on the development of Arduino, the cheap physical computing circuit boards [3.35].

Creative design agencies such as Poke, which moved from its first location in a Fulham basement to Shoreditch in the late 1990s, exploited the cheap rents of this then-underdeveloped area of London.[12] Realizing the potential of the new technologies, it pushed the boundaries of branding and advertising, building websites and creating marketing campaigns that used advanced and bespoke technologies to develop innovative brand identities and campaigns.

Benefiting from lower property prices and an increasingly networked design community, centres located outside the capital – such as those in Sheffield, Dundee, Brighton, Liverpool and Bournemouth – have also contributed to the digital-design landscape in the UK. Zoo Digital, based in both Sheffield and Los Angeles, provides digital post-production software services for the Hollywood film industry. Counting Warner Home Video and the television networks HBO and the BBC as its clients, Zoo Digital joins a host of substantial UK-based post-production houses, including the world-renowned London-based Framestore, The Mill and Cinesite. The National Centre for Computer Animation, based at Bournemouth University, featured on the CVs of more than 50 of the staff working on the Academy Award-winning film *Avatar* [3.36]. The film grossed more than $2 billion, becoming one of the most successful films of all time. Bournemouth University trained a number of the specialists involved in the production of graphics in the film, exporting British-trained talent to the film industry in Hollywood.

The extended network of agencies, studios, individuals and companies can draw on an expanding framework of open-source code; either fully functioning software, or components of it – a scroll bar, or a button need not be programmed from scratch, for example, but incorporated from elsewhere. Online repositories of 'creative coding' languages are freely available to designers to develop and produce technology-based projects. One such language, developed at MIT's Media Lab – 'Processing' – enables users to create images, animations and interactions. This open-source software, created by Casey Reas and Ben Fry, has been used by thousands of people globally, both professionals and hobbyists alike; it has been joined by a host of complementary open-source 'creative coding' environments, such as openFrameworks, which enable access to free code, thereby encouraging a sharing ethos. These provide access to anyone with a networked computer, from the interested amateur to the professional developer, and are helping to shift the design and production of digital-based work. Freely available coding languages, coupled with cheap electronics and the development of platforms such as Arduino, as advocated by British-based companies like Tinker, have enabled designers to develop and produce work that revives the tinkering ethos of the early kit-form computers.

Digital fabrication techniques have enabled designers to create objects that stretch the potential of production. A host of new processes allow designers to create intricate three-dimensional objects in a number of materials at rapid speed.[13] And the development and availability of new production tools such as rapid prototyping machines, together with cheap, easily available small-scale electronics, enable people to become increasingly involved in the production of their objects. Technological advances have revolutionized the design and manufacturing industry worldwide. A host of new software packages, along with a wealth of additive and subtractive manufacturing processes, have increased the opportunity to create prototypes at rapid speed. Objects can be modelled and built digitally in packages such as CAD (Computer-Aided Design). These objects can then be made using a host of digital technologies such as CAM (Computer-Aided Manufacture), CNC (Computer Numerical Control) milling, laser-cutting, rapid prototyping and manufacturing.

Zachary Eastwood Bloom, a graduate of the Royal College of Art ceramics MA, has been using subtractive methods such as CNC milling in the production of his furniture [3.37]. His chair, entitled 'Digital Decay', is a playful investigation into an information-driven society. His work uses advanced digital technologies to cut out a pixellated area of the object, as though a computer virus has become a physical parasite, eating away at the beech chair.

● 3.35 [OPPOSITE] 'Moanbot', Tinker, 2010 | Arduino-based robot with sound, light, temperature and acceleration sensors
● 3.36 [ABOVE] Still from *Avatar*, directed by James Cameron, 2009

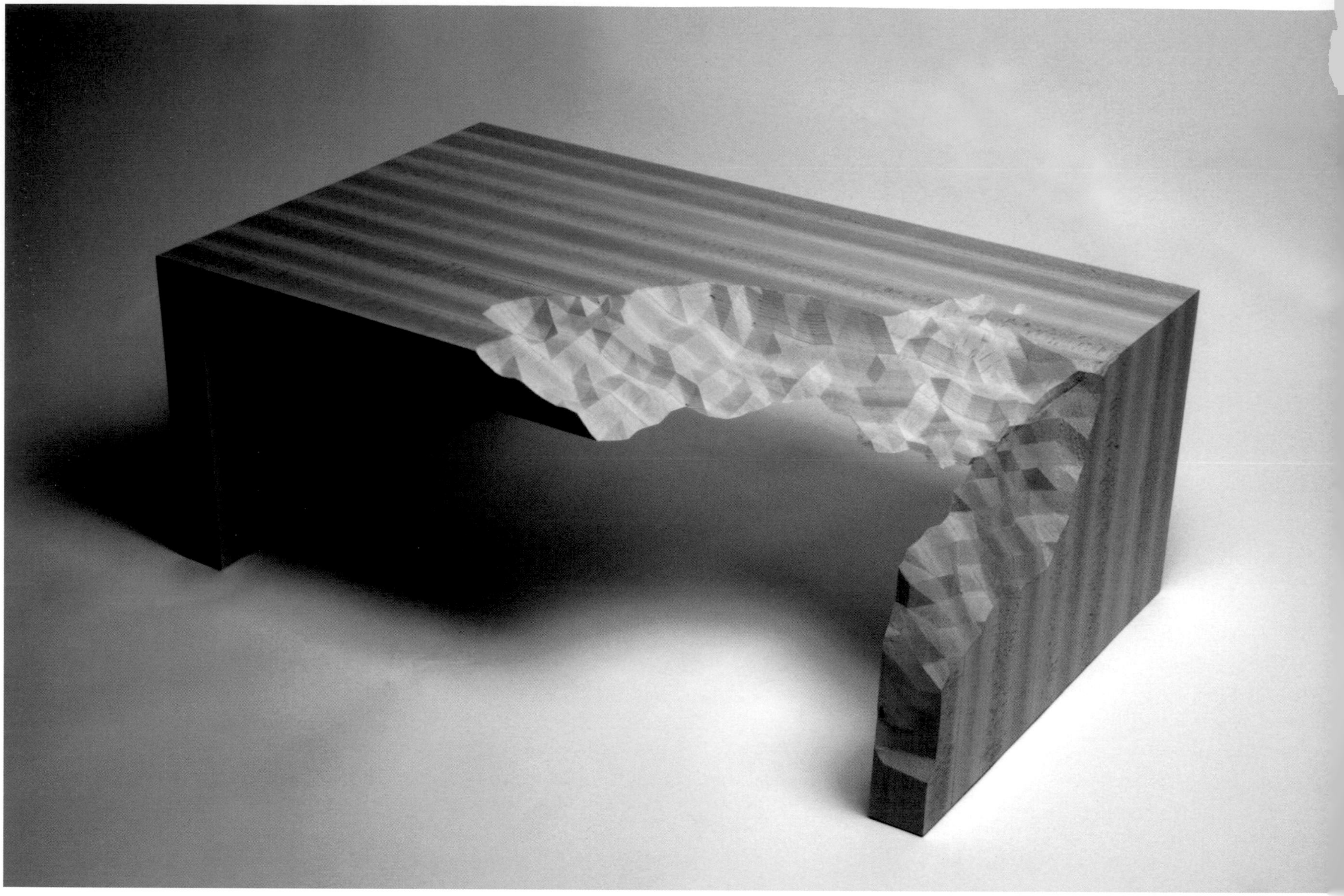

THE CULT OF THE LAB – A NATION OF INVENTORS

● 3.37 [OPPOSITE] *Information Ate My Table*, Zachary Eastwood Bloom, 2010 | CNC milled beech ● 3.38 [LEFT] *Study for a Mirror*, rAndom International, 2009 | Corian frame, glass, UV light, light-reactive ink, camera, PC, custom software | V&A: E.295–2011

HYBRIDS

New technologies are enabling designers to work collaboratively with engineers, scientists, programmers and technicians to produce pieces that mix experimental production techniques with traditional design practices. This lab-like approach and fusion of design practices ensures that the boundaries of design are stretched, blurring and cross-pollinating disciplines.

This approach creates works that investigate the space beyond product, furniture or moving image, often encouraging interaction with the viewer. The experimental London-based collective rAndom International describe their work as a combination of design practices, their studio providing a space for investigating interactions between humans and objects. Their work spans both performance and interaction design and combines the experience of three designers across multi-disciplines. The V&A acquired *Study for a Mirror* in 2010, following its inclusion in the exhibition 'Decode' and its award for 'Best in Show' at the Pavilion of Art and Design, London [3.38]. The 'Mirror' captures an image of the viewer, printing the image in ultraviolet light, which fades over a few minutes, leaving no trace.

The London-based design trio Troika show how contemporary designers are utilizing new technologies and traditional design practices to make hybrid objects that blur the boundaries between object and experience. Their practice fuses product design with interaction and communication, exploring the intersections of art, design and technology. Their work embodies a spirit of experimentation and playfulness, challenging contemporary design standards by discovering the machine within or, in the case of the Newton Virus (2005/9), turning the machine on its head. The Newton Virus works by 'infecting' the icons on an Apple desktop. The icons take on the properties of gravity, falling to the bottom of the screen, and roll around the desktop responding to physical movement in the computer.

As is the case with a number of designers who studied in London, Troika remained in the capital and benefited from the international platform that London provided for the international design market in the mid-2000s. New businesses were set up easily and were encouraged by the UK government. According to Eva Rucki and Sebastien Noel of Troika, commissions were – in comparison to other European cities – plentiful. The culture of commissioning new work in the UK, before the economic downturn, was commonplace among both public institutions and private industry, offering opportunities for developing ideas and new projects.[14] Troika have been commissioned by private industry and public bodies across the globe, with an important commission for London Heathrow's Terminal 5, hosted by British Airways. When launched in 2008, the new terminal featured a number of high-profile commissions, including Troika's award-winning designs *All the Time in the World* – a silk-screened electroluminescent digital clock – and *Cloud*, a kinetic sculpture [3.40]. These commissions offer an international platform for British-based design. And in 2010 the V&A commissioned Troika to create a semi-permanent sign in the tunnel entrance to the Museum. *Palindrome*, a kinetic work, is a mixture of hand-crafted components and playful communication design coupled with technology, woven throughout the piece to create a dynamic interpretation of the original Alan Fletcher-designed V&A logo [3.39].

● 3.39 [ABOVE] *Palindrome*, Troika, 2010 | Based on the original V&A logo by Alan Fletcher of Pentagram, mirror-polished brass, stainless steel and wood, in a clear acrylic case ● 3.40 [OPPOSITE] *All the Time in the World*, Troika, 2008 Made by Elumin8 Systems Ltd, Firefly modular electroluminescent display

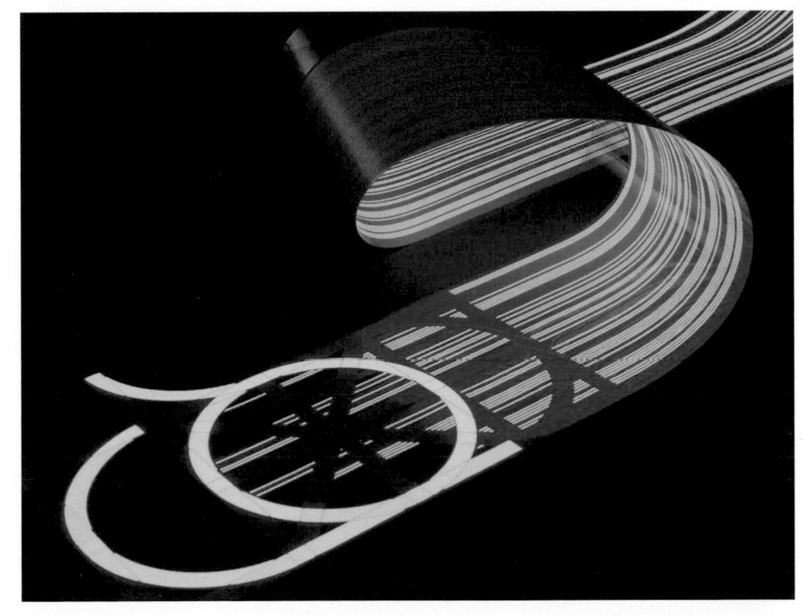

THE ART SCHOOL AS EXPERIMENTAL LAB

The UK's universities and research centres have provided educational labs for design and experimentation, encouraging inter-disciplinary practice.

The cross-fertilization of ideas and processes is in no small part down to the innovative approach to design education provided by tutors such as Ron Arad at the Royal College of Art (RCA). Arad has an innovative approach to cross-disciplinary learning and his establishment of the Platform system in 1997 [15] has inspired a generation of designers who have questioned the single-discipline approach, combining practices and approaches to develop new forms of design.

Centres such as the Material Beliefs unit, a two-year project, based at Goldsmiths, University of London, encouraged engineers and scientists to work together with designers in a research lab-based context, developing ideas and designs based on collective research. Their interests were not founded purely in the development of product design, but rather in speculative design, making connections between silicone and cells. Prototypes were developed using new technologies, making connections between biomedical engineering and everyday design. Projects developed as part of the Material Beliefs unit include *Carnivorous Domestic Entertainment Robots*, developed by the designers James Auger and Jimmy Loizeau [3.42]. As part of their speculative design development, they created self-sufficient robot prototypes that survive on fuel provided by trapping animals and pests that enter the domestic environment. Both the *Flypaper Clock* and the *Mousetrap Coffee Table Robot* use microbial cells to convert organic material into energy that, in turn, powers the robots and the motors in the devices. These self-sustainable machines prompt questions about the future role of technology and its impact on contemporary society that, according to the designers, offer an 'alternative take on how we live'.[16]

As we hurtle towards a digital-design-only process, a host of leading British designers are interrogating the role and impact of technology. Anthony Dunne and Fiona Raby have had a profound effect on contemporary British design. Their work 'uses products and services as a medium to stimulate discussions amongst designers, industry and the public about the social, cultural and ethical implications of emerging technologies.' [17] Design Interactions, led by Anthony Dunne at the RCA is a course devoted to the development of concepts and ideas. At the RCA, Dunne and his contemporaries have 'defined an approach to industrial design based on experimentation, scenarios, concepts and research on materials and technologies.[18] The *Faraday Chair* (1995), bought by the V&A in 2001, is an example of their approach to design and technology [3.41]. The chair is a transparent box designed to cradle the sitter in a foetal position, encased in Perspex with a breathing pipe as a lifeline. The object is a proposed retreat – an escape away from a world dominated by magnetic fields and electrical currents, a space that is both womb- and tomb-like, both nurturing and suffocating. Dunne and Raby's work reaches beyond investigations based purely on aesthetics or functionality and looks to the social and ethical questions posed to consumers on a daily basis.

The Design Interaction Department at the RCA has nurtured a generation of designers who are using technology and innovation to develop work that questions the role these technologies will play in our future. For example, as life becomes increasingly digitally led, what happens to this digital data after death? This question is posed by the designer Michele Gauler. Developed while Gauler was completing an MA at the RCA, *Digital Remains* is not only a repository for digital files, but a digital memory that re-creates our digital behaviours, enabling loved ones to experience the digital life of those who have died; re-creating online behaviours, painting a digital portrait of the deceased through their recorded internet activity [3.43].

● 3.41 [OPPOSITE] *Faraday Chair* | Dunne & Raby, 1995 | Welded-steel frame, acrylic box, silicone tube, cotton pillow | V&A: W.674:1-5-2001

● 3.42 [BELOW] *Flypaper Clock*, James Auger and Jimmy Loizeau, 2010 From the *Carnivorous Domestic Entertainment Robots* series, LCD clock, microbial fuel cell, motor, flypaper

RICK TERR
1964 - 2003

● 3.43 [OPPOSITE] *Digital Remains*, Michele Gauler, 2006 | Aluminium, wood, acrylic and electronic media

TOWARDS PERSONALIZED PRODUCTION

Through tinkering and the hacking of existing technologies, designers can create small-scale responsive and interactive objects using inexpensive kits containing simple sensors and circuit boards. Designers are increasingly a part of networked communities and global forums that promote the exchange and development of design tools, circumventing geographical boundaries. They are using these networks to share ideas, develop software and create new work.

Launched in 2011, the Fab Lab Manchester is a fully functioning lab focused on public engagement with making and personal production. The Fab Lab – devised by Professor Neil Gershenfeld, Director of the Center for Bits and Atoms at the Media Lab based at the Massachusetts Institute for Technology in Cambridge, Massachusetts – has been exported to a number of countries worldwide.

These production labs have resulted in an increased choice for designers, an alternative to the traditional manufacturing and modelling processes. Objects can be designed and tested within the computer program using CAD programs, printed out or rendered, laser-cut or milled, to be demoed at rapid speed. The ability to prototype and demo is fundamental to the development and experimental spirit of contemporary design. It, according to Tim Brown, CEO of IDEO, speeds up the process on innovation,[19] and as designer and academic Anthony Dunne confirms, this is a way of 'narrowing the gap between experimental design thinking and everyday life'.[20]

What we are experiencing in contemporary design is the possibility to shift, from mass to personal production, from large-scale manufacturing to user-generated design. New technologies have changed the way we communicate, the way we consume and, increasingly, the way we design. Designers are, according to Tim Brown, increasingly discovering the 'potential for participation'.[21] Users of products and services are investigating the 'shift from a passive relationship between consumer and producer, to the active engagement of everyone in experiences that are meaningful, productive and profitable'.[22] Echoing the revolution of web 2.0 and the consequent ability of web users to comment, participate, share and create content, this ethos is filtering into the design and manufacturing process, looking to a future when consumers will be able to design, modify and produce objects at rapid speed. Brown speculates that in fact design is at its most powerful 'when it is taken out of the hands of designers and into the hands of everyone'.[23] As Kara Johnson, a designer at IDEO, has commented, designers are acting as 'mediators between individual and corporate participation'.[24] There has been what she describes as the creation of 'Punk Manufacturing', intercepting and subverting the large-scale production process to enable small-scale, do-it-yourself design and production.

Government support for new design industries, combined with an encouraging and generous approach towards commissioning by cultural institutions and commercial clients, has ensured thus far an innovative design culture in Britain. These dynamic education centres are an important part of the creative economy of the UK and play a vital role in the development and training of both UK-based and overseas students. As the cultural landscape is facing economic challenges, an industry focused on innovation is vital if Britain is to remain relevant within global design markets.

As the designer Tom Dixon has stated, the economic recession of the 1980s provided a design environment in which you had to 'get things made yourself'.[25] Taking its inspiration and ethos from the music scene, the 'do-it-yourself' attitude that had permeated music, fashion and graphics also influenced the design and production of furniture. Thirty years later, the global recession has similarly affected design and manufacture. What the impact on the British design sector will be remains to be seen.

The Old Reliable: Contemporary British Design and the Resources of Craft

— Glenn Adamson

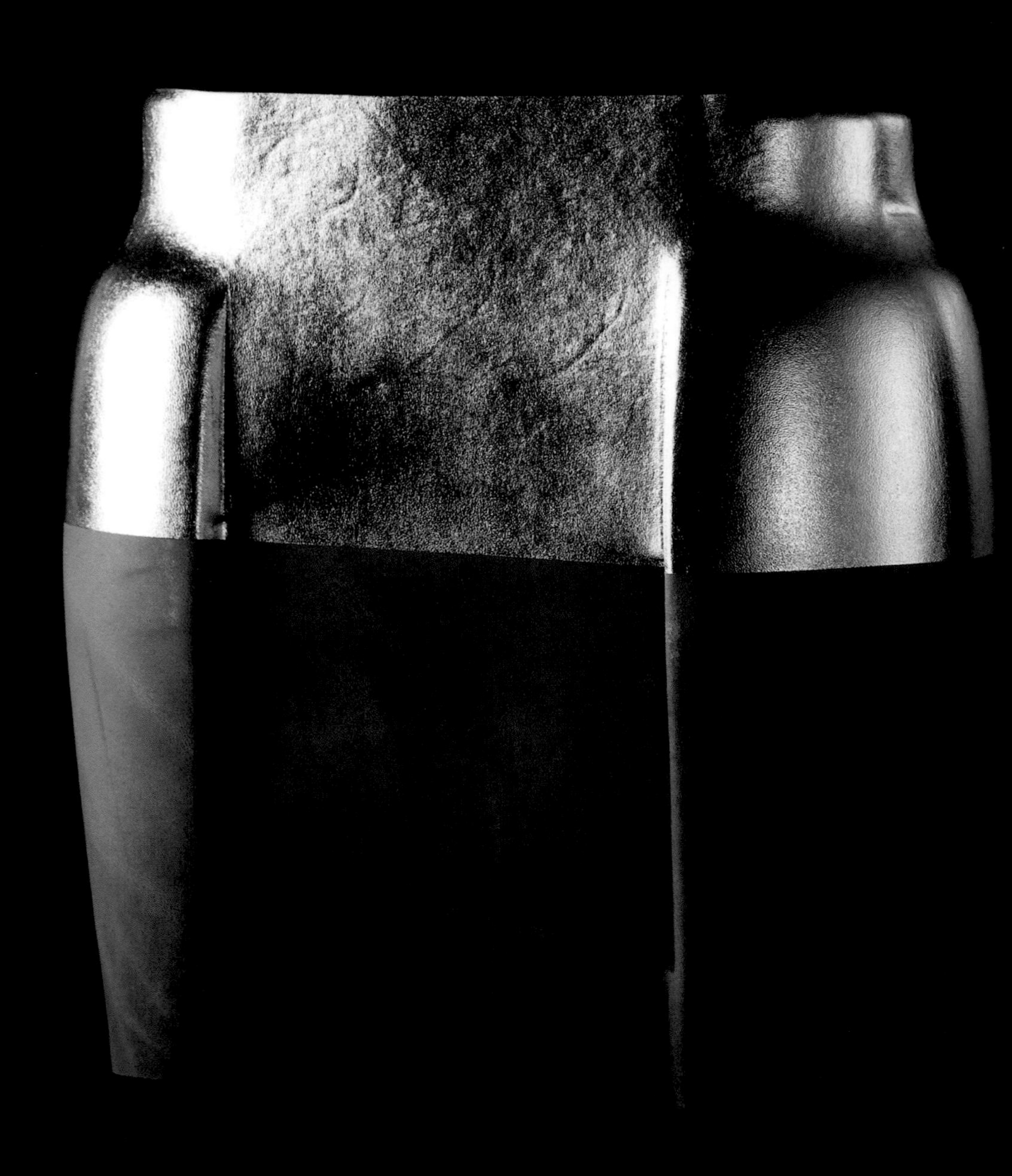

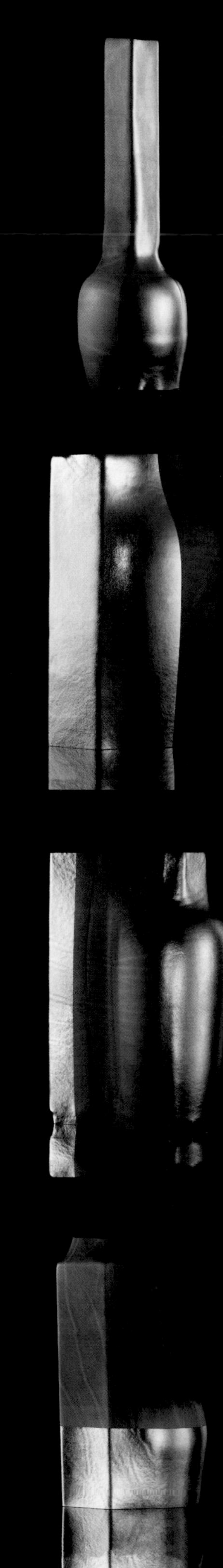

● 3.44 [OPPOSITE AND FAR RIGHT EDGE] 'Vase Family', Simon Hasan, 2009 | Boiled leather, polyurethane resin, gold or palladium oil gilding ● 3.45 [ABOVE] 'Sunray Easy Chair', William Warren, 2010 | Ash with jute webbing ● 3.46 [RIGHT] 'Kelp Constructs', Julia Lohmann, 2008 | *Laminaria japonica* seaweed

In tough times, where's a designer to turn? What to do when commissions dry up, when the market is awash with derivative imports, when sustainability trumps consumption and domestic manufacturing starts to seem a nostalgic (not to say quixotic) enterprise? That, roughly, is the situation faced by contemporary British designers today. What they need is a new means of attaining self-sufficiency – without creating a world even more full of junk in the process.

Fortunately there are many ways of making that achieve exactly that result. But they are not so new after all. In fact, they are the oldest we know. These are the techniques of craft, which has always been light on the land. And they are absolutely everywhere at the moment. Government ministers express concern for disappearing skills. Twenty-somethings in east London organize their social lives around knitting. And one designer after another is finding that the best pair of hands for the job might just be his or her own.

Like so many other repositories of value in modern times, craft has often found itself pressed into systems that dwarf it in terms of scale and power. Industrial processes don't so much do away with craft skill as displace it, from the making of finished products to preparatory and ameliorative activities such as prototype-making, repair and creative salvage. But Britain is now a post-industrial economy, in which knowledge and experience are the primary drivers of value. So more direct forms of craft have come back into play. Sure, designers can locate know-how easily enough – call it up from down the road or halfway across the world, just like anything else, hire skills rather than learn them. But can they afford to work that way? And even if they can, are they happy with the all-too-familiar dynamic of outsourced labour? In our infinitely word-searchable age, workmanship is one of the few remaining sources of productive friction. British designers are at the forefront of realizing this truth: they have begun to reap the benefits of taking craft seriously, not as a static, exploitable resource, but as a means of innovation in its own right.

A prominent recent example of this rediscovery was London-based Martino Gamper's project *100 Chairs in 100 Days*, undertaken in 2007 [3.47]. As the title suggests, this was an exercise in 'rapid forming', but all done by hand rather than by a huge and expensive piece of kit. To meet his self-imposed deadline, Gamper mainly used pre-existing parts (he could scarcely have done otherwise), an 'upcycling' strategy that was transformative rather than additive. The results have the crazed inventiveness of a stack of children's drawings, but also the solidity of old-fashioned joinery. Unlike the conceptual designs made in the Netherlands in the 1990s, which his work superficially resembles, Gamper doesn't treat craft ironically, as if it were the set-up for a punchline (as in Marcel Wanders's *Knotted Chair*, for example). It is instead a means of becoming – a seemingly desperate measure that becomes a source of certainty.

As more and more British designers have turned to craft as their best last resort, however, they have realized that it doesn't need to be a matter of DIY immediacy. As any potter or weaver knows, craft can be a matter of sustained, even lifelong research and investigation. The question is how to make such deep investment in skills compatible with design innovation. Craft is often celebrated as a cultural repository, but in the same breath it is maligned for being stuck in the past. Cognizant of this dilemma, designers who turn to artisanal processes tend to appropriate them, much in the manner of a sculptor incorporating a found object into an artwork. Yet this need not be a disrespectful act. It can involve collaboration as well as experimentation.

Julia Lohmann's boxes and lighting made of seaweed, for example, represent a good-faith effort to shape a traditional Japanese material into contemporary form [3.46]. They could not have been realized without the direct contributions of skilled artisans. Armed with a complete lack of preconceptions, she has stretched kelp across frames like kites and let it dangle in curling ribbons, and (working with a team of lacquerers) has structured thin sheaves of *kombu* seaweed into neo-Constructivist shapes reminiscent of architectural models. Similarly, Simon Hasan's experiments with *cuir bouilli* (boiled leatherwork) required him to undertake a reverse-engineering investigation of historical artefacts such as leather armour. After painstakingly recovering these processes, he mated them with another traditional craft – oil gilding – to create vessels that virtually glow with contemporary sensibility [3.44]. Both Lohmann and Hasan regard their work not as an exploitation of traditional skills, but rather as an affectionate tribute to the possibilities they engender.

A similar humility marked the project *Bodging Milano*, which represented new heights in terms of British designers' willingness to subject themselves to the demands of an unfamiliar craft. In the summer of 2010 Designersblock, a curatorial initiative based in London, led a group of nine British furniture designers out into the woods. There they were briefly apprenticed to Gudrun Leitz, a master of the craft of 'bodging' or rustic chair-making, requiring the use of a foot-powered pole lathe as well as several other basic hand tools. Like Gamper, the designers were working under time constraints and, given their inexperience with these fabrication processes, at the very limits of their skills. The statements issued by the group during and after the event are filled with reverence for the toughness and clarity afforded by this 'unplugged' workmanship. When the pale-wooden chairs they made – all variants on the traditional Windsor form – were put on display at the Milan Furniture Fair, they spoke of an ideal marriage between rural and urban, simple and sophisticated [3.45].

For those who have always valued crafts, the enthusiasm for traditional techniques among contemporary designers can sometimes be a little vexing. The tacit question is: where have you been all our lives? Then, too, there is the matter of historical asymmetry between the two fields. Rather like fine art, design has often treated craft as a silent partner, relying on its potency without granting it any form of authorship. But it doesn't need to be that way. If designers are willing to put their own hands to work, and to approach artisanal processes (and artisans too) with respect as well as curiosity, they will continue to find ways forward – by going back to basics and taking a good long look.

● 3.47 [ABOVE] *100 Chairs in 100 Days*, installation view, Martino Gamper, 2007

11 British Design Consultancy and the Creative Economy

— Guy Julier

● 3.48 [ABOVE] Drawing of a proposed livery for a Western diesel locomotive, Design Research Unit, early 1960s
Watercolour on paper | National Railway Museum

When the Yellow Pages were launched in 1966 there were just three design consultancies listed in central London. By 1999 there were 536. In 1994 there were about 8,000 design firms within the then 12 member-states of the European Union. Within the European market, the United Kingdom maintained the highest expenditure on design services during the 1990s.[1] In 1998 Britain had some 4,000 design consultancies employing more than 20,000. A further 3,000 worked as sole traders or in non-design-specific organizations – in other words, as in-house designers to companies and institutions.[2] By 2001, UK employment in design consultancies was recalculated at 73,000.[3] While it is widely acknowledged that calculating size and expenditure in the creative industries is difficult, a glance at the specialist news-stands of London will demonstrate that British design is unmatched in its scale and reach. Describing the patina of British design – the ways by which it functions – is an even harder task. It is useful, though, to understand its emergence and breadth as coming from a series of economic waves felt through the late twentieth century.

The astonishing rise of British design and advertising from 1980 must be understood in three ways. First, it was a response to changing economic (and therefore consumer) circumstances; but, second, it developed in relation to Britain's geographical (and therefore cultural) position. Third, while Britain has become progressively sharper in its commercial operations, its own craft ethic has produced wide variations in its working practices.

British design has often driven a middle ground between American and European approaches. On the one hand, it has drawn from commercial business models found in America. On the other, many British designers have embraced a more European studio ethic. Meanwhile, the business model of British design has also been interpreted as the craft of designing itself: plan ahead, and then make it up as you go along. Trusting your intuition while being seen to know what you're doing is the creative's survival technique. These factors have conspired to make design in Britain a heterogeneous field.

In Italy and Spain the emphasis has been on small-scale, individually led design studios, and it is more common in Germany and Nordic countries to find designers working in-house for companies. Much of British design is, however, practised on a consultancy basis. Here the consultancy usually works for an agreed fee on specifically outlined projects for clients, rather than being employed on a retainer or receiving a percentage of the client's sales income. It therefore works as a service providing outsider expertise. Its currency is the creativity and innovations that it can make on behalf of the client. As such, British designers are always keen to provide a differentiated product for their clients, but also, in a heatedly competitive marketplace, to differentiate themselves from each other.

British design consultancy has also been distinguished by two further, related aspects. As we have already seen, in terms of the sheer numbers of staff employed and its financial turnover, it has dominated the global field. This has contributed to its international, export-orientated character. Given that it outweighs its domestic market, competition within the British design industry is such that it has sought foreign markets within and far beyond Europe. Some 75 per cent of British consultancies were active in overseas markets, concentrating their efforts in the United States and northern Europe. Exports by British design consultancies rose from £175 million in 1987 to £385 million in 1997; in a survey carried out by the Design Council in 1998, 45 per cent of consultancies reported that exporting their services was more profitable than participating in UK projects. Developments in design-consultancy practices have often been in response to economic and social change within the UK. But the resultant specialisms, strengths and ways of working have also become highly exportable. This chapter therefore focuses on the ways in which British design imported working methods from outside, how it built consultancies in response to business and consumer practices and, ultimately, how it has faired in response to changing economic fortunes.

GO TO WORK
ON AN EGG

130
STANDARD

● 3.49 [OPPOSITE] 'Go to Work on an Egg', Mather & Crowther, 1964 | Designed for the Egg Marketing Board, art director Ruth Gill, photographer Len Fulford, copywriters Fay Weldon and Mary Gowing, colour offset lithograph | V&A: E.309–2011

FROM AD AGENCY TO DESIGN CONSULTANCY

The overall concept of a design consultancy had been hatched in the United States by groups such as Raymond Loewy Associates or Teague in the interwar period. These benefited from a relatively stable, affluent and homogenized market with a wide distribution base. They demonstrated that a design business can expand across design disciplines taking in graphics, interior and product design, but also marketing and management specialists. Raymond Loewy Associates reached some 150 employees by 1947, integrating the design of advertising, packaging, interiors and products of corporate clients. This model itself was derived from the rise of the American advertising agency, a model that had been established in the latter part of the nineteenth century. By the 1920s American ad agencies would typically include copywriters, art directors, account executives and media space buyers.

Partly responding to these American developments, graphic artist Milner Gray established what was arguably Britain's first multidisciplinary design consultancy, the Bassett-Gray Group of Artists and Writers in 1934, which became the Industrial Design Partnership a year later. During the Second World War they designed propaganda exhibitions for the Ministry of Information. Within this ambit, Milner Gray, architect Misha Black and writer and critic Herbert Read joined advertising agency chief Marcus Brumwell to establish the Design Research Unit (DRU) in 1943. The presence of Read within the group is notable. His influence on the DRU, and on British design more generally, comprised the injection of ideas found in European Modernism. After all, he was author of the influential book *Art and Industry* (1934), in which he argued that abstract art could be given social purpose through its application to 'industrial art'.[4]

The DRU anticipated the wide-scale need for design in the reconstruction of Britain after the Second World War, both in its commercial and public sectors. It proceeded to undertake important public commissions for such historically important events as the 'Britain Can Make It' (1946) exhibition and the Festival of Britain (1951) (see Chapter 2). However, the Modernist verve for visual coherence also found its way into large-scale commercial projects. Milner Gray developed the use of 'corporate identity' over its predecessor term 'house style'. He oversaw, for example, the wholesale makeover of identities of Watney Combe pubs, Ilford photographic materials and British Rail [3.48, 3.54].[5] The British government also proved to be an important client to design and advertising in these Keynesian reconstruction years. Ogilvy Benson and Mather's 1957 'Go to Work on an Egg' slogan for the British Egg Marketing Board – itself established by the government to stabilize and promote egg sales – subsequently became a £12 million campaign that ran through the 1960s [3.49]. The celebrated 1969 Cramer Saatchi 'pregnant man' campaign, promoting family planning for the Health Education Council, continued the tradition of public commissioning [3.50].

The post-war period saw the internationalization of American advertising agencies: in 1937 just four had branches outside the USA, while by 1960, 36 had foreign branches, with a total of 281 offices.[6] Again, this had a direct impact in Britain in that it encouraged designers to set up larger, more complex design consultancies. Examples of these included Allied International Designers and Fletcher Forbes Gill (which became Pentagram in 1972), both founded in 1959; Cambridge Consultants, begun in 1960; Minale-Tattersfield, founded in 1964; Wolff Olins, started in 1965; and Michael Peters and Partners, established in 1970. These were to remain the key design establishment names in the following decades.

By and large these studios had to invent their own working methods. James Pilditch's Allied International Designers was an important influence. Pilditch wrote influential books on product development and corporate identity, which helped to give a voice to the emergent multidisciplinary design industry in the UK.[7] Meanwhile one of its key participants, Wally Olins, admitted that it was mostly 'learning as it went along'.[8] Nonetheless, the strength of the British economy provided a firm footing for the growth of consultant design during the 1960s. This was also the decade when many corporate giants emerged, forcing either takeover, liquidation or the repositioning of many smaller businesses, and it was when designers learned to coordinate sizeable corporate projects. Wolff Olins' first major corporate-identity scheme in the early 1960s was for the paint manufacturer Hadfields [3.52]. With the emergence of ICI's Dulux brand and Hoechst's Berger – both with high-quality product, blanket distribution and massive advertising – a corporate identity for Hadfields had to be developed that made the company equally visible, but also emphasized its stealth and flexibility. Hence a fox motif was adopted for its corporate logo.[9]

DESIGN FOR THE CONSUMER ECONOMY

The decline of manufacturing in Britain from the 1970s was mirrored by the growth of the British service sector. Employment in manufacturing dropped in the UK from 38.4 per cent in 1960 to 22.5 per cent in 1990; Britain's share of world manufacturing exports dropped from 14.2 per cent in 1964 to 7.6 per cent in 1986.[10] Nonetheless, during the 'Thatcher decade' of 1979–89, employment in the service sector grew by two million, roughly the same figure as the decline in manufacturing employment. Output in the service sector grew by 28.8 per cent, as against nearly 10 per cent in manufacturing.[11]

It is useful to understand the resulting shifts in consumer patterns through this period in order to see how, also, the drivers of British design came from the retail and communications sectors. The 1970s were characterized by deep economic recession, precipitated by the rise in oil prices in 1973 and by severe worker unrest and frequent strikes experienced throughout manufacturing, extraction industries and the public sector. The socio-economic profile of the country was rearranged. Pay deals that were negotiated by the trade unions meant that traditionally lower-paid manual workers experienced significant rises in income. Added to this was the entry of many more women into the labour force. This meant that most lower-income households benefited from higher disposable income. The consumer preferences of this population sector were oriented more towards clothing and durable goods than food, and choices were more readily being made on considerations of price rather than quality. With inflation reaching 25 per cent by the mid-1970s, consumers were even more price-conscious. This in turn led to the growth of mass merchandisers as they extended their ranges and used their economies of scale to offer cheaper goods. Throughout the 1970s Peter Dixon, chief designer at the supermarket chain Sainsbury's, introduced modern Helvetica lettering on its food packaging to signal quality at reasonable prices [3.51]. Into the 1980s Tesco also learned that strong packaging design could do the work of shop-floor assistants in selling goods.[12]

As capital investment in manufacture in the Far East was consolidated, so cheaper durable goods of more reliable production standards were attainable. In turn this enabled multiples to become mass merchandisers.[13] Food-based multiples such as Asda and Tesco therefore moved into non-food-product markets, and specialist mass merchandisers such as Currys, Rumbelow, Dixon and Comet were also consolidated.[14] In fashion, new retail patterns also emerged. Wardrobes extended from 'a best suit' and a 'working suit' to two or three 'general-purpose suits' and an extensive range of leisure clothing. Thus high-street brands such as Topman (part of the Burton group), catering to younger consumers, were established in the late 1970s.

For the design sector, this meant significant new opportunities in packaging, retail interior and graphic design, as increased product variety and volume of sales began to transform the high street and the shopping centre. In this context, several larger-scale consultancies were established during the 1970s, including Michael Peters & Partners (founded 1970), Enterprise IG (founded 1976), Addison (founded 1978) and Fitch (founded 1972).

Rodney Fitch, founder chairman of Fitch, was keenly aware of the challenges that these trends implied. In a speech in 1984 he noted that there were by then 500 shopping centres in Britain, with 80 per cent of its population within a 15-minute drive of two. There were 380 superstores, all built in the previous 20 years, and this could rise to 800 in the coming 10 years. Department stores had lost their share of the market from 6 per cent to 4.5 per cent over the last 20 years. There had been a rise of multiples that concentrated on identified market sectors, such as Burton, Next and Habitat. As with the Body Shop, these also distributed their own-brand product, which put the emphasis on high-street recognition over advertising for market share. Fitch also noted the shift away from the traditional nuclear family buying unit amongst households. People were more style-conscious, but also more demanding on price. Shopping would have to be designed to be pleasurable both in its immediate experience and in the attainability of the goods on offer.[15]

Retail design thinking also found its way into other sectors during the 1980s. Hitherto, high-street banks had occupied architecturally prominent buildings that emphasized their historical pedigree and importance. The majority of their interior space was given over to back-room offices and archiving. Two important changes took place for banks in the 1980s. The first was in the move of accounting information to more centralized, digital storage facilities, thus freeing up space in individual branches.[16] The second was in deregulation. The 1986 Building Societies Act allowed building societies to act as banks. In turn, this introduced far greater competition for customers and diversification in terms of the services offered by both banks and building societies. As a result, banks were designed increasingly to be more outward-facing. Fitch's redesign for the Midland Bank branches in the mid-1980s made them look more welcoming – places to browse new financial products as much as undertake transactions [3.55]. The changes featured the introduction of soft furnishings, a brighter colour palette, multidirectional circulation (rather than the standard 'bank queue') and greater visibility of bank staff.

The UK retail boom of the 1980s set new standards in design. Consumer demand grew, but was tempered by the need for price-competition. Packaging design, as James Pilditch had advocated, was to take on a sharpened role as the 'silent salesman' in delivering the idea of quality, but at low prices. Meanwhile shopping was reinvented as a leisure activity by design consultancies such as Fitch and David Davies Associates. Retail outlets were not just there to shift products, but to provide an ambience that reinforced their brand image while encouraging shoppers to linger and form more lasting relationships with the outlet.

● 3.50 [ABOVE] 'Would you be more careful if it was you that got pregnant?', Cramer Saatchi, 1969 | Designed for the Health Education Council, art director Bill Atherton, photographer Alan Brooking, copywriter Jeremy Sinclair, offset lithograph | V&A: E.1704–2004

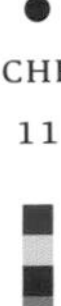

Printed Publicity
Symbol and logotype in colour for rail publicity

sheet no.	2/05
issued	Apr 1965

British Rail

a. Symbol and logotype in BR Publicity Red

British Rail

b. Symbol in BR Publicity Red with logotype in black

British Rail

c. Symbol and logotype within ruled rectangles all in BR Publicity Red

British Rail

d. Symbol and logotype in BR Publicity Red within ruled rectangles in black

British Rail

e. Symbol in BR Publicity Red with logotype in black within ruled rectangles in black

MANAGING THE DESIGN BUSINESS

As the retail landscape became more sophisticated, so clients and their design consultants were having to become strategic in what they had to offer. Fitch, for instance, acquired Retail Solutions, a consultancy specializing in retail trends, which would add further expertise to the design process. Many of the key design studios expanded in terms of the range of concepts they embraced, but also in terms of scale, as projects became ever larger. Following its establishment in 1982, David Davies Associates, specializing in retail and corporate identity, employed 150 staff by 1988.[17] RSCG was employing 300 by 1987, as was Fitch. At its height, the Michael Peters Group employed 720.[18]

With this massification within design studios came further challenges in their management. Prior to the 1980s most design consultancies worked in a rather laissez-faire way with regards to their accountancy systems. With larger-scale projects – particularly for retail design that involved the coordination of graphics, interior and product design – the design process had to be managed across several individuals and teams in the studio. Time-sheets, hitherto anathema to the long-houred but 'relaxed' culture of studio practice, were introduced. Workflows had to be devised and managed. Specialist teams within the studio became cost centres. New employees had to be inducted into the design consultancy's particular way of processing projects. The profit-motive was no longer a back-room issue for the account handlers. Rather, greater efficiency and quicker turnover of design projects became imperative. A new environment of commercial 'reality' took centre-stage. The need for tighter management of design in the studio precipitated the use of the account 'planner' from 1986, a practice adopted (again) from advertising. The planner's role was to undertake the research and analysis as part of the brief-writing, and to then articulate and clarify the brief both as a guide for the client and for the studio staff. Subsequently this helped to structure and clarify the details of the design process.[19]

During the 1980s many clients were experiencing work with a design consultancy for the first time, and so the need for designers to explain what they were doing (and thus charging for) was paramount. Fitch, for instance, coined its 'Perception, Concept, Action' structuring of projects, for the sake both of client understanding and its own staff training.[20] It is difficult to say whether or not this shift in working practices had an effect on the finished look of objects and environments. But it did ensure quicker turnaround of projects and an easier outflow of volume in design projects. It also helped build trust with clients and streamline the processing of retail design for foreign markets. British design, one might say, was being increasingly packaged for foreign clients.

The growing commercial orientation of the British design consultancy, the growth of studio size and its responsiveness to client demand were fuelled by the appearance in 1986 of the design magazine *DesignWeek*. At the time this was the only magazine that addressed all design disciplines. Its classified ads provided a one-stop resource when a consultancy needed to put multidisciplinary teams together quickly for specific projects. Its weekly publication meant that the quickening pace of the 1980s design bubble was made even more urgent. As *Campaign* reflected the commercial news of the advertising industry, so *DesignWeek* [3.52] did the same for design. Meanwhile monthly journals such as *Blueprint*, founded in 1983, concentrated on the more cultural aspects of contemporary design.[21]

The 1980s also saw design consultancies involved in more complex business arrangements, including the flotation of some of them on the stock market. The first of these was Allied International Designers: when Pilditch took the consultancy to the market in 1980 it had a turnover of £23 million, with 16 companies and a staff of 600. The move of design consultancies into public quotation allowed them to recapitalize, but it was also strategic in that it encouraged clients to view the design consultancy 'as a proper business' – it bought credibility with clients. When Addison took over Allied International Designers in 1984, it expanded it to a group of 1,600 employees offering market research, public relations and recruitment specialisms alongside design.[22] Following on, Fitch became publicly quoted in 1982, the Michael Peters Group floated in 1983 and Addison went to the City in 1984.

In some cases, acquisition worked in the opposite direction, when marketing-services groups took over design companies. These would include the WPP Group, Euro RSCG, Havas, Aegis, Gruner & Jahr and Saatchi & Saatchi. In 1983 when it began buying design businesses, the WPP Group encompassed 54 companies employing 22,500 staff.[23] Its portfolio ranged from advertising agencies, public-relations and public-affairs consultancies to media-planning and research groups. WPP wholly or part-owned companies, its payoff being increased capitalization and the sharing of clients across the group according to required specializations. During the 1980s many larger design consultancies were driven by the imperative for high profits, either coming from the stock market or from their parent group.

● 3.51 [OPPOSITE TOP LEFT] Packaging for Sainsbury's biscuits, Peter Dixon, 1967 ● 3.52 [OPPOSITE TOP RIGHT] *DesignWeek*, first issue, 26 September 1986 ● 3.53 [OPPOSITE BOTTOM LEFT] Corporate identity for Hadfields (Merton) Ltd, Wolff Olins, 1968 Art director Michael Wolff, designers Kit Cooper and Richard Peskett, artist Maurice Wilson ● 3.54 [OPPOSITE BOTTOM RIGHT] Page from the British Rail design manual, Design Research Unit, 1965 | Printed paper | AAD: 1999/8 ● 3.55 [ABOVE] The Broadmead branch of Midland Bank, Bristol, Fitch & Co., 1986

THE DESIGN CONSULTANCY AND THE DESIGN STUDIO

The design bubble was to burst in 1990 in spectacular ways. Following the global stock-market collapse of 1987, the British economy continued to perform relatively well. But the summer of 1990 saw the Michael Peters Group and Crighton go into receivership, while the Conran Design Group axed 43 staff. David Davies Associates followed in 1991. Fitch drastically reduced to fewer than 50 staff by 1991 and was rescued from receivership by a buyout from Terence Conran. For Fitch, the early 1990s recession coincided with problems with its high property costs. This raised a serious question concerning the economic resilience, when it came to downturns, of design businesses that took on high costs.[24]

Following on from the design-market crash, many smaller, more flexible design studios took the place of the large-scale consultancies. With lower overheads, these were able to appeal effectively to clients through lower fees. Needless to say, the introduction of the Apple Macintosh desktop computer in 1984 gave way to subsequent software packages that streamlined the design process. Desktop publishing, facilitated by MacPublisher (introduced in 1984) and then Aldus PageMaker (1987), and graphics programs such as QuarkXPress (1987), virtually cut out a complete typesetting industry. Designers were now able to prototype more easily and cheaply, allowing for closer and quicker consultations with their clients. With greater commissioning experience by now, many clients were themselves more cautious and critical of what they were getting.

Just as advertising had moved to greater outsourcing of media buying, design and video production in the late 1980s, so design followed suit in the early 1990s. One might typify this as a shift in the 1980s from a 'Fordist' mode of design production to a 'post-Fordist' system in the 1990s. The former involved large-scale studios with highly organized divisions of labour. The latter featured multitasking, small-scale teams acting in flexible networks to undertake design projects with large-scale, multinational corporations.

The economic recession of the early 1990s also allowed for a return to a studio ethic, where the careful crafting of forms retook precedence. Arguably, some design consultancies of the 1980s had themselves developed some recognizable signature styles of their own that were deployed across various commissions: Lewis Moberly's 'invented heritage' to be found in Asda's own-brand drinks; Minale Tattersfield's 'scribble' logos; Wolff Olins' Matisse-inspired identities for the Prudential, 3i and BT. Meanwhile there were several individual graphic designers in the 1980s who successfully championed an even more personal, authorial style. These would include the recherché Modernism of Peter Saville, with his record sleeves and posters for Factory Records, and that of Neville Brody as seen through his art direction of *The Face* [3.56].

Perhaps the big difference in the 1990s was that such designers found their way to a wider audience, beyond youth-culture media. Thus, for example, the studio Tomato originated via members of the electronic dance group Underworld. Following their foundation in 1991, they moved rapidly from undertaking experimental, multi-layered print graphics to moving-image work with clients such as Nike, Coca-Cola and Warner Brothers [3.57]. In such work, though, the results were typified by a nervous juxtapositioning of typefaces and images rather than the slick, mannered neatness of corporate work of the 1980s. Equally, Martin Lambie-Nairn's award-winning computer-animated TV idents for Channel 4 of 1982 gave way to his quirky, live-modelled stop-motion using balsa wood for his idents for BBC2 during the 1990s [3.59].

● 3.56 [OPPOSITE] *The Face*, issue 32, December 1982 | Designed by Neville Brody, cover photograph of Phil Oakey by Simon Fowler
● 3.57 [BELOW] Brand identity for TV Asahi, Tomato, 2002

● 3.58 [ABOVE] Brand identity for Orange, Wolff Olins, 1994
Creative director Doug Hamilton, project director Keith Kirby
● 3.59 [OPPOSITE] Ident for BBC2, Martin Lambie-Nairn, 1991

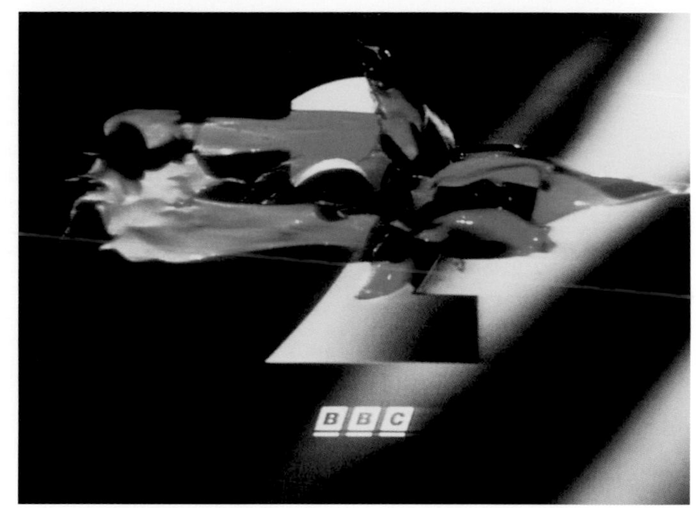

DESIGN UNLIMITED

The 1990s therefore saw increased flexibility in terms of design-consultancy size in relation to size of client; greater breadth of media with which designers could work; and more varied working relationships with other professional specialisms. Design began to overlap with advertising, management and marketing more frequently, to embrace branding as a central concern. Much British design had always aspired to orchestrating a perfect fit between its various platforms in order to produce coherence throughout a project. But within their day-to-day practice this was less often achieved. For example, with the division of the large-scale consultancy into product, interior and graphics departments, this often made them into individual cost centres, thus ensuring their accountability. The effect was occasionally to create internal competition with each wanting its own clients, thus, in effect, fragmenting the consultancy's operations further. Meanwhile, the rise of branding as the central spine of design thinking in the 1990s demanded an even closer fit across the various areas in which it was deployed. So, for instance, Wolff Olins's brand design for the mobile-communications company Orange in 1994 involved not only the design of its logo and literature, but also business advice on how to differentiate the company through its product offer [3.58]. On Wolff Olins' recommendation, in communicating its identity as 'honest' and 'straightforward', Orange then became the mobile-phone network to offer per-second billing.[25]

The ways in which British design consultancy works have thus continued to expand. If design is about innovating new forms, it has also innovated new ways of working and levels of engagement. Most recently British Design Innovation (BDI), an independent advisory and monitoring body for the creative economy, typefied the work of British design consultancies into 25 disciplines. While traditional categories such as interior design, graphics, product design and fashion figured here, BDI also identified such specialisms as 'innovation management', 'social responsibility', 'high-end consumerism' and 'proposition creation'.[26] Design has come to be recognized as much for its role in giving form to the aspirations of clients as for providing new ideas and directions for them.

By the late 1990s, when government policy-makers began to calculate the value of the creative industries, the design profession was firmly established as a significant player in the British economy. Between 1994 and 2001 employment in design (including fashion) had increased by 31.6 per cent, from 108,400 to 142,700, while overall employment in the creative industries also grew by 34.9 per cent, creating an additional 505,300 jobs.[27] Along with advertising and other sectors of the creative industries, it had become an object of serious academic, sociological analysis. With its emphasis on project-by-project working, speed of turnover and more flexible labour arrangements, the creative industries were seen to be emblematic of more general changes in working practices within the knowledge economy.[28]

British design has come to a mature state through experimentation with different studio scales and working methods. Changes in the economy in the late 1970s and '80s marked its extension to consumer-oriented design markets such as retail and communications design. More than anything, British design has demonstrated an ability to flex with market conditions, dodge and weave through changing business circumstances and reinvent itself to ensure its own continued expansion. In the challenging economic and political climate of the early twenty-first century the definitions of what British design could be will continue to be tested and stretched.

A Life in Advertising — John Hegarty

● 3.60 [ABOVE] Poster advertising Benson & Hedges cigarettes, Collett, Dickenson, Pearce International, 1977 | Art director Alan Waldie, photographer Brian Duffy, colour offset lithograph V&A: E.359–1982 ● 3.61 [OPPOSITE] Stills from 'Laundrette', advertisement for Levi's, Bartle Bogle Hegarty, 1982 | Art director John Hegarty, writer Barbara Nokes, director Roger Lyons

The arrival of commercial television in the mid-1950s took advertising from the margins of society and placed it firmly in the living room of the nation. It was now centre-stage. The cathode-ray tube transformed the impact and influence of the commercial world. Technology has always been the handmaiden of creativity. As we now wonder at the impact of digital technology and the phenomena of social networks, so that flickering black-and-white screen changed for ever the culture of Britain.

From its crude beginnings to its cultural flowering – informing, entertaining and challenging – advertising through the last 40 years has been instrumental in changing the outlook and fortunes of creative Britain. Advertising launched the careers of world-famous directors, such as Alan Parker, Ridley Scott and Michel Gondry. It showcased the creative skills of photographers, animators and illustrators.

It became an instrument of social change and political awareness. From Saatchi's Pregnant Man to its 'Labour isn't working' poster, from Hovis's yearning for nostalgia to Levi's hip-ness, advertising has captured the mood of the nation and opened up its cultural forces. Heineken's 'Water in Majorca' articulated brilliantly Britain's changing social scene. It was now cool to talk with an accent from the street. Power had shifted, and nowhere was that more evident than in the advertising we consumed.

It's only as we look back that we see changes mapped so clearly. When Fiat suggested we should buy a car 'Hand-built by Robots', they were capturing our disillusionment with union power and anticipating the collapse of the British car industry. And when Audi launched '*Vorsprung durch Technik*' we were readily embracing a European, if not a global view of manufacturing. Those Germans weren't really Teutonic overlords, but they could be beaten to the beach, especially if you owned an Audi 100.

The 1980s witnessed a transformation of Britain under Thatcherism. That transformation was spearheaded by the privatization of large tracts of industry. The 'Tell Sid' campaign for the privatization of British Gas became the talisman of that doctrine. As society grew in complexity, we saw the government emerge as the single largest advertiser – encouraging us to stay fit, stop smoking and drive carefully, while buckling up our seatbelts.

As we progressed into the 1990s and Noughties the growing globalization of our economy and the impact of technology were mirrored by an advertising industry that assured people that, whatever happens, 'the Future's Bright, the Future's Orange'. A drumming gorilla reassured us that life is still full of joy and that a thousand coloured balls spilling down a San Francisco street are the way to see colour. As more of our work crosses borders, we develop a visual narrative to unite a multicultural YouTube world.

History and culture are moulded not necessarily by the obvious, but often by the incidental. Power is transferred from the ruling elite to the street. Advertising's subliminal impact is only measurable in hindsight. If, that is, anything as public as advertising can be claimed to be subliminal. Its gift is that it is owned by us all. It's there to please us and entertain us. We judge it and value it on a daily basis. Because advertising only works if it interests us. That's what makes it so interesting.

● 3.62 [ABOVE AND FAR RIGHT] Poster advertising Silk Cut cigarettes, Saatchi & Saatchi, *c.*1990
Art director Paul Arden, colour offset lithograph | V&A: E.940–2002

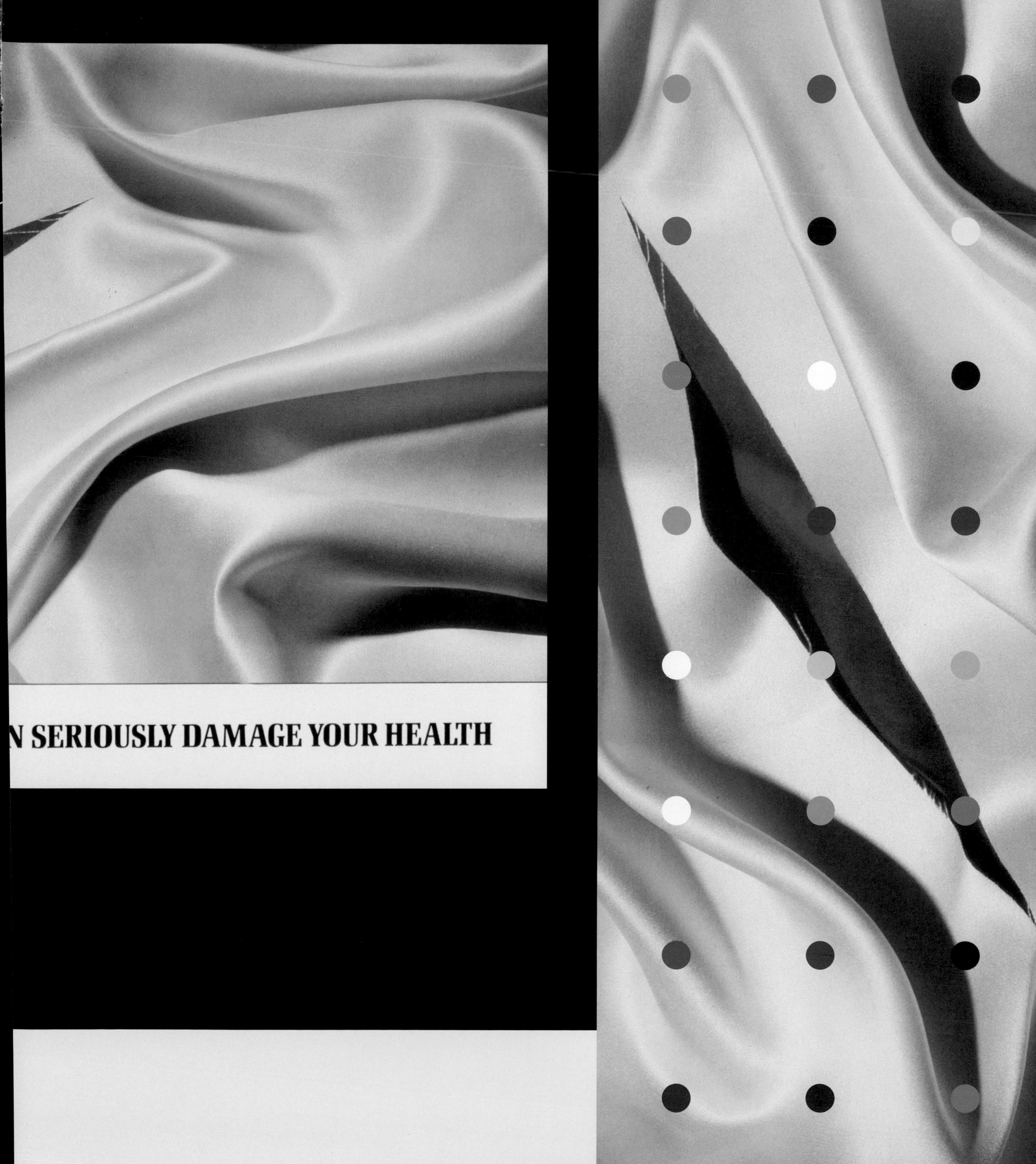
N SERIOUSLY DAMAGE YOUR HEALTH

12 Postmodernism to Ghost Modernism: Architectural Revenants 1979–2012

— Jonathan Meades

● 3.63 [LEFT] Alexandra Road, London, Neave Brown, designed 1968, built 1972–9

Modern architecture died on 16 May 1968 in Canning Town: an explosion in the kitchen of an 18th-floor flat caused part of the recently completed Ronan Point to collapse. According to an age-old tradition, celebrated in music-hall song, in East London gelignite (notoriously unstable) is kept in the fridge.

Modern architecture died on 16 March 1972 in St Louis: the Federal Department of Housing demolished the 16-year-old Pruitt-Igoe project, designed by Minoru Yamasaki – author, too, of the twin towers of the World Trade Center.

Modern architecture died on 16 October 1973 in Kuwait: OPEC cut the production of crude oil and raised its price by 70 per cent. By early 1974 that price had quadrupled.

Each of these versions, with its fatidic 16th day of the month, had its supporters: DIY pathologists who gleefully proclaimed the absence of signs of life. Calendrical coincidence is not, however, maintained by 3 May 1979 – the day that Margaret Thatcher attained power as Prime Minister. She would proceed to drive the final nail into Modernism's coffin by dismantling the economic and cultural apparatus that had supported it. No architectural idiom can survive without the armature of patronage. British Modernism was the material emblem of the cross-party, welfarist consensus that had endured since 1945. Indeed, during the period that Labour, at the 1964 election, decried as 'thirteen years of Tory misrule', the governments of Churchill, Eden and, especially, Macmillan had sanctioned the construction of an unprecedented volume of social housing. The Welfare State was *noblesse oblige* nationalized, and welfarism was *la pensée unique* – from which French locutions no decent person dared dissent in public. Its monuments served (and proclaimed) the democratization of tertiary education, the provision of cradle-to-grave healthcare and of a decent dwelling, the primacy of high culture, the beneficence of the nation.

With the early exception of a few soon-to-be-culled 'wets' (including Ian Gilmour, Francis Pym and Mark Carlisle), Thatcher's administrations were composed of self-made garagists, 'by-their-bootstraps' mini-tycoons and nabobs of estate agency who exuded an unmistakable whiff of Poujadism.[1] Had they even heard of it, these people were no more sympathetic to the idea of *noblesse oblige* than they were to the activities of trade unions. Institutionalized philanthropy was not susceptible to the new god of 'The Market'. Nor, according to the polls, was it what the public sought. The outgoing Prime Minister, James Callaghan, spoke memorably of a 'sea-change', thus revitalizing that expression of Shakespeare's and ensuring that, if he is recalled for anything, it is for his impotence in the face of the electorate's will; had he summoned the nation to the polls a few months previously, in the autumn of 1978, he would almost certainly have been returned to office.

Would British architecture consequently have taken a different course? Probably not. The exercise of suffrage is curt. The process of architecture is tortuously protracted. The same architects tend to flourish, no matter what the regime. While political power changes hands overnight, an architectural scheme conceived under one government's tenure will very likely not come to fruition until its successor is firmly ensconced. Thus Mrs Thatcher's accession followed close upon the completion of two architectural landmarks in London: Neave Brown's Alexandra Road (designed 1968, built 1972–9) and RMJM's Hillingdon Civic Centre (1976). [3.63, 3.64] The former would turn out to be the triumphant culmination of a tradition of inspired social housing, the end of the line, whereas the Hillingdon Centre – although it too was a *public* building, and had been planned as long ago as the first oil crisis – might have been commissioned as the bespoke herald of a cultural 'sea-change' commensurate with that which had occurred at the ballot.

These civic offices were uncannily predictive. But this was prophecy as apostasy. In the eyes of the Modernist establishment, represented by the *Architectural Review*, the unblemished practice of RMJM and its chief designer, Andrew Derbyshire (b. 1923, author in 1960 of New Zealand House) had committed an act that was ideologically heretical, aesthetically treasonable. Hillingdon was not even akin to the decorative, mannered late-Modernism of, say, Richard Seifert (1910–2001) or William Whitfield (b. 1920), which at least paid lip service to the holy orthodoxies [3.65]. Here, in the wilds of suburban Middlesex, was a town hall composed, apparently, of several dozen villas and bungalows, which had thrown their keys into the centre of the room and were now conjoined in cosily elephantine abandon. It broke so many rules, and was so wholly divergent from the precepts of canonical Modernism, that it was revolutionary – in the snuggest, homeliest, most carpet-slippers manner. It was the architectural equivalent of the style of British comedy typified by Benny Hill or Sid James: coarse, matey, undemanding, unthreatening and *accessible*. Inadvertently and fortuitously, then, just the ticket for a decade when we would be enjoined by Cabinet minister Norman Tebbit to 'get on our bikes' in search of work and to make contact with our inner barrow boy.

● 3.64 [OPPOSITE] Hillingdon Civic Centre, London, Robert Matthew Johnson-Marshall & Partners, 1976
● 3.65 [ABOVE] Design drawing of Space House, Kingsway, London, Richard Seifert, *c.*1965
Drawing by A.F. Gill, watercolour and gouache on paper | RIBA Library Drawings Collection

3.66 [RIGHT] St Mark's Road, London, Jeremy Dixon, 1975–9

Here was a building whose components (if not their wacky aggregate) were familiarly banal, instantly recognizable, utterly comprehensible. These properties, in a startling variety of guises, would define the architectural mainstream for years to come. High seriousness was buried beneath an avalanche of toy-town rustication, inverted Diocletian windows and distended columns. The Modernist hegemony was replaced by a pluralistic dressing-up box. The word 'irony', shorn of its literary and rhetorical meanings, was indiscriminately employed to signify smug knowingness and coyly daring playfulness. Jokiness became de rigueur. Just as battalions of unfunny comedians ensure a sycophantic response by laughing at their lame gags *before they tell them*, so do self-proclaimingly 'witty' buildings announce themselves with hyperbolic clashes of scale, a willed illiteracy and a children's entertainer's garrulous importunacy. Grown men – and they were nearly all men – went back to the playground, and to their history books. This was ultimately the architecture of contrition. Architects knew how much they had been despised. They were now eager to please. They were penitents: some equipped with nursery colours and elemental shapes, others with servility and forelock.

The clamorously bruited diminution in state spending during Margaret Thatcher's administrations was more notional than actual. It was cut by less than 5 per cent. Revenue was excised and books balanced by the privatization of utilities and by the sale to their tenants of council houses under Michael Heseltine's 1980 Housing Act. ('Selling the family silver' was Mrs Thatcher's own wary summation of her predecessor Harold Macmillan's misgivings. He himself did not use that precise expression, though having been instrumental in building 300,000 council homes per annum between 1951 and 1963, he might have entertained doing so.) These sales – what kind of *right* is the right to buy? – were effected for the short-term gain of electoral advantage. They were socially calamitous, the more so given the drastic reduction in the creation of new public housing. The private and housing-association developments of the 1980s were in signal contrast to both the towering megastructural schemes of the '60s and the impenetrably dense and labyrinthine low-rise projects of the early '70s.

Just as the exhilaratingly harsh Gothic monoliths of the 1850s and '60s had been succeeded by the genial warmth of the misnamed Queen Anne revival, so this new domestic revival conjured up a cosy sense of homeliness. The standard was set by Jeremy Dixon (b. 1939), who, a few years previously, had been co-designer of a regrettably unbuilt, confidently Modernist, prismatic glass pyramid for Northamptonshire County Council. Now, in a red-brick purlieu of Notting Dale he had designed a stylistically disparate, but equally startling terrace for a housing association [3.66]. It was a work of unmistakably reactionary inspiration, which drew on a generalized Dutch vernacular and, specifically, on De Stijl. And he had built it on a street, a form of thoroughfare that Modernists had scornfully cast aside, for it connoted both insanitary Victorian slums and despised interwar suburbia. One of the besetting problems of British and, indeed, European Modernism had been the relationship of the building to its immediate environs. Architects are not necessarily urbanists, any more than composers are conductors or playwrights are directors. The slavish crazes for tall buildings surrounded by parks and for cluster blocks accessed by novelty walkways, experimental alleys or untested tunnels had created ill-defined, semi-public, vulnerable spaces that were awkward, illegible and threatening. Deftly crafted projects such as Whicheloe Macfarlane's High Kingsdown in Bristol were the exception. The North American ideal of adherence to the building line had been largely rejected. With a revival of such building types as the terrace and the semi, it was inevitable that streets would return, along with curvy 'closes' and less accommodating cul-de-sacs.

Dixon's terrace would prove massively influential. That is to say, its design was sedulously ripped off. Architects' plagiarism is shamelessly bereft of cunning; these people seldom heed Montaigne's counsel to follow the example of the horse thief who dyes the creature's tail and mane and, sometimes, puts out its eyes. The London Docklands Development Corporation (LDDC), a Heseltine-appointed quango responsible for the redevelopment of the banks of the Thames downriver from the former Pool of London, was statutorily sanctioned to apply only the laxest planning stipulations: height and area only; 'aesthetic control' was forbidden as an illiberal contravention of the market's power. Thus the LDDC smiled beneficently on meretricious hackery. The area became a sprawling, infrastructure-less showcase for nicked ideas, second-hand wheezes and all the typologies that ever fell off the back of a lorry. It was a neat summation of London itself – a brick and stucco Klondike, ever mutating, ever chaotic, joined up only by chance and proximity. The most accomplished copier of Dixon (other than an entire generation of Dutch architects who relearned their idiolect from him) was Dixon himself. On the south-eastern perimeter of the Isle of Dogs he created an unusually coherent quarter of even more wholeheartedly Netherlandish semis and neo-Adelaide villas, laid out in crescents and squares, terraces and avenues. In less-sure hands this civil, understated urbanism was liable to teeter into insipidity: witness Arup's Lloyds TSB beside the Floating Harbour in Bristol, a crescentic building no doubt partially derived from that city's ponderous Council House, and one that is desperate to please by giving absolutely no offence to anyone – anyone at all.

3A

● 3.67 [ABOVE] China Wharf, London, Piers Gough of Campbell Zogolovitch Wilkinson & Gough, 1988
● 3.68 [BELOW] Neue Staatsgalerie, Stuttgart, Germany, James Stirling, completed 1984

A more usual stratagem for pleasing everyone was to follow the Hillingdon route: to borrow from the past's discards, to make art out of what had been calumnized as artless – this, after all, is what Richard Hamilton, Peter Blake, Andy Warhol, Mel Ramos, Roy Lichtenstein and countless others had been doing for years. But architecture is a tanker that turns torpidly, even though its crazes and fads shift with the speed of skirt-lengths: thus many buildings are out of date by the time they are finished; the bigger the building, the longer the construction and the greater the gap. Architecture is also predominantly practised by people who are still reckoned young at the age of forty or fifty – this is the age at which they tend to at last get their chance. The extraordinary flowering of pop music in the 1960s was achieved by war babies and baby-boomers. The architecture contemporary with that music was the work of their parents' coevals. The Modernist asceticism and straitened purity of these architects were there to be snubbed by filial insolence: one generation reacts against its predecessor. Baby-boomer architects embraced self-conscious impurity, high colour, loud ornament, unashamed façadism, burlesque frippery, (sometimes desperate) jollity, knowing vulgarity and, equally, unknowing vulgarity.

The cleverest and nimblest was Piers Gough (b. 1946); the most inescapable and ostentatious Terry Farrell (b. 1939). Both of them were incorrigible show-offs. Gough once described his work as 'B-movie architecture'. That merely gets part of it. He certainly displayed a fondness for obscure West Coast architectural subcultures, such as Borax and Googie – garish idioms that provided the decor, even set the mood, of countless *films noirs* and saturated Technicolor melodramas in the 1940s and '50s. But Gough was nothing if not catholic in what he stole, and from where: Viennese *Jugendstil*, Regency gewgaws (he was brought up in Brighton), Home Counties Arts and Crafts, nautical motifs, the Belgian seaside, arterial-road Metroland, officers' mess neo-Georgian, Wrenaissance, Edwardian free style, the Amsterdam school. And so on: any source that was marginally tainted or not quite respectable. Gough's invention was boundless. His method often appears to have been that of collage: stylistically disparate and temporally diverse components are juxtaposed. They elide. They collide. At his best – The Circle and China Wharf near Tower Bridge, the De Barones shopping centre in Breda, the Cascades in Docklands, the Black Lion development in Brighton – he has created, and continues to create, buildings that remain attached to the retina, images that carry an ineradicable emotional charge [3.67].

Terry Farrell's unmistakable work of the 1980s and early '90s is vast, hefty, glaring, squat, brooding. Like Gough and Dixon, Farrell had looked back, but to less-definable topos and eras, to unknowable generalized sites stored in his architectural back-brain – big sites, of course. Unlike them (and most American Postmodernists), he was unmoved by the picturesque, by sweetness and light. His set-pieces respond in kind to the Modernism he had briefly embraced at the start of his career, behemoth to behemoth. They have the scope and ambition of megastructures. Alban Gate bestrides London Wall with Brutalist confidence. Embankment Place is not *at* Charing Cross, it *is* Charing Cross; it derives from some dream of North American heavy engineering [3.69]. The laughably unsecret MI6 building at Vauxhall Cross is a brutal temple to necessary surveillance; it is formidable, overwhelming and undeniably powerful. Farrell embraced the cult of sullen ugliness with the gusto of such High Victorians as Pilkington and Teulon. He too possessed the drive and muscular vitality known then as 'go!'

No former Modernist was more penitently opportunistic than James Stirling (1926–92). In the late 1950s and '60s he had enjoyed among his professional peers an unrivalled reputation. Among those unfortunate enough not to be architects, among mere *lay* persons exposed to his buildings' manifold peculiarities, he was rather less feted. His Constructivist Leicester University engineering building was faintly praised by Anthony Burgess as '...functional. We can ... admire [it] without being moved.'[2] This was mild damnation in comparison to rebukes that became routinely vituperative. Calls were made for the demolition of his history library at Cambridge within a couple of years of its completion. The Florey Building at the Queen's College, Oxford fared little better. His buildings, like their bombastic maker, looked tough, but were perpetual invalids, basket-cases. By the end of the 1960s Stirling had become a byword for extravagant failure. Throughout most of the '70s he taught. When he returned to the actual practice of architecture he had (though he of course denied it) transformed himself into a fully fledged Postmodernist – it was akin to witnessing a man in late middle age dancing to the latest hits. His Neue Staatsgalerie at Stuttgart mixed Schinkel's classicism, fairground forms, wavy glazing, massive masonry (which, daftly, was considered rashly akin to Albert Speer's), brash colours and bunker-like voids [3.68]. Its exceptional incoherence did not prevent his career taking off again. A science centre in Berlin followed: it was as if de Chirico, another artist who famously lost his way, had devised a cylindrical cassata, baby-blue and baby-pink. He received commissions from Harvard and Cornell.

At last, after than more than a decade, Stirling was welcomed back to Britain; at least he was welcomed by the burgeoning and sycophantic architectural media, which didn't even entertain the idea that its esteem of him – and his esteem of himself – was inflated out of all proportion to his achievement. Charles Jencks, the taxonomically inclined cheerleader for Postmodernism, described the Clore Gallery as 'the greatest game of contextualism played to date... An architecture for all seasons.'[3] The ostensible purpose of this extension to the Tate was to house the gallery's collection of works by J.M.W. Turner. Its reception by those who were not groupies, not *parti pris*, was, quite properly, unanimously hostile – Marina Vaizey: 'These fun colours are not fun; they are shocking in the wrong sense. They are vulgar. The most subtle colourist in British art is defiantly shouted down.'[4] Gavin Stamp: 'An architect is showing off at the expense of England's greatest painter.'[5] John McEwan: 'A well upholstered bomb shelter.'[6] Richard Cork: 'The entire scheme had been conceived as Stirling's work of art, rather than as the most fitting vessel for Turner's long-abused bequest to the nation.'[7] And so on.

● 3.69 [RIGHT] Embankment Place, London, Terry Farrell, 1989
● 3.70 [BOTTOM] Willis Faber Dumas Building, Ipswich, Suffolk, Foster Associates, 1975
● 3.71 [OPPOSITE] David Murray John Tower, Swindon, Wiltshire, Douglas Stephen & Partners, 1976

Stirling died prematurely during a routine operation in 1992. His last building, No.1 Poultry, in the City of London, was not completed until six years later. By which time it looked hopelessly *retardataire*. Fashion had changed. Architecture, no matter how much architects deny it, is in absolute thrall to fashion.

British Postmodernism was, however, far from exhausted. While the epithet itself may have been buried sometime between Black Wednesday (16 September 1992) and New Labour's election (1 May 1997), the retrospective process that it signified has continued to flourish as the architectural norm. Instead of looking back to the Belle Epoque, or to primitive classicism, or to Tudor palaces (the bizarre Richmond House in Whitehall) or to Wurlitzer organs (Barclay's Bank in Lombard Street) or to Anton Furst's Gotham City in *Batman* (the 'Gothic' Minster Court in Mincing Lane) or to the Beaux Arts (Canary Wharf), architecture has, for the past decade and a half, contented itself with energetically recycling the Modern Movement in its many guises. Most – but certainly not all – of Modernism's stylistic history has been plundered, while the (possibly chimerical) ethical apparatus attached to it has been cast aside as an irrelevance. The quotes and allusions and citations and 'homages' that characterized 1970s and '80s Postmodernism are just as commonplace today, save that they tend to be occluded, they are deployed discreetly. They have been *synthesized*. Synthetic Modernism or neo-Modernism or IKEA Modernism (Owen Hatherley) or CABE-ism (Rory Olcayto) is as revivalist, as 'historicist', as neo-Georgian or the old English style or the baroque of 1900–10.[8] But unlike these idioms, it is loath to admit it: it adopts the pose of the 'modern Gothic' of the 1860s, which disclaimed medieval precedent. It pretends to originality. And its omnipotent, ubiquitous global practitioners possess both a PR machine and – hardly different – a deferential architectural press.

The volume and influence of that press increased with the advent in 1983 of *Blueprint*, a cleverly positioned glossy newspaper, which sought to make architecture attractive to a public that the worthy, rather ingrown *Architectural Review* and the cultist, jargon-splattered *Architectural Digest* could not reach. If architecture was for the people, then magazines about architecture ought to be for the people. Further publications appeared: *Wallpaper*, *Icon*, *Frame*, and so on. They were not perhaps the most strenuously critical of journals. The national press, too, had begun to pay attention. The broadsheets, as they then were – having largely neglected the subject, save to report on social catastrophes and crumbling concrete – appointed architectural correspondents, starstruck panderers who repeatedly eulogized the same big names.

In the late 1970s Philip Johnson (1906–2005), the wizened Talleyrand of New York architecture, then in his Chippendale phase, described his former pupil, the future Baron Foster of Thames Bank (b. 1935), as 'the last modern architect'. Good try. But wrong. Norman Foster was, rather, the first neo-modern architect. Or, anyway, the first neo-modern architect to get the timing right. It never does to be too far ahead of the game. It was the (literally card-carrying) communist Douglas Stephen (1923–92) who had in 1965 been the earliest British architect to return to the forms of early Modernism, when he adopted the rationalist idiom of the Lombardian fascist Giuseppe Terragni for a development of private flats on Campden Hill in Kensington, which retains a delightfully baffling timelessness. Stephen's marvellous David Murray John Tower (1975) in Swindon also looked back, to a 1920s platonic ideal of a tall building [3.71]. It's like the realization of an unmade project glanced at in a magazine – a far-from-uncommon instance of fiction made architectural fact, of 'paper architecture' given three-dimensional life. Foster's Willis Faber Dumas Building in Ipswich (1975) struck those who insouciantly came upon it as some unrecorded prodigy of the 1930s, specifically as an unknown work by Owen Williams (significantly an architect-engineer) whose black Vitrolite Daily Express plant in Manchester Foster must have known as a child [3.70]. Douglas Stephen went on to design a few largely unsung buildings in London.

Norman Foster (and his 1,400-strong practice under its succession of names, plus a brigade of civil engineers in the small print) went on to design many of the most-lauded and mediated structures in the world [3.72]. He belongs to a small cadre of masters of the architectural universe who create lumps of prestigious tectonite with promiscuous abandon. He is globally prolific, globally honoured. Astana, Barcelona, Berlin, Bordeaux, Frankfurt, Hong Kong, London, Madrid, Millau, New York, Nîmes, Rotterdam, Singapore... And Cosham, Finnieston, Gateshead, Norwich, Swindon, Woking. Whether they are orthogonal or geometrically delinquent or blobbily biomorphic, his work is characterized by sleekness, precision and jewel-like elegance. It is often glacially beautiful. These are machines for working in, for studying in, for creating in, for shopping in. And for living in – for living a life that's tidy, costive, ordered, rational, *fosterian*. His buildings may be emotionally affectless, heartless, but they are exemplary. They process and condition their users as though they are revenants from the age of architectural determinism. Although they are made for vast corporations, they retain a dilute utopianism, the hint of a will to improve the race.

Foster and his partner of long ago, Richard Rogers, are – due to the media's adhesive pairing of their names – as inseparably conjoined in the collective conscious as Chang and Eng. Foster's neo-Modernism had its provenance in buildings made before he was born, and in the moral Modernism of Pelican books, and in Frank Hampson's Dan Dare comic strip in *The Eagle* (whose oldest reader he must have been) and in the early oeuvre of his (and Rogers's) Yale teacher Paul Rudolph. In contrast, Rogers's and Renzo Piano's competition-winning scheme for the Beaubourg (1977) looked back only a decade to the sometimes fantastical, 'unbuildable' paper architecture of the Archigram group, to Cedric Price's proposed Fun Palace for Joan Littlewood and to the forms (if not the materials) of Paul Rudolph's design for Yale Architecture School.

● 3.72 [RIGHT] 30 St Mary Axe, London, Foster & Partners, 2004

● 3.73 [ABOVE] Law Courts, Antwerp, Belgium, Richard Rogers Partnership, 2006–7
● 3.74 [OPPOSITE TOP] Lords Media Centre, London, Future Systems, 1994
● 3.75 [OPPOSITE BOTTOM] Kunsthaus Graz, Austria, Peter Cook and Colin Fournier, 2003

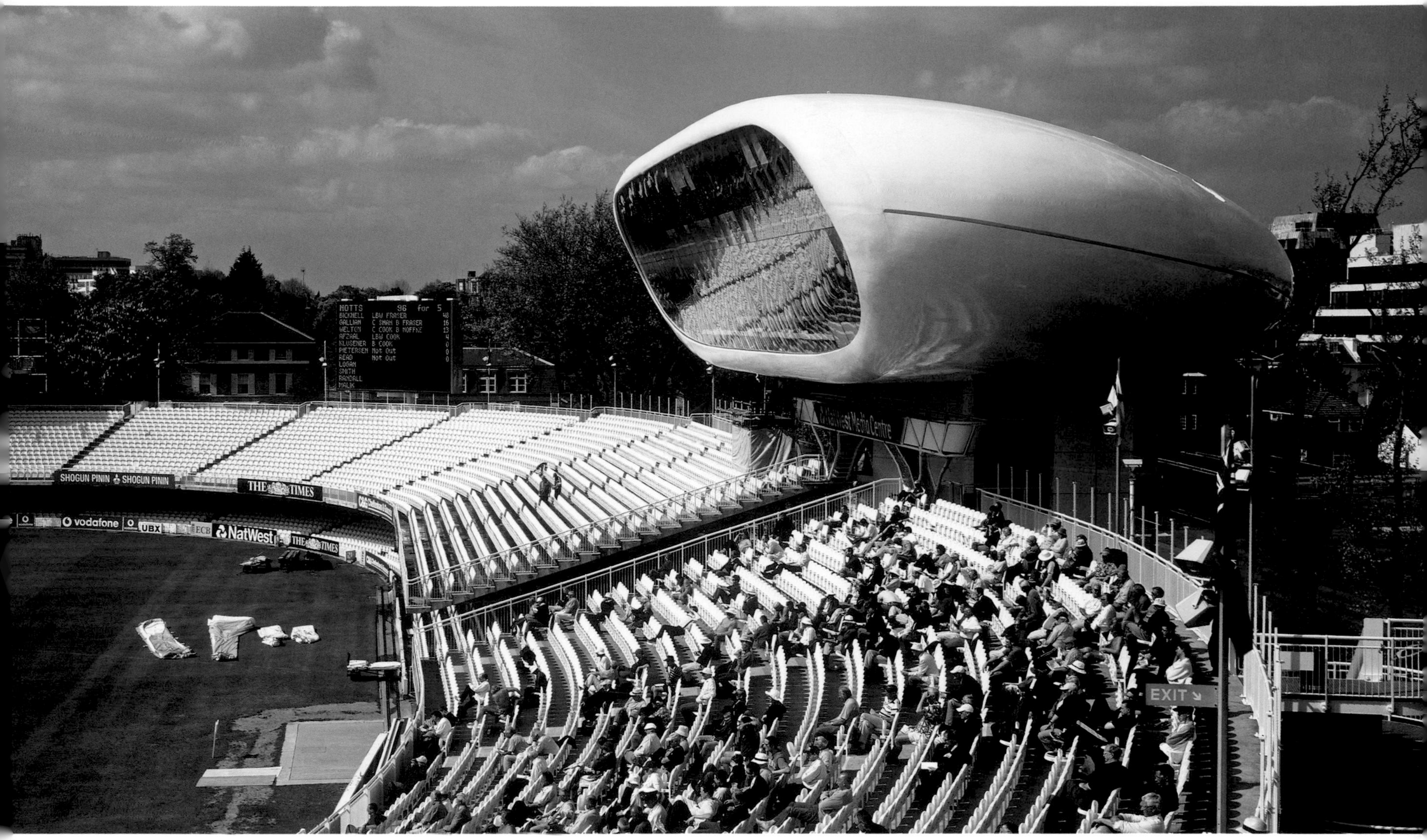

Rogers and Piano would also make the stratospheric leap to become global attractions, big pulls – the people to call in when, in defiance of economic discretion, gestural engineering and landmark beacons and iconic icons and 3D logos and lighthouse rebrands and vision hubcaps and regenerative torches are required to bolster megalopolitan vanities. Global architecture is trophy architecture, underwritten by base tribal primitivism, corporate one-upmanship, nationalistic boastfulness. It was always thus – the height of medieval spires, the vastness of fortresses, the lavishness of palaces. The clock may be digital, but it has been turned back. Architecture is once again for show and swank; mere building is once again for utility and shelter. This is the historic norm. The years of philanthropic welfarism were abnormal.

Unlike Foster, Rogers and Piano have been little imitated, no doubt because they share an unpredictability that is rare at this level of architecture, whose practitioners repetitively stick to a jealously forged 'signature' that renders them bankable, reliable, recognizable. Rogers's Lloyds building(s) in the City of London, the law courts in Bordeaux and Antwerp, the Hesperia hotel in Barcelona and the Beaubourg in Paris (1977) are entirely different from each other [3.73, 3.76]. What they have in common is that they are among the most viscerally thrilling structures of the past 50 years; his Knightsbridge flats for oligarchs and petro-Midases and his Millennium Dome are not. Piano has given London both the unmissable Shard (2012) and possible proof of colour-blindness at Central St Giles (2010).

A multi-teated amputee reptile with a prosthesis: 40 years after the heyday of Archigram its founder member Peter Cook (b. 1936) demonstrated, in collaboration with Colin Fournier (b. 1944), that he retained that group's power to astonish with yesterday's novelty [3.75]. The work in question was a civic art gallery in the Austrian city of Graz. Future Systems had existed for a decade and a half before it received, in 1995, the commission to build the media centre at Lords, a chunk of 1960s product design immeasurably magnified [3.74]. David Chipperfield's most significant projects are in Spain, Germany and China. Will Alsop built the startling offices of the Bouches-du-Rhône departmental council in Marseilles and a large ferry terminal beside the Elbe at Hamburg-Altona before he secured commissions in Britain [3.79]. The Olympic Aquatics Centre is Zaha Hadid's first major building to be completed in the country where she has lived and practised for almost two-thirds of her life [3.80, 3.81]. After he had completed the Beaubourg, Richard Rogers was so short of work, so broke, that he considered moving to America to teach. And so it goes on. It is impossible to deny the received idea of Britain's tawdry, risk-averse unwillingness to take a chance on 'new' talent. Especially given the generalized refusal to acknowledge that there is actually nothing remotely new or audacious about the notion of the avant-garde, particularly when it tends to feed predominantly on the avant-garde of many decades ago, merely saucing the dish with sustainabulous splashes of green piety and chromatic discord. And given that London is the most cosmopolitan, most polyglot city in Europe, it is odd that there should exist – alongside its resistance to architecturally indigenous daring – an equal disregard of foreign architects. Piano, Legoretta, Nouvel and Herzog & de Meuron are rare exceptions.

The mainstream of British architecture over the past decade and a half is notable for its blandness. Because the media, in any field, thrives on the atypical, and represents the atypical as typical, that which is actually quotidian, ubiquitous and commonplace is overlooked, save when its physical dimensions plead for attention. Synthetic Modernism is merely a stage of Postmodernism, it offends only by its cringing fear of offending. There is something of Uriah Heep about the mood and tenor of the monuments that New Labour, its PFIs and its quangos bequeathed to Britain. The most bellicose Prime Minister of the last 150 years and his mates were mere inheritors of the long-planned Falkirk Wheel and Jubilee Line stations, which opened under their tenure: these anyway, like the Millau viaduct, were essentially works of civil engineering [3.77]. What was more commonly built under that regime was block upon block of 'luxury' flats that pleaded to be liked. Block upon block – in London's Docklands and on Salford Quays, beside the Clyde, at Cardiff Bay, Ocean Village (Southampton) and Brindley Place (Birmingham), everywhere – were decorated with strips of oiled wood, terracotta-coloured tiles, translucent bricks, riveted Corten, titanium scales, random fenestration. But mostly it was just glass and funny angles. The gamut of devices was straitened.

The one idiom from the Modernist past that was not exhumed was Brutalism. It was presumed, no doubt, to be liable to scare the people. It was all too likely – as one of its practitioners, Owen Luder (b. 1928), put it – to say: 'Sod you!' [3.78] Luder and his designer, Rodney Gordon (1933–2008), could only watch from the sidelines as their masterful exercises in the sublimity of sculptural concrete were demolished to make way for an architecture of cosmetic vacuity and feeble consensus. An architecture that was all but official, governmentally ordained. This was the architectural monoculture sanctioned by CABE, the quango whose middle-of-the-road attachment to synthetic Modernism and avoidance of controversy left little space for the two extremes. The one extreme was represented by the 'new urbanism', by the Prince of Wales (b. 1948) and Quinlan Terry (b. 1937), a classicist whose devotion to pastiche is almost as fervid as Norman Foster's. The other by the genuinely modern, rather than the 'modern' – that is, that which is novel, which has not been done before, which does not obey rules evolved by an extant culture, which exhibits properties that are, perforce, yet unknown, which returns primacy to the imaginative artist and removes it from the people, the consulted community, who know only what they have already seen, what already exists. It is the role of the artist to produce what does not already exist and to exorcise the persistent ghost of the day-before-yesterday's architecture.

It is not difficult to surmise which of these two extremes is more likely to have flourished when the architecture of coalition government is assessed and exhibited some years hence.

● 3.76 [RIGHT] Lloyds Building, London, Richard Rogers Partnership, 1978–86

● 3.77 [ABOVE] Falkirk Wheel, Falkirk, Scotland, RMJM, 2002 | Project architect Tony Kettle
● 3.78 [OPPOSITE TOP] Tricorn Centre, Portsmouth, Owen Luder Partnership, 1965
● 3.79 [OPPOSITE BOTTOM] Hôtel du Départment des Bouches-du-Rhône, Marseilles, France, Will Alsop, 1994

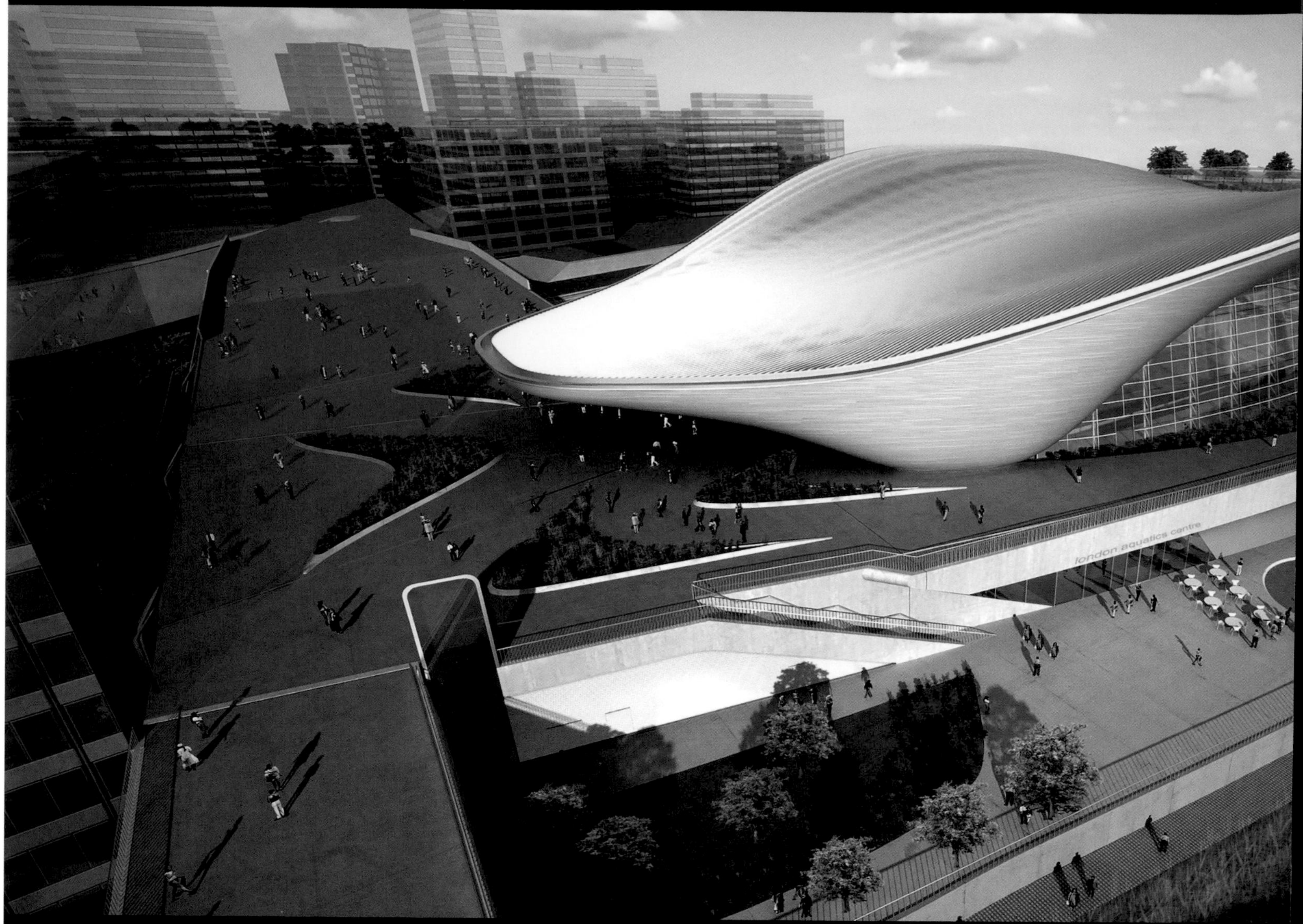

An Architect in London — Zaha Hadid

● 3.80 London Aquatics Centre, Zaha Hadid Architects | Completed 2011

I came to the UK in 1973 to study at the Architectural Association (AA) School in London. The AA's fantastic chairman at the time, the late Alvin Boyarski, believed the world would become much more international, so it was important to build a truly international school. He was considering the impact of globalization long before it actually began. Everyone at the school was on the brink of doing something new. The students, the staff and Boyarski were seminal to the past 30 years of architecture. It's still influencing current work today.

My own work developed entirely because I live in London. It is a very British situation; the UK has traditionally given a platform to those from around the world who want to research and experiment. London, in particular, has always welcomed and encouraged a tremendous degree of experimentation.

As an architect, one of the best things about living in London is the experience and skills of the consultants. This is very important to me. There's uniqueness to the city: the education, the amount of research and invention. Anything you want, you can get someone to advise you on. In the developing years of my career that was very critical. The seminal figure was Peter Rice. He was the first of that generation; matching innovative engineering with new, untried ideas and concepts.

London always inspires projects that are unpredictable. There are still all these quirky situations within the city. We did a project more than 20 years ago at the AA, where we drew lines through the city on a map and then travelled along these lines, documenting everything. It was a very interesting project because, first of all, it showed that certain things were aligned with each other, but that other things – when you jumped from one level to the next – were tremendously varied. These extreme adjacencies are what make the city so unique. It's a great city that has become very layered.

Unlike most European cities, there are still large gaps in London that allow for a major urban intervention on an interesting scale. Looking at the site for the Olympics, for example, we did a drawing more than 15 years ago about how London should be developed towards the east. It's fascinating to see this becoming a reality, with the Olympics as a catalyst for regeneration. It has offered the potential to do some very positive things with some interesting solutions.

The legacy that the 2012 Games will give the city is breathtaking. The new Olympic Park is one of the largest new public spaces in Europe, and the design of the London Aquatics Centre very much considers its legacy use by Londoners after the Games. It was important for us to conceive the building within its setting at the entrance to the park. The design establishes relationships that articulate this interplay between architecture and nature.

The design concept of the Aquatics Centre was informed by the fluid geometries of water in motion, creating spaces that maintain a dialogue with the surrounding landscape. A 159-metre undulating roof sweeps up from the ground as a wave, enclosing the pools of the centre with its unifying gesture, while also describing the volumes of the swimming and diving pools. This architectural language of fluidity and spatial complexity ensures that the Aquatics Centre retains the strongest sense of belonging to its riverside environment.

● 3.81 London Aquatics Centre, Zaha Hadid Architects | Completed 2011

Notes

NOTES

INTRODUCTION
British Design from 1948

1 Official Report of the Organizing Committee for the XIV Olympiad (London, 1948), p.221
2 Ibid., pp.196–7
3 Ibid., p.540
4 http://www.wolffolins.com/pdf/2012_case_study.pdf
5 Turner (1990)
6 Hoggart (1958); Thompson (1963); Hall and Jefferson (1975); Hebdige (1979); Samuel (1989); Hall (1993), pp.349–63
7 Colley (1992)
8 Pevsner (1956)
9 Matless (1998)
10 Anderson (1983)
11 Daniels (1993), p.5. See also Hobsbawm and Ranger (1983), and Goodrum (2005), pp.59–61
12 Wiener (2004)
13 Wright (1985); Savage (1991); Sinclair (1997); Ackroyd (2002)
14 MacCarthy (1982); Buckley (2007)
15 For surveys of British fashion, see De la Haye (1996); Breward, Conekin and Cox (2002); McDermott (2002); and Goodrum (2005). For film, see Cook (1996) and Street (1997). For craft, see Harrod (1999). The *Journal of Visual Culture in Britain* provides a number of useful essays on British art. Jeremiah (2000) offers a reading of state and private planning in twentieth-century Britain; and Powers (2008) constructs a polemical history of iconic projects and buildings.
16 McCay (1998); Hunt (1998); Bracewell (1998); Conekin, Mort and Walters (1999); Davey (1999); Walker (2002); Bracewell (2002); Conekin (2003); Hilton (2003); Harris (2004); Williams (2004); Donnelly (2005); Reynolds (2006); Sandbrook (2006); Sandbrook (2007); Marr (2007); Kynaston (2007b); Kynaston (2007a); Kynaston (2009); Harrison (2008); Hornsey (2010); Addison (2010); Harrison (2010); Hatherley (2010)
17 Bryson (1995); Paxman (1998); Fox (2004); Jack (2009)
18 Buckley (2007), p.118
19 Rosenthal, Norman, 'Circulation', *The Spectator*, 12 February 1977. V&A Archive, MA/19/13, Press Cuttings 1965–77
20 Both exhibitions were shown in 1969; Collingwood and Coper toured until August 1969
21 Note from Elizabeth Knowles (Underhill) to Joanna Weddell, 8 December 2010
22 'The new chintz tradition', *The Ambassador*, May 1960, p.103
23 Griggs Barbara, 'From a Museum – a design for the future', *Evening Standard*, 4 January 1960, 'Fashion News–Focus' Section
24 'Artists oppose V&A cut, by Our Arts Reporter', *The Times*, Thursday 16 December 1976, p.8
25 Boilerhouse exhibitions included 'Images for Sale 1983', 'Kenneth Grange at the Boilerhouse', 'The Good Design Guide' and '100 Best Ever Products'
26 Margaret Timmers's (Dept of Prints, Drawings and Paintings) exhibition 'The Way We Live Now: Designs for Interiors 1950 to the Present Day' was a groundbreaking survey of contemporary domestic design.
27 Huygen (1989), p.173
28 Sudjic (2009), p.7

SECTION ONE
Tradition and Modernity 1945–79

1 Marwick (1991), p.16
2 Gibberd et al. (1980), p.107
3 Marwick (1991), p.68
4 Quoted in Stephen Calloway's exhibition text for a John Fowler exhibition at the V&A
5 Lucia van der Post, *Daily Telegraph*, 1966. Photocopy from Max Clendinning file, National Museums of Scotland, 1987.367A-M

CHAPTER 1
In the Service of the State

1 Mort (2010), p.26
2 J.M. Richards, *Architectural Review*, vol.CIX, no.653, May 1951, p.278
3 Misha Black in Banham and Hillier (1976), p.82
4 The site is now occupied by the Ismaili Centre. Interview with Ghislaine Wood on 10 February 2011
5 In physics, the Coriolis effect is a deflection of moving objects when they are viewed in a rotating frame of reference. The building rotated to create the effect.
6 Richards (1951), p.278
7 See Crinson (2003), pp.113–14
8 Bevis Hillier, introduction to Banham and Hillier (1976), p.17
9 Misha Black, in Banham and Hillier (1976), p.82
10 Hugh Casson papers, '1951 Disposal of Works' list, Archive of Art and Design, AAD/2008/2/3/1/18
11 *Architectural Review*, vol.110, no.658, October 1951, p.216
12 The magnification of natural forms had been explored in the 1890s in the work of Ernst Haeckel and others, and was clearly seen as a metaphor for progress.
13 Banham and Hillier (1976), p.176
14 See the Terence Conran focus piece, 'The Legacy of the Festival of Britain', in this book, pp.138–41
15 Brown (1953), p.14
16 David Cannadine in Hobsbawm and Ranger (1983)
17 Hewison (1985), p.67
18 Hartnell (1955), pp.121–7
19 Ibid., p.122
20 Amy De la Haye in Wilcox (2007), p.106
21 Hugh Roberts in Lloyd (2003), p.86
22 Kuhn (1995), p.62
23 Brown (1953), p.10
24 Lacey (1977), p.156
25 Anne Sharpley, *Evening Standard*, 25 November 1960, p.7
26 See Crinson (2003)
27 Miles Glendinning has pointed to a similar raised design for the American Embassy at Accra in Ghana by Harry Weese (1956–9). 'Building for Modern Ceremony' in Long and Thomas (2007), p.79
28 Anne Sharpely, *Evening Standard*, 25 November 1960, p.7
29 Ian Nairn, *Daily Telegraph*, quoted in Ministry of Works file for the Rome Embassy, National Archives, WORK 10/612
30 Memo from J.H.S. Burgess, Ministry of Works, July 1961, Brasilia file, National Archives, WORK 10/505
31 *Architectural Review*, October 1975, p.224
32 Ibid.
33 Letter from Eric Bedford to Mr G.S. Knight, 11 March 1965, Brasilia file, National Archives, WORK 10/507
34 The British Embassy in Brasilia, designed by Alfred Coutts, was completed in 1983.
35 Letter from H. Glover, 8 December 1964, Advisory Committee on Decoration and Furnishing file, National Archives, WORK 10/700
36 Letter from the High Commissioner to Ceylon to the Minister, 25 May 1954, Colombo file, National Archives, WORK 10/313
37 Catherine Eagleton, 'Christopher Ironside and the designs for the decimal coinage', in Clancy (2008), p.23

38 Tony Benn, 'PMG Extraordinary', in Rose (1980), p.69
39 Christopher Frayling, 'Continuity through Change: The Royal Mint Advisory Committee', in Clancy (2008), p.57
40 Ibid., p. 61

Export Textiles in West Africa

1 Lovat Fraser (1948), p.103
2 Launert (2002), p.159
3 Lovat Fraser (1948), p.103
4 Launert (2002), p.156
5 Ibid., p.159
6 Picton (1995), p.28
7 V&A: T.236–1984 and T.186–1969
8 *Vogue*, April 1948, p.70
9 Spencer (1982), p.8

CHAPTER 2
Urban Visions

1 'Welfare State' is understood as the cumulative result of the provision of welfare as recommended in the Beveridge Report (1942), the Family Allowance Act (1945), the National Insurance Act (1946) and the National Health Act (1948).
2 This concept was launched by David Cameron, leader of the Conservative Party, in a speech in Liverpool on 19 July 2010.
3 In a speech to a conference on information technology of 8 December 1982 at the Barbican Centre, London, Mrs Thatcher declared: 'The Government itself also has a job to do. It must nurture, not nanny; stimulate, not stifle; it must not plan for people, but enable them to plan for themselves.' For further discussion, see Jonathan M. Woodham, 'Margaret Thatcher, Postmodernism and the Politics of Design in Britain', in Adamson and Pavitt (2011).
4 Sources include LeMahieu (1988)
5 Woodham (1966)
6 Edwards (2004)
7 For overviews, see Atkinson (2011); Conekin (2003); and Banham and Hillier (1976)
8 Matless (1998), p.167
9 Atkinson (2008), p.24
10 Conekin (2003), p.226
11 *Architectural Review* special issue, no.656, vol.CX, August 1951
12 Dümpelmann (2010), pp.94–113
13 Forgan (1998), pp.217–40; Cox (1950), pp.227–9. Scientific motifs were also widely seen elsewhere, as at the South Kensington site, in Brian Peake's screen at the entrance to the Science Museum and on many Festival posters. However, public interest in the Festival Pattern Group proved rather short-lived, perhaps due to British consumers' lack of enthusiasm for abstract motifs.
14 *Exhibition of Architecture: Poplar. Festival Guide* (London, 1951), p.5
15 Ibid., p.7
16 For a brief period Angus had been the wife of the Modernist architectural writer and critic J.M. Richards. Her tile work is addressed in Arber (2002).
17 Frederick Gibberd, 'Lansbury: The Live Architecture Exhibition', in Banham and Hillier (1976), p.141. For a fuller analysis of Lansbury, see Windsor Liscombe (2006), pp.317–48.
18 Reith Committee (1946)
19 *The Times*, 24 January 1992, cited by the anarchist writer Colin Ward in his detailed and revealing observations on New Towns: *Town, Home Town* (1993). Ward had worked for the architect Peter Shepheard, Deputy Chief Architect for the Stevenage Development Corporation (1947–8) in the 1940s and '50s, and later made a BBC documentary film on the New Towns for the 1979 series *Where We Live Now*.
20 Gibberd (1948)
21 July 1953
22 For a full discussion of many design dimensions of Milton Keynes, see *Urban Design*, special issue on 'Milton Keynes at 40', issue 104, October 2007
23 Originally built by the architects Derek Walker, Stuart Mosscrop and Chris Woodward, the shopping centre now attracts 30 million visitors annually, with more than 240 shops, cafés and restaurants. Early on in its life it won a number of architectural and design awards and was awarded Grade II listed building status in 2010.
24 In June 2008 it was named as the best location for combining value for money with high-quality life, on Channel 5's Property List.
25 Glendinning and Muthesius (1994)
26 It received a Festival of Britain Merit Award and, 10 years later, a Civic Trust Award. A number of blocks in Churchill Gardens also achieved Grade II listed building status in 1998.
27 For a committed account of Goldfinger's work, see Warburton (2005)
28 For a comprehensive account, see Saint (1987)
29 See Nicholas Bullock, ch.8, 'New ways of building for houses and schools', in *Building the post-war world: Modern architecture and reconstruction in Britain* (London, 2002), pp.169–97
30 The collected papers of David Medd and Bruce Martin are held at the Institute of Education, London, like those of the Photographic Archive of the Architects and Building Branch, Ministry of Education, where Marshall-Johnson, Medd and others moved from Hertfordshire County Council. See Martin (1951) and Stillman and Castle Cleary (1949) for early post-war thoughts.
31 For further information on schools furniture of the period, see, for example, Naylor (1957), pp.28–31; Arnold (2009); and, comprehensively, Saint (1987). By 2010 the Counties Furniture Group had more than 80 local-authority members.
32 Spence's practice also attracted numerous commissions from other universities and faculties in England and Scotland.
33 For an account of the railways' design policy considerations, see the special issue of *Design*, no.81, September 1955.
34 This was complemented by a special issue of *Design* magazine devoted to British Railways: *Design*, no.171, March 1963.
35 This was discussed by Robert Sparke in 'Face-lift for BR', *Design*, January 1965, pp.46–51.
36 Although it was not widely acknowledged, in practice Helvetica and Univers continued to be used in a range of printed materials for British Rail between 1965 and the 1980s. The Rail Alphabet font has been highly influential and, also being designed to be viewed from a pedestrian context, was adopted by hospitals and airports, as well as being taken up later by DSB, the Danish railway company.
37 For an overview of BOAC design in these years, see Jackson (1991), pp.167–85
38 Schreiber (1961), pp.109–11
39 'Designing a system for Britain's road signs', *Design*, May 1967, pp.69–71
40 Margaret Thatcher, opening speech at an information-technology conference at the Barbican, London, 8 December 1982, Thatcher Foundation; www.margaretthatcher.org/document/105067, accessed 24 March 2011
41 Reilly (1967), pp.255–7

Coventry Cathedral

1 Piper (1941), p.25
2 Because the building does not face east, its liturgical west corresponds to geographical south; liturgical directions are used here throughout.
3 Pevsner (1952), p.95
4 Banham (1962), p.768

CHAPTER 3
Nation, Land and Heritage

1 The significant developments in preservation and amenity societies in the post-1945 period are summarized in Harrison (2009), pp.159–60.
2 Hewison (1987). More sensitive to the wider issues is Wright (1985).
3 Mellor, Saunders and Wright (1990)
4 The case of the Euston Arch is discussed by Patrick Wright in Mellor et al. (1990), pp.25–6.
5 On the operas of Britten, see Carpenter (1992) and Seymour (2004)
6 Mandler (1997)
7 Mellor et al. (1990), p.10; Seebohm (1989)
8 Mandler (1997), pp.369–88; Bedford (1959); Montagu of Beaulieu (1967)
9 Mandler (1997), ch.8
10 Maeder (1987); Cook (1996)
11 Duncan Petrie, 'Innovation and Economy: The contribution of the Gainsborough Cinematographer', in Cook (1997), pp.118–36; Salwolke (1997), ch.8; Christie and Moor (2005); Barr (1998)
12 Blickling came to the National Trust at the death of Lord Lothian in 1940.
13 On Junge, see Salwolke (1997), Christie and Moor (2005), and http://www.oxforddnb.com/view/article/60591?docPos=1, accessed February 2011; on Heckroth, see Nannette Aldred, 'Hein Heckroth and the Archers', in Christie and Moor (2005), pp.187–206
14 A robust analysis of heritage film in the 1980s and '90s is found in the introduction to Vincendeau (2001), pp.xi–xxv.
15 On Fowler, see Cornforth (1985); Stephen Calloway, *John Fowler*, V&A file
16 Dutton (2001); Powers (1995), pp.51–8; O'Brien (1997), pp.43–7
17 For obituaries of Robin Jacques, see http://independent.co.uk/news/people/obituaries-robin-jacques-1612378.html/1613340.html, accessed 11 January 2011
18 For Susan Einzig's obituary, see http://www.timesonline.co.uk/tol/comment/obituaries/article7042899.ece, accessed 27 February 2011
19 For Pauline Baynes's obituary, see http://www.guardian.co.uk/books/2008/aug/06/booksforchildrenandteenagers, accessed 27 February 2011
20 On the neo-Romantic painters, see Mellor (1987)
21 Thistlethwaite, Miles, review of the Ninety-Third Annual Exhibition of the Royal Society of Painter-Etchers and Engravers, Royal Watercolour Society Galleries, *The Connoisseur*, June 1975, p.178
22 For Monica Poole's biography, see http://www.oxforddnb.com/view/article/92673?docPos=19, accessed 18 January 2011
23 Smith, Cook and Hutton (1976), with Smith's photographs, was published in his memory; see also http://www.oxforddnb.com/view/article/64202?docPos=26, accessed 11 January 2011
24 On Fay Godwin, see Drabble, Margaret, 'The wilderness years', *Guardian Review*, 8 January 2011, pp.14–15
25 Tufnell (2006); on Andy Goldsworthy in the Channel Islands, see Rushby, K., 'All will be revealed', *Guardian*, Travel, 16 April 2011, pp.2–3
26 On Bawden, see Bliss (1980); http://www.oxforddnb.com/view/article/39953?docPos=2, accessed 11 January 2011
27 Leach (1998); Harrod (1999)
28 Harrod (1999), p.38. Cardew's books included *Pioneer Pottery* (1969) and *A Pioneer Potter* (1988). For Cardew's biography, see http://www.oxforddnb.com/view/article/30897?docPos=2, accessed 18 January 2011
29 For Casson's biography, see http://www.oxforddnb.com/view/article/92791?docPos=5, accessed 18 January 2011

CHAPTER 4
At Home with Modernity

1 Barber (2009)
2 A fuller account of the relationship between taste and cultural capital is provided by Bourdieu (1986).
3 The formation, in 1944, by the coalition government of the day, of the Council of Industrial Design, headed by Gordon Russell who had previously led the war-time Utility scheme, set in motion a paternalistic drive to improve the taste of the British public, which was to remain in place for more than two decades.
4 Examples of popular publications included the women's magazines *Woman*, *Woman's Own* and *Woman's Realm* and the home-related magazine *Homes & Gardens*; influential exhibitions, especially 'Britain Can Make It' (held at London's V&A in 1946) and the Festival of Britain (constructed on London's South Bank in 1951), acted as interfaces between the CoID and the public; and the set of the 1950s television chat show *Joan Gilbert's Diary*, among others, utilized furniture in the contemporary style.
5 Barber (2009), p.22
6 The advertisement, which was for Olympus' 'Empire' furniture, was published in *House & Garden*, March 1967, p.7.
7 The term 'contemporary', rather than 'modern', was used by the CoID to distinguish anti-historicist post-war furniture and furnishings from the ideological associations of the interwar, progressive architecture and design movement known as 'Modernism'.
8 Bourdieu (1986), p.ii
9 The Royal College of Art, for example, was reorganized after the war and an environmental design course, led by Hugh Casson, was introduced in the 1950s.
10 *The Good Housekeeping Book of Home Decorating*, published in the 1950s, for example, combined 'do-it-yourself' advice relating to the practical side of 'painting and decorating', which included making loose chair covers and lampshades, with more aesthetic proposals relating to colour schemes and other taste-related decisions.
11 Rowntree (1964), p.11
12 The American-born Stanley Picker was the Managing Director of Gala Cosmetics (which produced the Mary Quant range), which was based in the Betty Joel factory building on the A3, designed in the 1930s. As well as commissioning Wood to design a modern house for him, he was also a collector of contemporary art.
13 An article in *Architectural Review* (November 1967, p.343), which discussed another of Wood's houses on Kingston Hill, described it as 'a more compact modern equivalent of the manor house'.
14 The design that David Hicks created for his house at 22 South Eaton Place, London, was published in *House &*

Garden in 1954. A few small commissions resulted from it. See Hicks (2003), p.34

15 *House & Garden*, March 1967, was dedicated to British Design and featured a range of innovative products in the areas of furniture, textiles, glass, ceramics and metalwork.

16 See 'Plastics and Pop Culture' in Sparke (1990)

17 Reilly (1967), pp.255–7

18 For more detail, see Sparke (1975), pp.118–25

19 Wolff, Michael, 'Life Enhancing', *SIA Journal*, January 1965, p.10

20 Archigram's Peter Cook elaborated the former tendency, which had its roots in the new informality and in the built-in furnishings of Modernist architecture. 'Chairs are on the way out,' he wrote. See Banham (1965), p.3

21 After studying at the Central School of Art in the late 1950s, Zeev Aram opened his first showroom in 1964, just before Conran opened Habitat on the Fulham Road. He was among the first to bring modern European classics into Britain, among them the work of Le Corbusier and, later, Eileen Gray. For an account of the presence of Italian furniture in Britain at this time, see Sparke (2008), pp.37–44

22 See *The Souvenir Book of Crystal Design* (1951)

23 See 'Conran's own Habitat', *Sunday Times Magazine*, 2 February 1968, pp.26–7

24 Elliott, J., 'Design–Function' *Sunday Times Magazine*, 15 April 1962, p.26

25 See Banham (1961), p.51

26 Reilly (1967), p.255

SECTION TWO
Subversion 1955–97

CHAPTER 5
Pop Goes the Art School

1 During the Second World War the Royal College of Art was relocated to Ambleside in the Lake District, where it was known as the 'potato-loft university'; the Slade School went to Oxford; and Chelsea and Camberwell Schools of Art to Northampton.

2 Ex-servicemen's grants were awarded under the Further Education and Training Scheme until 1950, with the purpose of helping to repair careers and training disrupted due to the war, and were similar to the grants provided by the GI Bill of Rights in the United States.

3 Strand (1987), p.6

4 Darwin (1949)

5 This was a move away from the fine-art focus of Darwin's predecessors, William Rothenstein and Percey Jowett, whose tenures he dubbed the 'Age of the Dodo' before his own 'Age of the Phoenix'.

6 The School of Painting remained a pinnacle of achievement at the RCA and an English tradition of urban realism emerged, headed by Rodrigo Moynihan and including the painters Colin Hayes, John Minton, Ruskin Spear and Carel Weight (Professor from 1957). This was particularly strongly expressed in the work of a group of former students known as the 'Kitchen Sink' painters: John Bratby, Edward Middleditch, Derrick Greaves and Jack Smith, whose uncompromising paintings were concerned with the commonplace and clutter of domestic life. Smith and Greaves had grown up on the same street in Sheffield, and their working-class, provincial origins and interests reflected the less-elitist make-up of British art schools after the Second World War.

7 Guyatt (1963), p.22

8 Kenneth Garland, quoted in Seago (1995), p.34

9 Johnstone (1980), pp.63–4

10 In particular the writer on psychoanalysis Anton Ehrensweig taught in the textiles department at the Central School, and his Freudian book *The Hidden Order of Art: A Study in the Psychology of Artistic Imagination* was to become an important text for the Basic Design movement in Britain.

11 Coleman (1959), p.1

12 At Leeds, Thubron established close links between the art college and the School of Fine Art at the University of Leeds, which enabled the university's Gregory Fellows in Fine Art to start teaching at Leeds College of Art. The tutors involved at Leeds included Sir Herbert Read, Sir Terry Frost, Alan Davie, Hubert Dalwood, Norbert Lynton, Tom Hudson, Maurice de Sausmarez and Wilhelmina Barns-Graham, among others. Thubron also helped to create a prototype for Britain's polytechnics by sending his students to work on collaborative projects with engineering students from Leeds College of Technology, out of which Leeds Polytechnic was formed. Hudson was subsequently appointed Head of Foundation Studies at Leicester School of Art, where he aimed to create a completely integrated system of art and design education. In 1963 an influential exhibition of students' work, entitled 'The Visual Adventure', toured to the Royal Festival Hall and the Museum of Modern Art in New York. Hudson became a consultant to UNESCO and an adviser on art education to the Brazilian government. In 1964 he moved his entire staff to Cardiff, where he was appointed Director of Studies, and led a radical programme of art education.

13 After the war Paolozzi and Turnbull had been resident in Paris, where they had met Alberto Giacometti, Fernand Léger, Jean Arp and Tristan Tzara, while Henderson also knew Max Ernst, Yves Tanguy and Marcel Duchamp through his mother, who had worked for the Guggenheim Jeune Gallery in London in the late 1930s.

14 Letter to Alison and Peter Smithson, 16 January 1967, published in Hamilton (1982), p.28

15 Wright had led an experimental typography course at the Central School during the 1950s, and encouraged a collage aesthetic informed by Dada and Kurt Schwitters. He was subsequently to become Head of Graphic Design at Chelsea College of Art in 1970. His students at the Central School included Theo Crosby and Germano Facetti, who became Art Director of Penguin Books in 1970.

16 Frayling (1987), p.167. An article in *ARK* by Alison and Peter Smithson in November 1956, entitled 'But Today We Collect Ads', in which they used the term 'pop art' as an abbreviation for 'popular art', was believed to be the first use of the term in print.

17 Quoted in Seago (1995), p.107

18 Colin Self and Jann Haworth were part of a slightly later wave of Pop artists who studied at the Slade in the early 1960s and were encouraged by RCA students such as Hockney and Blake.

19 Alloway (1961)

20 Hockney turned to graphic work as a student in 1961 because he could not afford painting materials. However, it coincided with an important moment for printmaking at the Royal College, when the artist Julian Trevelyan as Professor of Printmaking was encouraging his students to push the boundaries of the etching process.

21 Before studying in the Painting School of the Royal College from 1953 to 1956, Blake had studied typography, typesetting, hand-lettering and wood

engraving at Gravesend College of Art, which was to inform the graphic style of his paintings.

22 They included Syd Barrett (Cambridge College of Arts and Technology and Camberwell School of Art), Ray Brown (Hornsey School of Art), David Bowie (Bromley Technical High School), Ian Dury (RCA), Brian Eno (Winchester School of Art), Bryan Ferry (Newcastle), Dave Gilmour (Cambridge College of Arts and Technology), John Lennon (Liverpool School of Art), Keith Richards (Sidcup Art College) and Ronnie Wood (Ealing School of Art). Ferry has credited much of the visual styling of Roxy Music to the experience of studying with Richard Hamilton at Newcastle (see Bracewell [2007]). Ian Dury was even to write a song called 'Peter the Painter' in honour of his tutor, Peter Blake.

23 Coleman (1960)

24 Bernard Cohen and his brother Harold were tutors on the influential 'Ground Course' at Ealing School of Art from 1961 to 1963, together with Roy Ascott, Anthony Benjamin and R.B. Kitaj. The course explored cybernetics – the science of control and communication – and the imagery produced was often made up of fragmented images and concerned with the theory of signs.

25 William Turnbull, unpublished letter, 1966, in Robyn Denny Archive, quoted in Mellor (1993), p.75

26 Alloway (1962), p.41

27 Course description, 1962–5, printed in the sculpture department's prospectus, Central St Martin's School of Art and Design Archive, London

28 Ibid.

29 Taken from the course description, ibid.

30 Frank Martin, interviewed by Cathy Courtney for the National Life Story Collection of the National Sound Archive, 11–13 August 1995

31 Robertson (1965), p.8. At the same moment a younger generation of St Martin's sculptors, including Barry Flanagan, Richard Long and Bruce McLean, had become critical of the New Generation's hermetic abstract sculptures, which they saw as being presented without regard for the gallery context; instead they proposed ephemeral, process- and time-based sculptures. Questioning the materiality of sculpture, Richard Long asserted that a walk in the landscape could be sculpture, with his *Line Made by Walking* (1967), while Gilbert & George, who had met on the course, became *The Singing Sculpture* in 1969, singing the Flanagan and Allen standard 'Underneath the Arches'.

32 *The Times*, 18 January 1958

33 Ibid.

34 The Council was composed of 30 members, including the principals of leading art colleges, representatives of local-education authorities, educational organizations, the Arts Council, RIBA, the Society of Industrial Design Artists, the RA, the RSA, the Council of Industrial Design and the university sector.

35 Hamilton, however, was uneasy with the widespread application of teaching methods that had emerged from the personal approaches of the artists concerned and the creative exchange between teacher and student.

36 Quoted in Laughton (2004), p.203. These proposals reflected the changes that Coldstream had introduced at the Slade. He had been a founder of the 1930s Euston Road Group of artists, and their figurative approach to painting and adherence to close observation of the model endured at the Slade through key appointments given to former members of the group, including William Townsend, Claude Rogers and Lawrence Gowing, and the arrival of students who had previously studied under Coldstream at Camberwell School of Art, such as Patrick George, Patrick Symons and Euan Uglow. Coldstream restructured his organization with a belief in fine-art education as a humanitarian, liberal discipline that set the Slade apart from the RCA. History of art was given unprecedented prominence in the curriculum, with the significant appointment of the academic Rudolf Wittkower as Professor of History of Art (to be succeeded by Ernst Gombrich from 1956 to 1959).

37 'On the Reasons for a Revolution: A Study Paper by the Association of Members of Hornsey College of Art, England', in *Leonardo*, vol.2, no.2, April 1969, pp.193–8

38 Tickner (2008), p.11

39 Ibid., p.58

40 'The Structure of Art and Design Education in the Further Education Sector', Report of a Joint Committee of the National Advisory Council on Art Education and the National Council for Diplomas in Art and Design (London, 1970), paragraph 26

41 Tickner (2008), p.95

42 Ibid., p.86

43 Arts Against Cuts hosted an action-planning Long Weekend at Goldsmiths Student Union and occupied Tate Britain during the Turner Prize award ceremony. Art students from the Slade School of Fine Art were served a legal injunction and were taken to court by their university, following their sit-ins.

Paolozzi and the Krazy Kat Arkive

1 Paolozzi continued to add material regularly from 1987 until 1994.

2 See www.independentgroup.org.uk/paolozzi for a short film that features the collection.

CHAPTER 6

Staging Space

1 This collection of designs was given to the V&A by the Arts Council in 1977.

2 It took the Arts Council of Great Britain, the organization that succeeded CEMA, a long time to act on this knowledge, but when it finally grasped the idea, it provided subsidies for many artists and companies working outside traditional performance venues.

3 Gerald Barry quoted in M. Frayn, 'Festival of Britain', in French and Sissons (1963), p.312

4 Cook (1972), pp.17, 19

5 Jocelyn Herbert quoted in Findlater (1981), p.85

6 Jarka M. Burian, 'Contemporary British Stage Design: Three Representative Scenographers', *Theatre Journal*, vol.35, 2 May 1983, p.216

7 *The Crucial Years* (London, 1968), p.8

8 John Bury in an interview with Colin Chambers, quoted in Chambers (2004), p.35

9 Geoffrey Dench quoted in Pearson (1990), p.39

10 Ibid., p.40

11 Ibid., p.40

12 Ibid., p.40

13 Ibid., p.40

14 Ibid., p.39

15 Christopher Baugh, interviewed for the Theatre Archive Project by Lynsey Jeffries, 2003; http://www.bl.uk/projects/theatrearchive/baugh.html, accessed 20 December 2010

16 Peter Hall, quoted in Chambers (2004), p.37

17 Lynn Haill, head of publications at the National Theatre, talking

in an interview for the NT's magazine *Update*, November 2010

18 Interview with A.C.H. Smith conducted by Jamie Andrews, 4 August 2006; http://www.bl.uk/projects/theatrearchive/smithach.html, accessed 20 December 2010

19 Programme for *Henry VI*, Royal Shakespeare Company, 1964

20 *Flourish*, no.1, June 1964

21 Shaffer (1966), p.38

22 Jarka M. Burian, 2 May 1983

23 Chambers (2004), p.75

CHAPTER 7
Boutiques and Beyond

1 Banham (1966), p.21

2 Pevsner, Nikolaus, 'Architecture in Our Time: The Anti–Pioneers', *The Listener*,5 January 1967, p.9

3 Whiteley (1987), pp.7–8

4 Hall and Whannel (1964), p.282. Hall and Whannel's work follows the pioneering and much-cited M. Abrams (1959).

5 Whiteley (1987), p.272

6 *ARK*, no.36, Summer 1964, p.48

7 *RCA Calendar* (Prospectus), 1961–2, pp.82–3

8 *RCA Calendar* (Prospectus), 1967–8, p.80

9 *RCA Calendar* (Prospectus), 1969–70, p.93

10 *Sunday Tabloid*, 29 June 1966

11 Baynes (1967), pp.42–3

12 Ibid., pp.44–5

13 Aitken (1967), p.15

14 Quant (1966), p.35

15 Ibid., p.74

16 J. Lister, 'Mary Quant', in Breward, Gilbert and Lister (2006), p.40

17 Breward (2004), pp.155–7

18 Quant (1966), pp.48–9

19 Ibid., p.73

20 *Time*, 15 April 1966, p.32

21 Aquilina-Ross (2011). See also Bennett England (1967) and Cohn (1971). For a discussion of Savile Row in the early twenty-first century, see Cicolini (2005) and Sherwood (2007).

22 MacInnes (1961); Salter (1970); Cole (2000); Gorman (2001); and Reed (2010)

23 Webb (2009), p.137

24 S. Ashmore, 'I think they're all mad: Shopping in Swinging London', in Breward, Gilbert and Lister (2006), p.73

25 Fogg (2003)

26 Hughes-Stanton (1968), pp.42–3

27 Baynes (1967), p.45

28 Jencks and Silver (1973)

29 Hughes-Stanton (1968), p.43

30 Hulanicki (1983), pp.75–6

31 Aitken (1967), pp.17–18

32 Maitland (1988), p.36

33 Watt (2003), p.85

34 For commentaries on punk, see Savage (1991); Marcus (1989); Bracewell (1997); Sabin (1999); Haunch of Venison (2010)

35 Wilcox (2004); see also Vermorel (1996); Mulvagh (1998); and Davey (1999)

36 *Saint Martin's School of Art Prospectus*, 1981–3

37 Evans (2003), p.70

38 Ibid., p.73

CHAPTER 8
'A Danceable Solution to Teenage Revolution'

1 Interview with Bryan Ferry, *The New York Times*, 19 February 1975

2 Baudelaire (1964), p.28

3 York (1980), p.12

4 In conversation with the author, London, June 2003

5 In conversation with the author, London, November 2004

6 *Philadelphia Daily News*, 24 May 1975

7 Bracewell (2006), p.390

8 York (1976)

9 Ibid.

10 Marshall (2006), p.10

11 Crisp (1968), p.20

12 In conversation with the author, Sheffield, May 2000

13 Item 101, *Million Volt Light-Sound Rave!*, cat. no.1426, Maggs Bros, London (London, 2009)

SECTION THREE
Innovation and Creativity 1963–2012

1 Pilditch, James, 'The story so far', *Design Magazine*, April 1977, pp.28–31

2 'Design Council Awards for consumer and contract goods', *Design*, May 1978, p.64. The winners were the micro folding cycle, the SME series-III hi-fi pick-up arm, and the Micro-vision pocket television designed by John Pemberton and Sinclair Radionics.

3 Press release from David Gill, sent to Jana Scholze (Furniture, Textiles, Fashion Collection, V&A), for the 'Pyrenees' sofa by Fredrikson Stallard, 1 June 2011

CHAPTER 9
Workshop of the World?

1 See, for example, Barnett (1986); Maguire (1993), pp.97–113; Wiener (1981)

2 Stewart (1987), p.230

3 Ibid., p.229

4 J. McIntyre, 'The Department of Design Research at the Royal College of Art: Its Origins and Legacy 1959–1988', in Frayling and Catterall (1995), p.58

5 C. Frayling, 'Design at the Royal College of Art: The Head, the Hand and the Heart', in Frayling and Catterall (1995), p.12

6 See N. Cross, 'The recent history of post-industrial design methods', in Hamilton (1980), pp.50–56; and Cross (1984)

7 See Sparke (1986b), pp.167–70; P. Amphlett, 'The Hochschule für Gestaltung, Ulm', in Hamilton (1985), pp.39–44

8 Between 1963 and 1973 undergraduate courses in ergonomics were started at Loughborough and Nottingham and postgraduate courses in London, Aston, Hull and Birmingham, and the Institute of Consumer Ergonomics was established at Loughborough in 1970. See H. Murrell, 'How Ergonomics became part of design', in Hamilton (1985), pp.72–6

9 The establishment of a joint course in industrial design at the RCA with Imperial College of Science and Technology in 1980 further brought together design and engineering. See Stewart (1987), p.231

10 See Sparke (1983); J. Heskett, 'Industrial Design', in Ford, B. (ed.), *The Cambridge Cultural History of Britain: Modern Britain, Volume 9* (Cambridge, 1992)

11 See Blake (1969)

12 Huygen (1989), p.73

13 *Kenneth Grange at the Boilerhouse* (1983), p.25

14 MacCarthy (1979), pp.107–11

15 Design Council, 'Prince Philip Designer's Prize: 1959–1968'; http://www.designcouncil.org.uk/our-work/investment/Prince-Philip-Designers-Prize/19591968, accessed 18 February 2011

16 Stewart (1987), p.192

17 Whiteley (1987), p.41

18 For example, the Post Office took seven years to approve the Quickstep Deltaphone because it did not want to give its business to a single supplier – 'a delay that to the company compared

unfavourably with nine years to put a man on the moon'. Young (1983), p.200

19 For instance Twyfords, manufacturers of the recessed 'Barbican' hand-basin – designed by Munroe Blair at Twyfords with Chamberlain, Powell & Bon, architects of the new Barbican flats in London – were frustrated that builders' merchants did not promote the award-winning design. See Stewart (1987), p.193

20 Young (1983), p.197

21 Sandbrook (2007), p.69

22 Woodham (1983), pp.93–4

23 See Ryan (1997)

24 Woodham (1983), p.89

25 Buckley (2007), pp.171–80

26 Booth (2001), p.115

27 McIntyre (1995), p.59

28 Cross (2001), p.50

29 Ibid., p.51

30 This new material offered novel possibilities, which were exploited in other products such as Ian Proctor's 1977 Topper dinghy, which was originally made in glass-reinforced plastic, but was redesigned in injection-moulded polypropylene.

31 See Lyall (1981), pp.45–51; Jackson (2001), pp.118–22

32 Hille showed a similar commitment to R&D with its ergonomic 'Supporto' range of office chairs, designed by Fred Scott in 1982.

33 Edgerton (1991), p.101

34 Booth (2001), p.120

35 Ibid., p.121. Booth's and Edgerton's work challenges historians who see the post-war period as one of decline. See, for example, Barnett (1986) and Wiener (1981). The accusation that the failure of Britain's industries to Americanize contributed to the decline of manufacturing has been refuted. See Zeitlin (1995), pp.277–86

36 Huygen (1959), p.58

37 Evamy, M., 'Brain sells', *Design Week*, 8 August 1996, http://www.designweek.co.uk/news/brain-sells/1115035.article, accessed 21 February 2011

38 Quoted in Huygen (1959), p.60

39 See Dyson (1987)

40 Electronic engineers at Bristol University and David Butlion worked with Baylis on the technical development of the clockwork mechanism. See Baylis (1999). Baylis makes no mention of Andy Davey's work on the design, other than a reference to him as co-winner of the BBC Designer of the Year Award. See also Chick (1997), pp.53–6

41 Evamy, L., 'Why team play is often vital to individual skill', *Design Week*, 11 July 1996 (1996)

42 Relph-Knight (1996); http://www.designweek.co.uk/news/why-team-play-is-often-vital-to-individual-skill/1127294.article?sm=1127294, accessed 14 February 2011

43 Jackson (2000), p.57

44 Sparke (1995), p.219; J. Attfield, 'FORM/female follows FUNCTION/male: Feminist critiques of design', in Walker (1989), pp.199–225. For a discussion of streamlining, see Hebdige (1988), pp.45–76

45 See Harris, Hyde and Smith (1986), pp.148–9

46 'Products and Developments', *Design*, no. 245, 1 May 1969, p.73

47 H. Wilson, in BBC2's *Designing the Decades, Part I: Designing the '60s*, directed and produced by Nadia Haggar (2003)

48 Woodham (1983), pp.111–12

49 Hughes-Stanton (1968), p.42

50 See 'Plastics and Pop Culture', in Sparke (1990), pp.92–103; Whiteley (1987), pp.115–19, 197–200

51 'Duke of Edinburgh's prize for elegant design: Patrick Rylands for Trendon Toys', *Design*, no.258, 1 June 1970, pp.34–7

52 Berriman, D., 'Lecson AP3 MK2 Power Amplifier', *Practical Hi-Fi and Audio*, May 1977, p.93

53 '1974 Design Council Awards for Contract and Consumer Goods', *Design*, no.304, 1 April 1974, p.38

54 Hayman, M. and Faulkner, K., 'Keyboard Music', *Design*, no.299, November 1973, p.80

55 80 per cent of Meridian's products are sold outside the UK, mainly in the US. Meridian's founders have won the British Design Council Award for Outstanding British Products an unbeaten three times. See S. Curtis, 'A Brief History of Lecson Audio', http://www.lothar-kissinger.de/lecson-audio/pdf/Lecson-History%20by%20Stan%20Curtis, accessed 15 March 2011; L. Kissinger, 'The Meridian Story: Approaching three decades of audio innovation and superb sound', http://www.lothar-kissinger.de/lecson-audio/pdf/meridian, accessed 15 March 2011

56 The defibrillator was shown at 'Teamwork' (1975–6) and 'Profit by Design' (1977–8). Kenneth Grange also selected it for the British Council 'Best of British' exhibition held in Aspen, Colorado, in 1989. Brian McClelland, email to the author, 24 January 2011

57 Sparke (1983), pp.69–70

58 Jackson (2001), p.122

59 A. Nahum, 'Automotive: Breeding the Brand', in Sudjic (2009), pp.98–106

60 See Dixon (2008)

61 Papanek (1971)

62 See Fry (2008); Fuad-Luke (2009); Julier and Moor (2009)

63 Fairs (2009); Lovell (2009); Williams (2009)

64 Chapman (2005)

CHAPTER 10
The Cult of the Lab

1 Antonelli (2008), p.15

2 Kirkpatrick (2008), p.26

3 Reas (2011), p.23

4 http://www.bbc.co.uk/news/technology-12620077, accessed 15 March 2011

5 Reas (2011), p.23

6 http://www.dezeen.com/2009/12/08/super-contemporary-interviews-simon-waterfall, accessed 15 March 2011

7 Simons (2007), p.49

8 Loguidice (2009), p.256

9 Plunkett, Luke, 'What do Grand Theft Auto and Lemmings Have in Common?', http://kotaku.com/5830192/what-do-grand-theft-auto-and-lemmings-have-in-, accessed 6 September 2011

10 http://www.wired.co.uk/magazine/archive/2010/02/start/silicon-roundabout, accessed 27 March 2011

11 Georgina Voss, quoted in http://www.wired.co.uk/magazine/archive/2010/02/start/silicon-roundabout

12 http://www.dezeen.com/2009/12/08/super-contemporary-interviews-simon-waterfall, accessed 15 March 2011

13 Reas (2011), p.23

14 Interview with Eva Rucki and Sebastian Noel, London, 8 December 2010

15 Antonelli (2009), p.155

16 http://www.auger-loizeau.com/index.php?id=13, accessed 10 March 2011

17 Troika (2010), p.264

18 Antonelli (2009), p.151

19 http://blog.ted.com/2009/09/29/a_call_for_desi, accessed 1 April 2011

20 Troika (2010), p.264

21 http://blog.ted.com/2009/09/29/a_call_for_desi/, accessed 1 April 2011

22 Ibid.

23 Ibid.

24 Johnson, Kara, 'Punk Manufacturing, Technocraft, Manufactured Brands and Data Driven Design' in *Innovation*

Quarterly of the Industrail Designers of America, Spring 2011, p.34

25 http://www.dezeenscreen.com/2009/06/15/super-contemporary-interviews-tom-dixon, accessed 1 April 2011

CHAPTER 11

British Design Consultancy and the Creative Economy

1 Netherlands Design Institute (1994)

2 Creative Industries Task Force (CITF), (1998)

3 CITF (2001)

4 Kinross (1988), pp.35–55

5 McGuirk, Justin, 'Design Research Unit: The firm that branded Britain', *Guardian*, 12 October 2010

6 Nevett (1987), p.195

7 For example, Pilditch (1961); Pilditch (1970)

8 Olins (1982), pp.221–9

9 Ibid.

10 Barberis and May (1993), pp.31–2

11 Wells (1989), pp.25–64

12 Jeremy Myerson, 'The 1980s', in Vickers and Myerson (2002)

13 Walters (1983), pp.21–5

14 Walters (1981), pp.8–15

15 Sharples (1984), pp.10–16

16 Wilkinson and Balmer (1996), pp.22–35

17 Davies, David, 'My biggest mistake', *The Independent*, 15 August 1993

18 Jones (1991), pp.13–19

19 Southgate (1994)

20 Ian Cochrane (Managing Director, Fitch, 1979–90), interview with the author, 29 October 2010

21 Jeremy Myerson (Founding Editor, *DesignWeek*, 1986–9), interview with the author, 19 January 2011

22 Jones (1991), pp.13–19

23 Ibid.

24 Ibid.

25 Hamilton and Kirby (1999), pp.41–5

26 British Design Innovation (2008)

27 CITF (2001)

28 For example, Julier and Moor (2009); McRobbie (1998); McRobbie (2002), pp.516–31; Nixon (2003)

CHAPTER 12

Postmodernism to Ghost Modernism

1 Poujadism was a right wing, anti–corporatist, anti-big government movement of 'little people' in 1950s France.

2 Anthony Burgess, *The Listener*, 1 April 1965, p.499

3 Charles Jencks, *Los Angeles Times*, 20 December 1987, p.21

4 Marina Vaizey, *The Sunday Times*, 29 March 1987

5 Gavin Stamp, *Daily Telegraph*, 4 April 1987

6 McEwen (1987), p.32

7 Richard Cork, *The Times*, 30 November 1991

8 'Cabe-ism' refers to the type of architecture sanctioned by the Commission for Architecture and the Built Environment.

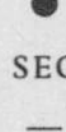

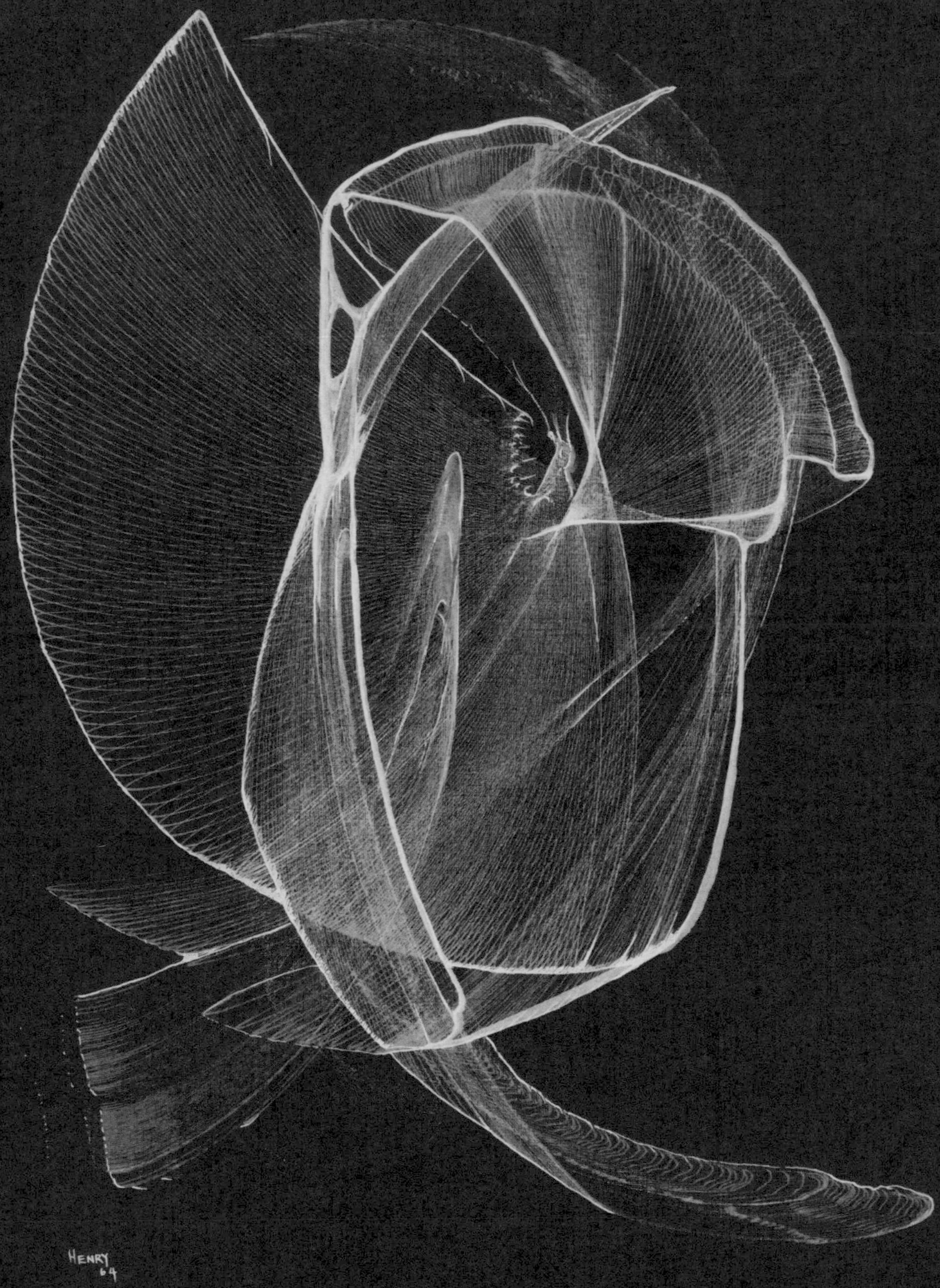

HENRY
64

Bibliography

BIBLIOGRAPHY

ART, ARCHITECTURE AND DESIGN

Primary Sources

- Alloway, Lawrence, 'Illusion and Environment in Recent British Art', *Art International*, February 1962, p.41
- Alloway, Lawrence, *Young Contemporaries* (London, 1961)
- Banham, Reyner, 'Arts in Society: Zoom Wave Hits Architecture' *New Society*, 3 March 1966, p.21
- Banham, Reyner, 'A Clip-on Architecture', *Design Quarterly*, May 1965, p.3
- Banham, Reyner, 'Coventry Cathedral', *New Statesman*, 25 May 1962, p.768
- Banham, Reyner, 'H.M. Fashion House', *New Statesman*, 27 January 1961, p.51
- Banham, Reyner, *New Brutalism: Ethic or Aesthetic?* (London, 1966)
- Baylis, Trevor, *Clock This: My Life as an Inventor* (London, 1999)
- Bennett England, R., *Dress Optional: The Revolution in Menswear* (London, 1967)
- Black, Misha (ed.), *Exhibition Design* (London, 1950)
- British Design Innovation, 'Design Industry valuation survey 2007 to 2008' (report) (Brighton, 2008)
- Cardew, Michael, *A Pioneer Potter* (London, 1988)
- Cardew, Michael, *Pioneer Pottery* (London, 1969)
- Cohn, N., *Today There Are No Gentlemen* (London, 1971)
- Coleman, Roger, *The Developing Process*, ICA exhibition catalogue (London, 1959)
- Coleman, Roger, 'Introduction', in *Situation*, Royal Society of British Artists exhibition catalogue (London, 1960)
- Cox, J., 'Science at the Festival', *Discovery*, July 1950, pp.227–9
- Crisp, Quentin, *The Naked Civil Servant* (London, 1968)
- Darwin, Robin, 'The Training of the Industrial Designer', *Journal of the Royal Society of Arts*, February 1949
- De Bondt, S. and Muggeridge, F., *The Master Builder: Talking with Ken Briggs* (London, 2009)
- Dixon, Tom, *The Interior World of Tom Dixon* (London, 2008)
- Dixon, Tom, *Rethink* (London, 2000)
- Dyson, J., *James Dyson: An Autobiography* (London, 1987)
- Fletcher, A., Forbes, C. and Gill, B., *Graphic Design: Visual comparisons* (London, 1963)
- Fry, M. and Drew, J., *Tropical Architecture* (London, 1964)
- Gentleman, David, *Art Work* (London, 2002)
- Gibberd, Frederick, *The Design of Harlow* (Harlow, 1980)
- Gibberd, Frederick, 'Landscaping the New Town', *Architectural Design*, March 1948
- Gibberd, Frederick, *Town Design* (London, 1953)
- Gibberd Frederick et al., *Harlow: The Story of a New Town* (Stevenage, 1980)
- Grange, Kenneth, *The Product Designs of Kenneth Grange of Pentagram* (Tokyo, 1989)
- Hamilton, Richard, *Collected Words: 1953–1982* (London, 1982)
- Hartnell, Norman, *Silver and Gold* (London, 1955)
- Hicks, David, *David Hicks on Living – with Taste* (London, 1968)
- Hirst, Damien, *I want to spend the rest of my life everywhere, with everyone, one to one, always, forever, now* (London, 1997)
- Hockney, David, *Hockney's Pictures* (London, 2006)
- Hulanicki, Barbara, *From A to Biba* (London, 1983)
- Institute of Contemporary Arts, *Growth and Form*, exhibition catalogue (London, 1951)
- James, Philip, *Sixty Paintings for '51* (London, 1951)
- Jencks, Charles and Silver, Nathan, *Adhocism: The Case for Improvisation* (New York, 1973)
- Johnstone, William, *Points in Time* (London, 1980)
- Kinneir, Jock, *Words and Building: Art and Practice of Public Lettering* (London, 1980)
- Klein, Bernat, *Design Matters* (London, 1976)
- Klein, Bernat, *Eye for Colour* (London, 1965)
- Leach, Bernard, *Beyond East and West: Memoirs, portraits and essays* (London, 1998)
- Machin, Arnold, *Artist of an Icon: The memoirs of Arnold Machin* (Kirstead, Norfolk, 2002)
- MacInnes, C., 'Sharp Schmutter', in *England: Half English* (Harmondsworth, 1961)
- Martin, Bruce, *School Buildings 1945–51* (London, 1951)
- Morrison, Jasper, *Everything but the Walls* (Baden, Switzerland, 2002)
- Newman, W.H. (ed.), *Design 46: A survey of British industrial design as displayed in the 'Britain Can Make It' exhibition* (London, 1946)
- Olins, Wally, 'How Wolff Olins Learnt about Corporate Identity', *Penrose Annual*, vol.74, 1982, pp.221–9
- Paolozzi, E. and Spencer, R. (ed.), *Eduardo Paolozzi: Writings and Interviews* (Oxford, 2000)
- *Pentagram: The work of five designers* (London, 1972)
- Pentagram, *Ideas on Design* (London, 1986)
- Pevsner, Nikolaus, 'Thoughts on Coventry Cathedral', *The Listener*, 17 January 1952, p.95
- Piper, John, 'The Architecture of Destruction', *Architectural Review*, July 1941, p.25
- Prizeman, John, *Living Rooms* (London, 1970)
- Quant, Mary, *Quant by Quant* (London, 1966)
- Reilly, Paul, 'The Challenge of Pop', *Architectural Review*, vol.xvii, October 1967, pp.255–7
- Reilly, Paul, *An Eye on Design* (London, 1987)
- Reith Committee, *New Towns Committee Final Report* (London, 1946)
- Reyntiens, Patrick, *The Beauty of Stained Glass* (London, 1990)
- Robertson, Bryan, *New Generation*, Whitechapel Art Gallery exhibition catalogue (London, 1965)
- Rous, Henrietta (ed.), *The Ossie Clark Diaries* (London, 1998)
- *Royal Designers on Design: A Selection of Addresses by Royal Designers for Industry* (London, 1986)
- Schreiber, Gaby, 'Furnishing and Finishing: Design Philosophy – the Consultant's Role', *Flight*, 27 January 1961, pp.109–11
- Smith, Paul, *You Can Find Inspiration in Everything (and if you can't, look again!)* (London, 2001)
- Smithson, Alison, *The Charged Void: Architecture – Alison and Peter Smithson* (New York, 2001)
- *The Souvenir Book of Crystal Design: The fascinating story in colour of the Festival Pattern Group* (London, 1951)
- Spence, Basil, *Phoenix at Coventry: The building of a cathedral* (London, 1962)
- Spence, B. and Snoek, H., *Out of the Ashes: A Progress through Coventry Cathedral* (London, 1963)
- Walker, Derek, *The Architecture and Planning of Milton Keynes* (London, 1982)
- Walker, Derek (ed.), *Derek Walker Associates: The View from Great Linford* (London, 1994)
- Walker, Derek (ed.), 'New Towns', special issue of *Architectural Design*, 1994
- Welch, Robert, *Hand and Machine* (Chipping Campden,

Gloucestershire, 1986)

- Whitechapel Art Gallery, *This is Tomorrow*, exhibition catalogue (London, 1956)
- Williams-Ellis, Clough, *Royal Festival Hall: The Official Record* (London, 1951)

Magazines and Periodicals

- *Ambassador*
- *Apollo*
- *Architectural Design*
- *Architects' Journal*
- *Architectural Review*
- *ARK*
- *Blitz*
- *Blueprint*
- *Ceramic Review*
- *Country Life*
- *Crafts*
- *Creative Review*
- *Design*
- *Eye*
- *The Face*
- *Frieze*
- *Fuse*
- *Guardian Space*
- *Harpers & Queen*
- *Homes & Gardens*
- *House & Garden*
- *i-D*
- *Ideal Home*
- *NATO*
- *Nova*
- *Octavo Journal of Typography*
- *Oz*
- *Sunday Times Colour Supplement*
- *Sunday Times Style Magazine*
- *Town*
- *Vogue*
- *Wallpaper*
- *World of Interiors*

Secondary Sources

- Adamson, Glenn and Pavitt, Jane (eds), *Postmodernism: Style and Subversion 1970–1990*, V&A exhibition catalogue (London, 2011)
- Aldersley-Williams, Hugh, *MoMA Design Series: British Design* (Milan, 2010)
- Aldred, Nannette, 'Hein Heckroth and the Archers', in Christie and Moor (2005), pp.187–206
- *Allen Jones* (London, 1993)
- Amies, Hardy, *Still Here: An autobiography* (London, 1984)
- Antonelli, Paola (ed.), *Design and the Elastic Mind*, MoMA exhibition catalogue (New York, 2008)
- Antonelli, Paola, 'Ron Arad, No Discipline', MoMA exhibition catalogue (New York, 2009)
- Aquilina-Ross, G., *The Day of the Peacock* (London, 2011)
- Arber, Katie, *Patterns for Post-war Britain: The Tile Designs of Peggy Angus* (London, 2002)
- Arnold, Damian, 'David Medd (1917–2009)', *Architects Journal*, 7 May 2009
- Atkinson, Harriet, 'A New Picturesque? The Aesthetics of British Reconstruction after World War Two', *Edinburgh Architecture Research*, no.31, 2008, p.24
- Backemeyer, Sylvia (ed.), *Ralph Koltai: Designer for the stage* (London, 2003)
- Bacon, C. and McGregor, J., *Edward Bawden* (Bedford, 2008)
- Baker, M. and Richardson, B. (eds), *A Grand Design: The Art of the Victoria and Albert Museum* (London, 1997)
- Banham, Mary and Hillier, Bevis (eds), *A Tonic to the Nation: The Festival of Britain 1951* (London, 1976)
- Bardsley, Gillian, *Issigonis: The Official Biography* (Cambridge, 2006)
- Barr, Charles, *Ealing Studios* (3rd edn, Moffat, 1998)
- Bayley, S. and Ward, J. (eds), *Kenneth Grange at the Boilerhouse*, V&A exhibition catalogue (London, 1983)
- Baynes, Ken, *Industrial Design and the Community* (London, 1967)
- Betsky, Aaron, *Zaha Hadid: The complete buildings and projects* (London, 1998)
- Birks, Tony, *Hans Coper* (London, 1983)
- Birks, Tony, *Lucie Rie* (Sherborne, Dorset, 1987)
- Blake, J. and A., *The Practical Idealists: Twenty Five Years of Designing for Industry* (London, 1969)
- Bliss, D.P., *Edward Bawden* (London, 1980)
- Bolton, Andrew, *Alexander McQueen: Savage Beauty*, Metropolitan Museum of Art exhibition catalogue (New York, 2011)
- Bowles, Hamish, *Stephen Jones and the Accent of Fashion* (Woodbridge, Suffolk, 2010)
- Brentnall, Margaret, *John Hutton: Artist and Glass Engraver* (London, 1986)
- Breward, Christopher, *Fashioning London: Clothing and the Modern Metropolis* (Oxford, 2004)
- Breward, C., Conekin, B. and Cox, C. (eds), *The Englishness of English Dress* (Oxford, 2002)
- Breward, C., Gilbert D. and Lister J. (eds), *Swinging Sixties*, V&A exhibition catalogue (London, 2006)
- Breward, C. and Wilcox, C. (eds), *The Ambassador Magazine: Promoting post-war British textiles and fashion* (London, 2012)
- Britton, A. and Swift, K., *Jim Partridge* (Aldershot, 2003)
- Brown, Linda, *The Modern Chair: Twentieth-century British chair design*, ICA exhibition catalogue (London, 1988)
- Brown, Susanna, *Queen Elizabeth II: Portraits by Cecil Beaton*, V&A exhibition catalogue (London, 2011)
- Buckley, Cheryl, *Designing Modern Britain* (London, 2007)
- Bullock, Nicholas, 'New ways of building for houses and schools', Ch.8 in *Building the Post-War World: Modern architecture and reconstruction in Britain* (London, 2002), pp.169–97
- Buruma, Anna, *Liberty and Co. in the Fifties and Sixties: A taste for design* (Woodbridge, Suffolk, 2009)
- Buruma, Anna, *V&A Pattern: Liberty & Co.* (London, 2012)
- Calloway, Stephen, *Twentieth-Century Decoration: The domestic interior from 1900 to the present day* (London, 1988)
- Campbell, Louise, *Coventry Cathedral: Art and architecture in post-war Britain* (Oxford, 1996)
- Campbell, Louise (ed.), *To Build a Cathedral: Coventry cathedral 1945–1962* (Warwick, 1987)
- Carpenter, Humphrey, *Benjamin Britten: A biography* (London, 1992)
- Chambers, Colin, *Inside the Royal Shakespeare Company: Creativity and the Institution* (London, 2004)
- Chapman, J., *Emotionally Durable Design: Objects, Experiences and Empathy* (London, 2005)
- Chick, A., 'The "Freeplay" radio', *Journal of Sustainable Product Design*, no.1, April 1997, pp.53–6
- Christie, I. and Moor, A., *The Cinema of Michael Powell: International Perspectives on an English Film-Maker* (London, 2005)
- Cicolini, A., *The New English Dandy* (London, 2005)
- Clancy, Kevin (ed.), *Designing Change* (Pontyclun, 2008)
- Coatts, Margot (ed.), *Lucie Rie and Hans Coper: Potters in parallel* (London, 1997)
- Cole, S., *Don We Now Our Gay Apparel: Gay Men's Dress in the Twentieth Century* (Oxford, 2000)
- Conran, Terence, *Terence Conran on Design* (London, 1996)
- Conway, Hazel, *Ernest Race* (London, 1982)
- Cook, Judith, *The National Theatre* (London, 1972)
- Cook, Olive, *Edwin Smith: Photographs 1935–1971* (New York, 1984)
- Cook, Pam, *Fashioning the Nation:*

Costume and Identity in British Cinema (London, 1996)

- Cook, Pam (ed.), *Gainsborough Pictures* (London, 1997)
- Cook, Peter (ed.), *Archigram* (Princeton, 1999)
- Cordwell, J.M. and. Schwarz, R.A., *The Fabric of Culture* (The Hague, 1979)
- Cornforth, John, *The Inspiration of the Past: Country House Taste in the Twentieth Century* (Harmondsworth, 1985)
- Creative Industries Task Force (CITF), *Creative Industries Mapping Document* (London, 1998, 2001)
- Crinson, Mark, *Modern Architecture and the End of Empire* (Farnham, 2003)
- Cross, N. (ed.), *Developments in Design Methodology* (Chichester, 1984)
- Crowther, Lily, *Award-Winning British Design* (London, 2012)
- Cullen, Oriole, *Hats: An Anthology by Stephen Jones*, V&A exhibition catalogue (London, 2009)
- Cullen, Oriole, *V&A Pattern: Pop Patterns* (London, 2011)
- Curtis, Colin, *The Routemaster Bus* (Tunbridge Wells, 1981)
- Curtis, William, *Denys Lasdun: Architecture, city, landscape* (London, 2004)
- Daniels, S., *Fields of Vision: Landscape Imagery and National Identity in England and the United States* (Cambridge, 1993)
- Davey, P. and Forster, K.W., *Exploring Boundaries: The Architecture of Wilkinson Eyre* (Basel, 2007)
- Dean, R. and Howells, D., *The Ultimate Album Cover Album* (London, 1987)
- De la Haye, Amy (ed.), *The Cutting Edge: 50 Years of British Fashion, 1947–1997*, V&A exhibition catalogue (London, 1997)
- Design Museum, *Super Contemporary: Celebrating visionary design from London's creative mavericks*, exhibition catalogue (London, 2009)
- Donovan, D. and Hillman, D. (eds), *Terence Donovan* (London, 2000)
- Dormer, Peter, *The New Furniture: Trends and Traditions* (London, 1987)
- Dümpelmann, Sonja, 'The landscape architect Maria Teresa Parpagliolo Shephard in Britain: Her international career 1946–1974', *Studies of the History of Gardens & Designed Landscapes*, vol.30, no.1, 2010, pp.94–113
- Dutton, Ralph, *Hinton Ampner, A Hampshire Manor* (revised edn, London, 2001)
- Dyson, James, *Against the Odds: An autobiography* (London, 1997)
- Edwards, Brian W., 'Sir Basil Unwin Spence', *Oxford Dictionary of National Biography* (Oxford, 2004)
- Elwall, Robert, *Building a Better Tomorrow: Architecture in Britain in the 1950s* (Chichester, 2000)
- Elwall, Robert, *Ernö Goldfinger* (London, 1996)
- Evans, Caroline, *Fashion at the Edge* (London, 2003)
- Evans, Mike, *The Art of British Rock: 50 Years of Rock Posters, Flyers and Handbills* (London, 2010)
- Fairs, M., *Twenty-First Century Design* (London, 2009)
- Farr, D. and Chadwick, E., *Chadwick* (Stroud, Gloucestershire, 1997)
- Favardin, P. and Bloch-Champfort, G., *Les Decorateurs des années 60–70* (Paris, 2007)
- Field, Marcus, *Future Systems* (London, 1999)
- Findlater, R. (ed.), *At the Royal Court* (Ambergate, 1981)
- Finn, David, *Henry Moore: Sculpture and environment* (London, 1977)
- Flood, Catherine, *British Posters: Advertising, art and activism* (London, 2012)
- Fogg, M., *Boutique: A '60's Cultural Phenomenon* (London, 2003)
- Forgan, Sophie, 'Festivals of science and the two cultures: Science, design and display in the Festival of Britain, 1951', *The British Journal for the History of Science*, vol.31, 1998, pp.217–40
- Fournier, Robert (ed.), *David Leach: A monograph* (Lacock, Wiltshire, 1977)
- Frayling, Christopher, *David Mellor: Master Metalworker* (Sheffield, 2006)
- Frayling, Christopher, *The Royal College of Art: One Hundred and Fifty Years of Art and Design* (London, 1987)
- Frayling, C. and Catterall, C. (eds), *Design of the Times; One Hundred Years of the Royal College of Art* (London, 1995)
- Fry, T., *Design Futuring: Sustainability, Ethics and New Practice* (Oxford, 2008)
- Fuad-Luke, A., *Design Activism: Beautiful Strangeness for a Sustainable World* (London, 2009)
- Gaillemin, Jean-Louis, *André Dubreuil: Poète du Fer* (Paris, 2006)
- Games, N., Moriarty, C. and Rose, J. (eds), *Abram Games, Graphic Designer: Maximum Meaning, Minimum Means* (London, 2003)
- Garlake, Margaret, *The Sculpture of Reg Butler* (Much Hadham, Hertfordshire, 2006)
- Garner, P. and Mellor, D.A., *Cecil Beaton* (London, 1994)
- Glancey, Jonathan, *Nigel Coates: Body buildings and city scapes* (London, 1999)
- Glendinning, Miles and Muthesius, Stefan, *Tower Block: Modern Public Housing in England, Scotland, Wales, and Northern Ireland* (London, 1994)
- Godden, Henrietta, *The Lion and the Unicorn: Symbolic architecture for the Festival of Britain 1951* (Norwich, 2011)
- Goodrum, A., *The National Fabric: Fashion, Britishness, Globalization* (Oxford, 2005)
- Gorb, Peter (ed.), *Living by Design: The partners of Pentagram* (London, 1978)
- Gorman, Paul, *The Look: Adventures in Pop and Rock Fashion* (London, 2001)
- Gorman, Paul, *Reasons to Be Cheerful: The life and work of Barney Bubbles* (London, 2008)
- Guyatt, Richard, 'Graphic Design at the Royal College of Art', in *Graphics RCA: Fifteen Years' Work of the School of Graphic Design* (London, 1963)
- Hall, Stuart and Whannel, Paddy, *The Popular Arts* (London, 1964)
- Hamilton, Doug and Kirby, Keith, 'A New Brand for a New Category: Paint it Orange', *Design Management Journal*, vol.10, issue 1, 1999, pp.41–5
- Hamilton, N. (ed.), *Design and Industry: The Effects of Industrialisation and Technological Change on Design* (London, 1980)
- Hamilton, N. (ed.), *From Spitfire to Microchip: Studies in the History of Design from 1945* (London, 1985)
- Harris, J., Hyde, S. and Smith, G., *1966 and All That: Design and the Consumer in Britain 1960–1969* (London, 1986)
- Harrison, M. and Traeger, T., *Ronald Traeger: New angles* (Munich and London, 1999)
- Harrod, Tanya, *The Crafts in Britain in the 20th Century* (New Haven, 1999)
- Harwood, E. and Powers, A. (eds), 'Festival of Britain', *Twentieth Century Architecture*, no.5, 2001
- Hatherley, Owen, *A Guide to the New Ruins of Great Britain* (London, 2010)
- Haunch of Venison, *Loud Flash: British Punk on Paper* (London, 2010)
- Hayes, John, *The Art of Graham Sutherland* (Oxford, 1980)
- Hebdige, D., *Subculture: The Meaning of Style* (London, 1979)
- Hebdige, D., 'Towards a Cartography of Taste 1935–1962', in *Hiding in the Light: On Images and Things* (London, 1988), pp.45–76
- Hegarty, John, *Hegarty on Advertising: Turning Intelligence into Magic* (London, 2011)
- Heskett, J., 'Industrial Design', in B. Ford (ed.), *The Cambridge Cultural History of Britain: Modern Britain, Volume 9* (Cambridge, 1992), pp.289–320

- Hewison, Robert, *Culture and Consensus: England, Art and Politics since 1940* (London, 1985)
- Hewison, Robert, *The Heritage Industry: Britain in a climate of decline* (London, 1987)
- Hicks, Ashley, *David Hicks: Designer* (London, 2003)
- Hughes, Graham, *David Watkins, Wendy Ramshaw: A life's partnership* (Polegate, East Sussex, 2009)
- Hughes, Graham, *Explosion: Talent Today* (London, 1977)
- Hughes, Graham, *Gerald Benney: Goldsmith* (Alfriston, East Sussex, 1998)
- Hughes, Graham, *Grima: A jeweller's world* (Alfriston, East Sussex, 2003)
- Hughes, Graham, *Modern Silver Throughout the World 1880–1967* (London, 1967)
- Hughes, Helen (ed.), *John Fowler: The invention of the country house style* (Shaftesbury, Dorset, 2005)
- Hughes-Stanton, Corinne, 'What Comes After Carnaby Street?', *Design*, no.30, February 1968, pp.42–3
- Hunt, L., *British Low Culture: From Safari Suits to Sexploitation* (London, 1998)
- *Hussein Chalayan* (Rotterdam, 2005)
- Huygens, F., *British Design: Image and Identity* (London, 1989)
- Hyman, B. and Braggs, S., *The G-Plan Revolution. A Celebration of British Popular Furniture of the 50s and 60s* (London, 2007)
- Ind, Nicholas, *Terence Conran: The authorised biography* (London, 1995)
- Jackson, Frank, 'The New Air Age: BOAC and Design Policy 1945–60', *Journal of Design History*, vol.4, no.3, 1991, pp.167–83
- Jackson, Lesley, *Alastair Morton and Edinburgh Weavers* (London, 2012)
- Jackson, Lesley, *From Atoms to Patterns: Crystal structure designs from the 1951 Festival of Britain: The story of the Festival Pattern Group* (London, 2008)
- Jackson, Lesley, *The New Look: Design in the Fifties* (London, 1991)
- Jackson, Lesley, *Robin & Lucienne Day: Pioneers of Contemporary Design* (London, 2001)
- Jackson, Lesley, *Shirley Craven and Hull Traders: Revolutionary fabrics and furniture 1957–1980* (Woodbridge, Suffolk, 2009)
- Jackson, Lesley, *The Sixties: Decade of Design Revolution* (London, 2000)
- Jeremiah, D., *Architecture and Design for the Family* (Manchester, 2000)
- Jones, Chester, *Colefax & Fowler: The best in English interior decoration* (London, 1989)
- Jones, Mike, 'Going Public, Going Bust', *Design*, January 1991, pp.13–19
- Julier, Guy and Moor, Liz (eds), *Design and Creativity: Policy, Management and Practice* (Oxford, 2009)
- *Kenneth Grange at the Boilerhouse: An Exhibition of British Product Design*, V&A exhibition catalogue (London, 1983)
- King, Emily (ed.), *Designed by Peter Saville* (London, 2003)
- King, Lucien (ed.), *Game On: The history and culture of videogames* (London, 2002)
- Kinross, Robin, 'Herbert Read's *Art and Industry*: A History', *Journal of Design History*, vol.1, no.1, 1988, pp.35–55
- Kwami, Atta, 'Textile Design in Ghana: Extracts From a Report', in *The Art of African Textiles: Technology, Tradition and Lurex* (London, 1995)
- Laughton, Bruce, *William Coldstream* (New Haven and London, 2004)
- Launert, Frederika, *The Role of Design in the Lancashire Cotton Industry, 1900–1939* (PhD thesis, University of Central Lancashire, 2002)
- Lauria, J. and Birks, T., *Ruth Duckworth: Modernist sculptor* (Aldershot, 2005)
- Leach, Dawn, *Richard Hamilton: The beginnings of his art* (Frankfurt am Main, 1993)
- Leslie, Fiona, *Designs for 20th-century interiors* (London, 2000)
- Lester, Richard, *John Bates: Fashion designer* (Woodbridge, Suffolk, 2008)
- Lichtenstern, Christa, *Henry Moore: Work, theory, impact* (London, 2008)
- Livingstone, Marco, *David Hockney* (London, 1996)
- Livingstone, Marco, *Peter Blake: One-man show* (Farnham, 2009)
- Loguidice, B., *Vintage Games, An Insider look at the History of Grand Theft Auto, Super Mario and the Most Influential Games of All Time* (Burlington, MA, 2009)
- Long, Philip and Thomas, Jane (eds), *Basil Spence: Architect* (Edinburgh, 2007)
- Lovat Fraser, Grace, *Textiles by Britain* (London, 1948)
- Lovell, S., *Limited Edition: Prototypes, One-Offs and Design Art Furniture* (Basel, 2009)
- Lutyens, D. and Hislop, K., *70s Style and Design* (London, 2009)
- Lyall, Sutherland, *Hille: 75 Years of British Furniture* (London, 1981)
- MacCarthy, Fiona, *British Design since 1880* (London, 1982)
- MacCarthy, Fiona, *A History of British Design 1830–1970* (London, 1979)
- McCay, G., *DIY Culture: Party & Protest in Nineties Britain* (London, 1998)
- McDermott, Catherine, *English Eccentrics: The textile designs of Helen Littman* (London, 1992)
- McDermott, Catherine, *Made in Britain: Tradition and Style in Contemporary British Fashion* (London, 2002)
- McDermott, Catherine, *Street Style: British Design in the 80s* (London, 1987)
- McEwen, John, 'Britain's Best & Brightest', *Art in America*, July 1987, p.32
- McEwen, John, *William Gear* (Aldershot, 2003)
- Mackley, George, *Monica Poole, Wood engraver* (Biddenden, Kent, 1984)
- McRobbie, Angela, *British Fashion Design: Rag Trade or Image Industry?* (London, 1998)
- McRobbie, Angela, 'Clubs to Companies: Notes on the Decline of Political Culture in Speeded Up Creative Worlds', *Cultural Studies*, vol.16, no.4, 2002, pp.516–31
- Maeder, Edward, *Hollywood and History: Costume design in film* (Los Angeles, 1987)
- Maguire, Patrick, 'Craft Capitalism and the Projection of British Industry in the 1950s and 1960s', *Journal of Design History*, vol.6, no.2, 1993, pp.97–113
- Maguire, P. and Woodham, J.M. (eds), *Design and Cultural Politics in Post-war Britain: The 'Britain Can Make It' Exhibition of 1946* (London, 1997)
- Massey, Anne, *The Independent Group: Modernism and Mass Culture in Britain, 1945–1959* (Manchester, 1995)
- Mellor, David A., *A Paradise Lost: The neo-romantic imagination in Britain 1935–55* (London, 1987)
- Mellor, David A., *The Sixties Art Scene in London* (London, 1993)
- Mellor, D.A. and Gervereau, L. (eds), *The Sixties: Britain and France, 1962–1973* (London, 1997)
- Mellor, D.A., Saunders, G. and Wright, P., *Recording Britain: A Pictorial Domesday of Pre-War Britain* (Newton Abbot, 1990)
- Miah, Andy, *Human Futures: Art in the Age of Uncertainty* (Liverpool, 2008)
- Milner, John, *Kenneth Rowntree* (Aldershot, 2002)
- Moore, Jenny, *Louis Osman (1914–1996): The life and work of an architect and goldsmith* (Tiverton, Devon, 2006)
- Muir, Douglas, *A Timeless Classic: The evolution of Machin's icon* (London, 2007)
- Muir, D. and West, R., *The Story of Definitive Stamps* (London, 1994)
- Muir, Robin, *David Bailey: Chasing rainbows* (London, 2001)
- Mulryne, Ronnie and Shewring, Margaret (eds), *Making Space for Theatre: British Architecture and Theatre since 1958* (Warwick, 1995)
- Mulvagh, Jane, *Vivienne Westwood: An Unfashionable Life* (London, 1998)

- Murray, P. and Trombley, S. (eds), *Modern British Architecture since 1945* (London, 1984)
- Myerson, Jeremy, *Gordon Russell: Designer of furniture, 1892–1992* (London, 1992)
- Myerson, Jeremy, *Makepeace: A Spirit of Adventure in Craft and Design* (London, 1995)
- Myerson, J., Poynor, R. and Gibbs, D., *Beware Wet Paint: Designs by Alan Fletcher* (London, 1996)
- Naylor, Gillian, 'Furniture for the Primary School, *Design*, no.222, June 1957, pp.28–31
- Netherlands Design Institute, *Design Across Europe: Patterns of Supply and Demand in the European Design Market* (Amsterdam, 1994)
- Nevett, T.R., *Advertising in Britain: A History* (London, 1987)
- Niblett, Kathy, *Dynamic Design: The British Pottery Industry, 1940–1990* (Stoke-on-Trent, 1990)
- Nielsen, Ruth, 'Wax Printed Textiles', in Cordwell and Schwarz (1979)
- Nixon, Sean, *Advertising Cultures: Gender, commerce, creativity* (London, 2003)
- O'Brien, Charles, 'Ralph Dutton and Ronald Fleming at Hinton Ampner House: Revivalist tastes in interior decoration', *Apollo*, April 1997, pp.43–7
- Ogilvy, David, *Confessions of an Advertising Man* (London, 2004)
- Osborne, June, *John Piper and Stained Glass* (Stroud, Gloucestershire, 1997)
- Papanek, V., *Design for the Real World: Human Ecology and Social Change* (New York, 1971)
- Parry, Linda, *British Textiles: 1700 to the present* (London, 2010)
- Pawley, Martin, *Norman Foster: A global architecture* (London, 1999)
- Pearson, Richard, *A Band of Arrogant and United Heroes* (London, 1990)
- Pevsner, Nikolaus, *The Englishness of English Art* (Harmondsworth, 1956)
- Phillips, Barty, *Conran and the Habitat Story* (London, 1984)
- Pick, Michael, *Be Dazzled! Norman Hartnell; Sixty years of glamour and fashion* (New York, 2007)
- Picton, John (ed.), *The Art of African Textiles: Technology, Tradition and Lurex* (London, 1995)
- Pilditch, James, *Communication by Design: A Study of Corporate Identity* (London, 1970)
- Pilditch, James, *The Silent Salesman: How to Develop Packaging That Sells* (London, 1961)
- Powell, Kenneth, *Powell & Moya* (London, 2009)
- Powell, Kenneth, *Will Alsop* (London, 2001)
- Powers, Alan, *Britain: Modern Architectures in History* (London, 2008)
- Powers, Alan, 'Ronald Fleming and Vogue Regency', *The Decorative Arts Society*, vol.19, 1995, pp.51–8
- Poynor, Rick, *Communicate: Independent British Graphic Design since the Sixties* (London, 2004)
- Prichard, Sue, *V&A Pattern: The Fifties* (London, 2009)
- Ransome Wallis, Rosemary, *Treasures of Today: Silver from Goldsmiths' Hall, London, 1980 to 2008* (London, 2008)
- Ransome Wallis, Rosemary, *Treasures of the 20th Century* (London, 2000)
- Rayner, G. and Chamberlain, R. (eds), *Austerity to Affluence: British Art and Design 1945–1962* (London, 1997)
- Rayner, G., Chamberlain, R. and Stapleton, A., *Jacqueline Groag: Textile and pattern design* (Woodbridge, Suffolk, 2009)
- Reas, Casey, *Form + Code in Design, Art and Architecture* (New York, 2011)
- Redhead, David, *Industry of One: Designer-Makers in Britain 1981–2001* (London, 2001)
- Reed, J., *The King of Carnaby Street: The Life of John Stephen* (London, 2010)
- Relph-Knight, L., 'Why team play is often vital to individual skill', *Design Week*, 11 July 1996
- Rennie, Paul, *Modern British Posters* (London, 2010)
- *Richard Rogers + Architects: From the house to the city* (London, 2010)
- Robbins, David (ed.), *The Independent Group: Postwar Britain and the Aesthetics of Plenty* (Cambridge, MA, and London, 1990)
- Rose, Stuart, *Royal Mail Stamps* (London, 1980)
- Rowntree, Diana, *Interior Design* (Harmondsworth, 1964)
- *Royal Shakespeare Company: The Crucial Years* (London, 1968)
- Ryan, Deborah Sugg, *The Ideal Home Through the Twentieth Century* (London, 1997)
- Sadler, Simon, *Archigram: Architecture without architecture* (Cambridge, MA; London, 2005)
- Safer, Samantha, *V&A Pattern: Modern British Designers* (London, 2012)
- Safer, Samantha, *Zandra Rhodes: Textile revolution: medals, wiggles and pop, 1961–1971* (Woodbridge, Suffolk, 2010)
- Saint, Andrew, *Towards a Social Architecture: The role of school building in postwar England* (London, 1987)
- Salter, T., *Carnaby Street* (Walton on Thames, 1970)
- Salwolke, Scott, *The Films of Michael Powell and the Archers* (London, 1997)
- Saunders, Gill (ed.), *Recording Britain* (London, 2011)
- Schoeser, Mary, *V&A Pattern: Heals* (London, 2012a)
- Schoeser, Mary, *V&A Pattern: Sanderson* (London, 2012b)
- Seago, Alex, *Burning the Box of Beautiful Things: The Development of a Postmodern Sensibility* (London, 1995)
- Sebba, Anne, *Laura Ashley: A life by design* (London, 1990)
- Sharples, Sue, 'Retailers rival strategies for the 1980s', *International Journal of Retail and Distribution Management*, July/August 1984, pp.10–16
- Sheffield Art Gallery, *Homespun to Highspeed: A Century of British Design 1880–1980* (Sheffield, 1979)
- Sherwood, J., *The London Cut* (Florence, 2007)
- Simons, I., *Inside Game Design* (London, 2007)
- Southgate, Paul, *Total Branding by Design: How to Make Your Brand's Packaging More Effective* (London, 1994)
- Spalding, Frances, *Dance Till the Stars Come Down: A biography of John Minton* (London, 1991)
- Spalding, Frances, *John Piper, Myfanwy Piper: Lives in art* (Oxford, 2009)
- Sparke, Penny, *As Long As It's Pink: The Sexual Politics of Taste* (London, 1995)
- Sparke, Penny, *A Century of Design: Design Pioneers of the 20th Century* (London, 1998)
- Sparke, Penny, 'A Classic and Original Italian Approach', in G. Bosoni (ed.), *Made in Cassina* (Milan, 2008), pp.37–44
- Sparke, Penny, *Consultant Design: The History and Practice of the Designer in Industry* (London, 1983)
- Sparke, Penny (ed.), *Did Britain Make It? British Design in Context, 1946–86* (London, 1986a)
- Sparke, Penny, *An Introduction to Design and Culture in the Twentieth Century* (London, 1986b)
- Sparke, Penny (ed.), *The Plastics Age: From Modernity to Post-Modernity* (London, 1990)
- Sparke, Penny, *Theory and Design in the Age of Pop: Problems in British Design in the 1960s* (unpublished PhD thesis, Brighton Polytechnic, 1975)
- Spencer, A.M., *In Praise of Heroes: Contemporary Commemorative Cloth* (Newark, 1982)
- Stallabrass, Julian, *Art Incorporated: The story of contemporary art* (Oxford; New York, 2004)

- Stallabrass, Julian, *High Art Lite: British art in the 1990s* (London, 1999)
- Stallabrass, Julian, *High Art Lite: The rise and fall of young British art* (London; New York, 2006)
- Stanfill, S. and Cullen, O. (eds), *Ballgowns: British glamour since 1950*, V&A exhibition catalogue (London, 2012)
- Steiner, Christopher B., 'Another image of Africa: Toward an Ethnohistory of European Cloth marketed in West Africa, 1873–1960', *Ethnohistory*, vol.32, no.2, Spring 1985, pp.91–110
- Stewart, R., *Design and British Industry* (London, 1987)
- Stillman, C.G. and Castle Cleary, R., *The Modern School* (London, 1949)
- Strand, Robert, *A Good Deal of Freedom: Art and Design in the Public Sector of Higher Education, 1960–1982* (London, 1987)
- Street, Sarah, *British National Cinema* (London, 1997)
- Sudjic, Deyan, *The Architecture of Richard Rogers* (London, 1994)
- Sudjic, Deyan, *Design in Britain: Big ideas (small island)* (London, 2009)
- Sudjic, Deyan, *Norman Foster: A life in architecture* (London, 2010)
- Sudjic, Deyan, *Norman Foster, Richard Rogers, James Stirling: New directions in British architecture* (London, 1987)
- Sudjic, Deyan, *Ron Arad* (London, 1999)
- Sudjic, D. et al, *Kenneth Grange: Making Britain Modern*, Design Museum exhibition catalogue (London, 2011)
- Taylor, Roger, *Landmarks: Photographs by Fay Godwin* (Stockport, 2001)
- Thackara, John (ed.), *New British Design* (London, 1986)
- Tickner, Lisa, *Hornsey 1968: The Art School Revolution* (London, 2008)
- Timmers, Margaret (ed.), *The Power of the Poster*, V&A exhibition catalogue (London, 1998)
- Timmers, Margaret, *The Way We Live Now: Designs for Interiors 1950 to the Present Day*, V&A exhibition catalogue (London, 1978)
- Treacy, P., Blow, I. and Bowles, H., *Philip Treacy: When Philip met Isabella* (New York, 2002)
- Troika (ed.), *Digital by Design: Crafting Technology for Products and Environments* (London, 2010)
- Tufnell, Ben, *Land Art* (London, 2006)
- Turner, G., *British Cultural Studies* (London, 1990)
- Vermorel, F., *Fashion & Perversity: A Life of Vivienne Westwood and the Sixties Laid Bare* (London, 1996)
- Vickers, Graham and Myerson, Jeremy (eds), *REWIND: Forty Years of Design and Advertising* (London, 2002)
- Victoria & Albert Museum, *British Art & Design 1900–1960* (London, 1984)
- Vincendeau, Ginette (ed.), *Film/Literature/Heritage: A Sight and Sound Reader* (London, 2001)
- Walker, John A., *Cross-overs: Art into pop/pop into art* (London; New York, 1987)
- Walker, J.A., *Design History and the History of Design* (London, 1989)
- Walker, J.A., *Left Shift: Radical Art in 1970s Britain* (London, 2002)
- Walsh, Victoria, *Nigel Henderson: Parallel of life and art* (London, 2001)
- Walters, David, 'The 1970s in retailing', *International Journal of Retail and Distribution Management*, March/April 1981, pp.8–15
- Walters, David, 'The 1980s in retailing: A prospective view, Part 2', *International Journal of Retail and Distribution Management*, January/February 1983, pp.21–5
- Warburton, Nigel, *Ernö Goldfinger: The life of an architect* (London, 2005)
- Ward, Colin, *Town, Home Town: The lessons of experience* (London, 1993)
- Watt, Judith, *Ossie Clark 1965/74* (London, 2003)
- Webb, I.R., *Foale and Tuffin, The Sixties: A Decade in Fashion* (Woodbridge, Suffolk, 2009)
- Webster, Helena (ed.), *Modernism Without Rhetoric: Essays on the work of Alison and Peter Smithson* (London, 1997)
- Wells, John, 'Uneven development and de-industrialisation in the UK since 1979', in Francis Green (ed.), *The Restructuring of the UK Economy* (Hemel Hempstead, 1989), pp.25–64
- West, Anthony, *John Piper* (London, 1979)
- White, Colin, *Edmund Dulac* (London, 1976)
- Whiteley, Nigel, *Pop Design: Modernism to Mod* (London, 1987)
- Whitworth Art Gallery, *1966 and All That: Design and the Customer in Britain 1960–1969* (Manchester, 1986)
- Wilcox, Claire (ed.), *The Golden Age of Couture: Paris and London 1947–57*, V&A exhibition catalogue (London, 2007)
- Wilcox, Claire, *Radical Fashion*, V&A exhibition catalogue (London, 2000)
- Wilcox, Claire, *Vivienne Westwood*, V&A exhibition catalogue (London, 2004)
- Wilhide, Elizabeth, *Terence Conran: Design and the quality of life* (London, 1999)
- Wilkinson, Adrian and Balmer, John M.T., 'Corporate and generic identities: Lessons from the Co-operative Bank', *International Journal of Bank Marketing*, vol.14, issue 4, 1996, pp.22–35
- Williams, Gareth, *The Furniture Machine: Furniture since 1990* (London, 2006)
- Williams, Gareth, *Telling Tales: Fantasy and Fear in Contemporary Design: Narrative in Design Art*, V&A exhibition catalogue (London, 2009)
- Williams, Gareth, *21/Twenty One: 21 designers for twenty-first-century Britain* (London, 2012)
- Williams, R.J., *The Anxious City: English Urbanism in the Late Twentieth Century* (London, 2004)
- Windsor Liscombe, Rhodri, 'Refabricating the Imperial Image on the Isle of Dogs: Modernist Design, British State Exhibitions and Colonial Policy 1924–1951', *Architectural History*, vol.49, 2006, pp.317–48
- Wood, Martin, *John Fowler: Prince of decorators* (London, 2007)
- Woodham, Jonathan M., *The Industrial Designer and the Public* (London, 1983)
- Woodham, Jonathan M., 'Managing Design Reform I: Perspectives on the Early Years of the Council of Industrial Design', *Journal of Design History*, vol.1, no.9, 1966
- Woodham, Jonathan M., *Twentieth-Century Design* (Oxford and New York, 1997)
- Wozencroft, Jon, *The Graphic Language of Neville Brody* (London, 1988)
- Wozencroft, Jon, *The Graphic Language of Neville Brody 2* (London, 1994)
- York, Peter, *Style Wars* (London, 1980)
- York, Peter, 'Them', *Harpers & Queen*, October 1976
- Yorke, Malcolm, *Keith Vaughan: His life and work* (London, 1990)
- Zeitlin, Jonathan, 'Americanization and its Limits: Theory and Practice in the Reconstruction of Britain's Engineering Industries, 1945–55', *Business and Economic History*, vol.24, no.1, Fall 1995, pp.277–86

Periodicals

- *Art History*
- *Costume*
- *Fashion Theory*
- *Home Cultures*
- *Interiors: Design, Architecture, Culture*
- *Journal of Design History*
- *Journal of Modern Craft*
- *Journal of Visual Culture in Britain*
- *Textile History*

CULTURE, HISTORY, SOCIETY

Primary Sources

- Abrams, M., *The Teenage Consumer* (London, 1959)

- Aitken, Jonathan, *The Young Meteors* (London, 1967)
- Barber, Lynn, *An Education* (Harmondsworth, 2009)
- Bedford, John, Duke of, *A Silver-Plated Spoon* (London, 1959)
- Cox, Ian (ed.), *Festival of Britain, South Bank Exhibition: A Guide to the Story It Tells* (London, 1951)
- Marshall, Bertie, *Berlin Bromley* (London, 2006)
- Montagu of Beaulieu, Lord, *The Gilt and the Gingerbread, or how to live in a Stately Home and make money* (London, 1967)

Secondary Sources

- Ackroyd, P., *Albion: The Origins of the English Imagination* (London, 2002)
- Addison, P., *No Turning Back: The Peacetime Revolutions of Post-War Britain* (Oxford, 2010)
- Anderson, B., *Imagined Communities: Reflections on the Origin and Spread of Nationalism* (London, 1983)
- Atkinson, Harriet, *The Festival of Britain: A Land and its People* (London, 2011)
- Barberis, Peter and May, Timothy, *Government, Industry and Political Economy* (Buckingham, 1993)
- Barnett, C., *The Audit of War: The Illusion and Reality of Britain as a Great Nation* (Basingstoke, 1986)
- Beckett, Andy, *When the Lights Went Out: Britain in the Seventies* (London, 2009)
- Booth, A., *The British Economy in the Twentieth Century* (Basingstoke, 2001)
- Bracewell, Michael, *England is Mine: Pop Life in Albion from Wilde to Goldie* (London, 1997)
- Bracewell, Michael, *The Nineties: When Surface Was Depth* (London, 2002)
- Bracewell, Michael, *Re-make/Re-model: Art, Pop, Fashion and the Making of Roxy Music 1935–1972* (London, 2006)
- Bryson, B., *Notes from a Small Island* (London, 1995)
- Colley, L., *Britons: Forging the Nation 1707–1837* (London, 1992)
- Conekin, Becky, *'The Autobiography of a Nation': The Festival of Britain* (Manchester, 2003)
- Conekin, B., Mort, F. and Walters, C. (eds), *Moments of Modernity: Reconstructing Britain* (London, 1999)
- Davey, K., *English Imaginaries* (London, 1999)
- Donnelly, M., *Sixties Britain* (London, 2005)
- Edgerton, D., *England and the Aeroplane: An Essay on a Militant and Technological Nation* (Basingstoke, 1991)
- Fox, C., *Watching the English* (London, 2004)
- Frayn, M., 'Festival of Britain', in French and Sissons (1963), p.312
- French, P. and Sissons, M. (eds), *The Age of Austerity* (London, 1963)
- Fyrth, J. (ed.), *Labour's Promised Land? Culture and Society in Labour Britain 1945–51* (London, 1995)
- Hall, S., 'Culture, Community, Nation', *Cultural Studies*, vol.7, no.3, October 1993, pp.349–63
- Hall, S. and Jefferson, T., *Resistance through Rituals: Youth subcultures in post-war Britain* (London, 1975)
- Harris, J., *The Last Party: Britpop, Blair & The Demise of English Rock* (London, 2004)
- Harrison, Brian, *Finding a Role? The United Kingdom 1970–1990* (Oxford, 2010)
- Harrison, Brian, *Seeking a Role: The United Kingdom 1951–70* (Oxford, 2008)
- Hilton, M., *Consumerism in 20th-Century Britain* (Cambridge, 2003)
- Hobsbawm, E. and Ranger, T. (eds), *The Invention of Tradition* (Cambridge, 1983)
- Hoggart, R., *The Uses of Literacy* (Harmondsworth, 1958)
- Hornsey, R., *The Spiv and the Architect: Unruly Life in Postwar London* (Minneapolis, 2010)
- Jack, I., *The Country Formerly Known as Great Britain* (London, 2009)
- Johnson, Paul (ed.), *Twentieth-Century Britain: Economic, Social and Cultural Change* (London, 1994)
- Kirkpatrick, G., *Technology and Social Power* (London, 2008)
- Kuhn, Annette, *Family Secrets: Acts of Memory and Imagination* (London, 1995)
- Kynaston, David, *Family Britain 1951–57* (London, 2009)
- Kynaston, David, *Smoke in the Valley: Austerity Britain 1948–51* (London, 2007a)
- Kynaston, David, *A World to Build: Austerity Britain 1945–48* (London, 2007b)
- Lacey, Robert, *Majesty: Elizabeth II and the House of Windsor* (London, 1977)
- LeMahieu, D.L., *A Culture for Democracy: Mass Communication and the Cultivated Mind in Britain between the Wars* (Oxford, 1988)
- Lloyd, Christopher, *Ceremony and Celebration: Coronation Day 1953* (London, 2003)
- Maitland, S. (ed.), *Very Heaven: Looking back at the 1960s* (London, 1988)
- Mandler, Peter, *The Fall and Rise of the Stately Home* (New Haven and London, 1997)
- Marcus, Greil, *Lipstick Traces* (London, 1989)
- Marr, Andrew, *A History of Modern Britain* (London, 2007)
- Marwick, Arthur, *British Society since 1945* (London, 1996)
- Marwick, Arthur, *Culture in Britain Since 1945* (Oxford, 1991)
- Matless, David, *Landscape and Englishness* (London, 1998)
- Mort, Frank, *Capital Affairs: London and the Making of the Permissive Society* (New Haven, 2010)
- Paxman, Jeremy, *The English* (Harmondsworth, 1998)
- Reynolds, S., *Rip It Up And Start Again: Post Punk 1978–1984* (London, 2006)
- Sabin, R. (ed.), *Punk Rock: So What?* (London, 1999)
- Samuel, R., *Patriotism: The Making and Unmaking of British National Identity* (London, 1989)
- Sandbrook, Dominic, *Never Had It So Good: A History of Britain from Suez to the Beatles* (London, 2006)
- Sandbrook, Dominic, *White Heat: A History of Britain in the Swinging Sixties* (London, 2007)
- Savage, Jon, *England's Dreaming: The Sex Pistols and Punk Rock* (London, 1991)
- Seebohm, Caroline, *The Country House: A Wartime History 1939–45* (London, 1989)
- Seymour, Claire, *The Operas of Benjamin Britten: Expression and evasion* (Woodbridge, Suffolk, 2004)
- Shaffer, Peter, *The Royal Hunt of the Sun* (London, 1966)
- Sinclair, Iain, *Lights Out for the Territory* (Harmondsworth, 1997)
- Smith, E., Cook, O. and Hutton, G., *English Parish Churches* (London, 1976)
- Thompson, E.P., *The Making of the English Working Class* (Harmondsworth, 1963)
- Wiener, M.J., *English Culture and the Decline of the Industrial Spirit 1850–1980* (Cambridge, 1981; Harmondsworth, 2004)
- Wright, Patrick, *On Living in an Old Country* (London, 1985)
- Young, P., *Power of Speech: A History of Standard Telephones and Cables 1883–1983* (London, 1983)

Object List

OBJECT LIST

NOTE: This list gives details of the objects included in the V&A exhibition 'British Design 1948–2012: Innovation in the Modern Age'. The objects are grouped according to their section in the exhibition. The list is correct at the time of going to press.

GALLERY 1 — Tradition and Modernity

CITY AND STATE
Festival of Britain

15 panels from *The Englishman's Home*, mural painting, John Piper, 1950–51. Ripolin paint on marine ply, entire mural (42 panels) 477 × 1547 cm. Courtesy of Liss Fine Art PLATE 1.31

'Antelope' bench, Ernest Race, 1951. Manufactured by Race Furniture Ltd, steel-rod frame and moulded plywood seat, 80.7 × 103.5 × 56.5 cm. V&A: W.35–2010 PLATE 1.25

Two stacking outdoor chairs, A.J. Milne, 1951. Manufactured by Heal & Son Ltd, perforated steel seat and back on a steel-rod frame, each 80 × 56.8 × 70.8 cm. V&A: W.33 & 34–2010 PLATE 1.26

'Kangaroo' rocking chair, Ernest Race, 1953. Manufactured by Race Furniture Ltd, painted steel rod and flat-section steel, 73.5 × 47.7 × 61.5 cm. V&A: W.36–2010 PLATE iv

Poster for the Festival of Britain, featuring the Festival emblem designed by Abram Games, 1951. Colour lithograph, 76.5 × 50.8 cm. V&A: E.307–2011 PLATE iii

Poster for the Festival of Britain, including the emblem designed by Abram Games, 1951. Printed by W.S. Powell Ltd for HMSO, colour lithograph, 76.3 × 50.9 cm. V&A: E.308–2011 PLATE 1.19

Poster advertising the Festival of Britain Exhibition of Industrial Power, Reginald Mount, 1951. Printed by the Scottish Co-Operative Wholesale Society for HMSO, colour offset lithograph, 76.6 × 50.2 cm. V&A: E.306–2011

Poster advertising the Festival of Britain Exhibition of Science, Robin Day, 1951. Issued by the London Press Exchange, colour offset lithograph, 73.8 × 49.1 cm. V&A: E.1923–1952 PLATE 1.24

Leaflet with a map of Festival of Britain events around the country, 1951. Printed paper, 42.9 × 30 cm. AAD: 1994/10/3/10

Presentation drawing of the Farm and Factory exhibition, Ulster, Willy de Majo, 1951. Gouache on watercolour paper adhered to millboard, 53.4 × 72.6 cm. The National Archives: WORK 25/69/B1/NI/4 PART 2

Presentation drawing of the South Bank with the Dome of Discovery, Douglas Stephen, 1951. Pen and ink, wax resist, coloured ink wash and wax crayon on paper, 50.1 × 69.4 cm. The National Archives: WORK 25/64/B1/SB GEN/5 PLATE 1.22

Map of the South Bank, 1951. Printed paper, 20.8 × 27.5 cm. V&A: E.300–1981

Poster promoting London Transport at the Festival of Britain, Abram Games, 1951. Designed for the London Transport Board, colour lithograph, 25.5 × 31.8 cm. V&A: E.311–2011

Guidebook to the Festival Pleasure Gardens, Battersea, Hans Tisdall, 1951. Printed paper, 25 × 18.9 × 0.5 cm. AAD: 1994/9/11/2

Leaflet for the Canterbury Festival, 1951. Printed paper, 231 × 296 mm. AAD: 1980/3/3

Presentation model of the 'Sea and Ships' Pavilion, Basil Spence, 1951. Painted wood, card, metal and glass, 21.5 × 122 × 79.5 cm. RIBA Library Drawings Collection: MOD/SPEN/2

Presentation drawing of the Skylon, Powell and Moya, 1951. Drawn by James Gowan, carbon-based ink on paper, backed onto millboard, with pen and ink drawing, pencil, and charcoal, 99.1 × 66.2 cm. The National Archives: WORK 25/77/B4/27 PLATE 1.21

Two designs for interiors in the Dome of Discovery, Stefan Buzas, 1951. Chalk and oil pastel on paper, each 48 × 63 × 3.5 cm. RIBA Library Drawings Collection: SC89/2(2) and (5)

'Plankton', furnishing fabric, Gerald Holtom, 1951. Manufactured by Gerald Holtom for the Design Research Unit, screen-printed cotton, 165 × 123.5 cm. V&A: Circ.225–1951 SEE PAGE 40

Three Hollow Men, maquette for *Stabile (Cypress)*, Lynn Chadwick, 1951. Cast copper, brass and iron, 104 × 31.5 × 19.5 cm. Sainsbury Centre for Visual Arts: 104

Autumn Landscape, William Gear, 1951. Oil on canvas, 196.2 × 138.7 × 4.5 cm. Laing Art Gallery, Newcastle upon Tyne (Tyne & Wear Archives & Museums): C10622 PLATE 1.1

Woman Resting, Reg Butler, 1951. Welded steel, 57 × 170 × 60 cm. Aberdeen Art Gallery & Museums Collections: ABDAG004596 PLATE 1.32

'Calyx', furnishing textile, Lucienne Day, 1951. Manufactured by Heal & Son Ltd, screen-printed linen, 214 × 123.5 cm. V&A: T.161–1995 PLATE 1.114

Room divider, Robin Day, 1950–51. Manufactured by Hille International Ltd, steel frame, with mahogany and ebony storage units, one decorated with an engraving by Geoffrey Clarke bonded in plastic, 182 × 188 × 40 cm. V&A: Circ.384-T–1974 PLATE 1.107

'Versalite', adjustable light fitting, A. B. Read, 1948. Manufactured by Troughton & Young, chromium-plated steel and painted aluminium. V&A: M.213–2011

'Chequers', furnishing textile, Terence Conran, 1951. Manufactured by David Whitehead Ltd, screen-printed cotton, 177 × 131 cm. V&A: Circ.283–1951 PLATE 1.125

Poster for the Festival Pattern Group display in the Regatta Restaurant, with a border based on the structure of polythene, 1951. Printed paper, 47.2 × 43.7 cm. V&A: E.169–1986

'Surrey' furnishing fabric, with a design based on the structure of afwillite, Marianne Straub, 1951. Jacquard-woven wool, cotton and rayon. V&A: Circ.73–1968 PLATE 1.30

Dress fabrics with a design based on the structure of afwillite, S.M. Slade, 1951. Manufactured by British Celanese, screen-printed spun rayon. V&A: Circ.75 and C–1968 PLATE 1.27

Wallpaper with a design based on the structure of insulin, Robert Sevant, 1951. Manufactured by John Line & Sons, screen-printed paper, 87 × 64 cm. V&A: E.888–1978 PLATE 1.58

Tile panel with a design based on the structure of zinc hydroxide, Reginald Till, 1951. Manufactured by Carter & Co., earthenware, 61 × 91.2 cm. V&A: Circ.38–1968

Plate with a design based on a Bernal chart, Hazel Thumpston, 1951. Manufactured by R.H. & S.L. Plant Ltd, printed bone china, 26.5 cm diameter. V&A: Circ.39–1968

Plate with a design based on the structure of hydrargillite, Hazel Thumpston and Peter Cave, 1951. Manufactured by E. Brain & Co. (Foley China), printed bone china, 26.5 cm diameter. V&A: Circ.40–1968

Two plates with a design based on the structure of beryl, Peter Wall, 1951. Manufactured by Wedgwood, printed bone china, each 22.7 cm diameter. V&A: Circ.41 & 42–1968

Carpet sample with a design based on the structure of resorcinol, R. Anderson, 1951. Manufactured by James Templeton & Co., wool, 43 × 47 cm. V&A: Circ.48–1968

Carpet sample with a design based on the structure of perovskite, L. Halliday, 1951. Manufactured by James Templeton & Co., wool, 15.5 × 31 cm. V&A: Circ.51–1968

Carpet sample with a design based on the structure of quartz, R. Anderson, 1951. Manufactured by James Templeton & Co., wool, 15 × 30.5 cm. V&A: Circ.49–1968

Carpet sample with a design based on the structure of insulin, G. Brown, 1951. Manufactured by James Templeton & Co., wool, 15 × 30.5 cm. V&A: Circ.50–1968

Panel with a design based on the structure of haemoglobin, Martyn Rowlands, 1951. Manufactured by Warerite Ltd, laminated plastic, 47.5 × 26.3 cm V&A: Circ.45–1968

Table linen with a design based on the structure of china clay, 1951. Manufactured by the Old Bleach Linen Company, jacquard-woven linen and rayon. V&A: Circ.71–1968

Tie silk with a pattern based on the structure of haemoglobin, Bernard Rowland, 1951. Manufactured by Vanners & Fennell Ltd, woven silk, 27 × 48 cm. V&A: Circ.72–1968

'Helmsley', furnishing fabric with a design based on the structure of polythene, Marianne Straub, 1951. Manufactured by Warner & Sons, woven cotton. V&A: Circ.308B–1951

Coronation

Flowers of the Fields of France, state gown, Norman Hartnell, spring 1957. Duchesse satin embroidered with pearls, beads, brilliants and gold thread, designed for the Queen's state visit to Paris, 165 × 120 × 38 cm. V&A: T.264–1974

'Queensway', furnishing fabric, Robert Goodden, 1952. Manufactured by Warner & Sons, woven silk, rayon, cotton and lurex, 256 × 128 cm . V&A: T.193–1953

Country Celebrations, Kenneth Rowntree, 1953. From the Royal College of Art's celebratory Coronation series of prints, lithograph, 38.3 × 56.1 cm. V&A: Circ.322–1953 PLATE 1.41

Life Guards, Edward Bawden, 1953. From the Royal College of Art's celebratory Coronation series of prints, lithograph, 56 × 38.3 cm. V&A: Circ.326–1953 PLATE 1.40

Design for Coronation street decorations for Whitehall, London, Hugh Casson, 1953. Ink and watercolour on board, 63 × 48 × 3.5 cm. RIBA Library Drawings Collection: SD158/5 PLATE 1.38

Design for Coronation street decorations for Hungerford Bridge, Hugh Casson, 1953. Gouache and pastel on paper, 48 × 63 × 3.5 cm. RIBA Library Drawings Collection: PA348/1 (37) PLATE 1.38

Design for Coronation decorations for the Oxford Street frontage of Selfridges department store, London, Edward Bawden and Richard Guyatt, 1953. Pencil, watercolour and bodycolour on paper, 63.2 × 75.5cm. V&A: E.440–2010 PLATE 1.37

Queen Elizabeth II on Coronation Day, Cecil Beaton, 2 June 1953. Photograph, printed 2011. V&A PLATE 1.33

Ruby venus brooch, Andrew Grima, 1966. Carved Indian rubies and diamonds set in gold and platinum. The Royal Collection

The Prince of Wales's Investiture Coronet, Louis Osman, 1969. The orb engraved by Malcolm Appleby, gold, platinum, diamonds and emeralds, with velvet and ermine cap of estate, diameter 15 cm. The Royal Collection PLATE 1.2

Relief portrait of Queen Elizabeth II for the obverse of coins, Mary Gillick, 1952. Plaster, 22 cm diameter. The British Museum: 2005,0806.8 PLATE 1.45

First competition designs for the reverses of 2-pence, 10-pence and 20-pence coins, Christopher Ironside, 1963–4. Pencil on paper, 17.4 × 18.5cm, 15.3 × 12.2 cm and 12.8 × 14.4 cm. The British Museum: 2006,0601.229, 2006,0601.227 and 2006,0601.238 PLATE 1.46

Final competition designs for the reverses of 2-pence, 5-pence and 50-pence coins, Christopher Ironside, 1966–8. Pencil on paper, 19.2 × 27.8 cm, 15.5 × 13.5 cm and 14.8 × 13.1 cm. The British Museum: 2006,0601.181, 2006,0601.177, 2006,0601.168

Definitive ½d. stamps, Enid Marx, 1952. Photograph by Dorothy Wilding, printed paper. The British Postal Museum & Archive

Imperforate registration sheet of Coronation-issue 1s. 3d. stamps, Edmund Dulac, 1953. Printed paper, 51 × 28 cm. The British Postal Museum & Archive PLATE 1.49

Relief portrait of Queen Elizabeth II for definitive stamps, Arnold Machin, 1966. Plaster, 46 × 41.7 × 5.3 cm. The British Postal Museum & Archive

Definitive 4d. stamps, Arnold Machin, 1967. Printed paper. The British Postal Museum & Archive

Page from the 'Gentleman Album' of proposed stamp designs, David Gentleman, 1965. Printed paper, 28.7 × 20.1 cm. The British Postal Museum & Archive PLATE 1.47

Coventry Cathedral

Interior of St Michael's Cathedral, Coventry, November 15th, 1940, John Piper, 1940. Oil on canvas, 70 × 80 × 6.5 cm. Herbert Art Gallery and Museum, Coventry: VA.1955.419

Elevation drawing of Coventry Cathedral from the east, Basil Spence, June 1952. Graphite on transparent paper, 61.7 × 133.1cm. RCAHMS: Sir Basil Spence Archive: SPE ENG/9/2/3/11/12 PLATE 1.78

Perspective drawing of the interior of Coventry Cathedral looking towards the Great West Screen, 22 August 1952. Mechanical copy, graphite and pastel on paper, 130 × 111.5 × 3.5 cm. RCAHMS: Sir Basil Spence Archive: SPE ENG/9/2/1/13

Model of the Baptistery window, John Piper and Patrick Reyntiens, 1958–9. Wood and stained glass, 366.4 × 218.4 cm. V&A: C.63–1976 PLATE 1.77

Panel for the Baptistery window, John Piper and Patrick Reyntiens, 1961–2. Stained and painted glass, 125.1 × 50.4 cm. V&A: C.10–1976

Madonna and Child, half-scale study for a panel in the Great West Screen, John Hutton, 1958. Engraved glass, 128.8 × 45.8 cm. V&A: Circ.109–1962

Design for one of the carved stone Tablets of the Word, Ralph Beyer, September 1960. Pencil on paper, 41 × 56 × 2 cm. Coventry Cathedral

First cartoon for the tapestry *Christ in Glory*, Graham Sutherland, 1953. Oil and gouache on board, 225 × 136 × 9.5 cm. Herbert Art Gallery and Museum, Coventry: VA.1974.50.46

Trial section of the tapestry *Christ in Glory*, showing the Eagle of St John, Graham Sutherland, 1958–9. Woven by Pinton Frères, Aubusson, France, wool, 295 × 198 cm. Herbert Art Gallery and Museum, Coventry: VA.1993.4 PLATE 1.80

Advent cope, John Piper, 1960. Manufactured by Louis Grossé, using silk made by West Cumberland Silk Mills, 160 cm neck to hem. Coventry Cathedral

Altar cross, Geoffrey Clarke, 1958. Cast silver, commissioned in relation to Clarke's altar cross for Coventry Cathedral, 101.5 × 43 cm. The Worshipful Company of Goldsmiths PLATE 1.79

Ciborium and two chalices, Gerald Benney, 1962. Silver, each 26 × 12.5 cm. Coventry Cathedral PLATE 1.75

Bishop's Jewel, Thomas Durant, 1963. Gold, silver, diamonds and enamel, 13 × 10.5 × 2.7 cm. Coventry Cathedral PLATE 1.76

Towers and New Towns

View of a Modernist housing development, Ernö Goldfinger, 1942. Print, watercolour and pastel on paper, 48 × 63 × 3.5 cm. RIBA Library Drawings Collection: PA626/1(1) PLATE 1.3

Elevation drawing of Balfron Tower, Rowlett Street, London, Ernö Goldfinger, 1965. Photomechanical print on drafting film, 63 × 48 × 3.5 cm. RIBA Library Drawings Collection: PA2062/1(4) PLATE 1.64

Design drawing of Space House, Kingsway, London, Richard Seifert, *c.*1965. Drawn by A.F. Gill, watercolour and gouache on paper, 80 × 112 cm. RIBA Library Drawings Collection: PA1086/2 (2) PLATE 3.65

Family Group, Henry Moore, 1954–5. Carved stone, 170 × 138 × 82 cm. Harlow Art Trust PLATE 1.60

Draft plan of Harlow New Town, Frederick Gibberd, 1947. Hand-coloured print, 63.5 × 89 cm. Gibberd Garden Trust PLATE 1.59

Design for The Dashes, Harlow, Gerald Lacoste, 1954. Drawn by Lawrence Wright, watercolour on card, 58 × 125 × 3.5 cm. RIBA Library Drawings Collection: PA677/6 PLATE 1.4

Model of The Lawn, Harlow, Frederick Gibberd, *c.*1951. Painted wood and mixed media, 26 × 115.5 × 77.5 cm. Gibberd Garden Trust

Design for Calverton End Adventure Playground, Milton Keynes, Ron Herron of Archigram Architects, 1972. Dyeline print with added colour felt-tip pen, film and collage mounted on board, 50 × 75 × 2 cm. Archigram Archive PLATE 1.61

Two posters, *Where is Milton Keynes?* and *Milton Keynes: The kind of city you'll want your family to grow up in*, Minale, Tattersfield, Provinciali, 1973. Designed for the Milton Keynes Development Corporation, printed by Westerham Press, colour offset lithographs, 101.5 × 76 cm. V&A: E.174 & 175–2011 PLATE 1.10

Aerial view of Milton Keynes city centre, planned by Derek Walker and Stuart Mosscrop, 1974. Drawing by Helmut Jacoby, pen and ink on paper, 65 × 65 cm. Private collection

Perspective view of the garden court, Milton Keynes shopping centre, Derek Walker, Stuart Mosscrop, Chris Woodward and Syd Green, 1973. Drawing by Helmut Jacoby, pen and ink on paper, 45 × 45 cm. Private collection

Perspective view of Milton Keynes town park, Derek Walker and Andrew Mahaddie, 1976. Drawing by Helmut Jacoby, pen and ink on paper, 32 × 70 cm. Private collection

Education and Culture

Model of Eveline Lowe School, Southwark, London, David and Mary Medd, 1967. Plastic, painted card, paper and wood, 11 × 55.3 × 39.4 cm. RIBA Library Drawings Collection: MOD/EDUC/7b PLATE 1.69

'Kings and Queens', curtain fabric for schools, Alice Roberts, 1951. Manufactured by Gerald Holtom, printed linen, 78 × 62.5 cm. V&A: Circ.223B–1951 SEE PAGE 96

Model of Norfolk Terrace, University of East Anglia, Denys Lasdun, 1963. Balsa wood, pine, chipboard, Perspex, felt, die-cast zinc alloy and cork. Sainsbury Centre for Visual Arts: 41435

Perspective drawing of the Albert Sloman Library, University of Essex, Architects Co-Partnership, 1964. Ink on architectural tracing paper, 55.5 × 75 cm. Architects Co-Partnership PLATE 1.65

Open University mace, Eric Clements, 1970. Made by Imperial Metal Industries, assembled and finished by Hamish Bowie and Sidney Perkins, cast, turned and anodized titanium, 103.2 × 18 × 10.1 cm. The Open University

'The New National Theatre is Yours', poster advertising the opening of the National Theatre, Tom Phillips, 1976. Printed paper, 74.8 × 50.8 cm. V&A: S.35–1994 PLATE 2.57

Set model for *As You Like It* by William Shakespeare, Ralph Koltai, 1967. Designed for the National Theatre Company, Perspex, acetate, paint, plastic and wood, 73 × 58 × 72 cm. V&A: S.474–1980 PLATE 2.53

Horse's head costume for *Equus* by Peter Shaffer, designed by John Napier for the National Theatre Company, 1974. Cane, foil, leather and wire, 40 × 31 × 85 cm. V&A: S.43:1–1993 PLATE 2.55

Poster for *Equus* by Peter Shaffer, Moura-George/Briggs, 1974. Designed for the National Theatre Company, illustration by Gilbert Lesser, printed paper, 76 × 51.3 cm. V&A: S.651–1996 PLATE 2.56

Transport

Model of the Routemaster bus, Colin Curtis, A.A.M. Durrant and Douglas Scott, 1947–56. Made at London Transport Chiswick Works, *c*.1960, painted aluminium and mixed media, 69.5 × 122 × 60 cm. Colin Curtis

Traffic light, David Mellor, 1966. Polypropylene and PVC-coated metal. Donated by Peek Traffic Ltd

'Children crossing' sign, Jock Kinneir and Margaret Calvert, 1964. Printed metal, 60 × 60 cm. Margaret Calvert PLATE 1.70

Four maquettes for directional road signs, Jock Kinneir and Margaret Calvert, 1957–67. Gouache on card. St Bride Library

British Rail logo from Bristol Temple Meads station, Gerald Barney of Design Research Unit, 1964. Enamelled steel, 70.5 × 113.4 × 6.5 cm. National Railway Museum: 1999-7716

Drawing of a proposed livery for a Western diesel locomotive, Design Research Unit, early 1960s. Watercolour on paper, 54.7 × 75 × 2 cm. National Railway Museum: 1977–7627 PLATE 3.48

Pages from the British Rail design manuals, showing logos, logotypes and train livery, Design Research Unit, 1965 and 1969. Printed paper, each 29.7 × 21 cm. AAD: 1999/8/113 and 118 PLATE 3.53

Poster showing the cab of the InterCity 125 train designed by Kenneth Grange, Peter Donnelly, 1976. Issued by the British Railways Board, colour offset lithograph, 101.2 × 63.3 cm. V&A: E.821–1980

LAND

Hidcote, Gloucestershire, England, Edwin Smith, 1962. Gelatin silver print, 25.3 × 20.5 cm. V&A: PH.844–1987 PLATE 1.93

Path and Reservoir from above Lumbutts, Yorkshire, Fay Godwin, 1977. Gelatin silver print, from the *Calder Valley* series, 40.5 × 30.5 cm. V&A: PH.15–1981 PLATE 1.91

Root, Monica Poole, 1977. Wood engraving, 26.1 × 41.5 cm. V&A: E.1687–1991 PLATE 1.89

Design for the cover of *Tom's Midnight Garden* by Philippa Pearce, Susan Einzig, 1958. Gouache and pen and ink on card, 44 × 37 × 2.5 cm. The Susan Einzig estate PLATE 1.88

Design for a poster map of J.R.R. Tolkien's Middle-earth for *The Lord of the Rings*, Pauline Baynes, 1971. Watercolour and pencil on paper, 76.5 × 54 cm. The Bodleian Libraries, University of Oxford: MS Tolkien drawings 100 PLATE 1.90

Life Began in Water, necklace, Sah Oved, *c*.1950. Gold, silver, agates, jasper and aquamarines, 20.4 × 16.5 × 1.3 cm. V&A: M.138–1984

Hare jewel made for *Masquerade*, Kit Williams, 1978. Gold, faience, ruby, citrines, mother-of-pearl, quartz. Private collection PLATE 1.17

Country-House Style

Outdoor seat, Edward Bawden, 1955. Manufactured by Bilston, cast iron, 96 × 124 × 51 cm. V&A: W.8–1986 PLATE 1.96

Dress, Laura Ashley, 1972–5. Printed cotton, 138 × 104 cm. V&A: T.94–2001

Child's dress and blouse, Laura Ashley, 1983. Printed cotton, 57 cm shoulder to hem. V&A: Misc.83-84–1983

'Girl in Tree', furnishing fabric, Olive Sullivan, 1956. Manufactured by Edinburgh Weavers, printed glazed cotton, 183 × 124.5 cm. V&A: Circ.850–1956

Design for 'Glade' furnishing fabric, Kenneth Truman for Arthur Sanderson & Sons, 1950s. Gouache on paper, 77 × 83 cm. Arthur Sanderson & Sons (Abaris Holdings Ltd) PLATE 1.87

Design for 'Pot Pourri' wallpaper, Antony Little for Osborne & Little Ltd, 1978. Gouache, pencil and dyeline print on paper, 42 × 26.1 cm. V&A: E.3640–1983 PLATE 1.86

Wallpaper from the Laura Ashley Decorator Collection, 1989. Colour screenprint on paper, 37.4 × 21.5 cm. V&A: E.1219–1989

Craft and the Land

Soft-tech House for the 1980s, John Prizeman, 1979. Pen and ink and felt-tip pens on paper, 41.9 × 29.6 cm. V&A: E.426–1980

Sylvan chair, John Makepeace, *c*.1985. English oak, 90 × 56 × 56 cm. Private collection PLATE 1.98

Coffee table, Alan Peters, 1978. Olive wood, 45.7 × 114 × 49.8 cm. V&A: W.61–1978

Flask, Michael Cardew, 1950. Stoneware with painted decoration on a grey glaze, 31.5 × 20.4 cm. V&A: Circ.426–1950 PLATE 1.95

Bowl, Michael Casson, 1975. Stoneware with inlaid decoration in porcelain on a ground of clay-ash glaze, and a tenmoku glazed interior, 16.5 × 18.7 cm. V&A: Circ.9–1976 PLATE 1.97

Plate, David Leach, 1980. Stoneware with wax-resist decoration in white over a tenmoku glaze, 5.3 × 29.5 cm. V&A: C.173–1980 PLATE 1.94

Storm chair, Stephen Richards, 2000. Various woods, including ash, oak, walnut, Douglas fir, sycamore, maple, elm and cherry, glued and jointed, 105 × 100 × 100 cm. V&A: W.1–2003 PLATE 1.101

'Block Seat', Jim Partridge and Liz Walmsley, 2004. Burr oak, hewn and charred, 71 × 45 × 35 cm. V&A: W.1–2005 PLATE 1.99

Tweed

Suit, Hardy Amies, *c.*1970. Mohair tweed designed by Bernat Klein, wool jersey. V&A: T.82:1&2–1992

Ensemble from the 'On Liberty' collection, Vivienne Westwood, Autumn/Winter 1994. Harris tweed and tartan. Westwood Archive

'Rowan' and 'Aspen' tweed furnishing fabrics, Bernat Klein, 1969. Manufactured by Margo Fabrics, 273 × 133 cm and 276 × 130 cm. V&A: Circ.717 & 720–1969

Monarch, model stag's head, Chloe Harrison, 2011. Harris tweed, antlers and embroidery, 150 × 62 × 65 cm. Studio gnu

HOME

House & Garden magazine, November 1953 and July 1954

Ideal Home magazine, January 1957

Design magazine, April 1957, issue 100. Cover by Peter Hatch, showing cruet set by Robert Welch. AAD: 745.205/DES

Her House, design for a home limited to 1,070 square feet and a cost of £3,000, John Prizeman, 1959. Pen and ink and Letratone on paper, 42 × 59.3 cm. V&A: E.1135–1979 PLATE 1.5

Design for a fitted kitchen, George Fejér, 1945. Dyeline print and coloured chalks on paper, 29.8 × 42 cm. V&A: E.791–1997

Fifties

'Homemaker', ceramic service, Enid Seeney, 1956–7. Manufactured by Ridgway Potteries Ltd, 1957–68, earthenware, glazed and printed, on 'Metro' shape designed by Tom Arnold, plate 22.8 cm diameter, coffee pot 18.3 × 19.7 × 11.5 cm, tureen 11 × 24 × 24 cm, sandwich plate 18 × 14.5 cm, coffee cup 5.1 × 8.8 cm, saucer 11.7 cm diameter. V&A: C.67–1982, C.18:1 & 2–1996, C.50–1991, C.205–1991, C.237–1991 PLATE 1.120

'Pride', cutlery, David Mellor, 1953. Manufactured by Walker & Hall Ltd, 1959, electroplated nickel silver, with stainless-steel knife blades and composition handles, table knife 21.8 × 1.7 × 1.5 cm, table fork 20.5 × 2.2 × 2.2 cm, cheese knife 18.8 × 1.6 × 1 cm, dessert fork 18.1 × 2 × 1.7 cm, fish knife 20.6 × 2 × 1.1 cm, fish fork 18.8 × 2.3 × 2.4 cm, table spoon 21 × 4.7 × 3 cm, soup spoon 20.1 × 4.8 × 2.5 cm, dessert spoon 18.7 × 4 × 2.4 cm. V&A: Circ.292-H–1959 PLATE 1.119

'Campden', candelabrum, Robert Welch, *c.*1957. Manufactured by J. & J. Wiggin Ltd, stainless steel with wooden feet, 23.5 × 13.5 × 9.9 cm. V&A: Circ.345–1959 PLATE 1.123

'Alveston', tea service, Robert Welch, 1962. Manufactured by Old Hall Tableware Ltd, stainless steel, teapot 11 × 24 cm, hot water jug 13 × 19 cm, milk jug 9 × 14 cm, sugar bowl 6 × 10 cm. V&A: M.19-C–1978

'Anniversary Ware' casserole, John and Sylvia Reid, 1960. Manufactured by Izons & Co., enamelled cast iron, 10.5 × 27 × 19 cm. V&A: Circ.447&A–1963

A Book of Mediterranean Food by Elizabeth David, illustrated by John Minton, 1950. Published by John Lehmann Ltd, cloth-bound hardcover. NAL: 38041800427502 PLATE 1.103

'Café', furnishing textile, Jacqueline Groag, 1951. Manufactured by Gerald Holtom for use in Kardomah Cafés, screen-printed linen, 66 × 76 cm. V&A: Circ.222A–1951 PLATE 1.115

'Cuban Fantasy', vase, Jessie Tait, 1957. Manufactured by W.R. Midwinter Ltd, earthenware, glazed and printed, 18 × 14.5 × 12 cm. V&A: C.65–1988 PLATE 1.121

'Cannes', tableware range, Hugh Casson, 1954. Manufactured by W.R. Midwinter Ltd, earthenware with printed and hand-coloured underglaze decoration, on the 'Fashion' shape designed by Roy Midwinter, *c.*1953, coffee pot 19 × 11 cm, sweetmeat stand 16 × 23 cm, plate 2 × 23 cm. V&A: C.94 & A, 98 & 102–1985 PLATE 1.102

Design for an interior furnished with G-Plan furniture, Leslie Dandy, 1960. Pen and ink and watercolour on paper, 39.1 × 57.5 cm. V&A: E.335–1978 PLATE 1.12

'Jason' chair, Carl Jacobs, 1951. Manufactured by Kandya Ltd, beech frame, beech-faced plywood seat and back, 74 × 52.5 × 43.5 cm. V&A: Circ.305–1970 PLATE 1.110

'Flamingo', furnishing textile, Tibor Reich, 1957. Manufactured by Tibor Ltd, printed cotton with a design derived from photographs of leaves using the Fotexur process, 254 × 122.5 cm. V&A: Circ.463–1963 PLATE 1.16

'Mambo' chair, Michael Inchbald, 1955. Iron frame with cane arms and back, and foam cushions with linen upholstery, 74.8 × 69.5 × 81.5 cm. V&A: W.13:1-3–1981 PLATE 1.7

'CS17' television, Robin Day, 1957. Manufactured by Pye Ltd, 17-inch screen, wooden cabinet and steel stand, television 53 × 47 × 51 cm, stand 46 × 43 × 40 cm. V&A: Circ.231 & A–1963 PLATE 1.6

Pendant lampshade, John and Sylvia Reid, 1956.Manufactured by Rotaflex (Great Britain) Ltd, cellulose acetate, 27 × 56 cm. V&A: Circ.387–1963 PLATE 3.12

Sideboard, David Booth, 1951. Manufactured by Gordon Russell Ltd, mahogany with rosewood veneer and white birch, 84 × 121.5 × 46.5 cm. V&A: W.43–1978

Carpet, Jean Finn, 1956. Tapestry woven wool. V&A: Circ.427–1956

Bowl, Ruth Duckworth, 1959. Stoneware, painted in black pigment on a green glaze, 40 × 9 cm. V&A: Circ.241–1959 PLATE 1.124

Bottle, Lucie Rie, 1959. Stoneware, with a flecked white glaze, 41.6 × 13.1 cm. V&A: Circ.126–1959 PLATE 1.124

Vase, Hans Coper, 1958. Stoneware, with black and white matt glazes, 49.2 × 38.1 cm. V&A: Circ.154–1958 PLATE 1.124

'The Fisherman', furnishing textile, Keith Vaughan, 1956. Manufactured by Edinburgh Weavers Ltd, screen-printed cotton, 169 × 118.5 cm. V&A: Circ.686–1956 PLATE 1.8

Sixties

Cabinet, Max Clendinning, 1965. Manufactured by Liberty, plywood, repainted by Clendinning for use in his dining room, *c.*1968, cupboard 107 × 61.7 × 50 cm, stand 107.3 × 76.3 × 48.3 cm. V&A: W.19:1 & 2–2011 PLATE 1.108

Chair, Max Clendinning, 1965. Manufactured by Liberty, painted plywood with tweed upholstery. Private collection PLATE 1.108

'Bricks' and 'Unica' vases, Geoffrey Baxter, 1965–6. Manufactured by James Powell & Son (Whitefriars Glassworks), 1965–74, mould-blown glass, 33.5 cm high, and 20.5 × 8.5 × 7.5 cm. V&A: C.240 & 241–1991, C.175–1996 PLATE 1.122

Carpet, Peter Collingwood, 1966. Horsehair core with mohair pile. V&A: Circ.799–1966

Designs for a bathroom and study, Max Clendinning, 1968. Drawn by Ralph Adron, published in the *Daily Telegraph* colour supplement, March 1968, poster-colour on paper, each 36.4 × 25.2 cm. V&A: E.827 and 829–1979 PLATE 1.104

Design for a living room for Milo Cripps, David Hicks, 1968. Pencil, ink, felt and paint on paper, 51.5 × 76.3 cm. AAD: 1986/4 PLATE 1.106

Three carpet samples, David Hicks, 1970 and 1978. Manufactured by Crossley Carpets and Arena Carpets, wool and nylon, 22 × 22.5 cm, 23 × 23.5 cm and 68.5 × 68 cm. V&A: T.348C&D–1988, T.123–1979

Panel of dimpled wall tiles, Michael Caddy, 1962. Manufactured by Wade Architectural Ceramics, glazed Dimex ceramic body, 42.5 × 63 cm. V&A: Circ.590-W–1963

Habitat catalogue, 1964. Printed paper, single sheet unfolding to 58.4 × 51.2 cm. AAD1995/12/5/2

Habitat catalogue, 1965. Printed paper with metal fastener binding. AAD: 1995/12/5/3 PLATE 1.127

'Prince of Quince', furnishing fabric, Juliet Glyn Smith, 1965. Manufactured by Conran Fabrics, printed cotton, 278 × 126.5 cm. V&A: Circ.119–1967 SEE PAGE 118

'Input', range of containers, Conran Associates, 1974. Manufactured by Crayonne Ltd, ABS plastic, ranging from 5 × 10 × 10 cm to 30 × 20 × 20 cm. V&A: Circ.99, 105, 106, 111, 114 & 116–1977 PLATE 1.129

Design for a dining room furnished with flatpack furniture, Conran Associates, 1976. Drawn by Chris Williams, felt-tip pen on paper, 42 × 29.5 cm. V&A: E.1544–1976 PLATE 1.126

Designs for the 'Viking' range of seating, Conran Associates, for Dual Furniture Ltd, 2 May 1977. Drawn by G.P. Wood, felt-tip pen and watercolour on paper, 29.6 × 41.8 cm. V&A: E.1127–1979 PLATE 1.128

'Chair Thing', self-assembly children's chair, Peter Murdoch, 1968. Manufactured by Perspective Designs, polyurethane-coated laminated paper, 49 × 44 × 36 cm. V&A: Circ.795–1968

'Mandarin', furnishing textile, Linda Harper, 1966. Manufactured by Hull Traders Ltd, printed cotton sateen, 121.5 × 128.5 cm. V&A: T.168–1989 PLATE vi

'T5' stacking chair, Rodney Kinsman, 1969. Manufactured by OMK Designs Ltd, chromium-plated steel-tube frame with upholstered plywood seat, 73 × 52 × 46 cm. V&A: Circ.359–1970 PLATE 1.111

'Colourtron', furnishing fabric, Eddie Squires, 1968. Manufactured by Warner & Sons, printed cotton, 275.5 × 127 cm. V&A: Circ.801–1968 PLATE 1.117

'Contour' chair, David Colwell, 1967–8. Manufactured by 4's Company Ltd, 1968, acrylic shell with nylon-coated steel frame. V&A: Circ.64–1970 PLATE 1.15

'Moiré', furnishing fabric, Dorothy Carr, 1964. Manufactured by Hull Traders Ltd, printed cotton satin, 120 × 124 cm. V&A: Circ.703–1964

'Torsion' prototype chair, Brian Long, 1970. Vacuum-formed ABS plastic shell, upholstered. V&A: W.15–2011 PLATE 1.112

'Galleria', furnishing fabric, Barbara Brown, 1969. Manufactured by Heal & Son Ltd, printed cotton, 276 × 126.5 cm. V&A: Circ.35–1969 PLATE 1.116

GALLERY 2 — Subversion

ART SCHOOL

Three posters for the exhibition 'This is Tomorrow' at the Whitechapel Art Gallery, Richard Hamilton, Nigel Henderson and Richard Matthews, 1956. Screenprints, each 76.3 × 50.8 cm. V&A: E.176, 179 & 181–1994 PLATE 2.1, 2.24

'Barkcloth', furnishing fabric, Eduardo Paolozzi and Nigel Henderson, 1954. Made by Hammer Prints, screen-printed cotton, 191 × 121 cm. V&A: T.111–2011 PLATE 2.39

'Pogo' chair, Peter and Alison Smithson, 1956. Manufactured by V.E. Edwards and Thermo Plastics Ltd, tubular steel with Perspex panels, 89.8 × 71.1 × 44.4 cm. V&A: Circ.81–1975 PLATE 2.2

Diana as an Engine I, Eduardo Paolozzi, 1963/6. Welded and painted aluminium, 163.7 × 97.5 × 53.3 cm. British Council: P1273 PLATE 2.38

Objects from the Krazy Kat Arkive of Twentieth Century Popular Culture. Various media and dimensions. AAD: 1985/3, 1989/5 & 1994/17 PLATE 2.41

Hers is a Lush Situation, Richard Hamilton, 1958. Oil, cellulose, metal foil and collage on panel, 100.5 × 140.9 × 7.6 cm. Pallant House Gallery (Colin St John Wilson through the Art Fund) PLATE 2.23

We Two Boys Together Clinging, David Hockney, 1961. Oil on board, 121.9 × 152.4 cm. Arts Council Collection, Southbank Centre, London: ACC5/1961 PLATE 2.28

The Diploma, David Hockney, 1962. Etching and aquatint, 57.1 × 39.8 cm. V&A: E.1084–1963

ARK, the magazine of the Royal College of Art, autumn 1958, summer 1960 and summer 1963. Printed paper and metal foil. NAL: 38041800727679 and 38041800727687 PLATE 2.26

Mirror, Frank Bowling, 1964–6. Oil on canvas, 350 × 250 cm. Tate: Lent from the artist 2010 PLATE 2.31

'Simple Solar', furnishing fabric, Shirley Craven, 1968. Manufactured by Hull Traders Ltd, printed cotton, 280 × 129.5 cm. V&A: Circ.791–1968 PLATE 1.118

'Gala', furnishing fabric, Zandra Rhodes, 1964. Manufactured by Heal & Son Ltd, screen-printed cotton, 260 × 127 cm. V&A: Circ.746–1964 PLATE 2.45

Don't Let the Bastards Grind You Down, handbill, Martin Walker of the Association of Members of Hornsey College of Art, 1968. Linocut on paper, 16.6 × 23 cm. V&A: E.139–2002 PLATE 2.32

Open Forum, poster, Association of Members of Hornsey College of Art, 1968. Screen print, 58.3 × 45.5 cm. Royal Watercolour Society

Chair, Allen Jones, 1969. Painted plastic and mixed media, 77.5 × 57.1 × 99.1 cm. Tate: T03244 PLATE 2.29

Necklace, Gerda Flöckinger, 1963. Gold, blister pearls, smoky quartz and aquamarine, 29.5 cm long. The Worshipful Company of Goldsmiths PLATE 2.22

Necklace, Charlotte de Syllas, 1965. Silver and tourmaline, 32 × 3.6 cm. The Worshipful Company of Goldsmiths PLATE 2.21

Necklace, Wendy Ramshaw, 1971. Gold and enamel, 18.5 × 1 cm. V&A: M.169–1976 PLATE 2.20

Large Pendant Body Piece, David Watkins, 1975. Acrylic, gold and aluminium, 60 × 25 × 6 cm. V&A: LOAN:WATKINS.1–2011 PLATE 2.4

12 Cubes, Glenys Barton, 1971. Bone china, slip-cast, with silk-screened decoration, each 5.3 × 5.3 cm. V&A: Circ.277-279–1973 PLATE 2.3

Dish and bowl from the 'Cushion' service, Carol McNicoll, 1972. Earthenware, transfer-printed with 'Button Flower' textile design by Zandra Rhodes, 5 × 26 × 28 cm and 5 × 18 × 17 cm. Private collection

Two bowls, Jacqueline Poncelet, 1976. Bone china, slip-cast and unglazed, 6.6 × 10.9 cm and 10.3 × 13.4 cm. V&A: Circ.255 & 256–1976 PLATE 2.33

Saxophone and Piano Duo, pair of vases, Elizabeth Fritsch, 1978. Stoneware with matt glazes, 21.5 × 12.5 × 9 cm and 26.3 × 11 × 7.5 cm. V&A: C.160&A–1979 PLATE 2.34

Yellow Triangle, vase, Alison Britton, 1981. Stoneware, slab-built with painted decoration, 27.8 × 21.5 cm. V&A: C.87–1981 PLATE 2.35

Drunk Punch, figure, Richard Slee, 1991. Earthenware, coiled, with coloured glazes, 56 × 35 × 50 cm. V&A: C.15:1-5–1992 PLATE 2.36

BOUTIQUE

Morris Mini-Minor, Alec Issigonis, 1959. Manufactured by the British Motor Corporation, 133.4 × 139.7 × 304.8 cm. British Motor Industry Heritage Trust PLATE vii

'Peachy', sleeveless dress, Mary Quant, 1960. Wool tweed, 105 cm shoulder to hem. V&A: T.27–1997

Mini dress, Mary Quant, 1966. Wool jersey, 91 cm shoulder to hem. V&A: T.86–1982 PLATE 2.65

Ankle boots, Mary Quant, 1967. PVC lined with cotton jersey, each 11 × 27.5 cm. V&A: T.59:1 & 2–1992 PLATE 2.66

'Double D', mini dress, Foale & Tuffin, 1966. Linen with a partial cotton lining, 81 cm shoulder to hem, 80 cm bust. V&A: T.29–2010 PLATE 2.77

Mini dress, John Bates, 1966–8. Manufactured by Jean Varon, viscose/nylon blend with rayon lining, 83 cm shoulder to hem, 79 cm bust. V&A: T.262–2009 PLATE 2.11

Platform sandals, Terry de Havilland, early 1970s. Plastic, snakeskin and diamanté. V&A: T.16&A–1983

Dress, Ossie Clark and Celia Birtwell, 1970–71. Printed chiffon and silk satin, 139 cm shoulder to hem, 84 cm bust, 75 cm waist. V&A: T.194–1997 PLATE 2.76

Jacket and skirt with accessories, Biba, 1971. Embossed velvet. V&A: T.56-M–1974

'Mexican Dinner Plate', evening dress, Zandra Rhodes, 1977. Screen-printed silk chiffon with sequins and satin sash. V&A: T.67–1978

PHOTOGRAPHER'S STUDIO

Poster advertising *Blow Up*, directed by Michelangelo Antonioni, 1966. Photograph by Arthur Evans, printed by Rotolito, Italy, 1967, photolithograph, 198 × 140 cm. V&A: E.463–2011

Thermodynamic, Terence Donovan, October 1960. Gelatin silver print, printed 2011, 60.5 × 50.7 cm. V&A: E.329–2011 PLATE 2.71

Secrets of an Agent I, Terence Donovan, March 1961. Gelatin silver print, 50.5 × 40.7 cm. V&A: E.330–2011

Jean Shrimpton, David Bailey, 1962. Published in *Vogue*, April 1962, gelatin silver print, 40.4 × 30.4 cm. V&A: PH.145–1983

Julie Christie, Terence Donovan, 1962. Published in *Women Throooo the Eyes of Smudger Terence Donovan*, 1964, gelatin silver print mounted on card, 30.3 × 38 cm. V&A: E.332–2011 PLATE 2.6

Jean Shrimpton, Terry O'Neill, 1965. Gelatin silver print, printed 2009, 51 × 40.4 cm. V&A: E.314–2011 PLATE 2.7

Twiggy, Ronald Traeger, 1967. Gelatin silver print, 75.5 × 50 × 1.5 cm. Collection of Tessa Traeger

E-Type Jaguar on the M1, Brian Duffy, 1960. Published in *Vogue*, 1960, gelatin silver print, printed 2010, 48 × 37.5 cm. V&A: E.673–2011

Queen, 22 June 1966. Cover photograph of Claudia Duxbury by Claude Virgin, printed paper. NAL: 38041800727695 PLATE 2.67

Nova, May 1971. Cover photograph of Amanda Lear by Brian Duffy, printed paper. AAD: 1985/3/2/549/1 PLATE 2.68

RECORDING STUDIO

Stage costume for David Bowie, Kansai Yamamoto, 1973. Knitted acrylic and lurex. Courtesy of the David Bowie Archive PLATE 2.94

Stage costume for Brian Eno, Carol McNicoll, 1972. Rayon jacket with feathers, satin trousers embroidered with silver thread. V&A: S.156 & 157–1977 PLATE 2.92

Stage costume for Bryan Ferry, Antony Price, *c.*1972. Sequined jacket and cotton trousers. Collection of Mr Bryan Ferry

Suit worn on stage by Marc Bolan, Granny Takes a Trip, 1970s. Gold lamé. V&A: S.75&A–1978

Sleeve for *Sgt Pepper's Lonely Hearts Club Band* by the Beatles, Peter Blake and Jann Haworth, 1967. Art direction by The Apple and M.C. Productions, photographed by Michael Cooper, printed by Garrod & Lofthouse Ltd, colour offset lithograph on card, 31.4 × 31.4 cm. V&A: E.577–1985 PLATE 2.30

Sleeve for *The White Album* by the Beatles, Richard Hamilton, 1968. Embossed card, 31.4 × 31.4 cm. PLATE 2.30

Original sleeve artwork for *Their Satanic Majesties Request* by the Rolling Stones, Michael Cooper, 1967. Lenticular transforming print, 35.5 × 35.5 cm. V&A: S.468–1984

'The Tongue', original artwork for the Rolling Stones logo, John Pasche, 1970. Gouache on light-gauge artboard, with drawing cell and brown tape, 32.6 × 39.3 cm. V&A: S.6120–2009

Mick Jagger, David Bailey, 1965. Photograph from *David Bailey's Box of Pin-Ups*, halftone print, 37 × 32 cm. V&A: E.2047:20–2004

David Bowie, Brian Duffy, 1973. Photographed for the sleeve of the album *Aladdin Sane*, dye transfer print, 45.7 × 35.5 cm. Duffy Archive PLATE 2.93

David Bowie, Terry O'Neill, 1974. Promotional photograph for the album *Diamond Dogs*, gelatin silver print, printed 2009, 50.4 × 40.8 cm. V&A: E.315–2011 PLATE 2.5

Nite Tripper, poster for the UFO nightclub, Michael English, 1966. Offset lithograph, 59.6 × 44 cm. V&A: E.1695–1991

Hendrix, poster, Martin Sharp, 1967. Printed paper, 93.3 × 69.8 cm. V&A: S.2176–2009

Mr Tambourine Man, poster, Martin Sharp, 1968. Screen print on paper, 77.1 × 53 cm. V&A: S.28–1978

Swingeing London 67 (f), Richard Hamilton, 1968–9. Acrylic, collage and aluminium on canvas, 84.8 × 103 × 10 cm. Tate: T01144

PUNK

Black bondage suit, Vivienne Westwood and Malcolm McLaren, 1976. Cotton, with metal zips, snap fastenings, D-rings and spring links. V&A: T.252-D–1989

'Tits' print T-shirt, Vivienne Westwood and Malcolm McLaren, 1976, and white bondage trousers and kilt, Boy, 1976. Shirt cheesecloth muslin, with metal D-rings, bust 94 cm, 62 cm shoulder to hem, trousers nylon and cotton. V&A: T.90–2002 and T.91:2-4–2002

T-shirt with the slogan 'Destroy', and black bondage trousers, from the 'Seditionaries' collection, Vivienne Westwood and Malcolm McLaren, 1976. Shirt cheesecloth muslin, screen-printed, with metal D-rings and catches, 63 cm shoulder to hem, sleeves 90 cm, trousers cotton. V&A: T.773–1995 and T.85:2–2002

Sleeveless T-shirt printed with a letter to Derek Jarman, Vivienne Westwood and Malcolm McLaren, 1977. Cotton, 58 cm shoulder to hem, 98 cm chest. V&A: T.104–2002

Sleeveless T-shirt printed with artwork from the Sex Pistols single 'Anarchy in the UK', Jamie Reid, Vivienne Westwood and Malcolm McLaren, late 1970s, worn and altered by Johnny Rotten. Cotton, 49 cm shoulder to hem, 84 cm chest. V&A: S.794–1990

Poster promoting the Sex Pistols single 'God Save the Queen', Jamie Reid, 1977. Offset lithograph, 70 × 99 cm. V&A: S.1286–1982 PLATE 2.95

Poster promoting the Sex Pistols album *Never Mind the Bollocks*, Jamie Reid, 1977. Screen print, 152 × 91 cm. V&A: S.760–1990

'Ian Dury with Love', poster, Barney Bubbles, 1977. Screen print, 152.3 × 101.2 cm. V&A: E.313–2011 SEE PAGE 12

Concert programme for Ian Dury & the Blockheads, Barney Bubbles, late 1970s to early 1980s. Colour offset lithograph, 59.1 × 83.8 cm. V&A: E.312–2011 PLATE 2.8

GRAPHICS

Artwork for a poster for the Factory nightclub, Peter Saville, 1979. Drawing, 28.7 × 21 cm. Peter Saville

Sleeve for the album *Unknown Pleasures* by Joy Division, Peter Saville, 1979. Printed by Garrod & Lofthouse Ltd, offset lithograph on card. 31.4 × 31.5 cm. V&A: E.2274–1990 PLATE 2.106

Sleeve design proof for the single 'Blue Monday' by New Order, Peter Saville, 1983. Print, 46 × 64 cm. Peter Saville

Two photographs taken for the sleeve of the single 'True Faith' by New Order, art director Peter Saville, photographer Trevor Key, 1987. Prints, 25.4 × 20.3 cm. Peter Saville

i-D magazine, designed by Terry Jones, issue 2, 1980, and issue 10, 1982. Issue 10 cover photo by Steve Johnston, printed paper, each 21 × 29.7 cm.

The Face magazine, art director Neville Brody, issue 49, May 1984. Printed paper, 30.2 × 23.4 cm.

TAILORING

Suit, Tommy Nutter, 1983. Wool, with a horizontal pin-stripe, with cotton shirt and silk tie. V&A: T.10-12–1983 PLATE 2.75

'Bird' jacket, Paul Smith, 1998. Printed velvet. Paul Smith PLATE 2.90

Purple suit, Ozwald Boateng, 1996. Wool, polyester and kid mohair, with cotton shirt and silk tie. V&A: T.22:1-6–1997 PLATE 2.74

Camouflage suit, Richard James, 1998. Printed cotton. V&A PLATE 2.72

DESIGN STUDIO

Studio doors, Mark Brazier-Jones, mid-1980s. Metal, painted in trompe-l'oeil verdigris, 305 × 335 × 11 cm. Courtesy of Mark Brazier-Jones PLATE 2.10

Chair made from Victorian railings and scrap metal, Tom Dixon, 1986. Welded cast iron, 112 × 76 × 38 cm. V&A: W.16–2011 PLATE 2.113

'Lyre' chair, Mark Brazier-Jones, mid-1980s. Steel, 120 × 40 × 50 cm. Courtesy of Liane Brazier PLATE 2.117

Design drawing for Caffè Bongo, Tokyo, Nigel Coates, 1986. Pencil and oil pastel on paper, 68.5 × 51 × 3 cm. Courtesy Nigel Coates Archive

Design drawing for Noah's Ark, Tokyo, Nigel Coates, *c.*1988. Pencil and oil pastel on paper, 68 × 87.5 × 3 cm. Courtesy Nigel Coates Archive

Northern Fleet, chandelier, Deborah Thomas, 1988. Glass shards, wired to a metal armature, with halogen lights, 148 × 100 × 60 cm. V&A: C.49–2011 PLATE 2.114

Desk, André Dubreuil, 1981. Wrought iron, leather and glass, 76 × 156 × 68 cm. Private collection, France, courtesy of Themes & Variations, London PLATE 2.112

'Medici', furnishing fabric, Timney Fowler, 1983. Printed cotton, 202 × 121 cm. V&A: T.210–1989

'Not in Arcadia', furnishing fabric, English Eccentrics, 1987. Printed cotton, 311 × 125 cm. V&A: T.303–1988 PLATE 2.14

'Thinkingman's Chair', Jasper Morrison, 1986. Manufactured by Cappellini, 1989, painted tubular steel and strip steel, 65.7 × 63 × 93 cm. V&A: W.15–1989 PLATE X

'Antelope Table', Matthew Hilton, 1987. Manufactured by SCP Ltd, stained MDF top with a stainless-steel insert, turned sycamore and cast-aluminium legs, 71 × 84 cm. V&A: W.17–1990 PLATE 2.15

'Little Heavy' chair, Ron Arad, 1989. Manufactured by One Off Ltd, 1991, beaten and welded stainless steel, 75 × 59 × 72 cm. V&A: W.17–1993 PLATE 2.12

FASHION STUDIO

Dress from the Spring/Summer haute couture collection, John Galliano for Christian Dior, 2000. Dior PLATE 2.80

Dress from the 'Horn of Plenty' collection, Alexander McQueen, 2009. Digitally printed silk. V&A PLATES 2.81, 2.82

Dress, Hussein Chalayan, 2011. Tulle. V&A PLATE 2.18

Brooch, Simon Costin, 1988. Red bream head, glass eye, glass beads, gold leaf, resin and paint, 7.9 × 13 cm. V&A: M.61–1988 PLATE 2.17

'Myra' hat, from the 'Poseur' collection, Stephen Jones, 2003. Plastic. Stephen Jones

PHARMACY

'Magazine Sofa', prototype, Michael Young, 1994. Aluminium frame, foam seat and arms, upholstered in vinyl, 65 × 151 × 55.8 cm. V&A: W.11–2011 PLATE 2.13

Three 'Jack' lights, Tom Dixon, 1996. Manufactured by Eurolounge Ltd, 1997, low-density rotary-moulded polyethylene with electric light fitting, each 53 × 63 × 63 cm. V&A: W.8-10–1997 PLATE 2.115

The Sleep of Reason, Damien Hirst, 1997. Metal, glass and pharmaceutical packaging, 250 × 368 × 25 cm. Private collection

Pain Killers, Damien Hirst, 2004. Lightboxes and duratrans, 113.7 × 156.2 × 15.2 cm. ARTIST ROOMS: Tate and National Galleries of Scotland. Lent by Anthony d'Offay 2011

Molecular structure from Pharmacy restaurant, Damien Hirst, 1997–8. Cellulose paint, aluminium and fibreglass, 100 × 180 × 222 cm. Private collection, USA

'Aspirin' stool designed for Pharmacy restaurant, Jasper Morrison from an idea by Damien Hirst, 1997. Moulded polyurethane foam seat, aluminium base, 67 × 45 cm. V&A: W.12–2011

Wallpaper designed for Pharmacy restaurant, Damien Hirst, 1997. Printed paper, each roll 53.8 cm wide

GALLERY 3 — Innovation and Creativity

FACTORY

E-Type Jaguar, Malcolm Sayer, 1961. Manufactured by Jaguar Cars Ltd, 122 × 165 × 444 cm. Jaguar Daimler Heritage Trust PLATE 3.3

Cutaway model of Concorde, British Aircraft Corporation and Aérospatiale, 1962–5 (first commercial flight 1976). Plastic and metal, 195 × 267 × 640 cm. British Airways Heritage Centre

'Rio TR70' transistor radio, Eric Marshall, 1961. Manufactured by Ultra Radio & Television Ltd, polystyrene cabinet and aluminium grille, 21 × 30 × 7.6 cm. V&A: Circ.293–1963 PLATE 3.1

'Courier' electric shaver, Kenneth Grange, 1963. Manufactured by Henry Milward & Sons, steel cutter screen mounted in chromium-plated brass with melamine casing and cellulose acetate carrying case, 13.4 × 6 × 5.5 cm. V&A: Circ.132–1965 PLATE 3.26

'Brownie Vecta' camera, Kenneth Grange, 1964. Manufactured by Kodak Ltd, plastic body with nickel-plated fittings, 11 × 6.5 × 7 cm. V&A: Circ.124–1965 PLATE 3.27

Three 'Mark II' chairs, Robin Day, 1964. Manufactured by S. Hille & Co. Ltd, injection-moulded polypropylene shells on metal bases with a range of finishes, each 73.7 × 53.3 × 41.9 cm. V&A: Circ.15-B–1966 PLATE 3.14

'Moulton Stowaway' bicycle, Alex Moulton, 1964. Manufactured by Moulton Bicycles Ltd, mild steel frame and rubber suspension, 101 × 157 × 53 cm. V&A: Circ.125–1965 PLATE 3.16

'Deltaphone', telephone, Martyn Rowlands, 1963. Manufactured by Standard Telephones and Cables Ltd, ABS plastic with polycarbonate switching bar and dial finger plate and rubber feet, 108 × 108 × 210 cm. V&A: W.65:1–2002 PLATE 3.11

'Barbican' hand basin, Chamberlin, Powell & Bon, 1966. Manufactured by Twyfords, Ceramant vitreous ceramic, 41 × 51.4 × 22.5 cm. V&A: Circ.395–1967

'Chefette' food mixer, Kenneth Grange, 1966. Manufactured by Kenwood, plastic with metal whisk attachments, bowl and stand 20 × 18 × 23 cm, motor for whisk 11.8 × 16.5 × 8.2, two whisk attachments each 17.5 × 3.5 cm, blender flask 19 × 8.5 × 6.5 cm. V&A: Circ.731-F–1968 PLATE 3.25

'Nova' tableware, David Harman Powell, 1968. Manufactured by Ekco Plastics Ltd, two-stage injection-moulded styrene acrylonitrile, milk jugs 8.5 × 13 × 8 cm. V&A: Circ.793-EE–1968

'Aurora', 'Vulcan' and 'Neptune', lamps, Martin Hunt and James Kirkwood, 1969. Manufactured by JRM Design Sales Ltd, ceramic, with glass diffusers and electric light fittings, 20 × 14 cm, 15.2 × 8.7 cm and 16 × 10 cm. V&A: Circ.75, 76 & 79–1977 PLATE 3.22

Range of toys, 'Mosaic', 'Little Men', 'Gyrosphere', 'Fish' and 'Bird', Patrick Rylands, 1967–70. Manufactured by Trendon Toys, ABS plastic, 'Mosaic' 6 × 40 × 27 cm, 'Little Men' 1.5 × 54 × 23 cm, 'Gyrosphere' 8 cm diameter, 'Fish' 7 × 13 × 6 cm, 'Bird' 13 × 9 × 14 cm. V&A: Circ.348-349 & 351-353–1970 PLATE 3.2

'Globoots', children's waterproof boots, Globoots Footwear, 1969. Manufactured by Plastic Coatings Ltd, PVC plastisol uppers and soles with removable PVC foam and nylon sock, each boot 15 × 8 × 20 cm. V&A: Circ.250-252–1971 PLATE 3.19

'Wharfedale Isodynamic' headphones, Oliver Hill with the Rank Radio Industrial Design Unit, 1973. Manufactured by Rank Radio International Ltd, ABS plastic moulded shell and stainless-steel headband, 22 × 21 × 12 cm. V&A: Circ.466–1973 PLATE 3.21

'AC1' and 'AP1', pre-amplifier and power amplifier audio units, Robert Stuart and Allen Boothroyd, 1973. Manufactured by Lecson Audio Ltd, matt-black aluminium and Perspex, pre-amplifier 4 × 37 × 26 cm, amplifier 30 cm high × 14 cm diameter. V&A: Circ.70 & A–1977 PLATE 3.20

'Topper' sailing dinghy, Ian Proctor, 1976. Manufactured by J.V. Dunhill Boats Ltd, injection-moulded polypropylene, 600 × 150 × 335 cm. National Maritime Museum Cornwall PLATE 3.5

'G-Force' vacuum cleaner, James Dyson, 1986. Manufactured by APEX Inc., Japan, plastic and electro-mechanical parts, 97 × 30 × 30 cm. V&A: M.64:1-5–1993 PLATE 3.18

'Baygen Freeplay' wind-up radio, Trevor Baylis and TKO Design, 1996. Manufactured by BayGen Power Group, South Africa, plastic, 19 × 10.5 × 6 cm. V&A: W.2–1997

'Wait Chair' prototype, Matthew Hilton, *c.*1997. Manufactured by Authentics, Germany, injection-moulded polypropylene, 77.5 × 47.4 × 51 cm. V&A: W.18–2005

'Eglu' chicken house, Omlet, 2007. Manufactured by Omlet, moulded plastic, 65 × 80 × 80 cm. PLATE xi

LABORATORY

Hardware to Software

'Sinclair ZX Spectrum', Richard Altwasser and Rick Dickinson, 1982. Manufactured by Sinclair Research Ltd, plastic shell with rubber keyboard, computer and electrical components, 23.3 × 14.4 × 3 cm.

'iMac G3', Jonathan Ive, 1998. Manufactured by Apple Inc., USA, moulded polycarbonate housing, computer and electrical components, 40.1 × 38.6 × 44.7 cm. V&A: W.29:1-4–2008 PLATE 3.30

Elite, David Braben and Ian Bell, 1984. Published by Acornsoft for the BBC Micro and Acorn Electron PLATE 3.34

Lemmings, David Jones and Mike Dailly of DMA Design, 1991. First published by Psygnosis for the Commodore Amiga

Tomb Raider, Toby Gard of Core Design, 1996. First published by Eidos Interactive for the Sega Saturn, Sony PlayStation and PC PLATE 3.31

Grand Theft Auto, Dan Houser, Sam Houser and David Jones, 1997. First published by BMG Interactive for the Sony PlayStation, PC and Nintendo GameBoy; published since 1999 by Rockstar Games PLATE 3.32

LittleBigPlanet, Media Molecule, 2007. First published by Sony Computer Entertainment Europe for the Sony PlayStation 3 PLATE 3.33

Advertising and Design Consultancy

'Go to Work on an Egg', poster, Mather & Crowther, 1964. Designed for the Egg Marketing Board, art director Ruth Gill, photographer Len Fulford, copywriters Fay Weldon and Mary Gowing, colour offset lithograph, 74.5 × 49.6 cm. V&A: E.309–2011 PLATE 3.49

'Would you be more careful if it was you that got pregnant?', poster, Cramer Saatchi, 1969. Designed for the Health Education Council, art director Bill Atherton, photographer Alan Brooking, copywriter Jeremy Sinclair, offset lithograph, 59.7 × 41.6 cm. V&A: E.1704–2004 PLATE 3.50

Poster advertising Benson & Hedges cigarettes, Collett, Dickenson, Pearce International, 1977. Art director Alan Waldie, photographer Brian Duffy, colour offset lithograph, 37.8 × 76.1 cm. V&A: E.359–1982 PLATE 3.60

Poster advertising Benson & Hedges cigarettes, Collett, Dickinson, Pearce International, 1977–8. Art director Neil Godfrey, photographer Jimmy Wormser, colour offset lithograph, 38.3 × 76.2 cm. V&A: E.1884–1990

Poster advertising Silk Cut cigarettes, Saatchi & Saatchi, *c.*1990. Art director Paul Arden, colour offset lithograph, 37.5 × 74.7 cm. V&A: E.940–2002 PLATE 3.62

V&A logo, Alan Fletcher of Pentagram, 1989 PLATE 3.39

Orange logo, Wolff Olins, 1994 PLATE 3.58

London 2012 Olympic Games logo, Wolff Olins, 2007 PLATE i

Brand identity for BBC2, Lambie-Nairn, 1991–2001. Screen-based PLATE 3.59

Redesign of the *Guardian* newspaper for Berliner for-mat and interactive platforms, Mark Porter, 2005–11. Various media and dimensions Brand identity for TV Asahi, Tomato, 2002. Screen-based PLATE 3.57

Technology and Design

Shade, Simon Heijdens, 2010. Light projection through transparent/opaque transforming membrane

Falling Light, Troika, 2010. Swarovski crystal lenses in suspended metal armatures, computer-controlled motors, LEDs. Swarovski

Video Dress, Hussein Chalayan, 2007. Engineering design by Moritz Waldemeyer, fabric over 15,000 LEDs. Swarovski

'Pyrenees' sofa, Fredrikson Stallard, 2007. Flocked CNC-routed foam on an aluminium frame, 80 × 220 × 100 cm. V&A: W.25–2011 PLATE 3.8

Shadow, chandelier, Paul Cocksedge, 2012. Manufactured by Baccarat, crystal glass. Baccarat *Study for a Mirror*, rAndom International, 2009. Corian frame, glass, UV light, light reactive ink, camera, PC, custom software, 42.7 × 36.7 × 6.9 cm. V&A: E.295–2011 PLATE 3.38

Chair, David David and Glass Hill, 2011. White beech with hand-drawn pencil crayon design, 76 × 34 × 49.3 cm. Collection of David David and Glass Hill PLATE 3.7

Relay, drawing, David David, 2011. Pencil crayon on cold-pressed illustration paper, 119.5 × 90 cm. Collection of David David and Glass Hill PLATE 3.7

ARCHITECT'S PRACTICE

Presentation model of the Lloyds Building, Richard Rogers, 1986. 87 × 110 × 110 cm. Lloyds of London PLATE 3.76

Presentation model of the Falkirk Wheel, RMJM, 2002. RMJM PLATE 3.77

Presentation model of 30 St Mary Axe, Foster & Partners, 2003. 213 × 110 × 110 cm. Foster & Partner PLATE 3.72

Presentation model of OCAD, Toronto, Canada, Alsop Architects, 2004. Mild steel, wood and vitreous enamel, 50 × 110 × 50 cm. Alsop Architects

Presentation model of Poole Harbour Bridge, Wilkinson Eyre, 2011. Wilkinson Eyre PLATE 3.10

Presentation model of the London Aquatics Centre, Zaha Hadid Associates, 2011. Wood and MDF with plastic cladding, 9 × 125 × 95 cm. V&A PLATES 3.80, 3.81

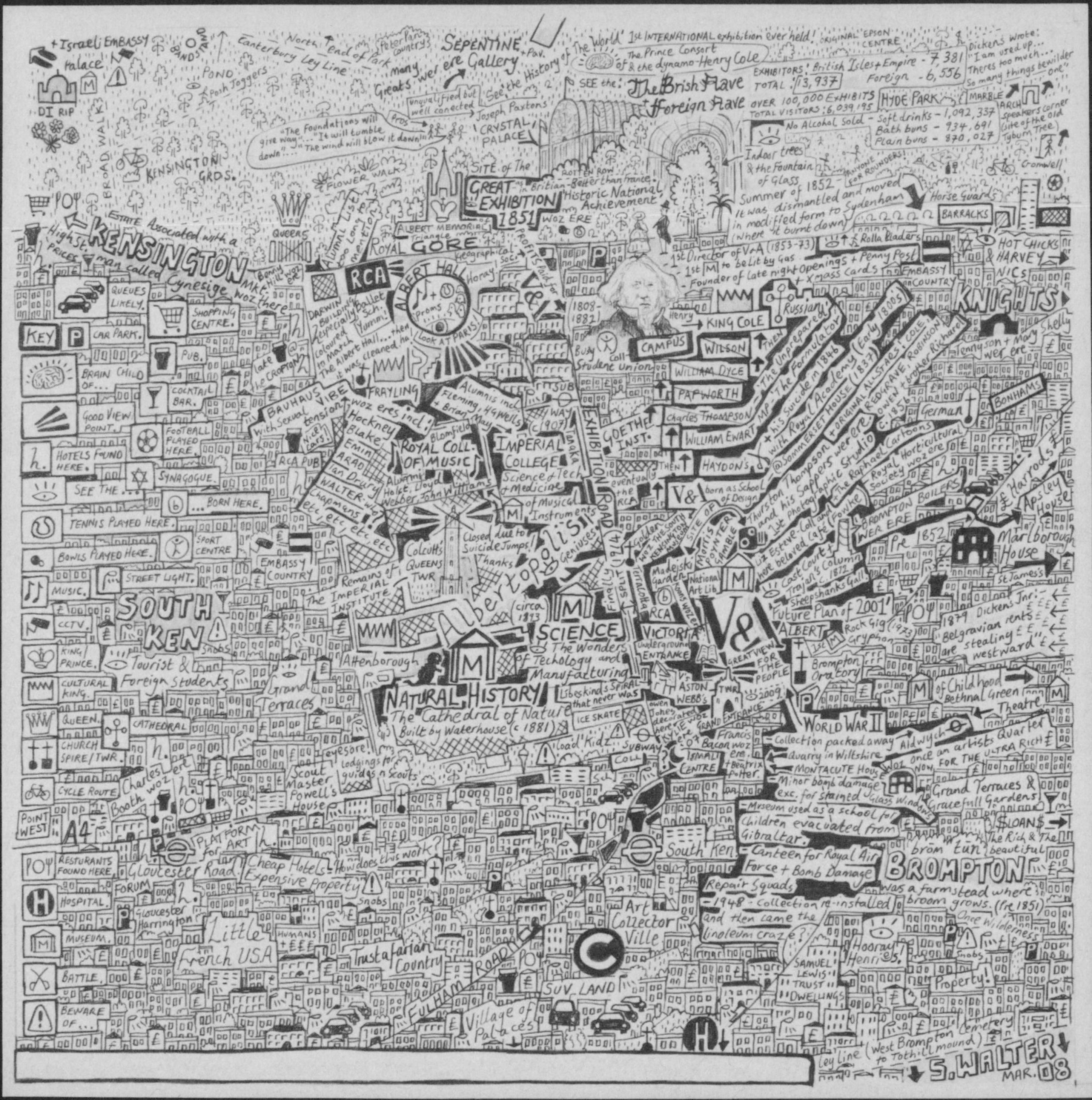
KENSINGTON GRDS.
SEPENTINE
CRYSTAL PALACE
HYDE PARK
SITE of The GREAT EXHIBITION 1851
KENSINGTON
ROYAL GORE
ALBERT HALL
RCA
KNIGHTS
ROYAL COLL. OF MUSIC
IMPERIAL COLLEGE
EXHIBITION ROAD
GOETHE INST.
Albertopolis
SCIENCE
NATURAL HISTORY
The Cathedral of Nature
VICTORIA & ALBERT
Brompton Oratory
SOUTH KEN
Marlborough House
Apsley House
Harrods
BARRACKS
Gloucester Road
South Ken
BROMPTON
Little French USA
Trustafarian Country
FULHAM ROAD
Village of Palaces
Art Collector Ville
SUV LAND
KEY
CAR PARK.
PUB.
SHOPPING CENTRE.
COCKTAIL BAR.
GOOD VIEW POINT.
FOOTBALL PLAYED HERE.
HOTELS FOUND HERE.
SYNAGOGUE.
TENNIS PLAYED HERE.
SPORT CENTRE
BOWLS PLAYED HERE.
STREET LIGHT.
MUSIC.
CCTV.
KING/PRINCE.
CULTURAL KING.
QUEEN.
CATHEDRAL
CHURCH SPIRE/TWR.
CYCLE ROUTE
RESTURANTS FOUND HERE.
HOSPITAL.
MUSEUM.
BATTLE.
BEWARE OF...
S. WALTER
MAR. 08

List of contributors

LIST OF CONTRIBUTORS

CHRISTOPHER BREWARD is Principal of Edinburgh College of Art, Vice Principal of the University of Edinburgh and Professor of Cultural History. He was previously Head of Research at the V&A and is co-curator of the exhibition 'British Design 1948–2012'. His many books on the history and culture of fashion include *The Culture of Fashion* (1995), *The Hidden Consumer* (1999), *Fashion* (2003) and *Fashioning London* (2004). He has also co-curated exhibitions including 'Twenty-First Century Dandy' for the British Council (2003), 'The London Look' at the Museum of London (2004) and 'Sixties Fashion' at the V&A (2006).

GHISLAINE WOOD is a curator specializing in twentieth-century art and design in the Research Department at the V&A, and co-curator of the exhibition 'British Design 1948–2012'. She has curated and co-curated several major international exhibitions including 'Surreal Things: Surrealism and Design' (2007), 'Art Deco 1910–1939' (2003) and 'Art Nouveau 1890–1910' (2000). She has written and lectured extensively on twentieth-century design and publications include *Surreal Things: Surrealism and Design* (2007), *The Surreal Body: Fetish and Fashion* (2007), *Art Deco 1910–1939* (2003) and *Art Nouveau and the Erotic* (2000).

GLENN ADAMSON is Head of Course at the V&A for the V&A/RCA Course in the History of Design. He is co-editor of the tri-annual *Journal of Modern Craft*, and the author of *Thinking Through Craft* (2007) and *The Craft Reader* (2009). His other publications include *Industrial Strength Design: How Brooks Stevens Shaped Your World* (2005). He was co-curator for the V&A exhibition 'Postmodernism: Style and Subversion 1970 to 1990' (2011).

MICHAEL BRACEWELL is the author of several novels and three works of non-fiction, *The Nineties: When Surface was Depth* (2003), *Re-make/Re-model: Art, Pop, Fashion and the Making of Roxy Music, 1953–1972* (2007), and *England is Mine: Pop Life in Albion from Wilde to Goldie* (2009). He writes extensively on modern and contemporary British art and is a regular contributor to *frieze* magazine.

SIR TERENCE CONRAN is one of the world's best-known designers, restaurateurs and retailers. He founded the Habitat chain of home furnishings stores that revolutionized the UK high street in the 1960s and '70s by bringing modern design within reach of the general population. Today he is Chairman of the Conran Group which has eight Conran Shops around the world, an international interior-design and architecture practice and a successful brand licensing company. Terence's latest ventures are Boundary in Shoreditch, a restaurant, café and boutique hotel, and Lutyens, a restaurant in the City of London. He has written more than 30 books, selling more than 20 million copies worldwide.

LILY CROWTHER is the research assistant for the V&A exhibition 'British Design 1948–2012'. She is the author of *Award-Winning British Design 1957–1988* (2012), exploring the eclectic objects recognized by the Design Council's awards schemes. She previously worked on the V&A's permanent galleries of design since 1945, and twentieth-century studio ceramics. She also has a research interest in the crafting of the built environment, and has published on craft and suburbia.

TOM DIXON was born in Sfax, Tunisia, and moved to England at the age of four. He dropped out of art school in 1980 to pursue a career as a musician with Funkapolitan, and three years later he learned to weld in order to repair his motorbike. He rapidly converted his new-found skill into a career fabricating and selling metal furniture, then opened a shop, Space, in 1991. He began manufacturing his own and other designers' products through his company, Eurolounge, in 1994. In 1998 he became head of design at Habitat. He was awarded the OBE in 2000, and launched the Tom Dixon design company in 2001.

KATE DORNEY is curator of modern and contemporary performance at the V&A. She is one of the editors of the journal *Studies in Theatre & Performance* and author of *The Changing Language of Modern English Drama 1945–2005* (2009) and *The Glory of the Garden: English Regional Theatre and the Arts Council* (2010, with Ros Merkin). She is currently working on *Modern British Theatre in 100 Plays*, a visual history of British theatre post-1945 for tablet and book publication.

KENNETH GRANGE began his career as an architectural draughtsman before becoming a design consultant in 1950. He was a founding partner of Pentagram Design Ltd, established in 1972. He won 10 Design Council Awards for his product designs, as well as the Duke of Edinburgh's Prize for Elegant Design in 1963 and the Prince Philip Designer's Prize in 2001. He became a Royal Designer for Industry in 1969, was Master of the Faculty of Royal Designers for Industry in 1982–4 and has collected five honorary doctorates. He was awarded the CBE in 1984. His work has been shown in solo exhibitions at the Boilerhouse at the V&A (1983), XSITE, Tokyo (1989), and the Design Museum, London (2011).

ZAHA HADID, founding partner of Zaha Hadid Architects, was awarded the Pritzker Architecture Prize in 2004 and is internationally known for her theoretical and academic work. Each of her innovative projects builds on over 30 years of experimentations and research in the interrelated fields of urbanism, architecture and design. Major projects include MAXXI: National Museum of Twenty-First Century Art in Rome (completed 2009) and the London Aquatics Centre (completed 2011).

SIR JOHN HEGARTY is Worldwide Creative Director and Founder of Bartle Bogle Hegarty (BBH). John started in advertising in 1965, becoming a founding shareholder of Saatchi & Saatchi in 1970. In 1973 he co-founded TBWA, London, and in 1982 he started BBH, where he has been responsible for iconic campaigns for brands including Levi's and Audi. BBH has won the Queen's Award for Export Achievement twice, and John has won Golds at industry awards including D&AD, Cannes and British Television, as well as the D&AD President's Award for outstanding achievement. He was knighted in 2007, and received the inaugural Lion of St Mark's Award at the 2011 Cannes International Advertising Festival. His book *Hegarty on Advertising – Turning Intelligence into Magic* was published in 2011.

MAURICE HOWARD is Professor of Art History at the University of Sussex and President of the Society of Antiquaries of London. He worked with Michael Snodin on the Gallery of European Ornament at the V&A in 1991–2 and subsequently as Senior Advisor on the Tudor and Stuart sections of the British Galleries, which opened in 2001. He is the author of several books on English architecture, most recently *The Building of Elizabethan and Jacobean England* (2007).

BARBARA HULANICKI was born in Poland and raised in England. She worked as a freelance fashion illustrator in the early 1960s, and founded Biba with her husband Stephen Fitz-Simon in 1964. The business began with mail order, and the first Biba boutique opened in Abingdon Road, Kensington, before moving to successively larger premises on Kensington High Street. By the time it closed in 1976 Biba occupied a five-storey department store. Hulanicki continued to work in fashion design, photography and illustration. In 1983 she wrote her memoirs, *From A to Biba*. She has been based in Miami Beach since 1987, working as an interior and architectural designer and continuing her involvement in fashion.

GUY JULIER is the University of Brighton Principal Research Fellow in Contemporary Design at the Victoria and Albert Museum, London. Formerly Professor of Design at Leeds Metropolitan University, from 2003 to 2010 he was also an Honorary Professor of the Glasgow School of Art. He has authored the following books: *New Spanish Design* (1991), *The Dictionary of Design since 1900* (1993; revised 2004) and *The Culture of Design* (2000; revised 2008). With Liz Moor of Goldsmiths, University of London, he co-edited *Design and Creativity: Policy, Management and Practice* (2009).

JOHN MAKEPEACE trained in furniture design and making during the 1950s and established his reputation working with wood. He was a founding member of the Crafts Council in 1972, and opened his own furniture college alongside his own studios at Parnham House, Dorset, in 1977. He later expanded the college to include Hooke Park, a 350-acre woodland nearby, where a programme of research explored the improved utilization of indigenous timber and resulted in a series of award-winning buildings. Makepeace was awarded an OBE in 1988, and in 2002 the American Furniture Society's Award of Distinction. A solo Arts Council exhibition, 'John Makepeace: Enriching the Language of Furniture', toured the UK in 2010–11.

SIMON MARTIN is a curator and art historian and Head of Curatorial Services at Pallant House Gallery in Chichester. He is responsible for the Gallery's collection of modern and contemporary British art and programme of temporary exhibitions. He has an MA in Cultural Identity and European Art from the Courtauld Institute and a BA in History of Art from the University of Warwick. His books and catalogues include *Poets in the Landscape: The Romantic Spirit in British Art* (2007), *Colin Self: Art in the Nuclear Age* (2008), *John Tunnard: Inner Space to Outer Space* (2010), and the monograph *Edward Burra* (2011).

ANNE MASSEY is Professor of Design History at Kingston University. She has published widely on the subject of the Independent Group, including *The Independent Group: Modernism and Mass Culture, 1945–59* (1995) and *Out of the Ivory Tower: the Independent Group and Popular Culture* (2012). Her writing on design includes *Interior Design Since 1900* (third edition, 2008), *Designing Liners: Interior Design Afloat* (2006) and *Chair* (2011).

JONATHAN MEADES is the author of, inter alia, *The Fowler Family Business* and *Pompey*. He has written and performed in some 60 television films. They include studies of the scrap cult of the Western Isles and Stalin's architecture, eulogies of Birmingham and the Baltic, essays on vertigo and Surrealism. Three shows about France will be transmitted on BBC4 in Spring 2012. His next book is a collection of topographical and architectural writing, to be published by Unbound.co.uk.

ZANDRA RHODES was born in 1940, and studied printed textile design, first at Medway, Kent, and then at the Royal College of Art in London. With her distinctive personal style, Zandra was one of the new wave of British designers who put London at the forefront of the international fashion scene in the 1970s. Her innovative approach to the construction of garments is dictated by the printed patterns of her fabrics. Zandra is now based in London and San Diego. She has seven honorary doctorates, is a Royal Designer for Industry, and was awarded the CBE in 1997. Zandra founded the Fashion and Textile Museum in London, which opened in 2003 and is Chancellor of the University of the Creative Arts.

PETER SAVILLE is an artist and designer best known for his work in music. As the art director and co-founder of Factory Records he created an iconic series of record sleeve artworks for Joy Division and New Order between 1979 and 1993. Since 2004 he has been working as consultant Creative Director to the City of Manchester. His achievements were celebrated in 'The Peter Saville Show' at the Design Museum, London, in 2003; the exhibition then travelled to Tokyo and Manchester. His first major show in a contemporary art museum was at the Migros Museum, Zurich, in 2005 and he continues to exhibit internationally. Monographs include *Designed by Peter Saville* (2003) and *Peter Saville Estate* (2007).

LOUISE SHANNON is a graduate of Sussex University. Since joining the V&A in 2003 she has worked in various collections in the Museum including Furniture, Textiles and Fashion and the Word and Image Department. Past projects include 'Spectres: When Fashion Turns Back' (2005), 'Twilight: Photography in the Magic Hour' (2006) and 'Volume' (2006). She has overseen the management of the Friday Late programme of live events and has developed a series of digital based commissions for the V&A. She co-curated 'Decode' (2009), the first exhibition devoted to digital art and design at the V&A.

SIR PAUL SMITH opened his first shop in Nottingham in 1970. He took evening classes in tailoring and developed his look with the help of his girlfriend (now his wife) Pauline, a RCA fashion graduate. In 1976 he showed his first menswear collection in Paris. Since then he has established himself as a pre-eminent British designer, combining a sense of humour and mischief with a love of tradition. The unique Paul Smith shops throughout Europe, America and Asia reflect the character of Paul and his designs. Paul Smith continues to be involved with every aspect of the company, both as designer and chairman.

PENNY SPARKE is Pro Vice-Chancellor, Research, and Professor of Design History at Kingston University, London. Her most recent book is *The Modern Interior* (2008).

NICOLA STYLIANOU is the AHRC Collaborative Doctoral Award Holder for TrAIN (the Centre for Transnational Art Identity and Nation) and the V&A. Her PhD is entitled 'Producing and Collecting for Empire: African Textiles at the V&A'.

DEBORAH SUGG RYAN is Senior Lecturer in Histories and Theories of Design at University College Falmouth. Her research is on the experience of modernity – particularly non-Modernist manifestations – in the twentieth century. She is currently extending her doctoral research on the Daily Mail Ideal Home exhibition in a forthcoming book *The Inter-War Home: The Design and Decoration of the Suburban House in England, 1918–1939*. She has also published several articles on the revival of historical pageants in Britain, the US and the British Empire, exploring spectacle, space, performance and communities.

JONATHAN WOODHAM is Professor of Design History at the University of Brighton, where he has also been Director of the Centre for Research and Development (Arts) since 1998. He has published widely over the past three decades and has also contributed as a keynote speaker to many major international conferences over the past 20 years. He has also been a member of the Editorial Advisory Boards of a number of leading periodicals in the field as well as a national and international peer reviewer for leading national research funding bodies. His best-known book is *Twentieth Century Design* (1997), which has sold more than 50,000 copies worldwide.

ACKNOWLEDGEMENTS

The *British Design* exhibition and book have been made possible by the support of a vast number of people. We are tremendously grateful to all those involved in bringing both the book and the exhibition to life.

We would especially like to thank the Assistant Curator, Lily Crowther, for her enthusiasm, dedication and invaluable research. We have worked closely with Alice Sedgwick of the Exhibitions Department, whose organization of the project has been brilliant. Special thanks also go to the contributors to the book, many of whom advised on the exhibition and object selection. They are listed on pages 384–5 and we are deeply indebted to them for their help and expertise.

British Design brings together works from all over Britain and beyond, and the exhibition would, of course, not have been possible without the support of our lenders. We would especially like to thank all the lenders to the exhibition; some are mentioned, but others wish to remain anonymous.

Numerous scholars, curators, private collectors, advisers and friends have generously given their time and expertise. The V&A is extremely grateful for the help of Ralph Adron, Simon Alderson, Will Alsop, Hannah Andrassy, Simon Andrews, Colette Anthon and Ruthie Burgess, Rosie Arnold, Henk van Aswegen, Bruce Barker-Benfield, Anna Bazeley and Ben Bisek, David Braben, Mark Brazier-Jones, Paul Briggs, Neville Brody, Cheryl Buckley, Margaret Calvert, Hussein Chalayan and Milly Patrzalek, Nicholas Chandor, Gerald Chevalier and Soizic Pfaff, John Clarke, Max Clendinning, Chantal Coady, Sheridan Coakley, Nigel Coates, Paul Cocksedge, Colin Curtis, Anthony d'Offay, André Dubreuil, Jacqueline Duncan, Catherine Eagleton, Hetty Einzig, Caroline Evans, Gerda Flöckinger, Tiffany Foster and Domenic Lippa, Patrik Fredrikson and Ian Stallard, Francesca Galloway, Ken Garland, Malcolm Garrett, Rafael Gomes, Henrietta Goodden, Paul Gorman, James Gowan, Paul Greenhalgh, Katy Harris, Hannah Hawksworth, Simon Heijdens, James Hester, Charles Hind and Fiona Orsini, Michael Horsham, Susannah Hyman, Courtenay Inchbald, Paul Jarvis, Mushi Jenner, Huw Jones, Stephen Jones, Laura Kiefer, Lucien King, Stephen Laing, Paul Liss, Ian Livingstone, Brian, Pauline and Sharon Long, Jules Lubbock, Fiona McCarthy, John Makepeace, Anne Marden, Corin Mellor, David A. Mellor, Peter Molyneux, Glenn Moorley, Clare Morris, Douglas Muir, Deirdre Murphy, Michael Paraskos and Kelly Lean, Michael Parry, Johannes Paul, Mark Porter, David Harman Powell, Karam Ram, Rosemary Ransome Wallis, Geoff Rayner and Richard Chamberlain, Siobhan Reddy and Luci Black, Alex Reich, Paul Rennie, Sarah Riddle and Andy Wyke, Nigel Roche, Andrew Saint, Linda Sandino, David Saunders and Michael Sawdayee, Richard Slee, Chris Stephens, Karl Stewart, Charlotte de Syllas, Alice Taylor, Jane Thomas, Rupert Thomas, Margaret Timmers, Philip Treacy, Derek Walker, Jess Wilder, Jane Woodward and Sharon Crofts, and Tom Woolley.

Joanna Weddell's work on the Circulation Department has brought to light much new and fascinating material and we are very grateful to both Joanna and the University of Brighton for supporting her research.

We have been ably assisted by many interns, who have provided invaluable research and administrative support and given their time so generously. We are grateful to Kathryn Braganza, Will Green-Smith, Hannah Gregory, Abigail Hampton, Nicolas Hatot, Katy Houston, Debra Lennard, Jessie Lingham-French, Harriet Louth, Julie Piskor and Gabriel Williams.

The exhibition book has been an enormous undertaking and thanks go to Mark Eastment, Frances Ambler and Clare Davis of V&A Publishing, to Daniel Slater and Vicky Haverson for the picture research, to Mandy Greenfield for her copy-editing, and to Barnbrook for the innovative design.

Ben Kelly Design and Graphic Thought Facility have provided the wonderful design and graphics for the exhibition. Thanks to Ben Kelly, Andres Ros-Soto, Sarah Escolme, Andy Stevens and Mike Montgomery for their skill and patience. Thanks also to Zerlina Hughes, Anna Sbokou and Jono Kenyon, of ZNA, and to Fiddian Warman, Jonathan Jones Morris and Kirsten Campbell-Howes, of SODA. Sor-Lan Tan of Flemming Associates has also carefully steered the project.

Finally, we are immensely grateful to all our colleagues within the Museum for their continuing support and enthusiasm. Few museums could undertake an exhibition of this complexity, and the success of *British Design* is testament to the tremendous professionalism exemplified by all departments of the V&A. We would especially like to thank Glenn Adamson, Sarah Armond, Clair Battison, Susanna Brown, Juliet Ceresole, Olivia Colling, Oriole Cullen, Richard Davis, Alice Evans, Catherine Flood, Marion Friedmann, Moira Gemmill, Alun Graves, Elizabeth-Anne Haldane, Sophie Hargroves, Ann Hayhoe, Anna Jackson, Mark Jones, Rebecca Lim, Linda Lloyd-Jones, Beth McKillop, Liz Miller, Matt Rose, Jana Scholze, Laura Sears, Sonnet Stanfill, Malcolm Sutherland, Abraham Thomas, Eric Turner, Alex Westbrook, Damien Whitmore, Claire Wilcox and many, many others.

— Christopher Breward & Ghislaine Wood

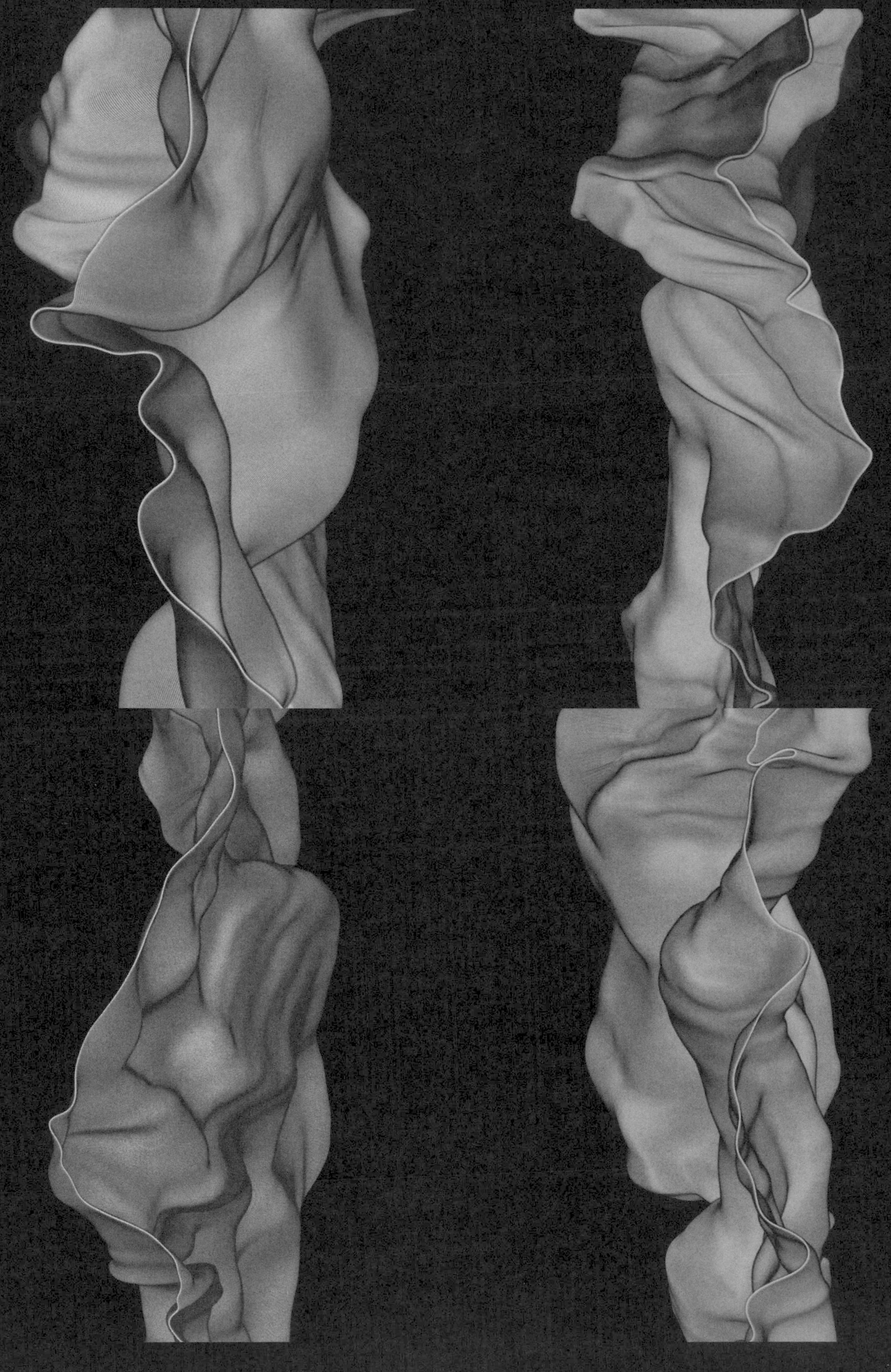

Picture credits

PICTURE CREDITS

All images are © The Victoria and Albert Museum, London, except:

- Michael Annals Estate: 2.50
- © Ron Arad: 2.12
- Adrian Arbib/Alamy: 3.15
- ARCAID: 3.76
- Image supplied by the ARCHIGRAM ARCHIVES 2011: 1.61
- Courtesy of Architects Co-Partnership: 1.65
- Architectural Press Archive/RIBA Library Photographs Collection: 1.28, 1.68, 1.93, 2.25, 3.64
- James Auger and Jimmy Loizeau: 3.42 (cover)
- Photo: Iwan Baan: 3.9
- © David Bailey: 2.42, 2.70
- Courtesy of Rowan S. Baker: 1.49 (cover)
- Glenys Barton: 2.3 (cover)
- Courtesy of the Edward Bawden and Richard Guyatt Estates: 1.38
- The Estate of Edward Bawden: 1.40
- BFI Stills Collection: 2.104
- © Peter Blake. All rights reserved, DACS 2011/Photograph courtesy of Pallant House Gallery: 2.27
- © Peter Blake/Estate of Richard Hamilton. All Rights Reserved, DACS 2011: 2.30
- BMIHT: vii, 3.24
- Ozwald Boateng: 2.74 (cover)
- Photography by Mike Bolam © Andy Goldsworthy: 1.92
- Crispin Boyle/RIBA Library Photographs Collection: 3.71
- Courtesy of David Braben and Ian Bell: 3.34
- Mark Brazier-Jones: 2.111, 2.117
- British Egg Board: 3.49
- © The British Library Board: 1.91
- © The Trustees of the British Museum. All rights reserved: 1.45, 1.46
- Photograph by Thomas Brown: 3.8 (cover)
- Scott Brownrigg: 3.54
- © June Buck: 2.10
- © Reg Butler Estate/Aberdeen Art Gallery & Museums Collection: 1.32
- Margaret Calvert: 1.70 (cover)
- © Michael Cardew: 1.95
- Courtesy of Sheila Casson: 1.97
- © Nigel Coates: 2.16
- Courtauld Picture Library: 1.56
- Photography by Anthony Crickmay: 2.54
- Crown ©: cover
- David David and Glass Hill: 3.7 (cover)
- Design Council Slide Collection at Manchester Metropolitan University: 1.42, 1.71, 1.72, 1.73 (cover), 1.119, 2.78, 3.5, 3.12, 3.17, 3.19
- Rick Dickinson: 3.29
- Photography © Tom Dixon: 2.116
- John Donat/RIBA Library Photographs Collection: 1.9
- © Terence Donovan Archive, courtesy of Diana Donovan: 2.6, 2.71
- © Duffy Archive: p.10–11, 2.93 (cover), 3.60
- Photograph by Sarah Duncan: 3.74
- Dunne & Raby: 3.41 (cover)
- Courtesy of the Estate of Ian Dury: p.12–13, 2.8
- Zachary Eastwood Bloom: 3.37
- Photograph by Timothy Eccleston: 1.75, 1.76
- Courtesy of Hetty Einzig: 1.88
- Richard Einzig/ARCAID/RIBA Library Photographs Collection: 1.67
- © Lucy Elder/patternlondon.com: 3.66, 3.67
- English Eccentrics: 2.14, p.228 (cover)
- © English Heritage. NMR: 1.13
- Courtesy of the Estate of Abram Games: 1.19 (cover), 1.20
- Amanda Gallant: 2.18
- Martino Gamper: 3.47
- Michele Gauler: 3.43
- Estate of William Gear/Laing Art Gallery, Tyne & Wear Museum Archives: 1.1
- Getty Images: 2.62, 3.4, 3.30, 3.68 (cover)
- Courtesy of the Gibberd Garden Trust: 1.59
- © Gilbert & George: 2.102
- The Goldsmiths' Company. Photography by Richard Valencia: 2.21, 2.22
- Courtesy of Andrew Greaves: 2.9
- FRANCOIS GUILLOT/AFP/Getty Images: 2.81 (cover)
- Estate of Richard Hamilton. All Rights Reserved, DACS 2011: 2.24
- Estate of Richard Hamilton. All Rights Reserved, DACS 2011/Photograph courtesy of Pallant House Gallery: 2.23
- Simon Hasan: 3.44
- © John Hedgecoe/Topfoto: 2.43
- Photograph reproduced with the permission of the Herbert Art Gallery & Museum, Coventry: 1.80
- The Estate of David Hicks: 1.14, 1.106
- © Matthew Hilton: 2.15
- Damien Hirst: cover
- HMSO: 3.50
- © David Hockney. Photo credit: Prudence Cuming Associates: 2.28
- Homes and Communities Agency: 1.10
- Christopher Hope-Fitch/RIBA Library Photographs Collection: 3.69
- Courtesy of HSBC Archives: 3.55
- Photography by Hufton + Crow: 3.77
- Alistair Hunter/RIBA Library Photographs Collection: 3.70
- Imagestate Media: 1.84
- IOC: ii
- Courtesy of Zaha Hadid Architects/ Photography by Hufton + Crow: 3.80, 3.81
- Jaguar Heritage: 3.3 (cover)
- Photography by Douglas H. Jeffery: 2.52
- © Allen Jones/TATE, London, 2011: 2.29
- © Elsbeth Juda: 1.53
- Ben Kelly: 2.79, 2.107
- Kobal Collection: 1.83, 3.36
- Ralph Koltai: 2.51, 2.53
- Sam Lambert/RIBA Library Photographs Collection: 3.78
- Courtesy of Lambie-Nairn: 3.59
- Lasdun Archive / RIBA Library Photographs Collection: 2.46
- Courtesy of John Leach Pottery: 1.94
- © Levi Strauss: 3.61
- © Liberty Ltd: 2.44
- By kind permission of LISS FINE ART © Piper Estate: 1.31
- Julia Lohmann: 3.46
- The London 2012 Emblem © LOCOG 2007: i
- Brian Long: 1.112 (cover)
- Angus McBean Photograph. © Harvard Theatre Collection, Houghton Library, Harvard: 2.49
- John McCann/RIBA Library Photographs Collection: 1.11
- Photograph © Craig McDean: 2.72
- Carol McNicoll: 2.92 (cover)
- © John Makepeace: 1.98, 1.100
- Courtesy of John Maybury: 2.105
- Estate of the Artist, Courtesy of The Mayor Gallery, London 2.1
- Estate of the Artist, Courtesy of The Mayor Gallery, London/National Portrait Gallery: 2.37
- Photograph by Roger Morton: 2.97
- National Archives: 1.21, 1.22, 1.24, 1.43
- National Railway Museum/SSPL: 3.28
- National Railway Museum/SSPL/Scott Brownrigg: 3.48
- © National Theatre: 2.56 (cover), 2.57, 2.59, 2.60
- National Trust Picture Library: 1.85
- Photo Courtesy of Omlet Ltd: xi
- © Terry O'Neill: 2.5, 2.7
- Orange: 3.58
- Trustees of the Paolozzi Foundation, Licensed by DACS 2011: 2.38, 2.40
- © Norman Parkinson Limited/courtesy Norman Parkinson Archive: 2.85
- © Jim Partridge & Liz Walmsley: 1.99
- © The Estate of John Prizeman: 1.5
- Courtesy of www.racefurniture.com: iv
- rAndom International: 3.38
- © RCAHMS: 1.39, 1.74, 1.78
- © Jamie Reid courtesy Isis Gallery, UK: 2.95
- REUTERS/Kieran Doherty: viii
- Rex Features: 1.82
- Patrick Reyntiens. All rights reserved, DACS 2011/The Estate of John Piper: 1.77
- RIBA Library Drawings Collection: 1.3, 1.4, 1.37, 1.62, 1.64, 1.69, 3.65
- RIBA Library Photographs Collection: 1.63 (cover), 1.109, 3.63

- © Stephen Richards : 1.101
- Lucie Rie, Hans Coper, Ruth Duckworth, Estate of the artists: 1.124
- Courtesy of Rockstar Games: 3.32
- Courtesy of the artist and ROLLO Contemporary Art: 2.31
- © The Estate of Kenneth Rowntree, Courtesy of Anderson & Garland Auctioneers: 1.41
- Royal Borough of Kensington and Chelsea Libraries: 2.64
- The Royal Collection © 2011 Her Majesty Queen Elizabeth II: 1.2, 1.34
- © Royal College of Art: 1.103, 2.26, 2.63, 2.67 (cover)
- Stamp designs © Royal Mail Group Ltd 2011, courtesy of The British Postal Museum & Archive. All rights reserved: 1.47, 1.48, 1.50 (cover)
- Image supplied by the Royal Mint Museum: 1.44
- Sainsbury Archive: 3.51
- Courtesy of Sanderson: 1.87
- Photograph by Jon Savage: 2.96
- Peter Saville: 2.108, 2.109 (cover), 2.110 (cover)
- Marion Schneider & Christoph Aistleitner: 3.75
- Science and Society Picture Library: 3.13
- Shakespeare Birthplace Trust: 2.48, 2.58
- Courtesy of Stuart Shave/Modern Art: 2.98
- Courtesy of Richard Small: 1.89
- © Grant Smith/VIEW: 3.73 (cover)
- © Paul Smith; 2.86–90
- Henk Snoek/RIBA Library Photographs Collection/Reproduced by permission of The Henry Moore Foundation: 1.60 (cover)
- © Sony Computer Entertainment: 3.33
- Photograph © Sotheby's Picture Library: 1.17
- Square-Enix/Crystal Dynamics: 3.31 (cover)
- Photo by Sukita © 1972/2011 The David Bowie Archive and Masayoshi Sukita: 2.94
- © Tate, London 2011: 1.18
- Courtesy of Themes & Variations: 2.112
- Emmanuel Thirard/RIBA Library Photographs Collection: 3.79
- Courtesy of the Tolkien Estate and HarperCollins, Photo © Bodleian Library: 1.90
- tomato: 3.57 (cover)
- Troika: 3.39, 3.40
- © Pierre Vauthey/Sygma/Corbis: 2.80
- VIEW: 1.66
- © Nick Waplington: 2.82
- Courtesy of William Warren: 3.45
- © David Watkins: 2.4
- Colin Westwood/RIBA Library Photographs Collection: 1.57
- Photography by Stephen White: p.8–9, 2.19
- Photograph: Tim White: 2.83
- Wilkinson Eyre Architects: 3.10
- © Stephen Willats, Courtesy of Victoria Miro Gallery: 2.100
- Collection; The Worshipful Company of Goldsmiths: 1.79
- Photograph by Nigel Young © Foster + Partners: 3.72

Section and chapter openers

PAGE 28
Layers: 'Plankton', furnishing fabric, Gerald Holtom, 1951 (shown in full p.40); 'Brussels', furnishing fabric, James Gardner, 1958 (shown in full p.68); 'Kings & Queens', furnishing textile for schools, Alice Roberts, 1951 (shown in full p.96); 'Prince of Quince', furnishing fabric, Juliet Glyn Smith, 1965 (shown in full p.118)

PAGE 142
Layers: 'Glitter', furnishing fabric, Judy Smith, 1968 (shown in full p.156); 'Age of Kings', printed cotton furnishing fabric, Pamela Kay for Tibor Reich, 1964 © Tibor Limited (shown in full p.184); 'Floating Daisy', dress fabric, Celia Birtwell, 1969 (shown in full p.202); 'Dada', dress fabric, Helen Littman, 1986 (shown in full p.228)

PAGE 254
Layers: design for 'Piazza' Vymura vinyl wallpaper, Sue Faulkner, 1975–6 (shown in full p.264); 'Decode' V&A exhibition identity, Karsten Schmidt, 2009 (shown in full p.288); special edition, inside jacket for *Barking* by Underworld, tomato, with additional drawing by Dexter, 2010. Used with permission of tomato, remixed, altered and collaged by Barnbrook (shown in full p.310); 'London Toile', furnishing fabric, Timorous Beasties, 2005 © Timorous Beasties (shown in full p.328)

Endmatter

PAGE 362
Untitled, Desmond Paul Henry, 1964
Pen and ink machine drawing on paper
V&A: E.378–2009

PAGE 372
Untitled, Computer Assisted Drawing, Paul Brown, 1975 | Plotter drawing on paper
V&A: E.961–2008

PAGE 382
Untitled (Subterranea), Stephen Walter, 2008
Pencil drawing (map of South Kensington)
V&A: E.562–2008

PAGE 386
Still from 'House of Cards' by Radiohead, 2008
Video | Directed by James Frost, courtesy of Xurbia Xendless Ltd

PAGE 388
Forever, Universal Everything, 2008
Generative digital artworks from installation at the V&A | Creative Director Matt Pyke/ Universal Everything; creative code Karsten Schmidt; post-spectacular audio Simon Pyke/Freefarm

PAGE 392
High Arctic, United Visual Artists, 2011
Mixed media installation © United Visual Artists. Photo by John Adrian

Index

INDEX

Page numbers in *italic* refer to the captions

C

D